FUNDAMENTALS OF LAW ENFORCEMENT

Problems and Issues

West's
Criminal Justice Series

WEST PUBLISHING COMPANY

St. Paul, Minnesota 55102

February 1980

CONSTITUTIONAL LAW

Cases and Comments on Constitutional Law 2nd Edition by James L. Maddex, Professor of Criminal Justice, Georgia State University, 486 pages, 1979.

CORRECTIONS

Corrections—Organization and Administration by Henry Burns, Jr., Professor of Criminal Justice, University of Missouri–St. Louis, 578 pages, 1975.

Legal Rights of the Convicted by Hazel B. Kerper, Late Professor of Sociology and Criminal Law, Sam Houston State University and Janeen Kerper, Attorney, San Diego, Calif., 677 pages, 1974.

Selected Readings on Corrections in the Community 2nd Edition by George G. Killinger, Member, Board of Pardons and Paroles, Texas and Paul F. Cromwell, Jr., Director of Juvenile Services, Tarrant County, Texas, 357 pages, 1978.

Readings on Penology—The Evolution of Corrections in America 2nd Edition by George G. Killinger, Paul F. Cromwell, Jr., and Jerry M. Wood, 350 pages, 1979.

Selected Readings on Introduction to Corrections by George G. Killinger and Paul F. Cromwell, Jr., 417 pages, 1978.

Selected Readings on Issues in Corrections and Administration by George G. Killinger, Paul F. Cromwell, Jr., and Bonnie J. Cromwell, San Antonio College, 644 pages, 1976.

Probation and Parole in the Criminal Justice System by George G. Killinger, Hazel B. Kerper and Paul F. Cromwell, Jr., 374 pages, 1976.

Introduction to Probation and Parole 2nd Edition by Alexander B. Smith, Professor of Sociology, John Jay College of Criminal Justice and Louis Berlin, Formerly Chief of Training Branch, New York City Dept. of Probation, 270 pages, 1979.

CRIMINAL JUSTICE SYSTEM

Fundamentals of Law Enforcement by V. A. Leonard, 350 pages, 1980.

Administration of Justice: Principles and Procedures by Garrith D. Perrine, Professor of Administration of Justice, Shasta College, Redding, California, 300 pages, 1980.

Introduction to the Criminal Justice System 2nd Edition by Hazel B. Kerper as revised by Jerold H. Israel, 520 pages, 1979.

Introduction to Criminal Justice by Joseph J. Senna and Larry J. Siegel, both Professors of Criminal Justice, Northeastern University, 540 pages, 1978.

CRIMINAL JUSTICE SYSTEM—Continued

Study Guide to accompany Senna and Siegel's Introduction to Criminal Justice by Roy R. Roberg, Professor of Criminal Justice, University of Nebraska–Lincoln, 187 pages, 1978.

Introduction to Law Enforcement and Criminal Justice by Henry M. Wrobleski and Karen M. Hess, both Professors at Normandale Community College, Bloomington, Minnesota, 525 pages, 1979.

CRIMINAL LAW

California Law Manual for the Administration of Justice by Joel Greenfield, Sacramento City College and Rodney Blonien, Executive Director, California State Peace Officers' Association, 800 pages, 1979.

Basic Criminal Law: Cases and Materials 2nd Edition by George E. Dix, Professor of Law, University of Texas, and M. Michael Sharlot, Professor of Law, University of Texas, 600 pages, 1980.

Readings, on Concepts of Criminal Law by Robert W. Ferguson, Administration of Justice Dept. Director, Saddleback College, 560 pages, 1975.

Criminal Law 2nd Edition by Thomas J. Gardner, Professor of Criminal Justice, Milwaukee Area Technical College and Victor Manian, Milwaukee County Judge, about 600 pages, 1980.

Principles of Criminal Law by Wayne R. LaFave, Professor of Law, University of Illinois, 650 pages, 1978.

CRIMINAL PROCEDURE

Teaching Materials on Criminal Procedure by Jerry L. Dowling, Professor of Criminal Justice, Sam Houston State University, 544 pages, 1976.

Criminal Procedure for the Law Enforcement Officer 2nd Edition by John N. Ferdico, Assistant Attorney General, State of Maine, 409 pages, 1979.

Cases, Materials and Text on the Elements of Criminal Due Process by Phillip E. Johnson, Professor of Law, University of California, Berkeley, 324 pages, 1975.

Cases, Comments and Questions on Basic Criminal Procedure 4th Edition by Yale Kamisar, Professor of Law, University of Michigan, Wayne R. LaFave, Professor of Law, University of Illinois and Jerold H. Israel, Professor of Law, University of Michigan, 790 pages, 1974. Supplement Annually.

EVIDENCE

Criminal Evidence by Thomas J. Gardner, Professor of Criminal Justice, Milwaukee Area Technical College, 694 pages, 1978.

Criminal Evidence by Edward J. Imwinkelried, Professor of Law, University of San Diego; Paul C. Giannelli, Associate Professor, Case Western Reserve University; Francis A. Gilligan, Adjunct Professor, Jacksonville State University; Fredric I. Lederer, Associate Professor, Judge Advocate General's School, U.S. Army, 425 pages, 1979.

Law of Evidence for Police 2nd Edition by Irving J. Klein, Professor of Law and Police Science, John Jay College of Criminal Justice, 632 pages, 1978.

Criminal Investigation and Presentation of Evidence by Arnold Markle, The State's Attorney, New Haven County, Connecticut, 344 pages, 1976.

INTRODUCTION TO LAW ENFORCEMENT

The American Police—Text and Readings by Harry W. More, Jr., Professor of Administration of Justice, California State University of San Jose, 278 pages, 1976.

INTRODUCTION TO LAW ENFORCEMENT—Continued

Police Tactics in Hazardous Situations by the San Diego, California Police Department, 228 pages, 1976.

Law Enforcement Handbook for Police by Louis B. Schwartz, Professor of Law, University of Pennsylvania and Stephen R. Goldstein, Professor of Law, University of Pennsylvania, 333 pages, 1970.

Police Operations—Tactical Approaches to Crimes in Progress by Inspector Andrew Sutor, Philadelphia, Pennsylvania Police Department, 329 pages, 1976.

Introduction to Law Enforcement and Criminal Justice by Henry Wrobleski and Karen M. Hess, both Professors at Normandale Community College, Bloomington, Minnesota, 525 pages, 1979.

JUVENILE JUSTICE

Text and Selected Readings on Introduction to Juvenile Delinquency by Paul F. Cromwell, Jr., George G. Killinger, Rosemary C. Sarri, Professor, School of Social Work, The University of Michigan and H. N. Solomon, Professor of Criminal Justice, Nova University, 502 pages, 1978.

Juvenile Justice Philosophy: Readings, Cases and Comments 2nd Edition by Frederic L. Faust, Professor of Criminology, Florida State University and Paul J. Brantingham, Department of Criminology, Simon Fraser University, 467 pages, 1979.

Introduction to the Juvenile Justice System by Thomas A. Johnson, Professor of Criminal Justice, Washington State University, 492 pages, 1975.

Cases and Comments on Juvenile Law by Joseph J. Senna, Professor of Criminal Justice, Northeastern, University and Larry J. Siegel, Professor of Criminal Justice, Northeastern University, 543 pages, 1976.

MANAGEMENT AND SUPERVISION

Selected Readings on Managing the Police Organization by Larry K. Gaines and Truett A. Ricks, both Professors of Criminal Justice, Eastern Kentucky University, 527 pages, 1978.

Criminal Justice Management: Text and Readings by Harry W. More, Jr., 377 pages, 1977.

Effective Police Administration: A Behavioral Approach 2nd Edition by Harry W. More, Jr., Professor, San Jose State University, 360 pages, 1979.

Police Management and Organizational Behavior: A Contingency Approach by Roy R. Roberg, Professor of Criminal Justice, University of Nebraska at Omaha, 350 pages, 1979.

Police Administration and Management by Sam S. Souryal, Professor of Criminal Justice, Sam Houston State University, 462 pages, 1977.

Law Enforcement Supervision—A Case Study Approach by Robert C. Wadman, Rio Hondo Community College, Monroe J. Paxman, Brigham Young University and Marion T. Bentley, Utah State University, 224 pages, 1975.

POLICE—COMMUNITY RELATIONS

Readings on Police—Community Relations 2nd Edition by Paul F. Cromwell, Jr., and George Keefer, Professor of Criminal Justice, Southwest Texas State University, 506 pages, 1978.

PSYCHOLOGY

Interpersonal Psychology for Law Enforcement and Corrections by L. Craig Parker, Jr., Criminal Justice Dept. Director, University of New Haven and Robert D. Meier, Professor of Criminal Justice, University of New Haven, 290 pages, 1975.

VICE CONTROL

The Nature of Vice Control in the Administration of Justice by Robert W. Ferguson, 509 pages, 1974.

Cases, Text and Materials on Drug Abuse Law by Gerald F. Uelman, Professor of Law, Loyola University, Los Angeles and Victor G. Haddox, Professor of Criminology, California State University at Long Beach and Clinical Professor of Psychiatry, Law and Behavioral Sciences, University of Southern California School of Medicine, 564 pages, 1974.

FUNDAMENTALS OF LAW ENFORCEMENT

Problems and Issues

V.A. Leonard, Ph.D.
Professor Emeritus of Police Administration
Washington State University
Volume Coordinator

West Publishing Company
St. Paul • New York • Los Angeles • San Francisco

50 West Kellogg Boulevard
P.O. Box 3526
St. Paul, Minnesota 55165

Printed in the United States of America

Library of Congress Cataloging in Publication Data

Leonard, Vivian Anderson.
Fundamentals of law enforcement.

(Criminal justice series)
Bibliography: p.
Includes index.
1. Law enforcement
I. Title. II. Series.

HV7921.L36 364 79-28735

ISBN 0-8299-0222-8

2nd Reprint—1982

Preface

Fundamentals of Law Enforcement was conceived by Dr. Harry W. More of the Criminal Justice faculty at California State University in San Jose, and President of Justice Systems Development, Inc. Currently, he is also President of the Academy of Criminal Justice Sciences.

On the basis of their combined academic and field experience, both Dr. More and the Volume Coordinator recognized the urgent need for a university and college textbook designed specifically for an introductory course in the criminal justice curriculum. Geared to the practical requirements of both instructor and student, *Fundamentals of Law Enforcement* provides a strong foundation for succeeding course work in the criminal justice program.

Assembled for this purpose is a distinguished panel of authors, whose achievements and contributions have attracted national and international attention.

Fundamentals of Law Enforcement is in reality, more than a textbook, in terms of study, instruction and research. It is indeed, prophetic of things to come in an emerging profession, and in the criminal justice system. It brings together between the covers of one volume the expertise of twelve authors in the considered treatment of those basic issues that confront the police enterprise as a major component of the system. Reference to Chapter titles and the detailed Table of Contents will reveal a comprehensive approach to major problems that today challenge the capabilities of law enforcement administration and research.

Fundamentals of Law Enforcement is unique in the literature of the field since it is designed and written as a text for an introductory course in criminal justice and will also be found useful as a reference work for courses in the upper division, as well as at the graduate and seminar level. Toward this end, each Chapter is supported by a list of Chapter Objectives, a

Chapter Summary, Suggested topics for Discussion, a detailed list of References, and an Annotated Bibliography.

The text is also written for use in Police Academies, In-Service Training and Executive Development Programs, and will prove of working interest to practitioners in related disciplines, including Sociology, Psychology, Political Science, Law Schools, Social Work, the Judiciary and Corrections.

In the opinion of one reviewer whose name is known throughout the field, the volume ". . . has synthesized the important contributions to police literature; it is an analytical work; it addresses structure and process; it blends theory and practice; and it focuses on humanism, change, and the future."

V. A. L.

Contributing Authors

W. FRED WEGENER (Chapter 1) is Associate Professor of Criminology in the Department of Criminology, and former Director of the Crime Study Center at Indiana University of Pennsylvania. In addition to his other responsibilities, he is also Director of the *Criminology Internship Program*. He holds the B. A., degree in Sociology/Political Science from Colorado State College; and the M. A., and Educational Specialist degrees in Sociology and Urban Sociology respectively, from the University of Northern Colorado. He completed additional graduate work at the University of Denver School of Law, and in the area of deviant behavior, at Indiana University of Pennsylvania. He is presently a doctoral candidate in public administration at Nova University in Ft. Lauderdale, Florida.

Professor Wegner's wide professional experience included service as Shift Commander in a 125 man urban Sheriff's Department (Adams County, Colorado), coordinating the activities of from 5 to 14 patrol units; Institutional Parole Agent in the Colorado Pre-Parole Release Center, Colorado Department of Adult Parole; Field Agent, Colorado Department of Adult Parole; Assistant Professor and Chairman of the Criminal Justice Program at Indiana University of Pennsylvania; Director of the Criminal Justice Training Center serving the Toledo, Ohio, area; Associate Professor of Criminology and Director of Continuing and Non-Resident Education in the School of Continuing Education. His services as a consultant in the general area of criminal justice administration are well known.

RICHARD A. MYREN (Chapter 2) is Professor and Dean of the School of Justice in the College of Public Affairs, The American University in Washington, D. C. He holds the B. S. degree in chemistry from the University of Wisconsin; and the L. L. B., (J.D.) degree from Harvard Law School. In April of 1978 he was granted the Distinguished Service Award by the School of Criminal Justice of the State University of New York at Albany for "academic leadership of the best kind." In 1976, Professor Myren was cited by the American Society for Public Administration for "integration of a broad interdisciplinary curriculum into a pioneering model at the university graduate level, thereby improving the study of criminal justice administration." He was awarded the Honorary Degree of Doctor of Laws at the University of New Haven in June of 1976. During the period 1966 to 1976, Professor Myren served as Dean and Professor of Criminal Justice, School of Criminal Justice at the State University of New York at Albany. From 1956 to 1966, he was Assistant and Associate Professor, Department of Forensic Studies at Indiana University in Bloomington.

As a Fulbright Research Scholar on sabbatical leave from Indiana University, Professor Myren served with the Institute of Sociology, National University (Research Associate) and with the Institute of Public Administration, Provincial Government (Visiting Professor Public Law and Government,) in Cordoba, Argentina. He conducted independent research for a descriptive monograph on the Argentine criminal justice system (now in manuscript) to be used in a long-range comparative study of such systems in federated nations. The manuscript, *Estudio Comparativo de los Sistemas de Justica en lo Criminal—Revista de Administracion Publica* (pp. 205), was published in *Govierno Uno* (Cordoba: Instituto Superior de Administracion Publica de Govierno,) in 1964. From 1952 to 1956, he was Assistant Director and Associate Research Professor in the Institute of Government at the University of North Carolina. Professor Myren is a Past-President of the Academy of Criminal Justice Sciences. His record as a professional consultant and author is extensive and impressive.

MICHAEL A. DOYLE (Chapter 3) holds the B. S., and M. S., degrees in criminal justice from Michigan State University in East Lansing. He served on the criminal justice faculties at Michigan State University, in the Police Administration Department at Sul Ross State University, Alpine, Texas, and at Glendale Community College in California.

He was a member of the Armed Services, commanding armor units in Germany and Vietnam, involving the operations of 60 to 245 man units in both combat and non-combat environments. He has also served in the Military Police, and in the Police Department of Lansing, Michigan, for a period of five years. Professor Doyle conducted victimization and attitudinal surveys as part of *Neighbors Against Burglary—A Multi-faceted Patrol Emphasis Project* funded by a LEAA grant to the City of Simi Valley, California. He is currently a member of the faculty in the Administration of Justice Department at California Lutheran College in Thousand Oaks, California.

GEORGE T. FELKENES (Chapter 4) is now Director of the School of Criminal Justice at Michigan State Unversity in East Lansing. He was consecutively, Professor in the Department of Criminology at California

State University in Long Beach; Professor and Chairman of the Department of Criminology at the same institution; and Professor and Chairman of the Department of Criminal Justice at the University of Alabama in Birmingham. He was chosen by faculties and students in the state of California as Professor of the Year (1969–1970). He is Past-President of the Academy of Criminal Justice Sciences and is recipient of the Academy's Founder's Award.

Professor Felkenes holds the B. S., degree from the University of Maryland; the M. A., degree from California State College in Long Beach; the L.L.B. degree from the University of Maryland; and the Ph.D., degree from the University of California in Berkeley.

He is Chairman of the Criminal Justice Accreditation Council of the Academy of Criminal Justice Sciences, a national accrediting agency for criminal justice programs at the University and College level. In addition, his services have been widely sought as a consultant in police organization and management.

JOEL I. GREENFIELD (Chapter 5) is currently the Associate Dean of Occupational Education at Sacramento City College. His criminal justice background includes positions as full-time administration of justice faculty member, Director of the Sacramento Center—Northern California Criminal Justice Training and Education System, Police Officer/Lieutenant—Sacramento Police Department. Mr. Greenfield is an active member of the Academy of Criminal Justice Sciences and is a past president of the California Association of Administration of Justice Educators. He is a graduate of California State University, Sacramento, and holds an MPA degree from the University of Southern California.

V. A. LEONARD (Chapter 6) founded the Department of Police Science and Administration, now the Department of Criminal Justice, at Washington State University in September of 1941. The program featured a four-year curriculum with a liberal arts emphasis, leading to the B. S., degree in the police major. The program became accredited with the Graduate School in 1944, and the M. A., degree was added in that year. Professor Leonard was Chairman of the Department until 1957; Professor of Police Science and Administration 1955–1963; and Professor Emeritus of Police Administration since 1963. He holds the B. S., degree from Texas Wesleyan College, the M. A. degree from Texas Christian University; and the Ph.D., degree from Ohio State University.

Professor Leonard is a Past-President of the Texas Division, International Association for Identification; Past-President, Academy for Scientific Interrogation, now the American Polygraph Association; Honorary Life Member, Texas Division, International Association for Identification; Honorary Life Member, Sociedad Cubana de Policiologia y Criminalistica, awarded through the U. S. State Department in 1949; Honorary Life Member, American Polygraph Association; Honorary Life Member, Academy of Criminal Justice Sciences and recipient of the Academy's Founders Award in 1976. At the invitation of the Central Chinese Government, he served as a visiting Professor of Police Administration at the Central Police College in Taipei, Taiwan, during the academic year 1971–1972. He is the author of some twenty-seven books, including the Fifth Edition of *Police Organization and Management*, now in its twenty-seventh year as a university text and police reference work.

JOHN P. KENNEY (Chapter 7) holds the A. B., degree in economics from the University of California at Berkeley; the M. S., in public administration from the University of Southern California; and the Ph.D., in political science from the University of California at Los Angeles. He has been a Professor of Criminal Justice since September 1966, and formerly Director of the Institute for Police Studies (now the Center for Criminal Justice) at California State University in Long Beach. He was Professor of Public Administration, University of Southern California, 1950–64, and Coordinator of the Police and Corrections Program; Professor in the Police Science Program at the College of the Sequoias in Visalie, California, in 1947. He was a continuing lecturer from 1948 through 1970 at the Delinquency Control Institute, University of Southern California.

Professor Kenney is the author of *Police Administration*, now in its third revised printing; *Police Work With Juveniles* (co-author), premier publication in the field of police work with juveniles; and with Professor Harry W. More, *Principles of Investigation*. Other publications include The *California Police, Police Management Planning, Police Writing, Police Operation: Policies and Procedures*. He is a former Director of the California Department of Justice, 1964–66, in charge of the Law Enforcement Division. Professor Kenney's services as a consultant continue to experience a steady demand in the area of police organization and administration. He was a two-term President, 1957 and 1958, of the American Society of Criminology, and founding member of the American Academy of Criminal Justice.

JAMES P. MORGAN, Jr. (Chapter 8) began his professional career with the New York City Police Department, and then served five years with the Federal Bureau of Investigation, including a two-year assignment as a Supervisor in the Training Division in Washington, D.C. His career next turned to academia where he spent two years as Administrator of the Police Science Division at the University of Georgia. In January of 1971, he assumed command of 900 men and women as the first Public Safety Administrator for the city of St. Petersburg, Florida.

Since 1973, Professor Morgan has also been involved in private consultant work. His clients have included cities, counties and states, as well as public and private organizations throughout the country. He is currently a member of the faculty at Virginia Commonwealth University, teaching primarily at the graduate level. Professor Morgan holds both the B.A., and M.P.A., degrees, and has completed additional study at the graduate level toward the D.P.A., and L.L.B., degrees.

DAVID E. BURNS (Chapter 9) has been an Assistant Professor in the Administration of Justice Department at San Jose State University since 1974. He received the B.S., and M.A., degrees in Public Administration from New Mexico State University. He is presently completing requirements for the Doctorate in Public Administration at Golden Gate University in San Francisco. Professor Burns served approximately six years as a police officer in the line. One of his major areas of professional interests is police policy formulation and execution.

RONALD L. ELTZEROTH (Chapter 10) is Assistant Professor in the Police Training Institute at the University of Illinois in Champaign. His primary teaching responsibilities include Police Science and Police Labor/Management Relations.

He served as an officer with the Indiana State Police in the positions of Trooper, Uniformed Sergeant, Detective Sergeant and Detective First Sergeant. His last assignment with the State Police was in the Division of Forensic Sciences. Professor Eltzeroth holds the Associate of Science degree in Law Enforcement Technology, and the B.S., degree in Criminal Justice Administration from Indiana University; and the M.A. degree in Law Enforcement Administration from Sangamon State University in Springfield, Illinois.

ERIK BECKMAN (Chapter 11) is Assistant Professor at the School of Criminal Justice, Michigan State University, East Lansing. Professor Beckman holds B.S. and M.S. degrees in Criminology from California State University, Long Beach, an M.A. in Correctional Administration from University of Detroit, and the Ph.D. in Educational Sociology from Wayne State University, Detroit.

Professor Beckman served as a police patrolman, detective and sergeant in Orange County, California until 1970 when he entered college teaching. He is the author of a law enforcement textbook, as well as numerous journal articles and newspaper columns. He is also the editor of a Criminal Justice Dictionary. Professor Beckman has served as a consultant for the Law Enforcement Assistance Administration.

WILLIAM P. BROWN (Chapter 12) was a sworn officer in the New York City Police Department from 1940 to 1962. During that time he went through the ranks from Patrolman to Inspector. At various times in his career he was in police, juvenile, staff and, most frequently, line patrol work. He commanded several precincts and, for some time, the New York City Police Academy. His final assignment was in charge of a patrol district in midtown Manhattan.

Professor Brown's academic work through the Ph.D. was completed at New York University during his police career. Since 1962, he has been a Professor, first in the School of Public Affairs and then in the School of Criminal Justice at the State University of New York at Albany. His major research interests have been in administration and in that area of administrative pathology designated as police corruption. His 1966-67 study of corruption in the United States was the first major nationwide study of that area and was conducted for the President's Commission on Law Enforcement and Administration of Justice. His most recent work, *A Reconciliation of Administrative Theory and Police Practice*, was published in 1979.

Contents

FUNDAMENTALS OF LAW ENFORCEMENT

Problems and Issues

1

THE POLICE AS A MAJOR COMPONENT OF THE CRIMINAL JUSTICE SYSTEM: Isolated or Integrated

Chapter Objectives

The study of this chapter should enable you to:

☑ Indicate the nature and extent of serious crime in the United States.

☑ Explain the concept of system as it relates to the Administration of Criminal Justice.

☑ Explain the need for Constitutional safeguards in the criminal justice process.

☑ Explain the justification of police power.

☑ Give reasons for the proliferation and stratification of police agencies in the United States.

☑ Explain how the police identify and introduce the suspected criminal offender into the system of justice.

☑ Explain the relationship between the police, the prosecutor, and the courts.

☑ Explain the police role in correctional administration.

☑ Discuss the milieu of law and order and the need for public peace and tranquility.

☑ Define the concept of crime prevention and give an explanation of why everything else is ex post facto.

Introduction

In spite of how they're often perceived, the police are not a self-sufficient and isolated entity; rather, they constitute but a single subsystem in a large and complex mosaic of social structures. The pronounced social upheavals which characterized the late 1960s, combined with the public's need for reassurance concerning personal security and safety in today's complex society, have made public safety administration a sensitive sociopolitical issue. This chapter views the law enforcement establishment within a systemic framework and places the police in perspective with respect to the criminal justice system.

Crime in American Society

Crime in modern American society is a visible, pervasive, and deadly reality. Table I and Figures 1-4, reprinted from Uniform Crime Reports (UCR), graphically illustrate this fact. In 1977 alone, 10,935,800 major crimes were reported to the police. Recent UCRs indicate that crime in this country is epidemic—yet even these astronomical figures, which only represent *statistical* crime, do not reflect the total crime picture. We can only estimate how many crimes go unreported. Thus, the nation's score on the crime front continues to be a cause for great concern. The Law Enforcement Assistance Administration (LEAA), supported by substantial social research, estimates that the ratio of *actual* to statistical crime is about four to one.[1] By design, and through a process of organizational evolution, the American criminal justice system has emerged as society's response to the problem of crime and the criminal.

Table I

National Crime, Rate, and Percent Change

Crime Index offenses	Estimated crime 1977		Percent change over 1976		Percent change over 1973		Percent change over 1968	
	Number	Rate per 100,000 inhabitants	Number	Rate per 100,000 inhabitants	Number	Rate per 100,000 inhabitants	Number	Rate per 100,000 inhabitants
Total	10,935,800	5,055.1	−3.3	−4.0	+25.4	+21.7	+62.7	+50.0
Violent	1,009,500	466.6	+2.3	+1.5	+15.3	+11.8	+69.7	+56.4
Property	9,926,300	4,588.4	−3.8	−4.5	+26.6	+22.8	+62.1	+49.4
Murder	19,120	8.8	+1.8	....	−2.6	−6.4	+38.6	+27.5
Forcible rape	68,020	29.1	+11.1	+10.2	+22.6	+18.8	+99.0	+83.0
Robbery	404,850	187.1	−3.7	−4.4	+5.4	+2.2	+54.0	+42.0
Aggravated assault	522,510	241.5	+6.4	+5.6	+24.2	+20.4	+82.2	+67.9
Burglary	3,052,200	1,410.9	−1.2	−2.0	+19.0	+15.4	+64.2	+51.3
Larceny-theft	5,905,700	2,729.9	−5.8	−6.6	+35.8	+31.8	+69.6	+56.3
Motor vehicle theft	968,400	447.6	+1.1	+.3	+4.3	+1.1	+23.6	+13.9

Courtesy of Federal Bureau of Investigation, *Uniform Crime Reports*, October 1978, p. 35.

The Criminal Justice System

The criminal justice system is best described as a grouping of relatively autonomous components which have been designed to accomplish common objectives through mutual effort. The objectives of the American criminal justice system are generally considered to be as follows:

- the protection of life and property;
- the preservation of the peace;

Figure 1.1

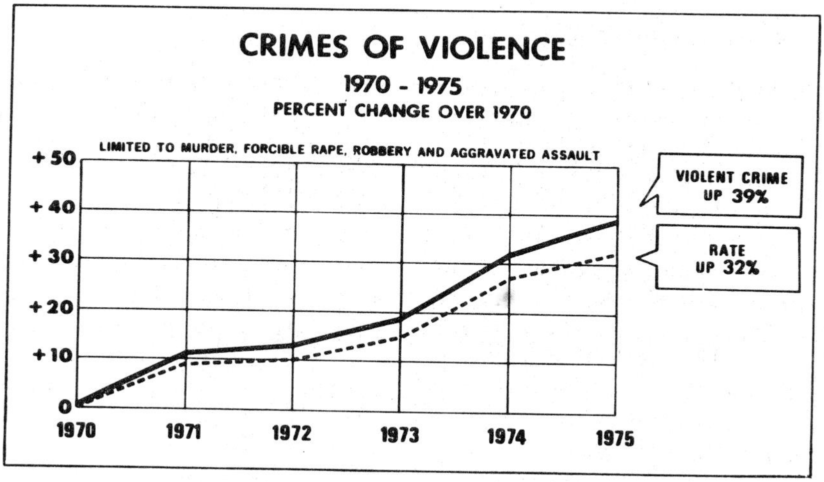

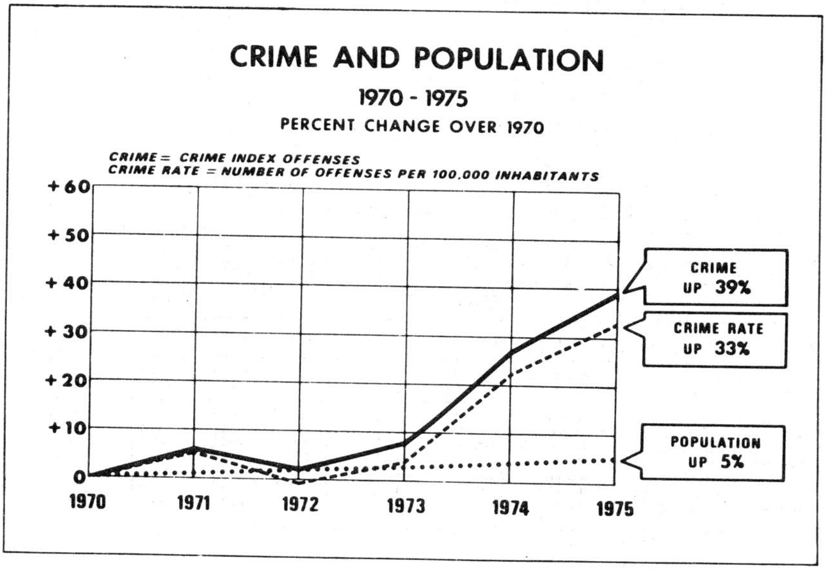

Courtesy Federal Bureau of Investigation, *Uniform Crime Reports.*

- the prevention of crime;
- the detection and arrest of violators;
- the enforcement of laws and ordinances; and
- the safeguarding of the rights of the individual.

Based on a structural and functional analysis of the criminal justice process, the following are identified as the major components (or subsystems) of the criminal justice system:

- politically-based legislative activity;
- the modern police establishment;
- the prosecutorial function;
- the judicial process; and
- corrections.

The President's Commission on Law Enforcement and the Administration of Justice has developed a schematic representation of the overall criminal justice system that can help us to better understand its parts and how they function. As is obvious from this schematic, shown in Figure 5, the

Figure 1.2

CRIME INDEX OFFENSES REPORTED

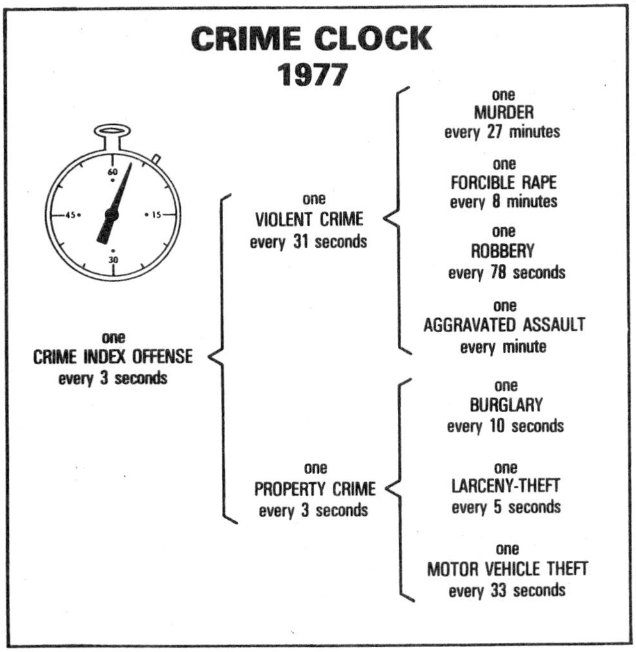

The crime clock should be viewed with care. Being the most aggregate representation of UCR data, it is designed to convey the annual reported crime experience by showing the relative frequency of occurrence of the Index Offenses. This mode of display should not be taken to imply a regularity in the commission of the Part I Offenses; rather, it represents the annual ratio of crime to fixed time intervals.

criminal justice system in this country is enormously complex and can be difficult to manage and control. There are, however, certain limits which have been imposed on the system; these will be discussed below.

Constitutional Controls

In order to ensure the quality of American justice (i.e., the maintenance or administration of what is just according to the law) and in an effort to define the powers of government, the people of the United States, through their duly elected representatives, adopted a formal Constitution in 1787 and a supplemental Bill of Rights in 1791. The Bill of Rights, which consists of the first ten amendments to the United States Constitution, was specifically designed to protect individual liberties. The basic rules and procedures set forth by the Bill of Rights have been synthesized and incorporated into local laws, and it is possible to determine the major substantive and procedural rights of a defendant in a specific state by scanning that state's penal code.

Figure 1.3

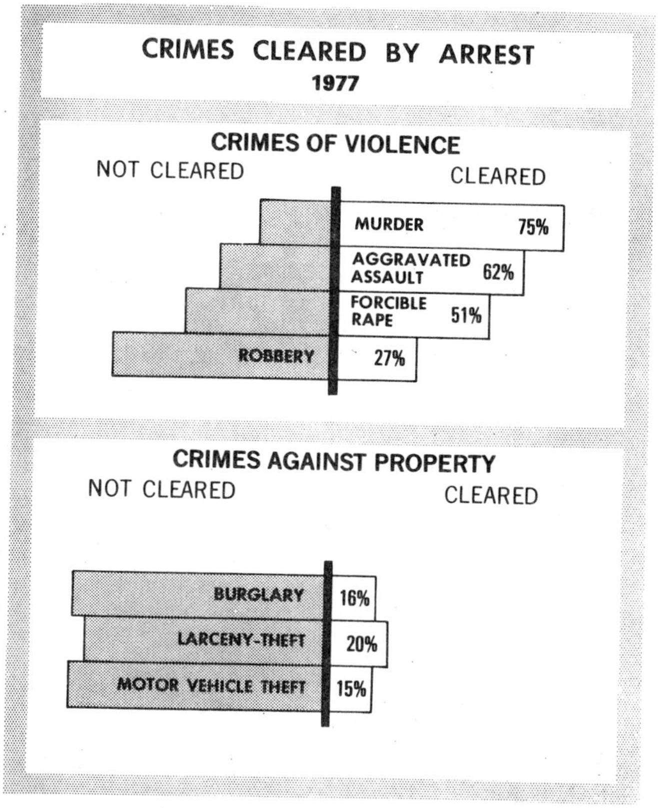

Source: Uniform Crime Reports (October, 1978), p161.

For example, the California penal code indicates that the defendant in a criminal action is entitled:

1. To a speedy and public trial.
2. To be allowed counsel or to appear and defend in person and without counsel.

Figure 1.4

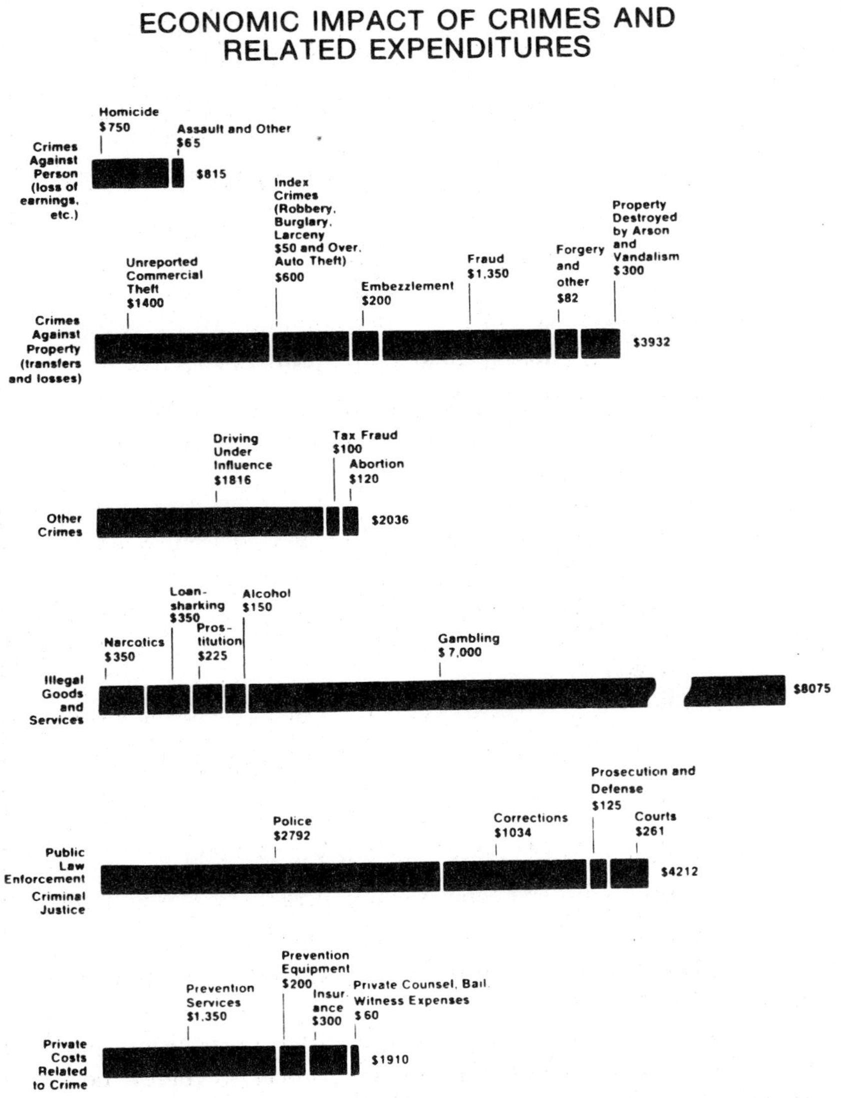

Courtesy Federal Bureau of Investigation, *Uniform Crime Reports*. (above figures expressed in millions of dollars.)

[A9857]

3. To produce witnesses on his behalf and to be confronted with witnesses against him in the presence of the court except:
   a. Hearsay evidence may be admitted to the extent it is otherwise admissible, and
   b. The deposition of a witness taken in action may be read to the extent that it is otherwise admissible.
4. Not to be prosecuted for a crime of which the accused person has once been prosecuted and convicted or acquitted.
5. Not to be restrained prior to conviction more than necessary for detention to answer the charge.
6. Not to be convicted of a crime (public offense) unless:
   a. By verdict of a jury accepted and recorded by a court.
   b. By finding of a court in a case where a jury has been waived, or
   c. By a plea of guilty.
7. To prosecution by indictment or information, except:
   a. For removal of state civil officers,
   b. For offenses arising in the organized militia,
   c. For offenses triable in municipal and justice courts,
   d. For misdemeanors triable in juvenile courts, and
   e. For felonies in which it is lawful for the defendant to plead guilty before a magistrate.
8. To preliminary examination of the case by an examining magistrate and an order holding the defendant to answer signed by such judicial officer, when prosecution is to be by filing of an information.
9. When prosecution is by indictment, the grand jury shall receive sufficient competent evidence to support the indictment and no other evidence than such as is:
   a. Given by witnesses produced and sworn before the grand jury,
   b. Furnished by writings, material objects or other things presented to the senses, or
   c. Contained in a deposition admissible under the laws of the state.
10. To release on bail if the offense charged is bailable.
11. To have a proceeding to conditionally examine material witnesses.
12. Not to be compelled to be a witness against himself.
13. The burden of proving guilt beyond a reasonable doubt must be borne by the "people."[2]

In addition, the United States Constitution was further amended in 1868 to guarantee *due process* and *equal protection* under the law. The Fourteenth Amendment, in part, states that:

> *All persons born or naturalized in the United States and subject to the jurisdiction thereof, are citizens of the United States and of the state wherein they*

A general view of The Criminal Justice System

This chart seeks to present a simple yet comprehensive view of the movement of cases through the criminal justice system. Procedures in individual jurisdictions may vary from the pattern shown here. The differing weights of line indicate the relative volumes of cases disposed of at various points in the system, but this is only suggestive since no nationwide data of this sort exists.

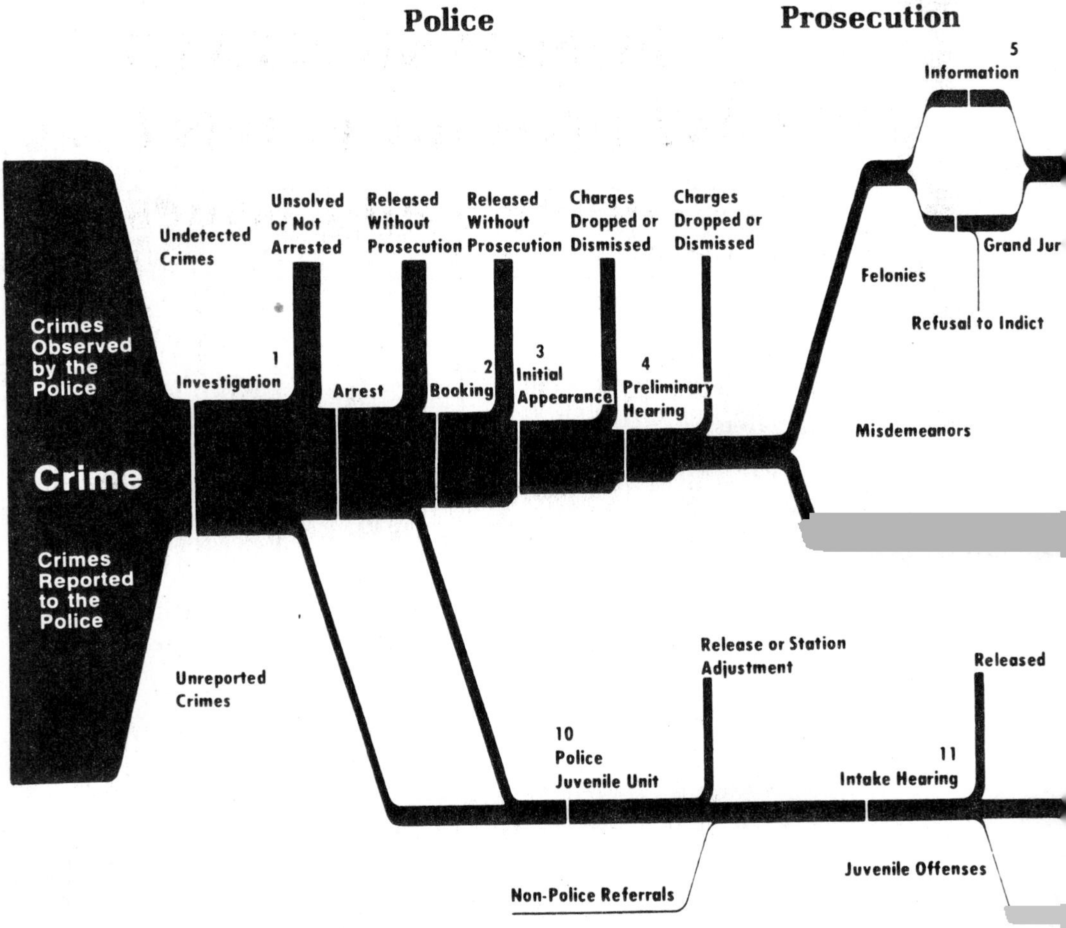

1. May continue until trial.

2. Administrative record of arrest. First step at which temporary release on bail may be available.

3. Before magistrate, commissioner, or justice of peace. Formal notice of charge, advice of rights. Bail set. Summary trials for petty offenses usually conducted here without further processing.

4. Preliminary testing of evidence against defendant. Charge may be reduced. No separate preliminary hearing for misdemeanors in some systems.

5. Charge filed by prosecutor on basis of information submitted by police or citizens. Alternative to grand jury indictment.

6. Reviews whether Government evidence sufficient to justify trial. Some States have no grand jury system; others seldom use it.

Figure 1.5 Adapted From *The Challenge of Crime in a Free Society*. The President's Commission on Law Enforcement (1967).

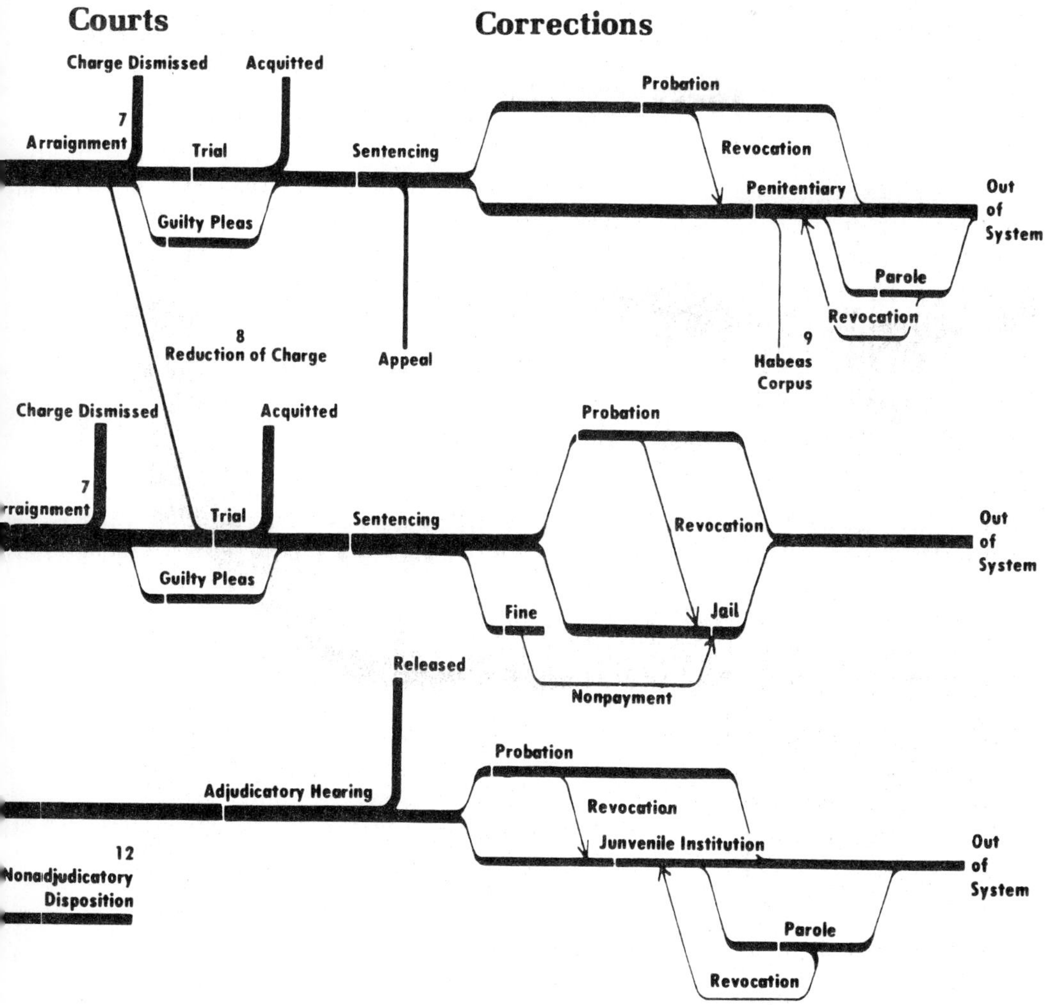

7. Appearance for plea; defendant elects trial by judge or jury (if available).

8. Charge may be reduced at any time prior to trial in return for plea of guilty or for other reasons.

9. Challenge on constitutional grounds to legality of detention. May be sought at any point in process.

10. Police often hold informal hearings, dismiss or adjust many cases without further processing.

11. Probation officer decides desirability of further court action.

12. Welfare agency, social services, counseling, medical care, etc., for cases where adjudicatory handling not needed.

> *reside. No State shall make or enforce any law which shall abridge the privileges or immunities of citizens of the United States; nor shall any State deprive any person of life, liberty, or property, without due process of law; nor deny to any person within its jurisdiction the equal protection of the laws.*

The Constitution and the Bill of Rights serve as blueprints for the general administration of criminal justice. They are designed to protect individual liberties while at the same time, ensuring the security of the community and its citizens. As interpreted by the United States Supreme Court, the Constitution has a direct impact on the manner in which the American police perform their duties. Supreme Court decisions in the area of criminal justice and procedure have been very significant, and their effects have been far-reaching. For example, *Mapp v. Ohio*[3] in 1961 prohibited the use of illegally obtained evidence in all criminal prosecutions, *Gideon v. Wainwright*[4] in 1963 guaranteed indigent defendants free legal representation in cases involving a serious crime, *Miranda v. Arizona*[5] in 1966 required the advisement of constitutional rights at the accusatory stage of a criminal investigation, and *Schmerber v. California*[6] in 1966 applied significant restrictions on the scope of a search incidental to a lawful arrest. This process of examining and occasionally changing existing laws is called *judicial review*. Combined with the application of judicially imposed procedural restrictions on police power, judicial review is and will continue to a controversial issue both within and outside of the criminal justice system.

Justification of Police Power Within the Social Order

No human society has ever been totally free of deviant behavior, and it's unlikely that any society ever will be. The more populated and complex a society becomes, the wider the range of social conduct which must be controlled by government through the exercise of its inherent *police power*. Police power is the legitimate authority of government to regulate the behavior of its population in order to achieve the common good. "In the exercise of its police power, government enacts laws designed to protect the health, welfare, and morals of its citizens."[7]

Certain kinds of deviant behavior are considered to be injurious to the social order and enough of a threat to the people that they are labeled *criminal behavior*. A *crime* is generally defined as an act or omission in violation of the criminal law. *Criminal laws* are group-shared expectations, or social norms, which have been translated into *statutes* through the politically-oriented legislative process. These criminal statutes are usually categorized and catalogued in a public document known as the *Criminal Code* or *Penal Code*. The criminal statutes provide the executive branch of government with the authority to enforce the law. The executive (whether a president, a governor, a county commissioner, or a mayor), in turn, delegates the criminal law enforcement function to the police.

According to the National Advisory Commission of Criminal Justice Standards and Goals:

> *The police in the United States are not separate from the people. They draw their authority from the will and consent of the people, and they recruit their officers from them. The police are the instruments of the people to achieve and maintain order; their efforts are founded on the principles of public service and ultimate responsibility to the public.*[8]

The police form an essential link in the chain of effective social control, community safety, and personal security.

Governmental Fragmentation and the Police

The American system of government is based on a political philosophy of decentralized power and local control. As a result, governmental structures, including police agencies, have proliferated and often overlap one another (see Figure 6).

Semiautonomous governments (for example, towns, villages, cities and the like) have established a wide variety of police agencies with differing formal structures and functions. These agencies have been designed to carry

Figure 1.6
Stratification of Police Agencies

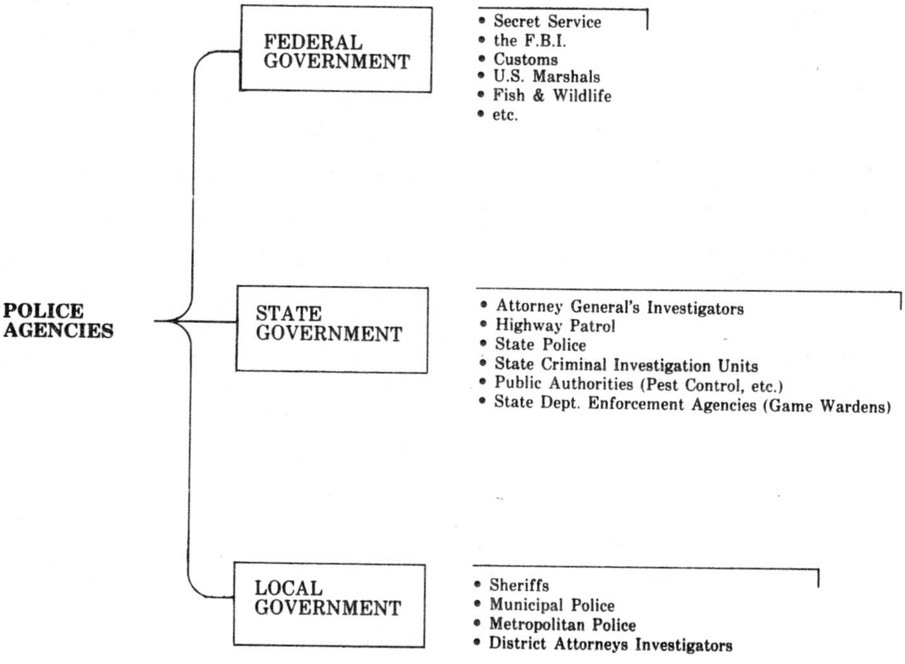

out specific government policy as well as enforce the criminal law. A superficial review of federal, state, and local governments will easily reveal the many and varied approaches to and structures for policing in the United States. These include:

- federal law enforcement agencies;
- state police departments;
- state highway patrols;
- state criminal investigation units;
- sheriffs' departments;
- county police;
- district attorneys' investigators;
- coroners' offices;
- metropolitan police;
- municipal police;
- public authority police;
- civil defense police;
- public safety agents;
- marshals;
- constables;
- auxiliary police; and
- other less significant approaches and styles.

This diversity in both structure and function makes generalizing about the police a very difficult task, yet there are enough common denominators to make the study of the police establishment worthwhile.

The Police Establishment

Collectively, the police represent the largest and most pervasive of the subsystems involved in the criminal justice process. They also play one of the most complex roles. Herman Goldstein, who served as Superintendent O. W. Wilson's executive assistant in the Chicago Police Department, says:

> *The police function is incredibly complex. The total range of police responsibility is extraordinarily broad. Many tasks are so entangled that separation is impossible. And the numerous conflicts among the different aspects of the functions cannot be easily reconciled. Anyone attempting to construct a workable definition of the police role will typically come away with old images shattered and with a new-found appreciation for the intricacies of police work.*[9]

The police role in modern society is, of necessity, multidimensional. The most popular image of the police as law enforcers and criminal investigators may be the least accurate. According to Donald J. Newman, a noted author and professor of Criminal Justice, State University of New York at Albany:

An ordinary patrol officer in a metropolitan police agency probably devotes no more than 10 to 15 percent of his time to activities directly related to criminal law enforcement. And, even here, "crime fighting" most often entails intervention in minor crime situations involving misdemeanant conduct and public order offenses.[10]

A dimension of police work which is often overlooked is that the police are involved in crime control only part of the time:

Much police activity has little to do with crime investigation, arrest, or interrogation of suspects. Most police work involves such things as directing traffic flow, providing emergency services for citizens who are injured or ill, maintaining an around-the-clock fire watch, locating missing persons, settling family and neighborhood disputes, handling chronic inebriates and mentally ill persons, and an endless list of other "service" functions. So much is expected and demanded of the police that the proper scope of policing has never been really defined. What a police agency does, should do, or should not do is literally unanswerable.[11]

The police organization in a given community generally develops in response to the needs, perceived needs, and demands of those segments of the community which have the power to shape public policy.

Police agencies vary in size, structure, jurisdiction, function, and ultimate authority. It's estimated that around 420,000 persons are currently working in approximately 40,000 separate police agencies. The combined expenditures of the police for personnel, equipment, and programming exceed $2.5 billion a year.[12] Police agencies vary in size and organizational complexity; they range from operations which have no full-time personnel and a strictly limited budget to organizations like the New York Police Department, which employs nearly 30,000 officers and works with a budget of millions of dollars.

Police agencies also differ in terms of sophistication and professional competence. Some agencies appear to be disorganized and incapable of performing even the most basic police functions, while other police organizations, such as the Los Angeles County Sheriff's Department and the Federal Bureau of Investigation, project a skilled, technically competent, and professionally-oriented image. American police agencies run the gamut with regard to basic organization and structure, ranging from the original police agent (or police generalist) concept employed in Lakewood, Colorado, where the individual officer performs a wide variety of different police tasks and follows up on almost all assigned cases, to the highly structured, paramilitaristic, and bureaucratic Pennsylvania State Police, with its emphasis on the functional specialization of personnel. The highly centralized Chicago Police Department—with its interconnected patrol, detectives, tactical squads, communications, and staff services—stands in sharp contrast to the Team Policing Project implemented in Dayton, Ohio or the Sector Patrol Plan used in Cincinnati, where policing is more or less decentralized with objectives, goals, and procedures determined by the police and the community groups being served. The modern police establishment is continuously experimenting with different approaches.

Finally, it should be noted that intergovernmental policing units are becoming increasingly popular. These units may be formed by specific design or through a process of consolidation. Special Law Enforcement Districts, formed by mutual agreement of a polity to increase their own taxes in order to generate more revenue to increase law enforcement activities within a specified geographical area; Metropolitan Enforcement Groups (MEG), in which local jurisdictions provide personnel to a central authority in a cooperative effort to combat criminal activities which cross municipal boundaries within a given metropolitan area; and regional Strike Forces, composed of federal, state, and local police personnel assigned to a coordinated unit designed to deal with a specifically targeted problem like organized crime, narcotics traffic, etc., have become a permanent feature of the modern approach to crime control and the enforcement of criminal law.

The Police and Criminal Law Enforcement

The police, viewed systemically, activate the criminal justice process. They are responsible for identifying the suspected offender and invoking official action to prosecute the matter further. Basically, the police serve as the catalyst which moves the criminal law out of the books and into social action (see Figure 7).

The criminal law enforcement/crime investigation process can be initiated in a variety of ways. The most common methods include:

1. A citizen makes a formal complaint to the authorities, stating that some type of criminal conduct is taking place or already has taken place; or
2. The police take action themselves based on information received and/or the observation of a suspected criminal act.

In the latter case, the police officer becomes both the complainant and the chief witness for the prosecution.

The police, like all of the other subsystems within the criminal justice process, possess a tremendous amount of *discretionary power*. Basically,

Figure 1.7

POLICE FUNCTIONS IN THE ADMINISTRATION OF JUSTICE

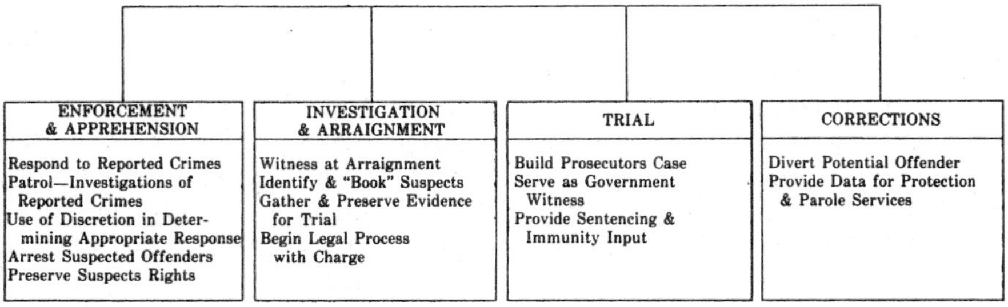

the individual police officer decides whether to intervene and pursue a specific matter or disregard it as unfounded or unworthy of further action. The nature and extent of police discretion can be described as follows:

> *Whether a criminal prosecution is initiated against an individual depends, in most instances, upon police judgment. Theoretically, this judgment is based upon a statutory definition of crime, although it is abundantly clear that there are many situations in which a violation has in fact occurred and is known to the police, but for which there is no effort by the police to make an arrest. Among the factors accounting for this discretionary decision not to invoke the criminal process are the volume of violations of a similar nature, the limited resources of the police, the overgeneralization of legislature enactments defining criminal conduct, and various local pressures reflecting community values and attitudes.*[13]

Once the police make the basic decision to formally invoke the criminal justice process, they have the authority to arrest the suspected offender. This authority is based on both custom and statutory law. An arrest may be defined as "the apprehending or restraining of one's person in order to forthcoming to answer for an alleged or suspected crime."[14] The police are empowered to make arrests with or without a written warrant, depending on the circumstances surrounding a particular crime or apprehension. *On-view* or *observed crime* arrests—the kind most often associated with ordinance violations and/or misdemeanor offenses—are very common. In almost all jurisdictions, a police officer has the authority to make a warrantless arrest if he or she has reasonable grounds to believe that a felony has been committed, and that the suspect actually committed the offense. This is generally true whether or not the criminal act was observed by the arresting officer.

Although warrantless arrests are made, arrest with a warrant, especially in a felony case, is preferable and is usually considered to be the most professional police practice. There are good reasons for this point of view:

1. Obtaining a warrant (pursuant to the provisions of the Fourth Amendment) virtually assures at least some degree of prior judicial inspection of the evidence or information which is being used to establish the probable cause required by the United States Constitution; and
2. A police officer who makes an arrest based on the conditions stipulated in an arrest warrant cannot be held responsible for false arrest.

"Probable cause" for an arrest is defined as "a combination of facts or apparent facts, viewed through the eyes of an experienced police officer, which would lead a man of reasonable caution to believe that a crime is or has been committed."[15]

From a strictly professional point of view, the planned and thorough pre-arrest investigation of the alleged criminal act is considered to be the best police procedure. Pre-arrest investigation gives the police ample time to develop enough evidence to prove their case beyond a reasonable doubt. Under these conditions, it is reasonable to assume that all of the important case-building steps will have been taken, that prior judicial inspection of the evidence has taken place, and that the prosecutor has had the opportunity to review the case (circumstances, suspect, and evidence) and has given some indication that the case is sound and is prosecutable. This is the calculated and procedurally sound manner in which the Federal Bureau of Investigation has traditionally operated.

From a much more realistic perspective, however, a large number of felony arrests are made at the spur of the moment and are surrounded by crisis circumstances; they often result from an on-view incident, a field investigation, or even pure luck. In cases of this type, an in-custody or post-custody criminal investigation is conducted so that the police can develop the evidence necessary to sustain the accusation and establish the evidentiary base required to support a conviction. In many cases, crucial and damaging evidence is developed by the police *after* the suspect has been apprehended and booked.

As is obvious by this time, it's very difficult to formulate consistent rules and/or procedures which can be applied to all police criminal law enforcement activities. Nevertheless, the quantity and quality of the evidence, the "chain of custody" (proof of who had control of and under what conditions the evidence was kept), and the reasonableness of the police case must be sufficient to establish the *corpus delicti* (or body of the crime) and to convince a jury (even though the vast majority of criminal cases never reach the jury trial stage) that there is reason to believe that a crime was committed and that the accused probably committed it.

The Police and Rules of Criminal Procedure

The federal and state governments are responsible for formulating and adopting rules of criminal procedure. These rules most generally stipulate *authority, objectives, appropriate procedure,* and *venue* (the geo-political jurisdiction within which the procedures apply). These are the rules of the game, so to speak. They regulate officer-violator contacts (such as the mechanics and techniques of arrest, the use of force, and so on) and outline the steps which must be taken to complete a successful prosecution. These procedural rules are extremely important; a violation can result in the loss of a case even when a conviction would be appropriate. According to American social and political thought, the end doesn't justify the means.

After being apprehended for a criminal act, the suspect must be advised of his or her constitutional rights. The police are required to safeguard those rights. The United States Supreme Court's *Miranda*[16] decision has been interpreted to require the following "warnings" at the time of the actual arrest, at the accusatory stage of a pre-arrest criminal investigation, and at the time of post-arrest interrogation:

1. You have the constitutional right to remain silent;
2. Anything you say can and will be used against you in a court of law;
3. You have the right to the services of an attorney while you are being questioned;

4. If you do not have or cannot afford to hire a lawyer, one will be appointed for you by the State.

If, after being warned, the accused chooses to cooperate by discussing the matter, the evidence is legal and admissible. Subsequent court decisions have emphasized the necessity for the above warnings in all felony cases; other decisions have emphasized their importance in significant misdemeanor investigations.

Once advised of his or her constitutional rights, a suspect may waive those rights and cooperate with the authorities. The waiver, which will eventually be evaluated by the prosecutor and the trial judge, must be competently made; this means that it must be given *knowingly, intelligently,* and *voluntarily.* A suspect, regardless of whether he or she is in custody, may change his or her mind and rescind the waiver at any time. If the waiver is rescinded, the questioning must stop. Violation of these procedures may result in the activation of the *exclusionary rule* and the suppression of any evidence gained from the suspect. The Exclusionary Rule is a legal concept which requires that illegally obtained evidence not be used against the suspect in a court of law.

Once the basic procedural and legal requirements related to an arrest have been met, the police, in most jurisdictions, have a reasonable amount of time to complete the booking process and to bring the accused before a magistrate on the initial charge. Booking usually involves confirming the identity of the suspect, searching, fingerprinting, photographing, and the recording of data. This interval is often used by the police to continue the investigatory process.

The initial appearance before the magistrate functions as a *prearraignment hearing* (except in minor cases, and then it may constitute a *primary trial* on the charges brought by the police). It is the magistrate's responsibility to review the police case and to determine whether or not *prima facie* evidence exists to justify the prosecution of the suspect. Prima facie refers to the apparent strength of the evidence. A prima facie case is one established by sufficient evidence but which can be rebutted and/or contradicted. The magistrate may also be called upon to make a determination as to the "reasonable grounds" standard in a warrantless arrest. The police are the prime (if not the only) prosecution witnesses at this stage of the criminal justice process. They may even act as a stand-in for the prosecutor. If they have done their job well, or if the magistrate is sufficiently pro-police, the decision will favor the police position and the suspect will be held for further processing.

It might be appropriate to note at this point that many jurisdictions are adopting *summons and citation systems* designed to improve on some of the negative aspects created by unplanned arrests. In these jurisdictions, the police are given authority, in select circumstances and for specific crimes, to issue citations. A citation is basically a summons which requires that the suspect appear in court to answer the charges brought by the police. He or she is not physically apprehended. The summons and citation gives the police more time for investigation, saves police time, saves money, and protects the community as effectively as an arrest and in-custody detention.

Once the pre-arraignment hearing has been held and the magistrate has concurred with the police action, the criminal case shifts into a new arena. This next subsystem, the prosecutorial function, is lawyer-dominated and is part of what has been called the "middle stages" of the criminal justice process. As a result, there are new concepts to deal with and new terms to learn. The prosecutor is responsible for officially determining the charge to be lodged; utilizing *nolle prosequi* (the decision, based on extra legal social and/or political considerations, not to initiate prosecution even when there is enough evidence to do so), when appropriate; referring the criminal case to the grand jury; initiating the information/preliminary hearing procedure; and representing the state in the criminal court trial. In this new arena, the police continuously interact with the prosecution. They play a decidedly different yet critical role.

The Police and the Prosecutorial Function

After the suspected offender has been introduced into the criminal justice process by some type of official police action, the prosecutorial subsystem comes into play. As a result, different roles are created, existing roles are reassigned, and new role expectations emerge. During the law enforcement/criminal investigation phase of the criminal justice process, the police—and, to a lesser degree, the magistrate—are preeminent. During the middle stages, the prosecutor (whether he or she is called the State's Attorney, the District Attorney, or by some other title) takes center stage and the police more or less become the supporting actors.

Following the pre-arraignment hearing in which the magistrate has concluded that there is probable cause to continue the prosecution of the defendant, the criminal case, in most jurisdictions, is referred to the prosecutor's office for processing. The prosecutor, considered to be the chief law enforcement officer in many parts of the country, is responsible for:

- reviewing the nature of the accusation;
- examining the circumstances surrounding the alleged crime;
- establishing the existence of the *corpus delicti;*
- studying police procedures employed in the apprehension through a review of the investigative report;
- considering the magistrate's findings;
- assessing the weight of the evidence;
- deciding if a prosecution is in order; and
- determining the official criminal charge to be lodged.

If the prosecutor finds that a *prima facie* case exists, the state may seek the continuation of the criminal justice process. If the decision is to prosecute, it is the prosecutor's job to determine the exact charge or charges which will be filed against the suspect. His or her decision is based both on evidence and criminal law.

In those states which still use the indicting grand jury, the case is reviewed by the appropriate judicial officer and placed on the jury's docket for formal action. A grand jury is a group of citizens impaneled to review the evidence and the actions of the magistrate for the purpose of issuing and/or declining to issue an indictment. An indictment is a finding of probable cause to proceed with the case and a directive to the criminal court to initiate formal proceedings. In those jurisdictions which utilize an information/preliminary hearing procedure, the prosecutor approves the information (or statement of charges) and schedules the preliminary hearing in the appropriate court. If the case is weak, or if the prosecutor is concerned about his or her ability to sustain the charge, the prosecutor may order the charge *nolle prosequied*, and the case will be dropped. This is an obvious example of the wide range of discretion inherent in the prosecutor's role.

The function of both the grand jury and the information/preliminary hearing procedure is to test the state's evidence and to establish probable cause to prosecute the case further. In theory, both serve as a filtering mechanism which is designed to divert unfounded and/or weak cases from the criminal justice system. It should be kept in mind, however, that the prosecutor's office is responsible for scheduling the cases which go to the grand jury and/or the preliminary hearing. In addition, the prosecutor is very active in coordinating, guiding, and monitoring the actual proceedings of the grand jury or the preliminary hearing. Only the state's case—evidence showing that a crime has been committed and that the accused probably committed it—is presented for review (although it may be tested by the defense counsel for content and for the quantity or quality of the evidence). It should come as no surprise, then, that most grand juries and preliminary hearings usually find probable cause to continue the case further. When probable cause is found to exist, the case is *bound over*, or passed on, to the appropriate court with jurisdiction to try the case.

The prosecution is almost totally dependent upon the data supplied by the police establishment. If that data is factual, accurate, and complete, the prosecutor (unless inhibited by corruption, incompetence, or politics) will be able to perform at a very high level. It is almost axiomatic to say that a highly trained, competent, and professional police component which operates within appropriate constitutional guidelines strengthens the prosecutorial function at its primary level (the level at which the decision to officially charge a suspect with the commission of a crime). On the other hand, if the police lack conceptual knowledge, professional skill, and credibility, they can have a negative impact on the prosecution.

Thus the police, in their supporting role, help to determine the strength of the state's case against the accused. In addition, the work they do during the criminal investigation assists the prosecutor in deciding which criminal cases should go to the grand jury or the preliminary hearing. The police serve as the eyes, ears, and official memory of the prosecutor. They help the prosecutor to establish venue, *corpus delicti*, and the circumstances surrounding the criminal incident (the who, what, where, when, why, with what, and how). The police are considered to be official witnesses and are empowered, under certain conditions, to give expert testimony.

The police and the prosecutor's office are intertwined in terms of function and, of necessity, have a symbiotic relationship with each other. It is the prosecutor who takes the results of the police investigation and translates them into acceptable legalese, a *prima facie* presentation, supportive evidence, and proof beyond a reasonable doubt. The prosecutor also uses information gathered by the police in suggesting punishment or an alternative correctional strategy for the accused.

The interrelationship between the police and the prosecution is becoming more and more important. In many jurisdictions today, the police actively participate in the plea bargaining process, which until quite recently was the sole domain of the prosecutor and the defense counsel. In addition, with the encouragement of the prosecutor, the police are taking an increasingly more active role in the immunity granting process and in sentencing recommendations.[17]

Competent, efficient, and rights-oriented police go hand in hand with effective prosecution. The same argument can be made with reference to the functioning of the judicial process.

As a case moves away from the street incident or the actual crime, the influence exerted by the police is less direct. This change does not negate the role of the police, but casts that role in a different perspective. The impact of the police on law enforcement and the arrest or physical apprehension of the suspected offender is, of course, great. An obvious and direct face-to-face relationship exists. The influence of the police establishment on the prosecutorial function, although somewhat different in orientation, is still substantial. The police perform a basic service for the prosecution by:

- producing the suspects;
- building the initial criminal case;
- invoking the criminal justice process;
- preserving the incriminating evidence; and
- acting as official witnesses for the state.

In addition, the police serve as consulting specialists for the prosecution and provide professional feedback to the prosecutor. It should not be forgotten, however, that the prosecutor is ultimately responsible for manipulating and managing the police input in such a way that the impact of the police reaches its maximum level.

The Police and the Judicial Process

Finally, the police role in the judicial process shifts even further. At this stage of criminal justice involvement, the police role as the official representative of the government and the role of the individual officer as an expert witness merge. A new role is created, one that is specifically designed to strengthen the prosecution's case against the accused.

This change is caused by the interjection of other subsystems—the prosecution, the judiciary, and the defense counsel—into the criminal justice process. In addition, as the case moves along, there is a perceptible change in the actual focus of the criminal justice system itself. Basically, it moves from *regulative* (regulating human behavior) through *resolutional* (resolving misunderstanding and conflict) to *adjudicative* (determining guilt or innocence and applying the appropriate sanctions).[18]

The primary functions of the police in the judicial process are as follows:

- they are expected to be impartial fact-finders;
- they are considered to be experienced evidence collectors;
- they are presumed to be efficient custodians of physical evidence;
- they are viewed as data collectors;
- they are information coordinators;
- they are seen as official representatives of government; and
- they are assumed, by the public, to be expert witnesses.

The police who appear in court are expected to play their supporting role in the judicial process in a thorough, competent, and professional manner. They are presumed to realize that the final judgment as to whether the suspect is or is not guilty is not theirs to make. That responsibility belongs exclusively to the jury (or the judge, in non-jury trials), and the appropriate exercise of this responsibility must be within select, rigidly enforced, guidelines.

The function of the defense attorney is to give his or her client the best defense available and to secure the client's release from the charge if at all possible. The defense counsel assumes an adversary posture and attempts to obtain his or her objectives by establishing doubt (or a lack of credibility) in the mind of the judge, who can order a directed verdict of acquittal, or in the minds of the jurors, who have the constitutional authority to find the defendant innocent of the charge.

One of the most effective methods of establishing the element of doubt is to successfully impeach not only the testimony but also the image of the police officer. The defense attorney who can show that the police are imperfect fact-finders, poor evidence collectors, incapable of effectively controlling the chain of custody, or unqualified to be expert witnesses can plant the seed of doubt in the minds of those persons who make the official determination of guilt or innocence. That seed of reasonable doubt can cost the state (especially the police, prosecution, and courts) hundreds of working hours, literally thousands of dollars, and the confidence of the community. The police role in the judicial process is of tremendous importance— yet the value of this role is often underestimated by the police themselves.

The police role as an informed and official witness is absolutely crucial to the judicial process. The testimony of a police officer is often the key to a successful prosecution. It should be obvious that a court appearance by a police officer is often an exercise in making a good impression, yet this is precisely where many good criminal cases are lost. The officer may present a poor professional image, by demonstrating a lack of bearing or professional poise, appearing uninterested, or being unable to project sincerity. This can happen because many police officers take the witness stand when they:

- are not sufficiently prepared to testify accurately about the matter under investigation;
- lack the necessary resources to refresh their memories;
- become confused by minor details of the case;
- demonstrate a lack of respect for the accused and/or the judicial process itself; and/or
- appear to be deceitful or dishonest.

The role of the police officer in the judicial process is a major contribution to the criminal justice system. While its importance cannot be measured by an objective test, it can be determined by a subjective review and evaluation of the entire criminal justice system.

When the police participate in the judicial process, they act as representatives of the state and the law enforcement profession. If they fail here, they have allowed themselves to be looked upon and criticized in a very unfavorable manner.

Effective participation by the police in the judicial process strengthens the prosecution, helps to eliminate doubt in the minds of jurors, and gives the community a sense of confidence in the police establishment and the criminal justice system as a whole.

In many jurisdictions across the country, the police are demanding more say in the sentencing of convicted criminals. In some areas, they have met with stiff judicial resistance. In those parts of the nation where the police are viewed as competent, efficient, and professional, however, opposition to their input into the sentencing process has decreased while police influence has significantly increased. It is logical to assume that the police obtain recognition, status, and influence in direct proportion to their professional qualifications and their image as protectors of society rather than oppressors.

The Police and Corrections

The term *corrections* refers to a loosely organized system of interrelated, semiautonomous agencies which share fairly common objectives. The most often cited correctional objectives are the protection of society, and the rehabilitation of the offender.[19] To obtain these lofty goals, there has been and continues to be an organized attempt to reduce *recidivism* (the repetition of crime by the criminal) through some type of behavior modification. As a result, several correctional strategies have been developed in the United States. They include, but are not limited to, the following:

- incapacitation of the offender through incarceration;
- alternative institutional treatment programs;

- surveillance, supportive guidance, and supervisory control of the offender while he or she is still in the community;
- the application of counseling and/or other clinical treatment procedures, on a voluntary or involuntary basis, in an attempt to change human behavior patterns; and
- utilization of the social casework method.

From a systemic viewpoint, several components which make up the correction subsystem can be identified. They are:

Probation: the conditional release of the offender back into the community, without any prolonged incarceration, but under the supervision and control of the probation service.

Institutionalization: the incapacitation of the dangerous offender through incarceration in an institution (a prison, reformatory, training school, Youth Development Center, etc.) designed to meet both security and treatment needs.

Parole: the conditional release of the offender, after he or she has spent time in a state prison or correctional facility, under the direct supervision and control of an agent appointed by the state.

After-care: a variety of semistructured, noninstitutional living environments (like halfway houses or transitional living centers) which are designed to help the ex-offender become reintegrated into society in an orderly manner.

Schematically, there are many correctional programs—such as work-release, furloughs, intermittent incarceration, probation without verdict, and so on—which fall under one or another of these major headings.

Most of these correctional activities appear to be far outside the purview of the police. Correctional strategies, for example, are applied to the offender by society and personally experienced by the individual long after the police have disengaged themselves from direct involvement with the crime. To presume that the police do not have an important impact on the correctional subsystem of the criminal justice process would be myopic, however. On the contrary, the police do a number of things which have a direct impact upon the correctional process. For example:

- they effectively divert potential offenders away from involvement in criminal activity and in the criminal justice process;
- they practice fundamental fairness in their dealings with the community at large and with the suspected offender in particular;
- they attempt to be as objective, accurate, and complete as they can when performing their official recordings and reporting roles;
- they demonstrate fundamental fairness in their relationship with those who have been labeled as criminal; and
- they serve as examples and/or role models for the community in general.

The police—who constitute society's first line of defense against crime and the criminal—are, as a result of continuous interaction with the community, in an excellent position to identify troublespots and potential offenders. Effective intervention can alter circumstances dramatically and may help to prevent an individual from developing into a delinquent or criminal offender. This is, of course, primary crime prevention. If it works, the potential offender can avoid the criminal justice process altogether and escape *labeling* (as a criminal) and the stigma which goes along with it.

Fairness is a fundamental prerequisite for effective police work in a free society. If the police are firm yet fair in their dealings with the public, they gain the respect and gratitude of the community. In addition, police fairness in the apprehending, processing, and prosecution of the accused helps to set the tone for the development of his or her attitudes toward self and society. If the accused is not robbed of dignity or self-esteem, and if he or she can be made to feel that the criminal justice process itself is fair, then he or she will be more open to the influences of the correctional subsystem. Effective, firm, and fair police action may well be the determining factor in the success or failure of the correctional effort.

The police investigative report is important not only to the prosecution (in deciding whether or not to file the charges) and the court (where it serves as an essential ingredient in the chain of evidence necessary to prove that the accused is guilty beyond a reasonable doubt) but is also invaluable to corrections. The police investigative report serves as a primary source of data for the probation service. It is often incorporated verbatim into the pre-sentence investigation records (PSI) and, as such, exerts a significant influence on the probation process. The pre-sentence investigation, which also contains sentencing recommendations, is given to the judge prior to final disposition of the case. In most jurisdictions, the judge bases his or her action on the pre-sentence investigation and the recommendations made by the probation officer. It's obvious, therefore, that the police indirectly influence the sentencing process itself; consequently, the police investigative report should be complete, thorough, and objective. Failure to meet any of these standards can distort the process and result in a person either being given probation on a "technicality" or being denied probation because of the inherent bias of a prejudiced police officer.

The same concept is true for the parole process. The police investigative report, the case summary, and the pre-sentence investigation are used in the development of the Pre-Parole Investigation Report (PPI). The PPI is only as good as the data it contains. If that data is faulty or incomplete, the decision-making process can be weakened and mistakes made. Here again, the police have a significant influence which should not be overlooked.

Finally, the manner in which the police treat the convicted offender is indicative of true professionalism—or the lack of it. Here, probably more than at any other juncture, the police serve as role models. If they forget the fundamental principle that once the penalty has been paid, the offender should be given a chance to demonstrate his or her worth—or if they stereotype and harrass offenders—they set the stage for others to acquire their attitudes. Ramsey Clark, the former United States Attorney General, summed it up this way: "No activity of a people so exposes their humanity or inhumanity, their character, their capacity for charity in its most generous dimension, as treatment they accord persons convicted of a crime."[20] To meet their responsibility as role models and opinion leaders, the professional police establishment must be objective and impartial while supporting the efforts of the convicted offender who is sincerely attempting to modify his or her behavior. Support in this area strengthens the ex-offender's resolve, boosts self-esteem, and benefits the society by preventing further crime. The importance of this pivotal police role cannot be overestimated.

An Overview of the Police Role

In its Task Force Report on the Police, the President's Commission on Law Enforcement and the Administration of Justice has concluded that:

> *Law enforcement has always been a difficult task. It is especially difficult in a society such as ours that has so heterogeneous and mobile a population; that has so prosperous an economy; that has so high a degree of urbanization, with its accompanying congestion and anonymity; that places so high a value on individual freedom, upon equality under the law, and upon local control over police power.*
>
> *The current widespread concern with crime and violence, particularly in large cities, commands a rethinking of the function of the police in American society. It calls for a reassessment of the kinds of resources and support that the police need to respond more adequately to the demands that we make upon them.*
>
> *While each person has a somewhat different impression of the nature of the police function, based primarily upon his personal experience and contacts with police officers, there is a widespread popular conception of the police, supported by news and entertainment media. Through these, the police have come to be viewed as a body of men continually engaged in the exciting, dangerous, and competitive enterprise of apprehending and prosecuting criminals. Emphasis upon this one aspect of police functioning has led to a tendency on the part of both the public and the police to underestimate the range and complexity of the total police task.*

Perspectives On Crime Prevention

Crime is a social reality, and the fear of crime is becoming a twentieth century human preoccupation. As the crime rate escalates, and as society's confidence in its own ability to control criminal activity declines, our frustrations are magnified. Mass frustration can lead to a lack of reason and a reliance on methods of social control which are inappropriate in a free society. Terms like "law and order" or "public safety" often mask society's inability to deal with the real issues in contemporary America, such as:

- the lack of confidence in government;

- the unequal distribution of political, social, and economic power;
- racial and social discrimination;
- the lack of appropriate means to attain legitimate human expectations; and
- the balance between individual freedom of action and the absolute need for some form of social control.

Unless these fundamental questions are addressed and basic structural adjustments are made, social deviance (including crime) will thrive and will continue to threaten the social order itself. Under existing conditions, the system of criminal justice is, according to some, merely a Band-Aid and cannot hope to ensure the tranquility and security Americans seek.

It is unreasonable to assume that American society will somehow miraculously deal with and solve these pressing social problems within the foreseeable future. Consequently, a reevaluation of the importance, structure, and function of the criminal justice system is in order. Fairness in the general administration of criminal justice must become a priority.

Conclusion

The administration of criminal justice is an essential yet complex function of government. If justice is administered in an impartial manner—fair but firm—the system safeguards the environment and contemporary social problems can be solved. Effectiveness and efficiency in the administration of criminal justice helps to prevent crime. If the police power of government is abused, criminal justice can become an instrument of oppression. Thus, the role of the criminal justice system must be that of a guardian of individual freedom.

In order to operate in an effective and impartial manner, the components of the justice system—the legislature, police, prosecution, courts, and corrections—must function in concert with one another. Each component, or subsystem, must make an effort to fulfill its basic responsibility. Each component must have an adequate number of qualified personnel and must be funded at a level which ensures quality performance. And finally, each of the subsystems must recognize its interdependence with the other components which make up the criminal justice system while recognizing a congruence of goals and overall philosophy.

The police must learn to recognize the centrality of their role within the criminal justice system. They have input into the lawmaking process; they invoke criminal justice procedures and introduce the suspected offender into the system; they actively assist the prosecutor; they appear in court as representatives of the government and in the capacity of an official or expert witness; and they set the tone for the entire correctional effort. All of these responsibilities must be carried out within the framework created by the Constitution of the United States of America. This very difficult task represents one of the true challenges for the 1980s.

Topics For Discussion

1. **What are the components of the criminal justice system, and how are they related?**
2. **What is a system? Explain how the concept of system is related to the criminal justice process.**
3. **What is the police role with relation to the other components or subsystems within the criminal justice system?**
4. **What is Police Power? Why is the exercise of police power by government essential in a complex society?**
5. **What is the role of the United States Constitution in relation to the delivery of criminal justice services?**
6. **Explain the basic methods used by the police to justify invoking the criminal justice process. For example, under what conditions can they make an arrest?**
7. **How do the police influence the correctional process? Discuss both the direct and indirect impact of the police on corrections.**
8. **Are the police, in concert with the rest of the criminal justice system, really the guardians of individual freedom? Why or why not?**

References

1. Donald J. Newman, *Introduction to Criminal Justice*, (New York: J. B. Lippincott Co., 1975), p. 13.
2. Paul B. Weston and Kenneth M. Wells, *The Administration of Justice* (Englewood Cliffs, N. J.: Prentice-Hall Inc., 3rd ed., 1977).
3. *Mapp v. Ohio*, 367 U.S. 643, 81 S. Ct. 1684 (1961).
4. *Gideon v. Wainwright*, 372 U.S. 335, 83 S. Ct. 792 (1963).
5. *Miranda v. Arizona*, 384 U.S. 436, 86 S. Ct. 1602 (1966).
6. *Schmerber v. California*, 384 U.S. 757, 86 S. Ct. 1826 (1966).
7. National Advisory Commission on Criminal Justice Standards and Goals, Washington, D.C., U.S. Government Printing Office, 1973.
8. N.A.C.C.J.S. and G., p. 9.
9. Herman Goldstein, *Police in a Free Society* (New York: Ballinger Publishing Company, 1977), p. 21.
10. Newman, p. 141.
11. Newman, p. 141.
12. Harry W. More, Jr., *Critical Issues in Law Enforcement* (Cincinnati: W. H. Anderson Company, 1972), p. v.
13. Arthur Neiderhoffer and Aberham S. Blumberg, *The Ambivalent Force: Perspectives on the Police* (Toronto: Ginn and Company, 1970), p. 93.
14. J. Shane Creamer, *The Law of Arrest, Search and Seizure* (Philadelphia: W. B. Saunders Company, 1975), p. 48.
15. Creamer, p. 9.
16. *Miranda v. Arizona*, 384 U.S. 436, 86 S. Ct. 1602 (1966).

17. Gilbert B. Stuckey, *Procedures in the Justice System* (Columbus, Ohio: Charles E. Merrill Publishing Company, 1976).
18. Robert P. Rhodes, *The Insoluble Problems of Crime* (New York: John Wiley and Sons, 1977), p. 47.
19. These objectives are cited by all published works within the correctional field.
20. Ramsey Clark, *Crime in America* (New York: Simon and Schuster 1970), p. 212.
21. President's Commission on Law Enforcement and the Administration of Justice, *Task Force Report: The Police*, 1967, p. 13.

Annotated Bibliography

Chamelin, Neil C., Vernon B. Fox, and Paul M. Whisenand, *Introduction to Criminal Justice* (Englewood Cliffs, New Jersey: Prentice Hall, Inc., 1975). This work contains a functional view of the fundamental structure of the criminal justice system with an emphasis on the processes involved in crime prevention and the delivery of public safety services.

Edelstein, Charles D. and Robert J. Wicks, *An Introduction to Criminal Justice* (New York: McGraw-Hill Book Company, 1977). An easy to read text which traces the development and function of the criminal justice system; it depicts the interrelationships necessary to preserve social order, detect criminals, and process the offender.

Kalmanoff, Alan, *Criminal Justice Enforcement and Administration* (Boston: Little, Brown and Company, 1976). A comprehensive textbook which covers the entire system of criminal justice with a specific emphasis on the role-expectations which have been deemed necessary to insure the delivery of effective service.

Lynch, Ronald G., *The Police Manager* (Boston: Holbrook Press, Inc., 1975). An overview of the management process which was designed to give the reader a comprehensive understanding of the background to and a review of the basic principles which make up today's approach to police administration.

More, Harry W., *The American Police* (St. Paul, Minn.: West Publishing Company, 1976). This text deals with basic police functions, the impact of day-to-day police work on the development of the police personality, a review of the variety of police behaviors, and police organization as a vehicle for the delivery of essential law enforcement services.

National Advisory Commission on Criminal Justice Standards and Goals, Police (Washington, D.C.: United States Government Printing Office, 1973). A thorough review of the current status of the police establishment in American society coupled with an analysis of specific problems related to law enforcement with very specific recommendations for improving police efficiency and service.

Souryal, Sam S., *Police Administration and Management* (St. Paul, Minn.: West Publishing Company, 1976). A systemic approach to the understanding of the components of effective police organization and the application of proven management principles in public sector administration.

Stuckey, Gilbert B., *Procedures in the Justice System* (Columbus, Ohio: Charles E. Merrill Publishing Company, 1976). A basic text dealing with specific procedures which are required to process the accused through the American criminal justice system.

Quinney, Richard, *Criminal Justice in America* (Boston: Little, Brown and Company, 1974). A radical view of the use and abuse of the criminal justice system with an emphasis on Marxist theory of criminal law and an examination of conflict theory as it relates to the role of law enforcement personnel in a changing society.

2

THE POLICE ROLE
Reactive or Proactive

Chapter Objectives

The study of this chapter should enable you to:

☑ Distinguish between police power and police powers.

☑ List the three main elements of the historical heritage that allegedly still shape the police role.

☑ Identify the major approaches of the recent past to the definition of police role and functions.

☑ Discuss the factors involved in a definition of the police role.

☑ Consider the possible relationships that might exist between individual police departments and the theoretical police role.

☑ Categorize the problems associated with the current police role.

☑ Reflect on ways in which the current police role might be modified to assist in achieving a higher quality of community life.

☑ Comment critically on suggestions for future definition of the police role.

Introduction

Police agencies the world over are social institutions. Each of them has been shaped by a heritage that goes back decades, generations, or even centuries, although some of the agencies themselves may be relatively new. Police departments in the United States share an Anglo-American heritage that is generally described as originating with the establishment of the Metropolitan Police of London in 1829 through the efforts of Sir Robert Peel. Almost every modern work on policing traces that history at least in broad outline, pointing out, for example, that the Peelian reform reached Toronto, Canada in 1835 and that the first unified day and night police department in the United States was established in New York City in 1884.[1]

Our police agencies have been molded by the people who created, led, and staffed them. Today's leaders recognize their agencies as being parts of the overall criminal justice system, but are not as often aware that their agencies are also parts of the economic, governmental, legal, political, and social systems of their particular regions. None of these systems is congruent with another, but all overlap to include segments of police agency operations. Police departments are integral to this complex system of systems.

Not all police agencies play the same role or perform all of the same functions, but a set of roles and functions can be described from which each agency takes those attributes that are required for its particular time and place. Regardless of the specific role assumed by a police agency, there are both strengths and weaknesses in its performance which can be attributed to its profile. Modifications are constantly being made in an attempt to maximize the strengths and minimize the weaknesses.

This chapter sketches the factors that influence police role definition in the United States today, describes the model that seems to best fit that role, points out some of the characteristics of that model, and suggests some possible changes for the future.

Police Powers

Powers that may be used by police agencies in performing their functions must be distinguished from the *police power* of the state, which is defined as, "The power vested in the legislature to make, ordain, and establish all manner of wholesome and reasonable laws, statutes and ordinances, either with penalties or without, not repugnant to the constitution, as they shall judge to be for the good and welfare of the commonwealth, and of the subjects of the same."[2] In short, police power is the power of the state to govern.

When we speak of police *powers*, on the other hand, we are referring to specific authority given to police agencies to carry out their functions and discharge the responsibilities that have been placed on them.

Defining a role for the police in the criminal justice system of the United States has been a historically complex process. During the last fifteen years, a number of wide-ranging studies have been made of criminal justice systems in North America and of the problems with which they deal.[3] In response to a January 1977 inquiry, the National Criminal Justice Reference Service of the Law Enforcement Assistance Administration's National Institute of Law Enforcement and Criminal Justice (LEAA/NILECJ) produced a printout listing and annotating 150 documents on the subject of police role, all of which had been published since 1964. This tremendous outpouring of literature has tended to focus primarily on specific, rather narrow police functions, such as dealing with public drunks,[4] problems in schools,[5] traffic problems,[6] or the very broad but somewhat different subject of police/community relations.[7] Relatively few of the reported documents are useful to this exploration of police role as a part of democratic government. Before attempting to summarize and discuss the content of this small group, it seems desirable to consider sources of police role definition in the United States today.

Defining the Police Role

Many mechanisms operate in definition of the police role.[8] In addition to forces within the police agency itself, at least four kinds of external influences must also be reckoned with: *private citizens,* both as individuals and as members of pressure groups; *legislative bodies; courts;* and *executive agencies.* Each of these influences merits further consideration.

Private Citizens Despite a great deal of political alienation on the part of U.S. citizens, they are still the effective arbiters of governmental function. This discussion might well not only begin but end with this same important factor. Citizens as individuals can and do influence their government at all levels—federal, state, and local. They do this with both formal and informal contacts, with the latter more common on the state and local levels and the former more frequently used at the federal level. At the local level, the interest and stated convictions of influential citizens can be and frequently are considered very seriously by police administrators at vital points in the decision-making process.

Private citizens also express their concerns and exert pressure on governmental agencies, including the police, through membership in organizations designed specifically for that purpose, such as the American Civil Liberties Union, the National Association for the Advancement of Colored People, the National Association of Manufacturers, the American Medical Association, the American Bar Association, and the John Birch Society, to mention just a few. There is strength in numbers, and that strength must be considered in a government which, like that of the United States, relies ultimately on the support of its citizens for legitimacy and source of authority.

Citizen pressure is applied not only to the police directly, but also to each of the other governmental entities engaged in police role definition. Even our courts, while interpreting legal provisions, must consider the changing moods and beliefs of the populace to which those provisions are being applied. It is probably true that most police executives pick and choose from among the various persons and organizations attempting to influence their decisions. Those persons and organizations who are unsuccessful at first, however, will frequently not give up, but instead will shift their pressure to some other center of influence.

Private citizens do, then, attempt to influence the role that police will play through both individual and corporate efforts. They aim both at police executives and at other governmental officials and institutions believed to play a roll in police function definition.

Legislative Bodies Perhaps the most obvious source of police role definition is *legislative action*. It may not be so obvious, however, that this legislative effort may be of three different types. Not only do legislatures enact statutes which deal directly with police organization and operation, but they also define the police role by enacting substantive criminal law provisions (the rules governing conduct) and controlling the purse strings.

Direct control of police organization and operation may be achieved by the enactment of individual city charters, each of which contains a section on that city's police department. It may also take the form of general statutes governing the organization and operation of cities according to their size, with the provisions for each size of city also containing a section on the police department. In addition, individual statutes may be passed dealing with specific problems in the organization or operation of the police department.

Legislatures also participate in police role definition when deciding which social problems will be handled through the vehicle of the substantive criminal law. A legislative determination, for example, that narcotics should be controlled without making their use criminal would have a tremendous impact on the police role. The same may be said of chronic alcoholism, sex offenses, and gambling. These legislative choices do determine, to an appreciable degree, the role the police play in the criminal justice system.

A third mechanism used by legislative agencies to influence police role definition is fiscal legislation. The power of the purse may be used to force a police executive to follow a favored course of action, or it may simply limit the possible scope of police action without influencing the content of specific programs. It must also be remembered that controls may be enacted not only by Congress and state legislatures, but also by legislative bodies at the county, city, and special district level.

In sum, legislative agencies at the federal, state, and local levels participate in police role definition through enactments defining the substantive criminal law, enactments dealing directly with police organization and operation, and enactments controlling the fiscal resources of police agencies.

Courts Although courts and the judges who preside over them do not handle fiscal matters of importance to the police, their influence does parallel the other two roles played by legislative bodies. Basically, they determine which areas will be brought under criminal jurisdiction by making decisions on, for example, chronic alcoholism and narcotic addiction. In establishing the content of due process, courts also have a very real impact on police operational procedures. For example, courts provide the rules governing how a confession may be obtained, when and how a house may be searched, and when an arrest can be made without a warrant.

Executive Agencies The definition of police role is also influenced by a number of different, separate executive agencies operating at several levels. Perhaps the most important of these is the office of the prosecutor. This official, whether elected or appointed, has almost complete control over deciding whether or not to prosecute a given case. The prosecutor's decisions depend on a vast variety of factors, some more justifiable than others. The net result of the prosecutor's action, however, is clearly that of determining what roles the police will play. If, for example, the prosecutor decides not to prosecute cases of assault that arise out of certain recurrent kinds of domestic disputes, the police will soon cease to make arrests in such cases. This action—or lack of action—can modify the police role just as strongly as legislative decisions can. In addition, the prosecutor determines the level of proof that must be in hand before proceeding with a given case. If that level is set too high, the police will begin to ignore violations, realizing that they can't possibly gather enough evidence to satisfy the prosecutor with the resources they have available.

Another way in which executive action can influence the police role is through the allocation of fiscal resources granted by legislative action. Although general outlines may be set by the legislature, some kind of executive control over the details of spending usually exists. Money originally intended for one use may be diverted to another.

Executive officers (such as the governor, county manager, or mayor) may also set policy for the police agencies under their control. A governor may decide, for example, that the state police shall not operate within the limits of any corporate town or city without a specific request from the municipality, even though such localities are included in the statutory grant of jurisdiction to the agency. A mayor might decide that certain enforcement techniques, such as the measuring of motor vehicles' ground speed from aircraft, may not be used even though experience proves them to be effective.

In these ways, executive officers outside the police agency do participate in police role definition. This process also continues within the police agency. The chief and his immediate assistants allocate the resources available to the department among the various line divisions, dictating by this action the broad limits of activity in each of the several areas. Further limitations may be imposed in the form of policy decisions aimed at compliance with the desires of public, legislative, judicial, or outside executive wishes. Additional policy decisions will reflect the professional judgment of administrators as to how they can best make their departments measure up to whatever standards the community uses for judgment—with the resources available to them.

When all of the above influences have made their mark, the officer who actually does the policing of the community adds final input to the definition of the police role. That input may differ from time to time, and from officer to officer, depending on a number of variables. The officer's input is usually designed to provide him with as much job satisfaction as possible. The content of this job satisfaction will vary with each officer within the permissible limits of the system. Part of that content will usually be determined by the reaction of the public, with which the officer must deal on a daily basis.

These examples make it clear that a variety of executive officers, both within and outside police agencies, participate in police role definition in direct and indirect ways.

Summary From the above, it's clear that there are many sources of police role definition, including private citizens, legislators, judges, and executive officers. It also seems apparent that the number of sources cannot be reduced, and that efforts to impose severe limits on the contribution of any particular source are apt to be effectively circumvented. Meaningful discussion of the police role must recognize the reality of an extremely complex definitional process.

Current Police Role

In his discussion of *The Function of the Police in Modern Society,* sociologist Egon Bittner points out that the cultural heritage of police departments in the United States has resulted in three *structural determinants* of the police role.[9] These are *structural character traits* which, according to Bittner, "control dealings between policemen and citizens on both sides." These traits are seen as unrelated to *ideal formulations* of what the police role should be.

Cultural Determinants The first character trait commonly seen as being associated with police work is that "police work is a tainted profession." Bittner explains the public view as follows:

> *In sum, the taint that attaches to police work refers to the fact that policemen are viewed as the fire it takes to fight fire, that they in the natural course of their duties inflict harm, albeit deserved, and that their very existence attests that the nobler aspirations of mankind do not contain the means necessary to insure survival. But even as those necessities are accepted, those who accept them seem to prefer to have no part in acting upon them, and they enjoy the more than slightly perverse pleasure of looking down on the police who take the responsibility of doing the job.*[10]

The second structural determinant that our heritage imposes on the definition of police role is that "the policeman is always opposed to some articulated or articulable human interest." This is in opposition to most occupations and professions that are seen as actively serving human interests. Bittner explains this role determinant as follows:

> *The fact that policemen are required to deal with matters involving subtle human conflicts and profound legal and moral questions, without being allowed to give the subtleties and profundities anywhere near the consideration they deserve, invests their activities with the character of crudeness. Accordingly, the constant reminder that officers should be wise, considerate, and just, without providing them with opportunities to exercise these virtues is little more than vacuous sermonizing.*[11]

Bittner proposes the following as the third social reality or structural determinant: "The ecological distribution of police work at the level of departmentally determined concentrations of deployment, as well as in terms of the orientations of individual police officers, reflects a whole range of public prejudices." He expands on this concept by stating:

> *The problem is not, however, whether the police have any responsibilities with regard to social injustice. The problem is that by distributing surveillance and intervention selectively they contribute to already existing tensions in society. That the police are widely assumed to be a partisan force in society is evident not only in the attitudes of people who are exposed to greater scrutiny; just as the young-poor-black expects unfavorable treatment, so the old-rich-white expects special consideration from the policeman.*[12]

Bittner considers these social attitudes toward the police as influencing their role definition and as being extremely difficult to do anything about. Their persistence is attributed by Bittner to the fact that they are deeply imbedded in our cultural heritage. It will be well to keep them in mind during the discussions that follow.

Police Function Examination of the activities of police agencies around the world reveals that they all perform six basic functions, albeit in different ways. These are:

- Combating violation of the traditional criminal law (murder, rape, robbery, arson, etc.);
- Combating violation of temporary convenience norms (traffic and health regulations, etc.);
- Performing a miscellaneous group of service functions (operating an ambulance service, operating a jail, escorting bank messengers, etc.);
- Preserving order in the population during its daily activity;
- Controlling or suppressing opposition to the government in power; and
- Maintaining forces for the repelling of possible military aggression against the nation-state.

In the United States, only the first four of these functions are regularly assigned to police agencies. Although the police do have an important role to play in civil defense in case of invasion, they don't have authority or responsibility for maintaining tank, paratroop, and similar military units, as do the paramilitary police organizations of some other countries. Police in the

United States are also not lawfully assigned the role of controlling and suppressing political opposition to the party in power, although there have been instances when they have seemingly assumed or been assigned this role illicitly.

Within the first four categories listed above, however, the police of the United States have assumed or been assigned a wide variety of activities. In addition to being responsible for preventing violations of the traditional criminal law and gathering evidence of the violations that do occur, police have been charged with achieving community conformity with the rules designed to make the close-knit life in industrialized, urbanized America acceptable despite the population densities involved (the second, third, and fourth items). Health practices relatively unimportant in rural areas have become vital in our cities; their supervision has been delegated to the police. The regulation of traffic necessary to our modern commercial life has also become an established police function. In addition, the police have been assigned or have voluntarily assumed responsibility for a wide variety of service activities, such as: operating ambulance services, jails, dog pounds, and recreational facilities; collecting delinquent taxes; furnishing chauffeurs for executive officers of the government; performing clerical functions for courts; licensing and regulating certain businesses (taxi cabs, pawnbrokers, night clubs, etc.); and escorting funerals and parades. Some of these are relatively widespread; others are almost unique to certain departments. Almost every department, however, has its share of both common and uncommon service responsibilities.

In addition, every department is charged with maintaining order in the community. Controlling crowds at political rallies, demonstrations, and sporting events; ensuring that the patrons of bars and other public facilities don't disturb neighborhoods; and making sure that private parties don't become public nuisances are all part of this order-keeping function. At least one commentator asserts that order maintenance is the essence of the police role: "In sum, the order maintenance function of the patrolman defines his role and that role, which is unlike that of any other occupation, can be described as one in which *sub-professionals, working alone, exercise wide discretion in matters of utmost importance (life and death, honor and dishonor) in an environment that is apprehensive and perhaps hostile.*"[13] [Emphasis in the original text] Although somewhat exaggerated, this sentiment does stress the importance of order maintenance as one element of the police role.

Facets of Police Agencies Regardless of the precise division of police time among these four categories (combating violation of the traditional criminal law, combating violation of convenience norms, performing miscellaneous service functions, and maintaining order in the community), it is essential to recognize that police do perform these four definitely different kinds of functions. It may also be helpful, however, to look at police agencies, as currently defined, from yet another perspective.

As one kind of unit in the criminal justice system, the police agency has four facets, all of which must be taken into consideration. One of these is the *legal prescription* as to what it should do. This describes the agency as it has been created and given responsibility by formal legislative enactment. A study of any particular agency should probably begin with this facet, but certainly it cannot end there. It must move on to the second facet, the *formal organizational and operational structure* as established by the top administrative officials of the agency. Still a third facet must be examined: the *informal structure* implemented by those who actually discharge the agency functions in day-to-day operation. And finally, in any study concerned with effectiveness of operation—a key element of which would be the extent of citizen support—still a fourth facet must be considered: the *image* of the agency held by differing segments of the society. Each of these four facets differs from the other three, and the image held by the public will itself vary according to the social subgroup whose view is being considered. Sometimes, this image of what the people *believe* the agency to be is actually more important than what it really *is*.

Each of these facets of a police agency will differ from the others for a variety of reasons. Human decisions, including legislative decisions, often suffer from a lack of omniscience or foresight. In addition to its intended and anticipated results, the legal prescription of the legislative process will have anticipated but intended results as well as results that are both unanticipated and unintended. Application of the written law to real life situations must take these facts into account. Then, too, the people who administer laws are subject to the usual frailties of humankind. For these reasons, discrepancies of at least the following types will exist between the legally prescribed and the officially planned organizational and operational structures of police agencies:

1. Differences attributable to the filling of gaps left, either intentionally or unintentionally, in the legal prescription (such gaps are sometimes intentionally left by the legislature, either because a matter is too controversial for a consensus to be obtained or because an honest belief exists that the executive or judicial branches can better make the necessary decisions; other gaps are inadvertent).
2. Differences attributable to ignorance of the pertinent legal provisions on the part of administrators.
3. Differences attributable to misunderstanding of the law by administrators.
4. Differences arising from an honest belief on the part of dedicated administrators that their way will better serve society, and that this end justifies any means that they might use.
5. Differences arising from a desire on the part of administrators to maximize their personal job satisfaction; and
6. Differences existing because of the corruption of administrators.

Usually, some combination of three or more of these possible causes will result in considerable differences between the legal prescription and what might be called the *actual-formal* organizational and operational structure.

For essentially these same reasons, the third facet (which here might be called the *actual-informal*, or the system established by those who really do the work) will differ from both the first facet of the police agency (the legal prescription) and the second (the formal organizational and operational structure). When the legislature pushes controversial decisions on to top administrators, these administrators in turn often push them down again to lower levels in their own organizations. It's then the line officer who's responsible for making the decision. And almost by definition one of the parties involved in a controversy of this nature will be displeased regardless of what the final decision may be. This sometimes means that the operating officers just looks the other way and never allow a situation demanding that kind of decision to come to their attention. In addition, the same qualities of ignorance, misunderstanding, belief that the ends justify the means, need for personal job satisfaction, and corruption also exist in the implementing structure.

Differing mental pictures of the same police agency will exist among different segments of the populace for at least the following reasons:

1. In some cases, the citizen will have no accurate information to use as a base for an image of the police. This may be because there is no information available, as will probably be the case when the system operates in secrecy, with no concern for the opinions of individuals, and with no felt need for their support. At the other extreme, the citizen may be uninformed simply because of apathy.

2. The citizen might lack the time and energy necessary for anything other than the daily fight for food and shelter. Someone who is faced with these problems probably won't be too concerned with more esoteric freedoms.

3. Misconceptions on the part of citizens may also result from unquestioning acceptance of rumor and stereotypes as fact, or from unwarranted generalizations drawn from isolated experiences.

Because of various combinations of these reasons, there will be appreciable differences between how the average citizen perceives the police agency and any of the above three facets of the system.

Thus, we see that police agencies are charged with four very different kinds of functions according to their role as it's currently defined in the United States. In carrying out these functions, they present four different faces. This complexity of current organization and operation must be considered by one who wishes to study the role of the police in our criminal justice system.

An Analytical Model of the Police Role Perhaps the most sophisticated recent analysis of the police role is the one which has been done by

William P. Brown. He characterizes his approach as a "three-dimensional task analysis."[14] The three dimensions are *problems*, *response*, and *process*.

In his analysis, Brown recognizes two broad problem areas, *individual victimization* and *community interest*. Individual victimization includes not only that which results from crime, but also that which stems from other "categories of emergency" typified by such occurrences as "illness, accidental injury, or misfortune." Community interest is defined as a much broader concept that comprises four kinds of troublesome situations involving potential for individual victimization (drunken driving, illegally carrying a revolver, etc.), community victimization (illegal use of city streets, natural disasters, etc.), non-victimization related but objectively specified community needs (giving information and minor assistance, enforcing traffic and other municipal ordinances, etc.), and mores maintenance (dealing with gambling, prostitution, alcohol and drug problems, etc.) Even this broad categorization cannot cover all police activity, requiring Brown to posit a reminder of miscellaneous activities:

> *The municipality does have the right to make such assignments and they are rather naturally given to the police with their 24-hour-a-day presence, their ordered appearance, and the transportation and communication facilities which are at their disposal. When such activities can be accomplished without undue interference with the police function, they may be appropriate. If they do interfere, it is still within the prerogative of the political authority to make the assignment. The point is that these are basically extraneous duties, and the police role is more usefully conceived as meeting the task that has been outlined.*[15]

In other words, Brown believes that these miscellaneous activities cannot be included in any scientific analysis of the police task.

Having stated the problems which he sees as demanding police attention, Brown goes on to analyze the response to those problems, which he defines as action leading the police either "(1) to control or (2) to give service." This problem-response model is further refined to distinguish between *incidents* and *issues*. One incident, such as burglary, requires immediate and specific police action; a series of such incidents, such as a rash of burglaries, raises an issue to which the proper police response is a program to meet the issue over time. That program may include such components as advice to the public on how to protect homes and business establishments against burglary.

Brown summarizes his analysis as follows:

> *In place of the conventional view of a single, indefinable police task, this analysis describes local policing as consisting of four distinct tasks, each definable in terms of community need and official response. The four community problem categories appear to be a comprehensive listing of issues that local police must meet. In each task area, problem and response can and should be considered both in terms of the isolated citizen-official contacts (incidents) and the broad themes (issues). The incident-issue discussion relates many police problem conceptualizations and response approaches which are normally seen without context.*

> *Since the task areas are distinct and comprehensive, we can offer a different formulation of the police task force from that which has been so often suggested: the protection of life and property, the prevention of crime, the detection and arrest of offenders, the preservation of the public peace, and the enforcement of all laws, etc. We can say, rather, that the police task is composed of four distinct segments: victimizing crime, victimizing emergency, regulation, and community service. The categories relate to police experience; the types of police work involved in the different categories are substantially different. Each of the four community problem categories is a reasonably well-defined sphere of community need and police activity. Each of these four kinds of police work is defined in terms of community need and official response and can be further analyzed in terms of the incident-issue dimension.*
>
> *The four task categories are mutually exclusive. Thus it is possible to distinguish among areas on the basis of clear lines of demarcation. This division would seem to allow theoretical consideration of the segments of police work at a different level of analysis and sophistication than has been possible while we thought of all police work as unitary in nature. Also, since the categories are distinct, it becomes theoretically possible to consider that the total function of the police is the sum of the four individual tasks.*[16]

Summary Regardless of how one looks at the police role, whether from a purely descriptive approach that seeks to categorize police activity, or from the standpoint of a sophisticated model-builder—the result is a view of agencies which perform a complex set of functions that comprise a varied role. Even when considering an analytical model of the police role, it must be remembered that there are four facets to any such model: the legally prescribed, that which the top officials *seek* to implement, that which the line officers actually *do* implement, and that which various segments of the population *believe* to be implemented in regard to their own specific needs. In addition, any attempt to change the police role must take into consideration the cultural determinants imposed by our heritage. Finding one's way among these complexities is the intellectual and operational challenge and opportunity accepted by the talented young men and women who today prepare themselves for careers in police agencies.

Current Problems in the Definition of Police Role

There is little doubt that at least some of the problems of the criminal justice system in the United States today can be attributed to current definitions of the police role. Elaboration of this assertion will consider first those difficulties which arise from the assignment of service tasks to police agencies; second, those which arise from enforcing convenience norms; and third, those which are encountered in the basic police tasks—combating violation of the traditional criminal law, and maintaining minimal order in society.

Problems of the Service Function Assignment of general service functions to police agencies raises the following kinds of problems: inflation of the police budget, along with distortion of the apparent cost of crime control and order maintenance; prevention of professionalism in the police career group; distraction of police attention from their primary assignments—combating violations of traditonal criminal law, and maintaining order; and prevention of a more satisfactory performance of the service functions by specially constituted agencies. Against these must also be considered three alleged benefits that might flow from such assignment of service functions to the police agency: generation of good will toward the police; the obtaining of information of value in combating traditional crimes; and achievement of governmental economy. Each of these issues merits further attention.

It is suggested that police stop providing miscellaneous services and that new units of city government be created to perform them instead. There are a variety of reasons for taking this position. If the police are going to perform miscellaneous general service functions, their budget must be larger. This budget is regarded by the average citizen as part of the cost of controlling crime and maintaining order. When citizens think about local police departments, they usually think in terms of crime control and order-maintenance functions. This means that the citizen weighs the department budget in its entirety against the success of the department in carrying out those functions. The outcome is almost certain to be an inflated view on the part of the citizen of the resources available to the police for these primary purposes, and a negative evaluation of the use of those resources when considered in the light of the results. This negative contribution to the community image of the police agency is serious; it adds to the list of cultural determinants described by Bittner.

Perhaps the most important argument *against* the assignment of general service functions to a police agency is that this custom prevents the evolution of a police *profession.* It does this in a number of ways, one of which is inhibition of the evolution of a unified "police task" concept for which preservice education can be implemented. When police officers are assigned a variety of tasks that run the whole gamut of non-police occupations and even some professions, in addition to being made responsible for maintaining order and combating violations of the traditional criminal law, no meaningful professional pre-service educational requirement can exist. This is the greatest single roadblock in the path of police professionalism today. The fact that many of these additional tasks are non-professional in nature (ranging from janitorial work through clerical assignments to automobile and radio maintenance tasks—any of which a patrol officer may spend an entire police career doing) makes it difficult to recruit persons well educated in the arts and sciences for police work.

In addition to the lack of challenge and job satisfaction in such positions for recruits who once thought that they were going to make a contribution to society by maintaining order and controlling traditional crime, the inclusion of such non-professional tasks results in the police role being demeaned in the eyes of citizens and governmental administrators alike. Consequently, provision for working conditions and salaries are more in keeping with the non-professional than with the police component. This adds to the difficulty of attracting educated and otherwise qualified personnel.

Assigning service functions to the police agency also dilutes the ability of the agency to concentrate on maintaining order and controlling crime—the police functions which pose the greatest problems today and form the basis on which police success or failure is judged. Some police administrators are convinced that accepting service responsibilities—with the resulting increases in budget—will make their positions seem more important, and that funds for more and better basic police work can be squeezed out of the service money. In fact, exactly the opposite is true. A common image of the police administrator today is one of an official who presides ineptly over a hodgepodge of activities carried out by persons who can't get or hold jobs elsewhere. Associating the basic police functions with a conglomerate of unrelated non-professional tasks has downgraded the former rather than elevating the latter. As is generally true in government, service tasks aren't adequately supported in the budget, and necessary additional funds generally come from the police function budget simply because the service activities must be performed. In addition to the fact that funds are diverted from the basic police task, once service tasks are taken on, executive effort is also diverted. Because it's more difficult to meet the challenges of the pure police functions than it is to perform service tasks, the mediocre employee will tend to prefer the easier way to do the job.

The assignment of service functions to police agencies also frequently leads to poor performance of those services. Education for and training in police agencies is directed at the performance of basic police tasks, *not* miscellaneous services. Even though some of those services are non-professional and are probably performed by police officers who are paid more than the work is worth, others would be better left to specialists whose training and education differ from that of the police. Some examples include operating a recreational program or one which licenses and regulates business. The results aren't good in any case. Oftentimes, the non-professional task is poorly carried out by one who thinks the task unworthy (and, in truth, these tasks are frequently used as punishment assignments). In addition, police officers who attempt to perform tasks for which they are not qualified will probably perform them poorly and only worsen the negative image of the police in the eyes of the public.

Against these obvious disadvantages of assigning miscellaneous service tasks to police agencies one must also weigh the alleged advantages. One of these is that police will build good will among people by performing these services: the public will see the police as helping people instead of getting them into trouble, which is often the way in which maintaining order and enforcing traditional criminal law are perceived. This argument assumes, of course, that the police perform these services well, which is not always the case when they take on responsibilities for which they haven't been trained and which they often don't like. Even assuming that a particular service is performed well and that someone becomes a police booster because of it, this is not enough to offset the general negative community reaction toward a police agency which seems to be doing everything but what it's supposed to be doing—namely, combating violations of the traditional criminal law and maintaining order. Concentrating effort on crime control would probably result in less crime, which in turn would probably earn the police more good will and citizen support than any service function could. The same would hold true for effective order maintenance. This kind of good will would be more important in the long run for two reasons. First, it would serve to suppress crime by enhancing the reputation of the police as an effective crime-fighting unit. Second, it would improve the quality of life for residents of the community by effectively maintaining order.

Another alleged advantage in performing service functions is that the police obtain information when doing them that assists them in solving crimes. It has never been documented, however, that the information obtained in this way even comes close to that which the police could glean by devoting even a small part of the time and resources they spend on service functions to the more specific task of gathering information. It's possible to get the same information from the non-police employees of the city who would regularly perform these services if the responsibility for performing them was taken away from the police. For example, the police could arrange informal chats with service personnel at regular intervals, or set up a formal interviewing program on a regular schedule, or even develop a carefully-designed personnel reporting system. It also could be valuable to assign an undercover investigator to a specific service team during those exceptional cases when police skills are needed to gather information from these sources.

Still a third argument is that it's cheaper to assign service functions to the police because the police and their administrative hierarchy are already there. In considering this argument, the first fact to remember is that removal of the service function would reduce the police budget, with the savings being reallocated to the new service agency. This argument is also outweighed by the values of developing a police profession, of properly allocating costs through program budgeting, of having the services performed well by persons educated and trained for such tasks, and of allowing police agencies to concentate on basic police responsibilities. In fact,the policy of having the police perform service functions is probably more costly than creating a new special agency to perform them. That agency could perform the service functions better than do the police, who would then be free to concentrate on good police work. And the police work must be done well in our large cities, the centers of our major crime and order maintenance problems.

There are enough of these service activities, examples of which are listed at the beginning of this section, in any city to warrant a separate organization. In the small rural town where the volume is smaller, adding service functions to the responsibilities of the police department might have some superficial logic. But even there, the non-police tasks could be concentrated in one person recognized as a service employee reporting directly to some other city official or, as a last resort, to the police chief.

In sum, assigning a wide variety of miscellaneous service functions to a police agency is extremely detrimental to that agency, and is responsible for at least part of the failure of police agencies to control traditional crime and maintain order.

Problems in Enforcing Convenience Norms Many difficulties that arise when service functions are assigned to police agencies also result when the police are made responsible for enforcing convenience norms. It is more difficult to generalize about this category, however, and the argument may differ depending on the nature of the convenience norm involved, but it does appear that general problems may arise when enforcement of convenience norms becomes a police responsibility. These include: inflation of the police budget with consequent distortion of the apparent cost of primary police functions: inhibition of the development of professionalism in the police career group; distraction of police attention away from their primary assignments; provision for an insidious source of police corruption; and development of ill will toward the police agency on the part of the community. Again, alleged advantages must also be mentioned: gaining of information by the police useful to them in their primary police tasks, and achievement of governmental economy through assignment of these functions to the police agency. Three of these alleged disadvantages and both of the alleged advantages have been discussed above and will not be dealt with further. However, the possibility that this activity is both a source of corruption and of ill will for the police merits further comment. It must also be remembered that what is being suggested is not only removal of the function from the police but also creation of new governmental units to which they would be transferred.

Traffic laws are typical of the convenience norms under consideration here. Traffic violations are, for the most part, distinctly different from burglary, murder, rape, and robbery in that convicted persons don't go to jail—they pay money. In addition, violators of this type usually aren't members of an aberrant minority in society; they can include any of us. When caught, we usually *know* that we committed the violation we're charged with, even though we may be reluctant to admit it. We also know that we have committed many similar violations in the past without doing injury to others and without getting caught—and that many of our friends have done likewise. This guilty knowledge doesn't cause us too much concern, however, since we know that little stigma is attached to conviction. Any genuine remorse that we might feel for committing the violation is usually replaced by chagrin at having been caught. We also end up resenting the officer for catching us instead of someone else.

Because experience has taught that being apprehended will probably cost a fixed sum of money, all too many violators of this sort attempt to settle the matter with the officer on the spot—either for the amount of money that would have to be paid anyway, but after considerable inconvenience, or for some lesser amount. Many police won't go along with this, but there are always some who will. In other words, upholding the traffic laws can be a source of police corruption.

Even if attempted bribery doesn't enter into the picture, motorists are often angry at having to pay a fine for what they don't really consider to be a serious antisocial act. The result may well be a lasting hostility toward the police. If an investigator should come by a few weeks later seeking information about a burglary, murder, rape or robbery, citizens may not be disposed to wrack their brains for knowledge which might help police to solve the case.

Similar examples might be given using other convenience norms which the police are responsible for enforcing. The result in any number of cases is often a new source of police corruption and ill will toward the police. Although corruption in any governmental agency is regrettable, it would be less dangerous in a purely service agency than it is in a police organization where it quickly spreads to the more important function of enforcing the traditional criminal law.

These arguments lead to a conclusion that the enforcement of convenience norms by the police is frequently detrimental to their primary responsibilities—maintaining order, and enforcing the traditional criminal law.

Problems in Enforcing the Law and Maintaining Order Not all of the problems arising out of the current definition of the police role in the criminal justice system stem from the fact that a variety of diverse elements are included in that definition. There are also problems associated with the execution of the primary police functions—enforcing the traditional criminal law, and maintaining order. These problems are of two fundamentally different types: those which arise when traditional criminal law and established order maintenance procedures are used to cope with social ills, and those which arise due to inefficient or poor organization on the part of the police for carrying out traditional police functions. Each will be discussed in greater detail.

Not all social evils can be handled best through the criminal law. In a number of areas, it's still necessary to classify persons as criminal before the state can provide them with needed educational, treatment, or welfare services. Since it's generally taken for granted today that government (both state and federal) must provide social services to some who can't otherwise obtain them, it would seem that we can now eliminate the necessity for criminal conviction before providing such services. A few examples should serve to represent the larger problem.

In many cases, monetary and other crimes against society are committed because young men and women are insufficiently educated for their roles as mothers and fathers in this complex economy. These crimes include fraud in connection with retail purchases, improper handling of mortgaged property, bad checks, and some thefts. In many instances the violation is a technical one that the individuals don't even know they are committing. In other cases, lack of the most rudimentary knowledge about budgeting and marketing for family needs is at fault. An aggressive governmental program of education and counseling for persons who are newly assuming responsibility for their own or family support would obviate the need for the same kind of education and advice now offered during probation following conviction.

Under our legal system as presently organized, it's necessary in many instances to convict individuals of a crime before they can be treated for a disease such as alcoholism or narcotics addiction. Compulsory or even voluntary civil commitment procedures can better handle these problems. At least, they couldn't fail any more miserably than our attempts to work through criminal statutes have.

Under the system presently operating in many cities, an unwed mother must be convicted of a sex offense and sentenced to a penal institution before she can be given care prior to, during, and after the birth of her child. Requiring that children be born in such settings is a questionable approach to the problem at hand. It seems obvious that cases like these can and should be disposed of outside the mechanism of the criminal law.

Order maintenance procedures have also gotten out of hand in recent years. Excessive zeal in attempting to anticipate civil disruptions has led to the keeping of dossiers on hundreds of thousands of citizens who simply disagreed in some way with governmental policies. Despite the fact that the keeping of such files has been condemned ever since their existence came to light, police agencies have been loathe to destroy them. This activity has led to less public respect for the police.

Problems also arise due to the unintelligent organization of police agencies. In this area, three primary challenges exist that police career group leadership has not yet met; the challenge of recognizing that the heart of the police task is judgment-making about crime situations and order maintenance problems; the challenge of providing the working conditions, salaries, and mobility necessary for the building of a police profession; and the challenge of defining the police task according to the discharge of primary police functions rather than support functions. The last of these challenges can be discussed in different contexts under a variety of headings. One solution might be the hiring of civilian personnel for service tasks necessary within the police agency. In the past, police officers—some of them high-ranking—have been known to sit in a chair and pound away at a typewriter for up to twenty years. These officers were uniformed, carried weapons, and were trained for the primary police functions—yet they were never called upon to use either their training or their equipment.

Among the principal arguments in favor of this seemingly illogical state of affairs were that sworn officers serving in clerical and other support services constituted a reserve for use in emergencies, that security reasons required the use of police personnel, and that these positions required great knowledge about police operations. All three of these stated reasons have been generally discredited. These officers were almost never used as a source of emergency power; civilian reserve forces, the National Guard, and federal troops were available. Concerning security, our most secretive national intelligence agencies all use civilians in large numbers. Finally, a civilian with an equal amount of time on the job will know just as much about an agency as a police officer. Police tasks must be recognized, staffed, and compensated for as such. Service tasks must be performed by individuals chosen from the service forces of the community, and these individuals must be recognized *not* as police officers but as police *employees*, and paid accordingly.

Police agencies must be reorganized so that judgement-making about crime and order maintenance situations is at the heart of the police task. Persons who aren't capable of making such judgments shouldn't be police officers, although they might be well qualified to be police employees. Officers who are skilled in decision-making regarding solving crimes and maintaining order should have an opportunity to receive higher compensation without having to become an administrator. If officers handle complex problems in difficult cases, they should receive the highest level of compensation possible and be recognized as a professional. Working conditions should be conducive to these creative activities, and sufficient financial security should make it possible for officers to give their full attention to the work at hand. In addition, they should be given the opportunity to move nationally to any position for which they quality. None of these circumstances is the case today.

Summary Problems arising from current police role definition can be associated with the functions from which they spring. Performance of service activities leads to police budget inflation and the consequent distortion of the apparent costs of police tasks; to prevention of professionalism in the police career group; to distraction of attention away from the primary tasks of combating traditional crimes and maintaining minimal order; and to prevention of more efficient performance of the service functions by specialized agencies. The good will that the police allegedly earn from these services is offset by bad will attributable to poorer performance of basic police tasks. Other more effective mechanisms can be devised for obtaining the information useful in crime control and order maintenance that is alleged to flow as a byproduct from service activities; governmental economy attributed to performance of service functions by the police is illusory.

In addition to the first three problems mentioned above as attributable to police performance of service functions, enforcement of convenience norms by police agencies also has two additional detrimental effects. It serves as a source of corruption, and it generates ill will toward the agency. Any resulting information useful in primary police tasks can again be obtained in other ways, and alleged governmental economy is again probably without foundation.

Problems which arise from enforcement of the traditional criminal law and established order maintenance procedures differ somewhat. One group stems from a less-than-careful consideration of which social problems should be assigned for solution to the criminal justice system. The prerequisite of criminal conviction before governmental units can offer certain educational, treatment, and welfare services is both unwise and unnecessary.

Police agencies have also been overzealous in attempting to anticipate civil disorder, confusing legitimate political dissent with unlawful subversive activity.

Another group of police problems associated with carrying out primary police tasks stems from poor police organization. Leadership of the police career group has not yet met the challenge of carefully differentiating the clearly *police* component in their basic tasks from necessary support services. A second unmet challenge is the recognition that the heart of the police task is judgment-making about crime and order maintenance situations. Yet a third is that of providing the working conditions, salaries, and mobility necessary for the building of a true police profession.

All of these problems arising from current definition of the police role as a unit of the criminal justice system are quite serious, and they must be given the attention they deserve.

Suggested Modifications of the Police Role

Probably the most important single movement in the recent past, in terms of long-range modification of police role in the United States, has been the building by universities of research and teaching programs concentrating on criminal justice systems as entities. The academic programs of the past which dealt with segments of the criminal justice system were reluctantly undertaken, narrowly conceived, poorly staffed and supported, and denied the insistence upon excellence that university administrators generally laid down for other university units. This is no longer true. After a decade of rapid growth in numbers, the new academic field of criminal justice studies has now turned its attention to improvement. Our colleges and universities now offer prototype programs in justice studies at all levels: two-year, four-year, and graduate. These programs set high standards of excellence which have not yet been met by all crime-related programs in higher education. The change in concentration from quantity to quality is definitely the mood of the late seventies, however.

Even in the prototype justice programs, there are still only a few outstanding research-oriented professors who are interested in police problems. And, because the strong research-oriented graduate students are drawn to the strong research-oriented professors, the best graduate students now frequently end up working on post-conviction problems. For this reason, the lack of concerted attention to police problems tends to be self-perpetuating. This situation probably stems from the fact that most of the empirically oriented professors in justice studies come to their positions with backgrounds in sociology and psychology, disciplines that naturally feel most at home dealing with post-conviction problems.

It is hoped that administrators of justice studies programs will recognize this problem and encourage talented young professors to concentrate their research and teaching on police problems. Perhaps the current buyers' market in academic employment will make this process easier. When this new research capacity is developed, one fruitful area for attention will be that of the redefinition of the proper role for a police agency in the criminal justice system of a democratic nation. Some of the avenues that might be explored in this reexamination of the police role are discussed below.

The Elimination of the Service Function A great deal of hard data exists today on the extent to which police agencies are spending their time and effort performing miscellaneous service functions. The consensus is that the percentage of time spent in this way is very high,[17] despite the fact that most studies have failed to take into account the police-initiated action that is more law enforcement than social-service oriented.[18] Although the time spent on service functions varies from department to department, the overall amount is appreciable. As William P. Brown points out in deriving his model, some service functions do not interfere with primary police tasks and should probably be kept. However, many do so interfere and should be assigned to a new Department of Public Services in the municipal government.

One of the principal advantages of such a change would be that education, treatment, and welfare costs would no longer have to be hidden in the police budget. This would reduce the inflation of that budget and the consequent distortion of the apparent costs of order maintenance and crime control. It would also contribute greatly to development of a true police profession, allow the police agency to concentrate on order maintenance and enforcement of the traditional criminal law, and allow others to perform the needed non-police services at greater economy and with greater effectiveness. Of the number of examples that might be used, one of the more controversial—jail operations—will serve to illustrate the point.

The proper operation of institutions for pretrial detention and for holding persons convicted of crimes is a complex function. Emerging emphasis on the rights of the accused will probably soon require that persons who have been accused but not yet convicted, and who cannot be released on bail pending trial, be held in institutions separate from those for persons already convicted. The fact that no one is considered to be a criminal until convicted by due process of law would seem to require that this be the case. Other nations even require it in their constitutions.

A modern view of the rights of the accused also seems to require that pretrial detention facilities interrupt the accused's normal life as little as possible. The fact that an appreciable number of persons accused of crimes are later acquitted and released demands no less. The pretrial detention institution should furnish facilities for the usual business or professional activity of the inmates, or, if this is not possible, for alternative employment that will allow the usual level of support for their families. Recreation and other customary amenities of life should also be provided. For those whose situations reveal an obvious lack of social adjustment, rehabilitative processes should begin immediately. Obviously, the police should not be responsible for operating such detention facilities.

It's equally clear that the police should not be responsible for operating jails which hold people who are serving short sentences. Again, some kind of rehabilitative action should be available to persons doing time in these jails. If it's true that a sentence is often too short for any kind of meaningful rehabilitative experience to take place, the criminal law is probably being used incorrectly as a mechanism of social control.

One raging controversy that could be largely eliminated by taking all detention facilities out of police stations is that which concerns improper police interrogation. If dispersed facilities were reasonably available to all police agencies through their modern communication and transportation capabilities, every person arrested could be taken immediately to a detention facility operated by the state correction agency. After being booked in a wing containing all the equipment necessary for this identification procedure, individuals would pass immediately into the custody of the director of the institution, to be held until their fate is decided by a court.

On the way to the institution and during the booking procedure, the police would have the right to question the accused with appropriate cautions, but they would *not* have the right to insist on answers. After booking and transferring the accused to the proper institution, the police would have access to the individual for further questioning or other procedures *only* according to detailed guidelines laid down by rules of the court having jurisdiction over the case.

Under these circumstances, all constitutional guarantees, including that against self-incrimination, would be made available to the accused. In those instances in which a particular right was waived, no question that the waiver was obtained by improper police action could arise. Such a plan might result in fewer admissions of guilt by accused persons; as the people gained respect for the criminal justice system because of its more fair and efficient operation, however, increased citizen support would soon make reliance on confessions much less necessary. The accused's knowledge that the underlying problem, of which the crime was a symptom, was going to be looked at fairly and with consideration would also reduce the resistance of the accused to governmental action and encourage cooperation.

Effective arguments can also be made in favor of eliminating many of the other service functions currently being performed by the police.

Eliminating the Enforcement of Convenience Norms In addition to condemning serious antisocial acts, most societies have established many convenience norms. Conformity to these norms is necessary in order for a society to achieve maximum freedom for all. It doesn't do any good, for example, to give the members of a society freedom to travel the roads on Sunday if the roads are so choked with traffic or so dangerous that it's practically impossible to get anywhere on them.

In modern industrialized and urbanized life, this example can be multiplied many times over. Conformity to convenience norms means maximum freedom for all. Again, hard data indicates that an appreciable amount of police time and effort is spent on controlling violations of these norms.[19] It isn't, however, as easy to argue against this kind of police activity as it is to argue against police performance of service functions.

Careful attention should be given, therefore, to the possibility of establishing a Department of Inspections in city government that would be responsible for enforcing the vast majority of convenience norms. The elimination of these regulatory costs from the police budget would provide a more realistic picture of the police cost of order maintenance and crime control; development of a police profession would be encouraged; police agencies could concentrate on maintaining order and enforcing the traditional criminal law; and a source of corruption within and ill will toward the police would be eliminated.

A single example might serve to illustrate the general point of this suggestion. Enforcement of traffic regulations is not necessarily "police" work. Some countries having a considerable amount of vehicular traffic don't assign municipal police any responsibility at all for its control. In such cases, a separate city department regulates traffic, and their enforcement officers wear uniforms entirely different from those of the police, who are charged with maintaining order and enforcing the traditional criminal law. This idea is worth a try in the United States as well. Traffic control has many facets. Planning traffic flow patterns and surpervising street construction are engineering specialties for which professional education has long been available. Traffic enforcement should be similarly treated. Cities which allocate any of this activity to police, who don't have the specialized education necessary, are being poorly served.

Traffic control deals with open, *not* clandestine, conduct. For example, there is usually no problem of identity of a parking violator. Liability for nonconformance rests with the owner of the vehicle, regardless of who actually parked it. There is also no problem involved with gathering evidence of such a violation, since the violation remains unknown unless an officer sees it. Usually, there is no risk of harm to any individual citizen—only an indication of an uncooperative attitude toward society. The same is true of moving violations which don't result in accidents. In other words, it's possible to use enforcement officers who are less trained and less educated to enforce traffic without also expecting them to also enforce the traditional criminal law and to maintain order.

Investigation of moving violations which do result in accidents poses a more difficult problem. In situations like these, a violation almost always results in property damage and frequently in injury and death to individuals. In most of these cases as well, however, there's no problem involved in identifying the participants. The problem is rather one of reconstructing the collision, a task requiring skills more akin to those of an engineer or physicist than of an investigator of traditional crimes.

It's true that in some of these cases (such as hit-and-run accidents) there can be a problem in identifying a participant. It's also true that an occasional case like this will involve willful injury or conduct in such reckless disregard for the safety of the lives of others as to warrant a charge of manslaughter or even of murder.

This description of the problem might well support an argument that planning for traffic flow should be a responsibility of the city engineer rather than of the police, that traffic direction and control should be a responsibility of the city Department of Inspections rather than of the police, and that only traffic cases which involve an unknown participant or willful or reckless injury should be handled as police matters.

Similar arguments can be made in favor of eliminating much police responsibility for enforcing other convenience norms.

The Decriminalization of Social Problems A careful look at the success of past efforts to cope with certain social ills by means of criminal law processes may indicate that other social control mechanisms may be more effective. For example, court decisions leading to questions of constitutional validity have provided the added incentive for making the cases of the narcotics addict and the chronic alcoholic applicable for this kind of consideration. The use of sex offense convictions to provide welfare services to unwed mothers might well be another. Because these areas lie outside the direct focus of this chapter, they won't be discussed further here.

The Modification of Police Organization and Operation Perhaps the most difficult question to be faced is that of whether police can or should be both peace officers and general public servants. It's suggested that they should primarily be peace officers. This view argues that better attention to the basic police tasks will do more than social service to eliminate some of the major upheavals in our urban centers.

If most service functions and some convenience norm enforcement were eliminated from police responsibility, as recommended above, many of the more friction-generating situations would be handled by the new Departments of Public Services and Inspections, both of which would have personnel available to answer such calls. It would also be necessary to strengthen other social control mechanisms in our cities that lie outside the criminal justice system. General governmental social and welfare services would have to be brought to the point where many of the friction-inducing conditions no longer existed.

Then, too, self help would have to remain an element of life in these United States. Learning how to live together peacefully is a process that must continue. Government can never carry the entire load.

All of these factors together would reduce the number of situations that result in calls to the police. But there would always be some calls made by citizens to report emergency situations that would require the police to perform their order maintenance and crime control functions. These must be considered a part of the police task, and reorganized policing must find a method of servicing them.

Eliminating most service functions and much of the responsibility for enforcing convenience norms would in turn eliminate many of the boring, unstimulating, and unchallenging activities that now plague the police career group. It would also make it possible to carry out organizational changes that would provide working conditions compatible with the newly-defined police role. One of the first such changes would be the abandonment of the quasi-military structure of police organization.

With the elimination of routine tasks that are best performed by persons under close supervision, the need for military organization would also be eliminated. In fact, the concept of military organization is incompatible with that of professional agents who operate independently on problems requiring mature judgment. For this reason, the tall triangle of military hierarchy should be done away with, and a much flatter organizational structure with fewer supervisory levels should be adopted. Military rank, uniforms, and the usually stultifying authoritarian mental attitude that goes along with them should be abandoned.

Along with these organizational changes must come a realization that there are areas within the police task in addition to those of administration and management that require the exercise of mature judgment. Management is an important area, and it should have its high level of compensation, but it should also be possible for a police officer to remain in one of the other areas of specialization, moving from lesser to ever more complicated and serious kinds of cases, and be compensated accordingly. This means that there would be a number of compensation hierarchies equivalent to that of administration.

To put it another way, there should be a number of positions available within a police department that pay as much as or only a token amount less than that of the chief. It should be possible, for example, for officers who make a career of combating professional burglars or organized crime to be paid a progressively higher salary if they show aptitude for and success in ever more complicated and serious cases. In terms of today's market, an agent who chose to stay in the field of specializing against professional burglars might be offered a salary range of from $12,000 to $30,000, the former a starting figure, the latter that for the unit leader with responsibility for the entire effort of the agency against professional burglars. There could be a number of such ranges, all of which, in the top figure, might be just $500 or so below the salary of the chief.

These areas are outside those of administration and management, so this kind of salary structure would put an end to transferring individuals out of their chosen specialty solely for the purpose of obtaining an increase in pay. They could then remain in their area of interest and develop greater expertise. Basically, it's suggested that a police agency should be able to offer a potential recruit a variety of specialized careers. There is no obvious need for every officer to be able to perform every police task; each should be able to serve and progress in a chosen field of interest.

In addition to changes that would make it possible for agents to enter policing with a particular career in mind, or to make such a choice early in their service, other changes should be made to enhance career opportunities by allowing national mobility. Police officers should be free to practice their profession anywhere in the country. For this to occur, requirements of residence prior to appointment must be eliminated. Opportunities for lateral transfer to a higher level of responsibility in other jurisdictions should also be created. This would mean that all individuals could compete for every position for which they are qualified, and that every community could hire the best qualified person for every position that became vacant.

A serious obstacle to such mobility today, in addition to residence requirements, is the retirement picture for the police career group. Each agency, no matter how large or how small, has its own retirement system, and benefits are lost or greatly reduced if one leaves the agency prior to retirement. In such a system, it's impossible for an administrator to fill a vacancy with the best available person. In addition, it means that frustrated officers must be kept in a department even when both they and the agency would be better off if they were to leave. Creating a nationwide retirement system for police, such as that now enjoyed by college and university teaching and research personnel, would allow the mobility needed for proper development of a police career group.

If this newly-defined police task were carried out in a reorganized department, some drastic modifications of procedure would also be required. Every department should work toward an ideal in which all police officers would have a specific order-maintenance or crime-situation-oriented reason for being where they are and doing what they are doing at every moment. For example, the question exists as to whether routine patrolling is worthwhile. That activity has often been carried on only in the hope that it will effect some unmeasured and unmeasurable quantity of deterrence from crime.[20] Police personnel are simply too expensive for this practice to continue. When an adequate data base has been built up about the crime pattern of a given community, all police personnel not required for order maintenance should be concentrated on solving previous crimes and intercepting persons attempting to commit new offenses.

One aspect of this activity would be the answering of citizens' calls for assistance. All such calls could come to a central city switchboard. This switchboard, in turn, would relay service calls to the Department of Public Services, convenience norm enforcement calls to the Department of Inspections, and crime and order maintenance calls to the Police Department. If a call for police action required only minor activity, such as taking a bit of volunteered information about a case already under investigation, the answering officer could return at once to his or her principal assignment. If the call developed into a major investigation, the anwering officer could be assigned to the new case.

Summary

Police agencies in the United States play roles dictated at least in part by structural determinants imposed by their cultural heritage. Defining that role is a complex process in which many influences are felt. The current role is described differently by different analysts, but all agree that it is not ideal. Changes are necessary.

It's been suggested in this chapter that our colleges and universities must create first-class research and teaching programs concentrating on police problems within their otherwise rapidly improving academic programs in justice studies. Such programs should carry out the research necessary prior to eliminating service functions and enforcement of some convenience norms from police responsibility. They should also assist police executives in organizing their departments so that they can discharge the newly-defined police task, converting departments into agencies staffed by professionals skilled in judgment-making in crime situations and order-keeping emergencies. Their research would also be helpful in devising new operational mechanisms for implementing the "new look" in policing. None of these changes can be made overnight. We must begin with the resources we have and then work toward the newly-established goals.

One result of this recommended restructuring of municipal police agencies and their operational procedures would be the emergence of a true police profession. This profession would be capable of handling its assigned task with greater insight.

Realization that the criminal justice system is an entity in which all segments are interrelated would result in new relationships among police professionals and those at all other levels in the system, from prosecution through court decision to correction.

There is no more interesting, stimulating, challenging or important endeavor being made in the United States today than that of the criminal justice system. Within that system, the most vital element, the police agency, stands at the threshold. The effectiveness of its functioning affects all other units of the system. An effective reassessment of the role of the police agency in the criminal justice system by the talented young men and women currently being educated for justice system careers is imperative.

Topics For Discussion

1. **Discuss the relationship of police agencies with other governmental and nongovernmental agencies and institutions.**
2. **Consider the relative importance in impact of the several factors which influence the definition of the police role.**
3. **Determine what sociologist Egon Bittner means when he refers to police work as "a tainted profession."**
4. **Comment on the different facets of police agencies that are alleged to exist.**
5. **Categorize the problems caused by police enforcement of convenience norms, and relate the impact of those problems to overall police effectiveness.**
6. **Discuss whether the operation of jails is a proper police function.**

References

1. Egon Bittner, *The Functions of the Police in Modern Society*, Washington: U.S. Government Printing Office, 1970, pp. 8-12.

2. Henry C. Black, *Black's Law Dictionary*, St. Paul, Minnesota: West Publishing Co., Third Edition, 1933.

3. William P. Brown, "Local Policing: A Three Dimensional Task Analysis," *Journal of Criminal Justice*, Vol. 3, No. 1, Spring 1975, pp.9-15.

4. E. Byrne, "Police Role in Traffic Engineering," *Law and Order*, Vol. 21, No. 6, June 1976.

5. S. A. Chapman and T. E. St. Johnston, *The Police Heritage in England and America*, East Lansing, Michigan: Institute for Community Development and Services, Michigan State University, 1962.

6. A. W. Cohn and E. C. Viano, *Police Community Relations: Images, Roles, Realities*, Philadelphia: J. B. Lippincott, 1976.

7. J. F. Elliott, *The "New" Police*, Springfield: Charles C. Thomas, 1973.

8. Herman Goldstein, *Policing a Free Society*, Cambridge, Massachusetts: Ballinger Publishing Co., 1977.

9. G. M. Janeksela and T. M. Nida, "Attitudes Toward Police," *Police Law Quarterly*, Vol. 5, No. 4, July 1976.

10. E. J. Keller, "School Security: The Role of the Police," *Law and Order*, Vol. 20, No. 12, December 1972.

11. George L. Kelling, Tony Pate, Duane Dieckman and Charles E. Brown, *The Kansas City Preventive Patrol Experiment: A Summary Report*, Washington: The Police Foundation, 1974.

12. William and Nora Kelly, *Policing in Canada*, Toronto: The Macmillan Co. of Canada, Ltd., 1976.

13. Roger Lane, *Policing the City: Boston 1822-1885*, Cambridge, Massachusetts: Harvard University Press, 1967.

14. C. P. McDowell, *Police in the Community*, Cincinnati: W. H. Anderson Co., 1975.

15. John C. Meyer, Jr., and Winthrop E. Taylor, "Analyzing the Nature of Police Mobilizations," *Journal of Criminal Justice*, Vol. 3, No. 2, Summer, 1975, pp.141-145.

16. Richard A. Myren, "Decentralization and Citizen Participation in Criminal Justice Systems," *Public Administration Review*, Vol. 32, Special Issue, October 1972.

17. Richard A. Myren, *The Role of the Police*, Washington: U.S. President's Commission on Law Enforcement and Administration of Justice, 1967.

18. R. Nimmer, "Public Drunk: Formalizing the Police Role as a Social Help Agency," *Georgetown Law Journal*, Vol. 58, No. 6, June 1970.

19. President's Commission on Law Enforcement and Administration of Justice, *Task Force Report: The Police*, Washington: U.S. Government Printing Office, 1967.

20. Charles Reith, *A New Study of Police History*, Edinburgh: Oliver and Boyd, 1956.

21. James Q. Wilson, *Varieties of Police Behavior: The Management of Law and Order in Eight Communities*, Cambridge, Massachusetts: Harvard University Press, 1968, p. 30.

Annotated Bibliography

Bittner, Egon, *The Functions of the Police in Modern Society*, Washington: U.S. Government Printing Office, 1970. A review of background factors, current practices, and possible role models for the police.

Brown, William P., "Local Policing: A Three Dimensional Task Anslysis," *Journal of Criminal Justice*, Vol. 3, No. 1, Spring 1975. An article that analyzes the police function and discuses the relevance of the model developed for police operations.

Elliott, J. F., *The "New" Police*, Springfield; Charles C. Thomas, 1973. A description of a possible form of what the municipal police may evolve into, why they must change, and how this evolution may be accomplished.

Goldstein, Herman, *Policing a Free Society*, Cambridge, Massachusetts: Ballinger Publishing Co., 1977. Deals with the complex, yet remediable problems that thwart the most determined efforts to achieve a high level of policing.

Kelling, George L., Tony Pate, Duane Dieckman and Charles E. Brown, *The Kansas City Preventive Patrol Experiment: A Summary Report*, Washington: The Police Foundation, 1974. Describes what may well be the most significant research project on the police in modern times which leads to question of the effectiveness of routine police patrol.

Kelly, William and Nora, *Policing in Canada*, Toronto: The Macmillan Co., 1976. A detailed and critical discussion of the role of the police in Canada's law enforcement structure.

Myren, Richard A., *The Role of the Police*, Washington: U.S. President's Commission on Law Enforcement and Administration of Justice, 1967. A discussion of the sources of the complex role police play in the United States and how it might be modified.

President's Commision on Law Enforcement and Administration of Justice, *Task Force Report: The Police*, Washington: U.S. Government Printing Office, 1967. Embodies the research and analysis of the staff and consultants to the Commission which supported the findings and recommendations of the Commission relating to the problems facing the nation's police.

Reith, Charles, *A New Study of Police History*, Edinburgh: Oliver and Boyd, 1956. The standard modern work on the history of policing.

Wilson, James Q., *Varieties of Police Behavior: The Management of Law and Order in Eight Communities*. Cambridge, Massachusetts: Harvard University Press, 1968. A description of the patrolman and the problems he faces that arise out of constraints imposed by law, politics, public opinion, and the expectations of superiors.

3

THE POLICE CULTURE
Open or Closed

Chapter Objectives

The study of this chapter should enable you to:

☑ Identify three factors contributing to the "closed" police culture.
☑ Explain the existence of political conservatism among the police.
☑ Cite six characteristics of the police personality.
☑ Characterize the nature of police authoritarianism.
☑ Explain the cause of police alienation.
☑ Summarize the impact on the police personality created by: a. danger; b. suspicion; c. cynicism; d. stress.
☑ Identify at least three psychological consequences of the police role for the individual police officer.
☑ Characterize the similarities between the police in the United States and police in other countries.

Introduction

Most occupations contain a number of unique characteristics. When the characteristics of a particular job are combined in the context of the working environment, they often affect persons performing the tasks related to the occupation in a unique way. Such an interaction of job-related and job-derived traits produces an *occupational culture.*

The existence of such an occupational uniqueness in the police service has been recognized, and elements of the police culture have become fairly well reported in recent years. Among the elements of the culture that have been addressed are: the informal code of the police,[1] the police code of secrecy,[2] the use of authority,[3] and the police socialization process.[4] Thus, the question of whether or not a police culture exists seems fairly well settled, and the real emphasis should lie in understanding how it affects the individual police officer and the quality of police service provided to the public.

Along with identifying the performance impact of the police culture, an ability to define causative factors will also be advantageous. For example, is the current police distrust of non-police persons caused by some departmental practice, the background of the police recruit, or the manner in which certain tasks are performed, or is it a result of the public's misconception of the police officer's role?[2] Answers to these questions may result in an improved police selection process, better managerial practices, more clearly-defined tasks, and the enactment of necessary legislation to provide guidelines for better performance of the police task. These answers aren't, however, easily obtained. This chapter, although not claiming to provide definitive answers, should indicate some of the problems by discussing the police culture, police personality, and the individual and professional impact of existing characteristics and relationships on the police and their role.

Characteristics of the Police Culture

The police have been provided with numerous visible symbols which are used to identify them as a distinct subculture within society. Recruiting methods, the backgrounds of police applicants, training, the types of duties which police perform, visible symbols of office (i.e., uniform, badge and gun), and common experiences all provide assistance in identifying distinct beliefs, perceptions, values, traditions, and customs among the police. Generally, scholars who study the police agree that the police culture may be characterized as a politically conservative *closed group,* with a high degree of *loyalty, solidarity, respect for authority,* and a fair measure of *cynicism.* A discussion of these characteristics will help us to obtain a clearer picture of the police culture.

The Police as a Closed Group Before attempting to understand the creation of a closed police group, it's necessary to first consider the background of police officers, the traditional entry procedures and practices, and the common tasks performed by virtually all police officers after entering the police service.

The typical police applicant comes from a working-class background, has completed high school, and frequently is a veteran of the military service.[5] The attraction of the police service as a steady job, regular income, and a guaranteed pension accounts for only a portion of the magnetism of a police career. Researchers have reported that police applicants are individuals who are attracted to the occupation because of the lack of routine believed inherent in the job, the opportunity to work outdoors, and the prevailing stereotype of police work as exciting, somewhat romantic, and adventuresome.[6] In addition, applicants see the occupation as a service to the community that has genuine social value. In short, the expectations of police applicants have a number of elements in common, and this commonality of expectations has important consequences for the police applicant after entry into the police agency. In essence, the commonality of expectations often becomes the commonality of unfulfilled expectations.

If the background of police applicants can be considered as a predominately unifying characteristic, so too is police training. The police applicant becomes the police *recruit*. The label of recruit is applied by all other members of the department and remains until some unspecified time shortly after the completion of the police training academy. As recruits, the new police officers are first exposed to the reality of the police occupation. They are at the bottom of the departmental social order and are generally left to the attentions of the training academy cadre. During training, recruits have virtually no contact with other departmental members as they perform the day-to-day police functions. The world of the recruit consists of endless lectures, films, demonstrations, and examinations on a variety of topics. Finger-printing, report writing, constitutional law, traffic control, firearms training, arrest procedures, defensive tactics, and departmental policy are normal fare.

The only similarities the recruits can see between the aspirations that drew them to the department and the department itself are the shared boredom, discipline, rewards, and after-hours socialization. Left in limbo, away from the mainstream of the agency, recruits easily learn the value of identification and association with other members of their recruit class. In shorty, *unity* and *solidarity* are encouraged by the training practices of the academy and the social requirements of the recruits.

In addition to instilling a sense of "oneness" among recruits during the training phase, the content of the curriculum at the academy often provides an indirect lesson in distinguishing between real and unreal expectations concerning police work. Frequently, training instructors provide examples of situations they have encountered on the job, quickly pointing out to the class that in spite of the fact that these solutions are not taught in the classroom, "real police work" requires more than textbook learning. With exposure to repeated examples, recruits begin to perceive a disparity between what they are being taught and what they will be expected to actually do to succeed on the job. The effect is a reduction in idealism and the initiation of a view that whatever works is the best solution to any problem. After graduation from the academy, the new police officer trades the label of recruit for that of *rookie.* In order to continue the rookie's training and socialization, the normal practice is to assign an experienced police officer to serve as a mentor and trainer. The rookie learns from the experienced officer that knowledge and skills only recently required at the academy aren't highly valued by most police officers. In fact, they're frequently perceived as detrimental to good police performance. Many rookies begin their first day of patrol with a training officer with instructions from the senior officer to "just sit still and watch." Those instructions are literally intended to cover all activities from filling out the daily log to communicating with a motorist during a traffic stop.

The training officer is frequently the sole source of evaluation of the rookie's capabilities. Departmental supervision via formal means is minimal, and the efficiency of the new officer is heavily dependent on the opinion of the training officer. It's in the new officer's best interests to internalize all the information gained from the training officer. Through continued demonstration and explanation, the rookie learns many of the intricacies of police work, i.e., the practice of selling traffic tickets to unhappy motorists, the locations and descriptions of "potential troublemakers", how to successfully resolve a domestic disturbance, how to complete an acceptable report, and some distinctions between "good" and "bad" policework.

The experience with the training officer shapes and socializes the new police officer into the police culture. Slowly, the new officer learns to associate geographic areas of the beat with specific police problems and the training officer's solutions to the variety of police business. Additionally, and importantly, the new officer learns that not all members of the public like the police, nor do they appreciate their interference.

The motorist who's issued a citation for speeding frequently berates the new (and old) police officer for not paying attention to truly serious matters, such as narcotics pushers and burglars, and being interested only in filling a "ticket quota". The participants in a domestic dispute either view police officers as intruders and their common enemy, or ask them to take some action that they have no legal ability to take. The store and tavern owner encountered in their places of business during routine patrols want the police to leave immediately so that their establishments don't get a bad reputation. Frequent encounters with such store and tavern owners may result in a formal complaint to the department against the officer.

The new officers are left in a quandary. Their efforts are often unrewarded, and their reception by the public is, at best, cool. Slowly, the new officers begin to withdraw from extensive interaction with the larger society. Their single and unanimous source of acceptance becomes other police. In short, the rookies learn that they are perceived in a negative way by most of the public. The primary source of their positive self-image lies within the department, and particularly in other patrol officers. The more rapidly the new officers experience the disparity between how they perceive the police task and how this task is perceived by the public, the more rapidly they become isolated from the mainstream of society. Along with this isolation from the rest of society goes an increase in solidarity and loyalty among and to other police officers. Subscription and adherence to the values learned while a rookie enhance acceptance and recognition by other police officers.

It's worth noting at this point that the traditional route of promotion to all levels of the police department begins with performing as a patrol officer. Thus, the sergeant, lieutenant, captain, inspector, and chief have all begun their careers as patrol officers and have all shared common experiences, frustrations, isolation, and reliance on other police officers. This commonality of experience strengthens the isolation of the police from society.

To summarize the factors which have contributed to the closed nature of the police culture we must first recall that most police applicants come from similar backgrounds. Second, the teaching and learning of entry-level police skills provides both a common experience and a rigidly controlled socialization process. Finally, the patrol tasks themselves encourage the police officer to withdraw from the larger society and to become isolated within the safety of the police culture.

Political Conservatism and the Police Among the various police missions — such as crime prevention, protection of life and property, and the maintenance of order, to name only a few — much police effort is devoted to *preventing* events from occurring. It's hoped that the police presence prevents crime, discourages neighborhood disturbances, and inspires a sense of social order. The police provide a unique public service because their primary reason for existence is that of preventing events from happening.[7]

The traditional police method of preventing crimes and disruptive behavior has been via the patrol function. Typically, the allocation of police patrol personnel within a jurisdiction is made on the basis of need. Those areas within a community which receive large amounts of police patrol resources are those which evidence the greater amounts of crime and disorder. This means that proportionately more police resources are devoted to the policing of ghettos and slums than to policing the middle- and upper-class neighborhoods. Lower-income and ghetto residents statistically represent the largest proportion of crime victims and perpetrators.

The police are thus heavily involved in providing protection and service in areas which are populated by individuals who frequently are minority group members or at least representative of society's lower socio-economic levels. This situation is compounded by the fact that the police as a group represent or at least aspire to be members of the middle class. In effect, the lower class receives middle-class law enforcement, or at least law enforcement which is provided by representatives of the middle class. Reference was made earlier to the background of the police, and it's worth noting that ample evidence exists that social and economic classes often subscribe to different values, norms, beliefs and practices. Stated another way, class might well be equated with subculture.[8]

The result is that the police, who represent the middle class and who possess the values and characteristics of the middle class, spend a major portion of their time in the lower-class environment attempting to enforce the law and maintain order.[9] The reception of the police by the ghetto or slum resident is similar to that granted an occupying army during a war.[10] When police officers perceive the hostile and negative reception by the citizens they are attempting to protect and serve, they become confused, alienated, withdrawn, and isolated from the ghetto. With frequent exposure to such hostility, both real and implied, police officers easily comes to equate the ghetto dweller with a threat to their safety. Frequently, to offset such a threat, aggressive activities by the police are deemed necessary for protection. Activities such as stop and frisk, "general" traffic stops, and extensive enforcement are often employed to offset the perceived danger of policing the ghetto.

Given the police perception of and reception by the ghetto resident, *conservatism* is encouraged by political efforts in the larger society. Numerous groups (such as The American Civil Liberties Union and the National Lawyers Guild) are engaged in varied activities meant to ensure protection under the law for all citizens. Frequently, the focus of such activities is on the police, and attempts to regulate the police concentrate on restricting the power of the police to interrogate and detain criminal suspects. From the police perspective, the right to counsel at seemingly every juncture of the police process is frequently cited by police officers as evidence that the politically liberal forces in the society are attempting to make the police task more difficult and more dangerous. The relatively low conviction rates and unsuccessful rehabilitative efforts of individuals known to the police as "hardened criminals" are often linked by the police to the efforts of "soft-hearted" liberals. For example, the "Free Angela Davis" movement was seen as threatening by many police departments.

Conversely, popular conservative political figures and campaign slogans typified by law and order themes become very appealing to the threatened police officer. George Wallace was publicly endorsed by the president of the Fraternal Order of Police as a presidential candidate. The popular "Support Your Local Police" slogan adopted by the John Birch Society tended to generate far more police sympathy than the slogans of most liberal causes. They view such causes and slogans as strengthening police efforts to contain the criminals in the society.

Having been charged with the task of identifying and apprehending criminals in a frequently hostile environment, the police gravitate toward political affiliations that offer the most support for their efforts.[11] To do otherwise would be inconsistent with human nature.

Police Loyalty The method of providing a police service to the public also enhances and encourages a high degree of loyalty among police officers; they tend to work either individually or in pairs. In either case, the police officer on duty is frequently functioning independently of the department. When the officer is working alone, much of a typical tour of duty is spent away from direct contact with other officers and the department, in spite of the advanced communications technology. The result is that many situations which require a decision by an officer are dealt with in the absence of supervision by the department. These situations often require the police officer to act rapidly without consulting a supervisor who may be several miles away. In spite of this job requirement, a wrong decision made by a patrol officer is likely to be strongly criticized by a supervisor at a later time. Such a dilemma — i.e., the requirement for a rapid decision, and the possibility of negative repercussions from the supervisor — forces patrol officers to seek approval of their actions from their peers. Other patrol officers constantly face the same dilemma, and this acts as a unifying force.

Another source of increased loyalty among the police involves those instances in which the only assistance the police officer can expect in a particularly hazardous or dangerous situation is that of other officers. The media has reported numerous cases in which an unresponsive citizenry has observed a police officer in a life-threatening situation without offering any assistance. Police officers rapidly learn this and grow accustomed to receiving help only from other officers. They must rely heavily on other officers to provide a margin of safety and protection. Reliance of this type reinforces a sense of loyalty and solidarity among the police.

A negative aspect of such unification and loyalty is the reluctance of one police officer to report the misconduct of another. The loyalty to the group tends to become so important that even serious misbehavior by an officer may go unreported. Despite common knowledge of an officer's misconduct, many police officers are often unwilling to break the bond of loyalty and report the offender. To do so would result in the reporting officer being labeled as a "fink" and ostracized by other officers.

Intense loyalty among the police can be observed at another level. Although many officers within a department may have misgivings and complaints about the department, that information is seldom carried beyond the department itself. Although police officers frequently gripe and complain about the agency to their peers, any external complaint against the department tends to act as a unifying force. Public complaints against the department or adverse publicity often result in an increased sense of solidarity among all members of the department. Loyalty and solidarity afford protection against outside attacks on the agency. Frequently, any external threat results in the department and its members taking an "us against them" stance.

To summarize this brief discussion of the characteristics of the police culture, it's been pointed out that the police are a closed group. The background, training, and commonality of duties are some of the unifying experiences that produce a high degree of similarity among police officers. Secondly, the nature and place of performance of the police task, combined with external political efforts, tend to encourage political conservatism among police officers. Finally, the police culture can be characterized as evidencing a high degree of group loyalty and solidarity.

The Police Personality

A police officer's personality might best be characterized as *multi-faceted.* While a variety of personality traits can be attributed to the police, it is somewhat difficult to determine which traits are inherent in individuals who become police officers, and which traits appear as a result of performing the police task. The following discussion is not an attempt to comprehensively report on all aspects of the police personality, but rather to highlight the commonly cited police personality characteristics.

Authoritarianism The police are frequently described as being more authoritarian than individuals in other occupations. This authoritarianism has been attributed to the police training and police role.[12] On the other hand, some research on police authoritarianism indicates that the police are *less* authoritarian than others.[13] Most researchers agree, however, that it's necessary for the police patrol officer to assert and assume authority because of the nature of the police role and the varied situations which he or she encounters. Further discussion of the patrol task will aid in explaining why the police assume authoritarian characteristics in performing their role during police-public encounters.

Police service is provided in a variety of social settings, ranging from the inner office of a bank president to the basement of a shabby tenement in the most economically deprived area of a city. Between these two extremes are other settings; city street corners, parking lots, taverns, factory assembly areas, and public schools. What's common to all these locations and situations is the likelihood that the nature of the police involvement in them is not governed by clear legislative and departmental guidelines. The majority of requests for police service, including criminal complaints, don't result in the police utilizing the power of arrest to resolve the situation. The typical tour of duty for a police officer doesn't involve an arrest.[14] The implication is that the police must and do resolve the variety of situational demands by some means other than arrest. It should be noted that an arrest is also the least desirable alternative for resolution of many encounters between the police and the public.

When police officers don't utilize the arrest power, they must develop alternative ways of resolving the conflicts and demands by the public that have resulted in police intervention. A primary technique is to come up with a reasonable solution to whatever problem exists and then get the involved parties to agree to accept the solution. The domestic disturbance provides an excellent example of this type of situation. Frequently, the police are asked to intervene in a husband-wife quarrel and are requested by the persons involved to remove one of the parties from the residence. Unless an assault or some other crime is committed in the presence of the officers, the police have no real authority to resolve the dispute except the willingness of the disputants to let the police referee the situation. The police are unable to legally and forcibly remove the husband or wife from the residence, and must find an alternative solution to the problem. One technique may be to convince the husband or wife to leave voluntarily. Another way may be to simply permit the disputants to "talk out" the problem. Whatever solution is proposed requires that police obtain the consent and compliance of the involved parties. Obtaining that consent and compliance may result in the police being labeled as authoritarian.

To obtain the compliance, the police must be heard by the disputants and must have a measure of control over the situation. To establish control and attentiveness, the disputants may be ordered to sit, be quiet, or leave the immediate room. The actions of the police in this instance are seldom based on an intrinsic need to dominate other people; rather they are based on a job-related need to resolve a difficult situation without using officially recognized and designated tools.

Clearly, in this example, the police task requires behavior that can be described as authoritarian. When the elements of this example are examined in the light of the numbers of requests for police intervention that don't involve a clear violation of the substantive criminal law, an authoritarian label may be seen as appropriate. The point to remember is that the label is likely to be appropriate because of the job requirements, *not* because of the characteristics of individual officers.

Suspicion Throughout police academy training, and continuing daily in the peformance of the police task, the individual officer is taught and learns to be alert to unusual behavior. Behavior that is considered unusual by the police officer is not necessarily classified as such by the casual observer. Police officers need to be alert to activities that appear normal yet represent a departure from the daily routine of events with which they are familiar. Clean automobiles with muddy license plates, persons who appear out of place or who don't conform to the general character of the neighborhood, individuals who become nervous in the presence of a police officer, and persons who exhibit atypical unconcern at the appearance of a police officer are examples of abnormal activity and present situations to be viewed with suspicion by the police officer. Patrol officers who fail to acquire the ability to identify suspicious persons and situations worthy of additional police observation and inquiry are usuallly considered poor police officers by the department and by other officers as well.

Experience also assists the police officer in developing a suspicious view of people and their activities. Frequently, citizens encountered by a police officer fail to be truthful and, depending on the situation, may even attempt to mislead the officer. The motorist about to receive a traffic citation usually offers numerous explanations and reasons for the violation, some of which are ludicrous or impossible. The patrol officer who conducts a traffic accident investigation involving two motorists seldom hears the same story from both parties. Clearly, the job of the officer is to determine which story is most true, but the effect of exposure to frequent untruths and half-truths makes the officer reluctant to accept the citizen's word at face value.

Similarly, the individual stopped by the patrol officer at four o'clock in the morning in a residential neighborhood represents a suspicious situation.

Even though the individual may offer a perfectly logical explanation for presence in the neighborhood, experience again tells the officer that accepting the story at face value may result in a prowler or burglar remaining free.

Citizens who are overly friendly to the police also tend to make the officer suspicious. Again, experience has taught officers that the majority of the public doesn't want to be involved with the police. A question arises in the officer's mind as to the motives of the overly friendly citizen. Frequently, these motives include a request for a favor or special treatment. Thus, the friendliness of the citizen represents something less than genuine interest in the welfare of the officer and may actually be detrimental to the officer's performance of duty. Such favors may take the form of requests for non-enforcement, special attention to a business or residence, or information not normally available to the public.

With daily exposure to similar situations and activities, suspiciousness becomes an integral and perhaps necessary part of the police personality.

Aggressiveness In the previous discussion of the police culture, mention was made of aggressive patrol tactics. Such tactics were described as the result of the need felt by the police to provide themselves with a measure of protection in a hostile environment. Prior to further discussion of police aggression, a clear definition of the meaning of aggression is helpful. Aggression has been defined as "an unprovoked attack or the practice of making attacks." Such a definition of aggression is inappropriate, however, when one considers the behavior of the police which is usually cited as evidence of the aggressive police personality.

Police aggression is something less than the negative connotation which is brought to mind by the dictionary definition. A better definition might be "the frequently unanticipated interference by the police in the activities of citizens." As such, that interference is normally less than a physical assault on a citizen; most frequently, police interfere only verbally. Again, discussion of the police function is helpful in understanding the type of police behavior often labeled as aggressive.

Deterrence and prevention of crime and social disorder require that the police assume a *pro-active* stance. Essentially, this means that the police must initiate contact with the public in observable situations that may, in the experience of the police, deteriorate into a criminal event or socially disruptive behavior if the police don't interfere. To function pro-actively means that the individual officer must not merely wait for an event to occur and be reported to the police before taking action. During the course of routine patrol, the individual officers may observe situations which seem to warrant police attention; i.e., disorderly persons and suspicious circumstances may result in the officers interjecting themselves into the situation. Such an interjection is usually considered unwelcome by the persons involved. In that sense, the interference by the police is "unprovoked" or at least unanticipated, and may be held as an example of police aggression.

No attempt is being made here to claim that all reports of police aggression are of the type described above. No one would deny that there have been instances of unprovoked physical attacks on the part of the police. The point being stressed here is that aggressive police behavior is job-related and somewhat overstated when used to support the theory that the police are naturally aggressive.

Masculinity Another commonly cited characteristic of the police personality, especially as it concerns the male officer, is the "macho" or "he-man" trait. Observers of the police have noted the value placed on traditionally "tough" behavior by members of the police profession. An officer who's been involved in physical violence is usually faced with endless requests by his peers to recount the incident. In addition, the listeners feel a sense of satisfaction when they hear that "just deserts" have been doled out and that "police toughness" is no myth. Officers who don't display a traditionally "macho" image are often considered unable to perform as a police officer by their contemporaries.

This type of behavior is also seen as being part of the defense mechanism which the police have created to deal with the variety of legally ambiguous situations they encounter. Toughness and unwillingness to "take any guff" aid the individual officer in establishing control of a situation, thus reducing the danger in it.

From both historical and sociological perspectives, law enforcement officers have always been portrayed as physically large and able to effectively deal with violent situations requiring a physical response. Until only recently, most police agencies had stringent height requirements. Requirements like these were based on the notion that large physical size improved the performance of the police officer. Large policemen were believed to be less likely to be open to physical attack and would be more capable of responding if they were attacked. Although height requirements are being modified today, many people – officers and civilians alike – still maintain that police work requires large physical size. Recent research demonstrates that some individuals, even in the face of overwhelming evidence to the contrary, won't concede that physical size is relatively unimportant to the police role.[15] As long as such stereotypes and beliefs are perpetuated by police officers and members of the public, the police will probably continue to be labeled as overly masculine.

Alienation Withdrawal and hostility are police personality characteristics that may well be directly proportionate to the amount of time the individual police officer spends performing the patrol function. This may in part be due to the disparities between the social class which receives the most police service and the social class of the police themselves; the police possess middle-class values, beliefs, and expectations, while the major recipient of police service is the lower-class citizen who isn't likely to share the same values as the police officer.

Day after day, patrol officers face situations that are culturally different from their own lifestyle. Demands are made on the police to handle neighborhood disturbances, disperse crowds of youths congregating on street corners, stop pick-up basketball games being played under a street light at two o'clock in the morning, and other types of human behavior that may be foreign to the police officer. In essence, the police officer is asked to function according to a set of values and rules which may be inconsistent with the norms of the neighborhood being policed. Added to this is the fact that the police officer's actions are usually viewed by the affected persons as interference.

The alienation that results from the performance of the patrol task is a product of two factors. First, at the level of individual police officers, alienation tends to result from the perception that they are being asked to monitor, assist, and direct a group of people who appear incapable of caring for themselves. The evidence for such a position is contained in the numerous calls for police service in the lower-income neighborhoods. The police are expected to provide services of all descriptions, including providing emergency transportation to the hospital, obtaining financial assistance for needy persons, handling abandoned children, and mediating the recurring family disturbance. Calls for services of this type are not common in middle- and upper-income neighborhoods. The police officer can easily begin to perceive the lower-income community as a group of people very different from the mainstream of society. The differences are sometimes seen as so great that an attitude of hostility and special treatment becomes justifiable. Taken to an even further extreme, it's possible that the police can perceive the ghetto resident as a second-class citizen.

At the organizational level, the performance of the patrol function enhances the alienation of the patrol officer. Most police departments evaluate individual officers on their ability to perform the law enforcement function of the police. Such an evaluation is usually based on the number of felony and misdemeanor arrests made by a patrol officer. Some departments also count the number of motor vehicle violations handled by the officer. Only rarely is an attempt made to evaluate the patrol officer's performance of the order maintenance and service function, which occupies the most time.

The dilemma created by the demands of the public being served and the evaluation techniques frequently used by the department itself produces the second source of alientation for the patrol officer. Not only is the majority of time occupied with what is commonly called "social work" but the manner in which the "social work" is performed appears immaterial to the department. In spite of the fact that the officers spend most of the time performing tasks unrelated to law enforcement, they receive no recognition for these efforts. From a career perspective, it's actually detrimental to an officer to provide services to ghetto residents, and this can be seen as justification for hostility toward that group of citizens.

Cynicism Much of what the police are asked to do during the normal day can be viewed as the "dirty work" of society. Recovering bodies of deceased persons in various forms of decomposition, informing the suicide victim's next of kin of the death, and facing the armed and mentally deranged person barricaded inside a building are all examples of the "dirty work" performed by the police. Police cynicism can be closely related to several issues surrounding duties of this nature. Using the example of the mentally deranged and armed individual barricaded inside a building, the problem of occupational prestige can be addressed.

The public expects the police to handle situations of this nature, and the possibility that a police officer may be injured or even killed is usually considered simply as one of the risks of the job. Yet, in spite of the public's expectations of the police, public opinion generally grants the police occupation relatively little status in comparison to other occupations. For example, teachers and social workers are granted more prestige in the eyes of the public than the police are. From the perspective of the police officer, this is *prima facie* evidence of the high expectations and low regard accorded the police occupation. The disparity between the demands of the job and the low prestige accorded it assists in producing a cynical police attitude.

Cynicism also tends to result from what the police often observe as a double standard applied to their profession. The police are expected by the public to regulate morality. They're responsible for enforcing moral standards concerning sexual conduct, alcohol consumption, and various gambling laws. As a result both the public and the police department expect the police, as individuals, to live exemplary lives both on and off duty. Failure of the individual officer to meet the high expectations—by becoming intoxicated in public, for example, or by having an extramarital affair—is likely to get the officer fired. The police view this as very unfair, especially when compared with the lesser penalties and sanctions to which other public servants are liable. If a state legislator is arrested for drunk driving, there is probably little chance of the legislator being dismissed from the legislature; police departments, on the other hand, cite driving while intoxicated as grounds for dismissal of the erring officer.

The individual officer perceives this unequal application of moral standards as evidence that the police are subjected to a double standard. The police are apt to become cynical when they realize that although various types of behavior are considered immoral and are classified as crimes, the same persons who clamor to enact the laws governing morality engage in violations of those laws without suffering the consequences.

A Summary of the Police Personality The six personality characteristics of authoritarianism, suspicion, aggression, masculinity, alienation, and cynicism all appear to be closely aligned with the police role. The extent and degree to which each personality trait is acquired and comes to play a major part in the behavior of the police officer seems related to the length of time spent on the force and the nature of the duties performed by the officer. Patrol officers tend to display more of these personality traits than do officers who are assigned to other duties. Police officers who perform the patrol function, however, represent the major portion of most police agencies. The potential impact of the personality traits which the officer developes during performance of the police patrol task is great, as is the impact on the individual officer.

The Impact Elements of the Police Personality

Danger The potential for violence and harm to the police officer is a constant threat present in each radio call and each contact with the public. Police officers tend to exhibit a mixed reaction to the danger present in their job. Depending on their audience, danger may be minimized and everyday safety hazards such as traffic accidents, may be pointed out instead. Another audience may hear about the hazardous aspects of the police as the focal point of the discussion. Police officers explaining away the job-related fears of their spouses are very likely to minimize the danger of the job. Conversely, in a public relations campaign intended to generate support for the police, much emphasis may be placed on the numbers of police officers injured and killed while performing their duties. The truth is that police work is not as dangerous as some other occupations. During a study of injuries to city workers in New York City, it was found that fire fighters were injured three times as often as police officers, and garbage collectors were injured four times as often.[16] This study indicates that both public and police perceptions of the hazards of police work are probably incorrect.

In spite of the fact that the dangers inherent in police work are often exaggerated, the unpredictability of the police work can be cited as strengthening the police perception of the dangers inherent in the job. The threat, although not visible and constant, is nevertheless always present.

The presence of this threat forms the basis for the individual officer developing a "shorthand" technique for identifying potentially harmful situations.[17] Basically, the police officer learns to associate certain situations, types of persons, and calls with a greater potential for harm. Bar fights, gang disturbances, geographical locations known to be frequented by troublemakers, and even specific residences and persons are associated with increased amounts of danger. A series of unfortunate experiences – some gathered individually, and some gathered via the experiences of other officers – gradually evolves into a stereotyping of certain individuals and locations as likely to represent more danger than others. One advantage of stereotyping is that it helps to increase the officer's level of alertness, and this alertness tends to provide a measure of protection.

One disadvantage of stereotyping is that the indicators of danger that create the stereotype are frequently displayed by non-threatening individuals. For example the correlation between race and crime provides a police stereotype that a black man is likely to be a criminal or a threat to the police. The association between long hair and beards with the civil disturbances of the late 1960s and early 1970s stereotyped such persons as potential troublemakers. Obviously, not all blacks are criminals, nor are all males who wear a beard and long hair disorderly demonstrators. The stereotyping developed in response to the danger of the policing job is often dangerously incorrect.

The second difficulty associated with the element of danger is the response of the police to a perceived increase in the hazard of the situation. In order to balance a potential threat with the need for a measure of safety, police officers often assumes a more aggressive stance than they might take in a less threatening situation. As previously mentioned, aggression is a defense mechanism, but from the perspective of the citizen who's the victim of police aggression such behavior is likely to be viewed as an unreasonable attack by the police. This is a particularly acute problem when the shorthand identification by the police officer is incorrect. The law-abiding black man who's the object of a "stop and frisk" by the police is unlikely to be sympathetic with the police. Instead, a chain of actions and reactions takes place. The police officer, acting on the basis of perceived danger, displays aggressive behavior in dealing with the citizen. The citizen subjected to police aggression experiences fear and counteracts with aggression toward the officer. What may have been a peaceful situation can erupt into a violent encounter between the citizen and the officer. The impact of the encounter frequently continues beyond the emotions of the immediate situation and tends to perpetuate further separation between the public and the police. Officers dealing with the agressive citizen obtain reinforcement for their stereotyping, and the citizen belief that the police are overly aggressive is also supported.

The Impact of Suspicion The effect of suspicion also requires additional explanation in terms of the consequences for the behavior of the police officer. As was noted earlier in the chapter, a healthy measure of suspicion is a requirement for effective performance of the police task. The problems lie in the extent to which suspicion fails to be balanced by an ability to objectively view situations, circumstances, and individuals.

Deep-seated suspicion, like the perception of danger, can become a catalyst for negative police practices and is also a cyclical and self-perpetuating phenomenon. Police officers see their experiences as providing evidence that the motives of many people are other than honorable. In turn, this reinforces the officers' belief that most citizens are law violators at some time. The longer officers are exposed to human transgressions, the more they conclude that people are basically dishonest.[18] If such an attitude is continually reinforced, an officer's suspicious view of the world can extend to all aspects of his or her life. Family, friends, and departmental associates are not beyond the bounds of suspicion. The unexplained absences of the patrol officer's spouse may lead one officer to suspect that the spouse is unfaithful. Acquaintances of long standing are met with reservation and coolness because of the officer's unwillingness to become closely involved with individuals who may later prove to be law violators.

The actions of police supervisors and administrators are also suspect, and for two reasons. First, experience tells the officer that many departmental policies are mere words and only haphazardly enforced. Departmental sanctions against various types of personal conduct are applied only if the transgressor is caught and there's sufficient public clamor to force the department to take disciplinary action. Second, the officer is aware that a type of behavior likely to be punished is practiced by many of the individuals who would bring action against it. The departmental policy concerning alcohol abuse is one example of this. At numerous police functions, officers can observe superiors demonstrating the type of conduct while intoxicated that would result in disciplinary action being taken against them under different circumstances. Distrust of people in general is unlikely to facilitate a willingness to be closely involved and concerned with people. This lack of concern can become sufficient justification for minimal police service, since people continue to behave poorly regardless of what the police do or fail to do. With time, suspicion breeds cynicism.

The Impact of Cynicism Not only does suspicion contribute to the development of a cynical outlook, but the daily fare of the police officer's duties also reinforces a low expectation of people. The demands for police intervention occur when people are confronted with problems they're unable to handle on their own. As such, the individuals involved in police business are seen by officers at their very worst. They daily view the victims of assaults, rapes, and other forms of violence. It often seems that the world of the police officer involves a continuous whirlwind of human tragedy. In the face of daily tragedy and human failing, an attitude of cynicism is difficult to avoid.

The development of cynicism is also facilitated by the police officer's observations of the criminal justice process. The police officer is charged with detecting and apprehending offenders so that they may be punished in accordance with the law. Experience quickly demonstrates that the wheels of justice turn very slowly and sometimes fail to turn at all. Arrested persons are often released on bail while awaiting trial. Frequently, these individuals are arrested for other offenses before being tried for the first violation, and they may end up being convicted for a lesser offense and receive lighter sentences. Typical sentences include probation or minimal confinement, which rapidly returns the offender to the streets. In essence, the police officer often sees the criminal justice system as behaving so erratically that the offender receives little or no punishment. Such a view encourages disbelief in the justice system of which the police officer is a part. It also supports a view that the general public is unconcerned about the problem of crime and of the problems facing the police. If the public were concerned, the officer argues, such practices would not be tolerated.

Cynicism may be a defense against the human inequities and failures which are seen daily by the police officer. In light of the realities of the police officer's world, it becomes increasingly difficult to retain an idealistic attitude and positive outlook.

The Impact of Stress Many of the day-to-day requests for police service and demands made on the police officer can be considered uneventful and rather mundane. The danger element is absent from the majority of encounters between the police and the public. The fact that danger is not inherent in all police activities doesn't negate its existence, however. It's precisely because of the infrequency of danger that police officers are left in perpetual uncertainty. They must be prepared to face an unknown hazard at any time, and this produces a constant strain. Along with the humdrum activities the police officer frequently performs is the knowledge that the next encounter may be physically violent and result in injury or death. Such a strain frequently becomes a mental and physical tension that permeates the officer's behavior.

Another stress-producing factor of the police task relates to the irregular work schedule of the police officer. Police service is provided twenty-four hours a day and requires the assignment of officers to work shifts that neither correspond to the normal work hours of the larger society, nor do the hours match the routine of the officer's family. Frequently, officers working a night shift are going to bed while their spouses and children are arising and beginning the day's activities. The mid-watch shift usually means that it's not possible to spend an evening with one's family; the police officer is working when children are returning from school, is working during the evening family meal, and returns home long after the family has retired for the day. Leave days are irregularly scheduled, and seldom is the police officer free on weekends or holidays. Instead, days off occur during the week when family members are busy. Frequently, too, the police occupation is a seven-day-a-week job when leave days are spent testifying in court. The strain on the personal life of the police officer increases the amount of work-related stress.

In conclusion, the total work environment of the police officer encourages a high degree of tension and stress. The presence of danger is a major contributor to stress, as is the abnormal work schedule of most police officers.

The Psychological Consequences for the Police

Frustration The way in which most police officers – especially new ones – prefer to see themselves is as "helpers."[19] Tolerance, sympathy, and a measure of altruism are unspoken qualities that officers see themselves as possessing and demonstrating during daily contact with the public.[20] Much of the police task consists of helping the public, particularly those segments of the society which have the fewest resources with which to obtain help from non-police individuals and agencies. The problem with the "helper" self-image is that those being helped are frequently unappreciative and, as was pointed out earlier, view the police as intruders. Police officers, faced with a contradiction between their motivation and their reception by the public, experience confusion. The unspoken but existing question is: "Why don't these people appreciate what I'm doing for them?" Through continued exposure to the contradiction between motivation and reception, the confusion experienced by the police officer becomes frustration. This relatively high level of frustration can then contribute to other psychological consequences.

Willingness to Use Force The frustrated officers, who encounter nothing but distain and lack of appreciation for their efforts may strike back at those who come to represent the source of the frustration. The officer experiencing a large amount of frustration may use unnecessary physical force in dealing with suspects and the public. Unnecessary force amounts to an improper use of police power and, simply stated, is the same as physical abuse. One study of the improper use of force by police during a seven-week period reports that these incidents occurred at a rate of over 41 per 1000 suspects.[21] These were cases of actual police brutality, which tells nothing about the extent of verbal abuse or harassment.

In addition to the role frustration plays in promoting the use of unnecessary force, police managerial practices tend to encourage the use of force by rewarding officers involved in violent encounters with law violators. The highest recognition a police officer may receive from his or her department is usually an award for heroism. During one year in New York City, twenty-six patrolmen received the department's highest award for participating in gun battles with armed criminals.[22] Interestingly, no other awards for other types of police service were made.

Police Delinquency The potential for the police recruit to be socialized into deliquent behavior can be partially related to the method of training new police officers. Delinquent police behavior often means police corruption. The development of extensive loyalty to the police culture can also encourage deliquent behavior and corruption in departments where such practices are common. Police secrecy makes the detection and correction of corrupt police practices difficult. An alternate cause of police corruption has been related to the existence of police cynicism.[23]

Essentially, cynicism tends to reduce the police officer's commitment to the larger social system and aids the development of a *replacement commitment* to an alternate set of values, beliefs, and practices. The replacement commitment is to an occupational subculture consisting of other police officers who engage in deliquent or corrupt practices. Corruption is unfortunately a logical type of deliquent behavior for police to engage in. Police authority and opportunities provided by the police task can easily be converted to financial gain. Police loyalty can sometimes encourage corruption, but the same loyalty makes corruption extremely difficult to ferret out when practiced by large numbers of police officers.

Anomie Anomie, the state of normlessness described by Merton,[24] has been used to explain one disastrous effect of alienation and cynicism on the police.[25] In the model described by Arthur Niederhoffer, anomie leads to severe psychological problems and often to suicide. Support for this model is contained in the finding that the suicide rate among police officers in New York is approximately 50% greater than the suicide rate for other males in New York. It should be restated that the development of anomie as a product of cynicism and alienation is not the only possible outcome for the cynical police officer. Suicide represents the ultimate negative result of what appears to be job-related and developed attitudes and beliefs of police officers.

Alcoholism Little factual information is presently available concerning the general causes of alcoholism, but some clinical observations support the contention that alcoholism among police officers exists to a significant extent. The National Council on Alcoholism estimates that one individual in ten living in the United States is an alcoholic. If that national average can be applied to the police occupation, it would imply a large number of alcoholic police officers. Two notes of caution are necessary when engaging in a discussion of this nature. First, the definition of alcoholism is very flexible and varies depending on who's doing the defining. Second, the cause of alcoholism is unknown. What is being suggested here is that the police task produces a high degree of stress, frustration, and retreat from the larger society. Alcohol use and abuse is a means of withdrawing from reality. It may well be that the police task contains a larger concentration of job related factors that may contribute to alcoholism than many other occupations. Suffice it to say that alcoholism does occur among police officers, and that some observers attribute the cause to the nature of the police occupation.

Professional Bonds and International Boundaries

The United States is not the only nation to identify a police culture. The police have been recognized as being the only institution in the world which is really international in scope. The presence of a police culture and elements of the police personality have been identified in studies of other nations. The suspiciousness of the police has been noted by the French and has been characterized as the major function of the police in that country.[26]

Police authority is commonly viewed as a tie which strengthens policing as an international profession. Except in totalitarian states, an ongoing struggle to define the limits of police authority is a concern of the public in many nations, and the debate heard frequently in the United States is echoed by other countries as well.

The isolation of the police in England closely parallels the experience of the police in the United States. British police officers have the same self-perception as Americans concerning the disparity between the importance of the police occupation and the low status accorded it by the public. Both British and American police see the public as less than cooperative. Both see the occupation of police officer as the reason why the public maintains a social distance, from police officers and their families. Both also see the public as failing to provide the level of support and assistance necessary to reduce crime and accomplish other police goals.[27].

Courses taught in Swedish police schools emphasize the conflict present in the police role in a democratic society.[28] The same conflict is the source of many difficulties associated with the police role in the United States. The restrictions placed on the police in the United States are very similar to those placed on the police in other nations. Limitations on the right to hold public office without first resigning from the police force and prohibition of the right to strike are only two of the common restrictions applied internationally to the police.

The police culture seems to exist wherever the police exist. Germany, France, England, and the United States all have differing political, social, and economic cultures. The one culture that's common to all is that of the police.

Summary

The police culture has the potential for tremendous impact on the performance of the police role. The potential impact is not reserved for the police alone, but also clearly affects the public. The causative factors producing the police culture also exceed the bounds of of the police, and part of the responsibility for causation belongs to the public. It may well be that the causes of a police culture are built into the very structure of the police task.[29]

It frequently seems as if an intentionally dysfunctional and counterproductive police system has been created. The interaction between the police and the public is so interrelated that focus on a single aspect or element of the complex cause-effect relationship is not possible. Pessimistically, the prognosis for eliminating the negative aspects of the police culture is dismal. Optimistically, the prognosis is that the constantly improving quality of police personnel may bring about a new critical awareness of the hazards and benefits of the police culture. An emphasis on recruiting better-educated police officers with a balanced perspective of the police task and the police environment is one step toward awareness and improvement. Education alone, however, is not a panacea. An improved police organization capable of minimizing the detrimental effects of existing police managerial practices must also be encouraged, along with a public which exhibits increased awareness of the complexity of the police task.

Topics For Discussion

1. **Discuss the impact of "unfulfilled expectations" on the police officer.**
2. **Explain the potential difficulties in performing the police tasks which are created by current police training practices.**
3. **Describe the class differences between the police and the recipients of the majority of police service. Explain the "culture shock" experienced by some police officers and its effect on police behavior.**
4. **Consider the causes of police alienation. Debate the potential for reducing police alienation. What must change and how can the change occur?**
5. **Describe the psychological consequences of the police role for the individual police officer.**

6. **Present a summary of the relationship between danger and stress. Provide examples of how the interaction between the two affects police behavior.**

References

1. William A. Westley, *Violence and the Police: A Sociological Study of Law, Custom and Morality*, Cambridge: MIT Press, 1970.
2. Police secrecy is addressed by all of the following authors: Albert J. Reiss, Jr., "Police Brutality — Answers to Key Questions", *Transaction*, Vol. 5, July-August, 1968, pp. 10-19, L. Savitz, "The Dimensions of Police Loyalty", *American Behavioral Scientist*, (May-June, July-August) pp. 693-704 and E. R. Stoddard, "The Informal Code of Police Deviancy: A Group Approach to "Blue-Coat' Crime", *Criminal Law, Criminology and Police Science*, Vol. 59, June 1968, pp. 201-213.
3. Jerome H. Skolnick, "A Sketch of the Policeman's Working Personality", *The Ambivalent Force: Perspectives on the Police*, Niederhoffer and Blumberg (Eds.), Hinsdale, IL., The Dyden Press, 1976, pp. 89-90.
4. John Van Maanen, "Working the Street: A Developmental View of Police Behavior", *The Potential for Reform of Criminal Justice*, Herbert Jacob, (ED.,) Beverly Hills, CA: Sage Publications, 1974, pp. 83-129.
5. President's Commission on Law Enforcement and the Administration of Justice, *Task Force Report: The Police*, Washington, D. C. : Government Printing Office, 1967, Arthur Niederhoffer, *Behind the Shield: The Police in Urban Society*, Garden City, New York: Doubleday, 1967, pp. 103-151 and Harlan Hahn, "A Profile of Urban Police", *The Police Community*, Goldsmith and Goldsmith, (Eds.), Pacific Palisades, CA: Palisades Publishers, 1974, pp. 15-35.
6. Van Maanen, "Working the Street," Jacob, (Ed.), op. cit, pp. 87-88.
7. James Q. Wilson, *Varieties of Police Behavior*, Cambridge, Harvard University Press, 1968, pg. 9.
8. Walter B. Miller, "Lower Class Culture as a Generating Milieu of Gang Delinquency", *The Sociology of Crime and Delinquency*, 2d.ed., Wolfgang, Savitz and Johnston, (Eds.), New York: John Wiley and Sons, 1970, pp. 351-363.
9. Jacob Chwast, "Value Conflicts in Law Enforcement", *Crime and Deliquency*, Vol. 11, April 1965, pp. 151-161.
10. Joseph Lohman, "Law Enforcement and the Police", *Riots and Rebellions: Civil Violence in the Urban Community*, Mosotti and Bowen (Eds.), Beverly Hills, Ca: Sage Publications, 1968, pp. 359-372.
11. Seymour M. Lipset, "Why Cops Hate Liberals — and Vice Versa", *The Police Community*, Goldsmith and Goldsmith, (Eds.), Pacific Palisades, Ca.: Palisades Publishers, 1974, pp. 183-196.
12. The empirical research was done by John H. McNamara, "Uncertainties in Police Work: The Relevance of Police Recruits Background and Training", *The Police: Six Sociological Essays*, David Bordua (Ed.), New York: John Wiley and Sons, 1967, pp. 211-212, and the experimental and observational research report by Albert J. Reiss, Jr., *The Police and the Public*, New Haven, Yale University Press, 1971, pp. 1-62 and Niederhoffer, *Behind the Shield*, op. cit, pp. 103-151.
13. David H. Baley and Harold Mendelsohn, *Minorities and The Police*, New York: the Free Press, 1969, pp. 17-18.

14. Reiss, *The Police and the Public*, op. cit., pg. 19.
15. David L. Cockrun and Michael A. Doyle, *Measuring and Changing Attitudes Toward Female Patrol Officers*, Alpine, TX: Unpublished Manuscript, 1975.
16. David Burnham, "Police Violence: A Changing Pattern," Niederhoffer and Blumberg (Eds.), op. cit., pp. 188-192.
17. Skolnick, "A Sketch of the Policeman's Working Personality," Niederhoffer and Blumberg, (Eds.), op. cit., pp. 84-85.
18. Niederhoffer, *Behind the Shield*, op. cit. pp. 103-151.
19. Chwast, "Value Conflicts in Law Enforcement", op cit., pp. 151-161.
20. Elaine Cumming, Ian Cumming and Laura Edell, "Policeman as Philosopher, Guide and Friend", Niederhoffer and Blumberg, op. cit., pp. 204-205.
21. Reiss, "Police Brutality — Answers to Key Questions", op. cit., pp. 188-192.
22. Burnham, "Police Violence: A Changing Pattern", op. cit., pp. 188-192.
23. Niederhoffer, *Behind the Shield*, op. cit., pp. 103-151.
24. Robert K. Merton, "Social Structure and Anomie", *The Sociology of Crime and Deliquency*, 2d ed., Wolfgang, et. al. (Eds.), New York: John Wiley and Sons, 1970, pp. 238-246.
25. Niederhoffer, "Police Cynicism", Niederhoffer and Blumberg, (Eds.), op. cit., pp. 193-196.
26. George Berkley, *The Democratic Policeman*, Boston: Beacon Press, 1969, pg. 6.
27. John P. Clark, "Isolation of the Police: A Comparison of the British and American Situations", *The Journal of Criminal Law Criminology and Police Science*, Vol. 56, September, 1965, pp. 307-319.
28. Berkley, *The Democratic Policeman*, op. cit., pp. 76-78.
29. John F. Galliher, "Explanations of Police Behavior: A Critical Review and Analysis", *The Sociological Quarterly*, Vol. 12, Summer, 1971, pp. 308-318.

Annotated Bibliography

Berkley, George E., *The Democratic Policeman*, Boston: Beacon Press, 1969. Analysis of the problems of the police in a democratic society; comparison of the American police with the police of several European nations demonstrates the difficulty of providing police service is not restricted to the United States.

Chwast, Jacob, "Value Conflict in Law Enforcement", *Crime and Delinquency*, Vol. 11, April 1965, 151-161. A discussion of the conflicting values held by police administrators, police officers and the public receiving the majority of police services; stress results for the police officer because of the value conflict; understanding of competing values is recommended for improving police service.

McNamara, John H., "Uncertainties in Police Work: The Relevance of Police Recruits Backgrounds and Training", *The Police: Six Sociological Essays*, David J. Bordua (Ed.), New York: John Wiley and Sons, Inc., 1967, 163-252. Using the New York City Police Department recruits in the study, conflict between law enforcement and other police tasks is analyzed. The impact on the police recruit and the resulting difficulty with role adjustment is described.

Neiderhoffer, Arthur, "Police Cynicism", *The Ambivalent Force*: Perspectives on the Police, 2d ed., Niederhoffer and Blumberg (Eds.), Hinsdale, IL.: The Dryden Press, 1976, 193-196. Presentation of a model to depict the importance of cynicism as a critical point between professional commitment and anomie in the career of the police officer. Included are a number of hypotheses concerning the extent of police cynicism in relation to the individual and job related characteristics of the policeman.

Reiss, Albert J., *The Police and The Public*, New Haven: Yale University Press, 1971. A study of the interaction between the police and the public in three large cities in the United States. Focus is on the difference in police behavior depending on the source of mobilization of the police. Citizen-initiated and police-initiated interactions are analyzed.

Skolnick, Jerome H., *Justice Without Trial: Law Enforcement in A Democratic Society*, New York: John Wiley and Sons, Inc., 1966. An in-depth examination of the police in a contemporary society; special attention is directed to describing the "working personality of the policeman" and the variables leading to development of that personality.

The President's Commission on Law Enforcement and the Administration of Justice, *Task Force Report: The Police*, Washington, D. C.: Government Printing Office, 1967. An encompassing survey of police practices and the environment in which police service is provided. Included are recommendations for enhancing the provision of police service and the modernization of approaches to the multiple goals of the police.

Van Maanen, John, "Working the Street: A Developmental View of Police Behavior:, *The Potential For Reform of Criminal Justice*, Herbert Jacob (Ed.), Beverly Hills, CA: Sage Publications, Inc., 1974. A description of the socialization of police based on the author's participation in recruit training and performance of the police task. Evolution of the police personality through continued exposure to the police role.

4

POLICE AND THE LAW
Enforcement by the Letter or the Spirit

Chapter Objectives

The study of this chapter should enable you to:

☑ Explain the three functions which law serves in a society.

☑ Demonstrate the complexity of law in a society in which the person is of paramount importance.

☑ Explain the nature of law as a social concept and demonstrate how the criminal law fits into the social order.

☑ Discuss the decision-making process concerned with what conduct should be designated criminal, including some theories of punishment for prohibited acts.

☑ Define, discuss, and distinguish the common law from statutory enactments, to present various common rules of interpretation of criminal statutes, and to review some of the theories of legal reasoning.

☑ Differentiate civil liberties from civil rights by reviewing constitutional doctrine regarding both, but especially focusing on criminal procedural matters.

☑ Develop an understanding of the classification and definition of crimes, and to explore the concept of criminal responsibility.

☑ Distinguish federal crimes and procedure from those found in the states, by discussing the primary responsibility of the courts and the criminal law at both levels.

☑ Explain the steps and some of the problems in the criminal process, from filing of a complaint or making an arrest to the completion of the appellate process.

☑ Explain the doctrine of *stare decisis*.

Introduction

As a functionary in the criminal justice system, the police officer needs to have an intimate knowledge of the theories behind the criminal law as well as a detailed understanding of the technicalities unique to its administration. Law is not just a series of rules to be memorized. No criminal justice practitioner can perform his or her job as a true professional without fully understanding the law, how it is carried out, what its goals are, and how it is supposed to function as opposed to how it does function.

In order to maintain the strength of our society, which is based on the rule of law, it is likewise imperative that all citizens understand the nature of law. Because of their unique responsibilities this is especially true for police officers, whose function is to enforce laws — even disagreeable ones.

This chapter focuses on the general nature of the law and some of the basic principles of American law. It examines the different classifications of law and describes the institutions and procedures used to handle a criminal case under our system of law.

The Nature and Functions of the Law

Law is a creation of society. It is necessary for society's continued existence. Society, whether a small tribal group or a great nation, is made up of individuals who have come together for their mutual advantage. These individuals will, however, have competing interests. Two of them may want the same piece of land or access to the same water supply. If the society is to survive as a cohesive group, it must find a way of regulating these competing interests. This need to order the interaction of individuals in society gives birth to law. When society becomes concerned enough with a certain activity to want to prohibit, modify, or encourage it, laws are made.

Law has three functions. First, *the law educates.* It molds moral and legal attitudes by holding out a standard of right and wrong. Much of what we do or do not do is determined by our knowledge of what is legal or illegal. We refrain from doing certain things not because there is a police officer watching us, but because we know they are against the law.

Second, *the law helps to maintain social order.* It not only defines what is right and wrong, but also provides penalties for disobedience. Knowledge of the legal consequences of violating the law encourages obedience. Motorists know that a traffic fine may result from failure to stop for a red light. Anticipation of the fine encourages them to obey the law. Further, law enables individuals to predict how their neighbors will act, since legal sanctions apply to them also. This allows people to interact in a secure atmosphere; they know what the normal bounds of behavior are and also know that their neighbor will usually stay within those bounds. Thus, the law encourages voluntary compliance with society's values and provides security and stability.

Finally, the law furnishes a *means for resolving differences and settling grievances.* Disagreements can be worked out without resort to violence or private vengeance. Society's unity is not disturbed.

Government exists as society's instrument for making and enforcing the law. The legislative branch writes the laws, the judicial branch determines their application, and the executive branch enforces them.

Deciding what the law is or what it should be is complicated, because law-making is a process of choosing among conflicting moral, political, social, and economic values. As an example, consider the situation of a man who burglarizes a grocery because his family is starving. Society has determined that burglary is a crime that must be punished. This reflects a value placed on private property. In this case, however, there is a competing value that society also considers important: the value of human life. Society could decide that human life is of paramount importance and should be preserved by any means, even at the cost of allowing a burglary. On the other hand, society could decide that the burglar could have obtained help for his family by some other action and must, therefore, pay a penalty for his crime. Actually, a court faced with this issue could take the position that the burglar *does have* a right to steal when he or his family is faced with eventual starvation. Thus, the court recognizes that there is a defense of necessity available to the person charged with a crime. By recognizing necessity as a defense, the court is stating that while it is socially desirable to protect property from burglary, it is more desirable that citizens not die from starvation. The courts are constantly faced with having to decide what constitutes acceptable conduct in the context of unique fact cases.

The current law basically identifies and prohibits serious misbehavior (substantive crimes) and less serious misbehavior (misdemeanors). Criminal law is a means of punishing wrongdoers. The theories of punishment found in criminological literature relate directly to the effectiveness of criminal statutes. One of the most frequently cited theories for punishing a deviant act is that of *deterrence*: discouraging future conduct of the same kind. According to this theory, would the threat of imprisonment have deterred the father from the above burglary? Probably not. Even if the law provided for death as the punishment for burglary, it is still likely that the father would have burglarized the grocery in order to feed his children. This discussion about one punishment theory is important to an understanding of the nature of criminal law as it operates in a society. As stated previously, the courts have the responsibility of interpreting and applying the law to the unique facts in a case. If the courts were severely circumscribed by the legislature as to the kind and severity of punishment allowed, justice would suffer. As a consequence, criminal laws normally allow judges some leeway. When imposing a penalty, a judge may consider the seriousness of an offense and the circumstances surrounding it.

As the values of a society change, both legislatures and courts are faced with competing values. The legislature continues to weigh competing interests and makes laws that are applicable to society as a whole. As already demonstrated, the courts take these rules of general applicability and apply them to the facts in individual cases. Thus, the solutions to particular legal problems reflect current political and social values.

There is an assertion frequently heard in the United States that laws are made by and for the "ruling class." This is a gross oversimplification. The "ruling class" does not get everything it wants from the law, nor do the many other groups within our society. Not only is the process of enacting the law greatly complicated by moral, political, and pragmatic considerations, but also, in a society as complex and diverse as ours, laws are seldom enacted to benefit the whole. Rather, laws result frequently from pressures by interest groups. Criminal law is, however, grounded upon the idea that society as a whole is sufficiently concerned about certain types of activities to want to prohibit or modify them.

Because society's values change through time, conflict in the meaning and application of criminal law is inevitable. A quick review of the history of obscenity laws in the United States makes this clear. Changes in morality, social permissiveness, constitutional philosophy, and political ideology have resulted in questions over not only whether obscenity should be a criminal offense but also over what the word means. The laws reflect such conflicts. To the extent that laws do not reflect the values of society, the law breaks down because the members of society will not abide by it.

However, courts are guided by what is called the rule of *precedent*, the process of arriving at new court decisions by analogy with previous ones having the same general facts. The use of precedent maintains continuity and stability in administration of the law. It also recognizes new societal conditions by overruling previous cases. Breaking with precedent may be a direct result of new societal values.

When discussing precedent in its legal context, a review of the doctrine of *stare decisis* clarifies how precedent works in our legal system. The rule of *stare decisis* essentially means that once a point has been settled by a decision, that decision forms a precedent which should not be departed from easily by overruling it, even though the rule may seem to be old and not well suited to the conditions at the time of a similar case requiring a new decision.

Stare decisis provides for uniformity, certainity, and stability of the law. Once courts have pronounced certain controlling legal principles for the guidance of governments and individuals, the latter should be able to rely on those principles in carrying out their business and personal activities. *Stare decisis* is based on public policy and should be followed unless there are extremely compelling reasons for change, i.e., the precedent is clearly erroneous, manifestly causes serious problems, or causes more harm than good. While *stare decisis* gives great weight to precedent, it does not demand that courts blindly adhere to it if satisfied that the precedent is wrong.

In areas of constitutional and criminal law, the doctrine is especially important. Court decisions construing the Constitution or legislative acts should be followed in the absence of cogent reasons to the contrary, because both the basic laws of the land and the statutory laws must have a consistent, certain meaning as well as a fixed interpretation. However, in the application of *stare decisis* to constitutional interpretation, some legal scholars take the position that the rule has no real place in constitutional law where the validity of a statute is concerned. They contend that *stare decisis* should not prevent a court from reviewing a constitutional question in which the facts before the court are slightly different from those in former decisions. In short, they argue that precedents have little validity when interpreting the Constitution. This argument, however, has not been widely accepted by the state or federal courts.

In summary, some acts threaten the peace and well-being of society. In order to protect itself, society enacts laws to curtail these undesirable acts. In order for the law to be effective as a deterrent, punishments are provided. However, the deterrence concept needs to be examined very critically because of the many unique situations that arise in the application of the criminal law.

Common Law and Statutory Law: Principles of Legal Application

When America was founded, the English colonists brought with them the common law of England as a foundation for the law in the New World. The term *common law* is used to designate laws made by judges as opposed to legislation enacted by governing bodies. The common law is found in the reports of judicial decisions, while statutes are enacted by legislatures. The common law is based on the premise that judges have the authority to create law while resolving disputes between parties in civil matters or in deciding criminal cases. A criminal or penal statute is an act of a legislature relating to crime or its punishment.

Common law, frequently defined as "unwritten law," is founded on the laws of nature and the dictates of reason based on custom and usage. It is comprised of those maxims, principles, and forms of judicial proceedings which are not prescribed or warranted by written law. Common law is based on the idea that when acts are harmful, undesirable, and tend to injure the community, they must be repressed if the social order is to be maintained. Common law has, over a period of time, been interwoven with statutory law through incorporation into state codes and local ordinances.

There are four rules of statutory interpretation and construction. The first states that *English common law is to be strictly construed.* This means that a statute enacted to change the common law will not be interpreted to alter the common law in any way other than that intended by the statute. The courts are also guided by another rule of statutory interpretation which is of special importance in contemporary society. This rule states that where *remedial legislation is enacted to cure some social ill, a criminal statute will be liberally interpreted* to carry out the goal of correcting that ill. This form of interpretation is evident in the voting rights cases of the 1960s in which the United States Supreme Court consistently interpreted congressional legislation liberally to strike down discriminatory state voting laws. Busing to integrate schools is another situation in which the federal courts have consistently provided a liberal interpretation of statutes in order to eliminate a social evil. Statutes are often enacted to correct some condition in society; in other words, some economic or philosophical objective serves as the underlying justification for a statutory enactment. Frequently, when dealing with applying and interpreting such statutes, judges will look elsewhere for assistance in determing what the statutory language means. They may study related laws, or examine the historical underpinnings of the statute, legislative committee reports, revisions of the statute, legislative debates, and the like.

A third rule quite often accepted in the interpretation and application of the criminal laws is "the rule of *ejusdem generis*." According to this, when general words follow enumerations of particular classes of persons or things, the general words shall be construed as applicable only to persons or things of the same general nature or kind as those enumerated. For example, if a statute forbade the concealment on one's person of pistols, revolvers, derringers, or *other dangerous weapons*, the italicized general words would be construed to mean only dangerous weapons of the type enumerated: firearms, or even more narrowly, handguns. This rule of statutory construction is generally accepted in both federal and state counts.

Criminal justice functionaries, especially the police, should be aware that law, particularly the criminal law, is largely developed through a process of legal reasoning called *reasoning by analogy*, the fourth rule of statutory interpretation. This is based on the idea that where there is no precedent in point on cases of the same subject, lawyers have resources to cases on a different subject matter but governed by the same general legal principle. Reasoning by analogy involves the similarity of relationships which exist between the points compared.

Reasoning by analogy is a definite benefit in deciding criminal cases because seldom can a precedent be found which is an exact duplicate of the case to be decided. Also, reasoning by analogy continues the legal concept that law should have some stability and *provide guidance*. Analysis of prior decisions on the same general subject matter can help keep a person from running afoul of the law.

In summary, the common law developed from custom and tradition. It was brought to America by the English colonists who adapted their common law to the needs of the New World. Today, many states have turned to codified or statutory law for regulation of social intercourse. Statutes are generally very specific in regard to what is prohibited. Courts have developed aids to assist them in interpreting and applying the statutory laws. These include the doctrine of strict construction, liberal interpretation of remedial statutes, the rule of *ejusdem generis*, and reasoning by analogy.

This brief discussion of the basis of our law and of several legal principles which guide the courts in interpreting the law leads to a question: What is a crime? At its basic level a crime is composed of an act prohibited by law of either commission or omission coupled with a specific state of mind. The latter is often referred to as criminal responsibility. The next section discusses the classifications of crimes and some of the more commonly found mental (intent) states found in the criminal law.

Definition and Classification of Crimes

In early stages of the criminal law, many of the acts labelled as crimes today were then called *torts*. A tort was a wrong against an individual for which the victim sought some form of redress. There were very few crimes in the common law; today's most serious crimes, such as murder, rape, or robbery, were torts for which the victim or his next-of-kin sought compensation — too often through violent retribution.

The common law as it developed in England permitted the judges to define what would be a crime. In the United States, the legislatures now perform this function. Thus, in most American jurisdictions, an act not prohibited by some statute is not a crime no matter how unethical the conduct may be. We have written laws because of a belief that individuals are entitled to know in plain and explicit language what constitutes any offense charged so that they may govern their conduct accordingly.

What constitutes a crime? In the American legal system, a crime is an act or omission forbidden by law and punishable according to the law in a particular jurisdiction. The prevailing penal philosophy in the United States will not permit the punishment of acts or omissions which were not clearly defined as offenses at the time the act was committed.

Classification of Crimes

Crimes may be classified in several ways. The first and most common categorizes according to the seriousness of the crime—felonies as opposed to misdemeanors. A special classification, "petty offenses," is found in federal law. Some jurisdictions are adopting still another classification for minor, non-serious, transgressions of the law called "violations" or "infractions". This classification is most frequently used for minor traffic offenses. In the common law treason was set off as the most serious of crimes but today does not assume the same significance.

The felony, the highest classification of crime, is reserved for the most serious offenses such as murder, robbery, rape, or arson. With respect to potential punishment, it provides for death or imprisonment in state prisons plus payment of a fine. The felony is most often prosecuted by grand jury indictment, although some states (California and Michigan for example) permit the local district attorney to initiate criminal prosecution through the use of an information. An information is similar to an indictment, only it is filed at the initiation of a prosecutor rather than a grand jury.

Misdemeanors are less serious crimes which do not call for the more severe felony penalties. A misdemeanor is punishable by incarceration in a jail for up to a year. In some states the misdemeanor has been further subdivided into gross and petty misdemeanors. The former is sometimes an indictable offense with a punishment of over six months and a specific minimum fine, while petty misdemeanors usually carry a short period of jail incarceration or only a fine. At the federal level, the "petty offense" category provides for punishment not to exceed "imprisonment" for six months or a fine of not more than $500 or both.

Violations or infractions is the last classification based on the seriousness of offenses. This classification is presently being used in some states and being considered in others. These offenses are usually very minor and are punishable by less than 30 days in jail and/or a small fine. For this kind of offense, a citation or summons is usually issued instead of an arrest being made.

A second major way of classifying crimes involves identifying criminal acts as either *Malum in se* or *Malum prohibita* offenses. The former classification refers to those crimes which are wrong in themselves and deserve punishment. This classification depends to a great extent on the moral and ethical norms of a country, but universally included are such offenses as murder, rape, robbery, and larceny. *Malum prohibita* offenses are those established by legislation. These offenses are not morally wrong, but are enacted in order to regulate social intercourse. The area of the law encompassing *malum prohibita* offenses has expanded during the past hundred years, primarily because the complex nature of our society has mandated certain controls in the form of legislation. For example, the automobile plays a significant part in the American way of life. Suppose a person drives through a stop sign. There is nothing morally wrong with this. However, it is clearly necessary to have such traffic controls because if there were no type of regulation, many persons would be killed or injured while the damage to property would be staggering. *Malum prohibita* offenses are frequently referred to as public welfare, regulatory, or administrative crimes because they are not based on any moral principle.

A third scheme for classifying offenses depends on the *kind of social harm* involved. This category is often followed in state codes to identify separate classes of crimes. Included are crimes against the person, crimes against property, offenses against the habitation, crimes against morality and decency, and crimes against the executive, legislative, or judicial authority. The police officer is most likely to be concerned with the third classification scheme since it has to do with the way most law enforcement agencies are organized to investigate crimes. (The investigative division would include a crime against persons unit, a crime against property unit, and so on).

Criminal Responsibility

Several legal phrases permeate the criminal law and serve to express ideas or concepts of importance when determining the criminal responsibility of a person. The police officer must be familiar with these concepts because they arise daily in crime investigation and case preparation.

Mens rea means "guilty mind" although the term is not entirely synonomous with criminal intent. It has been used to mean "willfully" as in the crime of murder, to mean "maliciously" as in arson, or to refer to guilty knowledge—not necessarily knowledge or foresight of a particular consequence, but of some bad or illegal consequence. *Mens rea* may also consist of criminal negligence, as in second degree manslaughter, or wantonness or reckless conduct, as in first and second degree murder. *Mens rea* requires a power of volition. The person must be able to "keep from doing what he does." "Blameworthiness" has often been the practical definition of *mens rea*.

The general rule in criminal law is that there is no crime unless there is criminal intent, guilty knowledge, or criminal negligence. The common law recognized three general kinds of *mens rea*: general intent, specific intent, and criminal negligence.

A *general intent* means that a person commits an offense aware of both the conduct involved and the results which are likely to follow. This means that when a person does an act which he means to do and which causes an injury, it is generally not relevant that he did not mean to cause the particular injury which followed provided that the injury was substantially certain to flow from his conduct. When one comes into contact with statutes requiring "willful," "deliberate", or "intentional" conduct, only this general intent is usually required to be proven. A general intent includes the whole field of blameworthiness.

Specific intent indicates an actual intention as distinguished from a general criminal intent. The accused person must not only have intended to perform an act, but must have done it with a particular state of mind. For example, some crimes require a specific intention in addition to commission of the proposed act. The crime of burglary often requires a breaking and entry into a dwelling *with the intent* to steal or commit a felony. The breaking and entry can be done deliberately with full knowledge of the consequences of the act. But if the breaking and entry were not done with the specific intent to steal or commit a felony there is no crime of burglary—only the crime of breaking and entering. The decision to steal *only after* the culprit has broken into the dwelling is not sufficient because the entry and breaking were not made with this specific idea in mind. Many other crimes also require specific kinds of intent.

Specific intent is sometimes couched in terms of specific knowledge that a perpetrator must have. For example, the offense of uttering a forged instrument usually states that there must be knowledge on the part of the utterer that the instrument was forged. If there is no knowledge, the defendant cannot be convicted. In this situation it is generally adequate to show that a reasonable man in the same circumstances would have known the facts involved. Courts have sometimes held it to be sufficient if a reasonable man would have been suspicious or would have launched an inquiry about the facts involved. For example, a person offering goods at a ridiculously low price would presumably have knowledge of their stolen nature. The person could then be charged legally with the offense of receiving stolen property.

Criminal negligence is included in the *mens rea* concept of criminal responsibility. It often serves as a substitute for a general criminal intent. The concept of negligence becomes the basis for criminal negligence when a person, through gross lack of care, allows a situation to develop or commits an act which results in injury. Thus, the individual becomes guilty of a criminal act.

The starting point of inquiry is whether there is a duty to a person if harm has resulted. For example, a stranger has no duty to come to the aid of a person in distress. But, should the stranger give aid, he or she then has a duty to act with a reasonable degree of care. It is important to note at this point that the degree of negligence is determined by referring to "reasonable man standard"—the duty of care owed by a reasonable, prudent person exercising ordinary caution under similar circumstances. The reasonable man standard will vary according to the skills of each individual. For example, a medical doctor would be held to a higher degree of care than a layperson when involved in a situation where medical attention is required.

When a person's actions involved a high probability of injury or a very substantial deviation from socially accepted conduct, criminal negligence may be involved. If there is a lesser degree of negligence, the individual may be sued in a civil action for acts of simple negligence. The difference between criminal and civil negligence is basically a matter of the degree of the negligence and depends on the facts and circumstances in the particular case. The fact finder must determine the degree of negligence from the severity of the breach of the duty, not from the severity of the harm that resulted.

In those crimes requiring a specific intent, criminal negligence cannot serve as a substitute. For example, burglary cannot be committed by negligence because of the requirement that there must be an intent to steal or commit some other felony when the breaking and entry occurred.

The police officer must bear in mind that criminal negligence involves an unconscious disregard of a potential harm to others. A *conscious* disregard of a known risk is governed by the actual state of mind of the accused and is more than a criminally negligent act. It is legally designated as "*recklessness*." In many states the element of "recklessness" permits a more severe punishment of an offense. Recklessness is wanton and willful conduct adequate to satisfy the general intent requirements in most statutes. For example, should "X" fire a gun into a moving passenger train and injure a passenger, he would have performed a criminally negligent act even though he thought the gun was unloaded. If the accused had known that he was firing at a passenger train and that his gun was loaded, or purposefully had not checked to determine if it was loaded, he would have engaged in willful and wanton conduct. In this example, the accused could be convicted of murder should the passenger die as a result of the wound inflicted.

In summary, crimes are classified as felonies, misdemeanors, and in some jurisdictions, as a lesser category of offenses called infractions, petty offenses, or violations. Second, crimes may also be classified according to the moral wrongness of the offenses, such as those crimes *malum in se* and those *malum prohibita*. A third classification, frequently used, depends on the kind of social harm involved, such as offenses against the person or property. The concept of *mens rea* permeates the criminal law and implies the idea of some blameworthiness. General intent, specific intent, criminal negligence, and recklessness are legal concepts included within the *mens rea* requirements.

Federal and State Jurisdictional Issues

In the United Sates there is a dual system of courts and laws, the federal and the state. The fifty state systems are independent of each other for most purposes despite the fact that they share a common ancestry. State courts are largely independent of federal courts, although the systems are tied together in a loose fashion by the supreme law of the land, the Constitution. A student who is bewildered by the multitude of federal courts will be even more amazed at the proliferation of courts authorized within each state by the state legislatures.

At the federal level there are numerous "special" courts having jurisdiction over specific subject areas, e.g. Tax Court, Court of Military Appeals, and the Court of Customs and Patent Appeals. All of these courts have different jurisdictions—matters about which each court is competent to decide. For example, one court may hear misdemeanor cases only. It cannot pronounce a decision—speak the law—in felonies because it is not competent (does not have jurisdiction) to decide that matter. A brief discussion of some concepts concerning the dimensions of federal and state jurisdiction follows.

First, *federal courts primarily enforce federal laws.* Article III, Section 2 (1) of the Constitution states that the judicial power of the United States extends to all cases and treaties made, or which shall be made, under the authority of the Constitution and laws of the United States. This provision has been interpreted broadly to include questions involving federal laws either by way of a claim under federal law or a defense based on federal laws. To carry out the constitutional requirements, the Congress establishes federal courts and sets their precise jurisdictional limits by statute.

Second, *federal courts adjudicate cases in which the parties are residents of different states.* The diversity of citizenship jurisdiction of the federal courts is found in Article III, Section 2 (1) which provides for the extension of the judicial power of the United States to cases between citizens of different states. This provision is designed to provide a neutral forum for out-of-state residents who are in the courts of a sister state. The federal statute which implements this constitutional provision provides that federal courts may hear civil actions involving the citizens of different states when the amount in the case exceeds $10,000.

Third, *state courts primarily enforce the laws of their respective states.* For the police officer and the other criminal justice functionaries this basically means that the state courts hear cases involving violations of state penal and regulatory laws. By far the overwhelming number of criminal offenses are found in state laws. Consequently, the jurisdiction of state courts is very broad.

Fourth, *state courts generally adjudicate cases involving persons resident in their own state.* However, it often happens that a state court will be presented a case in which one or both of the parties is a state resident, but the suit is based on the law found in another state. This common situation occurs for several reasons. First, Article IV, Section 1, of the United States Constitution mandates that full faith and credit be given in each state to the public acts, records, and judicial proceedings of every other state. Second, under the principle of comity, one sovereign expects another sovereign to give effect to its laws in return for the expectation that the second will do likewise. In short, the principle expresses the idea that mutual respect will be given to the laws of separate jurisdictions by each state. Third, a strong practical reason exists for a state to apply the law of another state within its borders—the most convenient forum for the adjudication of a case is frequently a state different from that where the cause of action arose.

From the above brief sketch, one can note that the *jurisdiction of federal courts is much more narrow than that of the state courts.* The federal courts' jurisdictional limits are set by the Constitution and federal statutes, and these limits generally provide that a substantial question of federal law be involved. The "diversity of citizenship" cases are an exception to the concept that a federal question needs to be involved. In these situations, the applicable state law is applied by the federal court.

In the area of criminal law, state courts have the responsibility of applying not only state statutory penal laws, but also applicable common law. At the federal level, however, there is no federal common law. Therefore, the federal courts deal almost exclusively with federal laws except in those diversity of citizenship cases where the appropriate state common law might be applied.

Turning from the issue of jurisdiction, the organization of the legal system, especially at the federal level, needs some explanation. The federal system has at its apex the United States Supreme Court, which has original jurisdiction (the power to hear cases for the first time) and appellate jurisdiction (the power to review the decisions of another court). The specific areas in which the Supreme Court has jurisdiction are stated in Article III of the Constitution. However, Congress has the power to control the court's jurisdiction through the use of legislation. The Supreme Court can exercise a great controlling check on federal courts by the grant of power given to it by the Constitution.

As a general rule, before the United States Supreme Court can review decisions of state courts, the highest court in the state in which a decision on the matter can be made must have considered or acted on the case. Usually this involves the state supreme court, although some states permit a final appeal of a case to be decided by a lower state court.

In some cases, a state court will hold that a federal statute is unconstitutional. When this occurs the United States Supreme Court must review the state court decision if it is appealed. Such a review must also take place when a federal treaty is determined to be unconstitutional or when a state court upholds a state law which is challenged as being in conflict with a federal law. These are just some of the cases involving federal questions. In all such instances the person may petition the Supreme Court to review the state court's decision. The Supreme Court, if it decides that the person's position is meritorious, will issue a *writ of certiorari* meaning that the court has decided to hear the appeal. The writ also serves as an order to the state court telling it to send all of the case records to the United States Supreme Court.

As noted above, many cases involving *federal questions* originate in state courts. The Fourteenth Amendment has done much to increase the number of state cases coming before the federal courts on appeal. Before the Thirteenth, Fourteenth, and Fifteenth Amendments were adopted after the Civil War, the Supreme Court, in *Barron v. Baltimore*, 32 U.S. (7 Pet.) 243 (1833), interpreted the Bill of Rights as being directed only to the federal government even though, with the exception of the First Amendment, each of the Bill of Rights was written so that it could be applied to the states. However, such application would have to wait many years for the Supreme Court to overturn the *Barron v. Baltimore* decision. The Fourteenth Amendment states, "Nor shall any State deprive any person of life, liberty or property without due process of law." It should be noted that the language in the amendment is extremely broad. Therefore it is easily susceptible to various interpretations by different people. This has been the situation throughout the history of the Amendment. Politically, the exact meaning of the clause has caused confusion over whether all of the Bill of Rights apply to the states. The position taken by the Supreme Court of today is that the due process clause of the Fourteenth Amendment incorporates selected provisions of the Bill of Rights. This "selective incorporation" doctrine has been interpreted to apply most of the provisions of the Bill of Rights to the states just as they apply to the federal government.

Civil Rights and Civil Liberties

The terms civil rights and civil liberties are frequently used synonymously. However, they do have different meanings. Civil rights are rights given, defined, and restricted by laws enacted by civilized governments. In the United States civil rights help to insure equality under the law for every individual. These rights include, among others, the rights of property, marriage, protection by the laws, freedom to contract, trial by a jury, and speedy trial. Generally speaking, civil rights belong to a person by virtue of citizenship in a state or country.

Civil liberties insure the greatest amount of liberty possible for every citizen of a state. Civil liberties include freedom of religion, freedom to travel, and freedom of expression. Civil liberties imply freedom from government interference by being a guarantee of protection against restriction by government. It must be emphasized, however, that civil liberty does not imply freedom from interference or actual restraint by private parties. For this reason, during the past several decades federal, state, and local laws have been enacted to regulate both governmental and private conduct which may inhibit equal opportunity for all citizens. States have enacted laws prohibiting private persons or companies from discriminating because of race, creed, or national origin in such areas as housing, employment, travel, access to public accomodations, and education. These laws, known as *civil rights acts*, protect civil liberties from interference by private persons.

Civil rights issues have resulted in numerous Supreme Court interpretations aimed at protecting individual civil rights.

In the field of constitutional law, the United States Supreme Court has held that the Constitution prohibits state action which infringes on a right guaranteed by the Constitution. Actions by persons acting with the apparent authority of the law but actually in contravention of it fall under the constitutional prohibitions. For example, the Constitution has been interpreted as forbidding state actions based solely on race, creed, or color. State sanctioned school segregation based on race has been held to be in violation of the equal protection; therefore, actions by state officials enforcing state segregation laws were in contradiction of the Consitution's Fourteenth Amendment. The federal government and its officers are similarly prohibited from discriminating under apparent authority of federal law because of the due process clause of the Fifth Amendment. These kinds of decisions have most often been called civil rights matters, although the right not to be discriminated against is a basic freedom (civil liberty) protected under the Constitution. The first ten amendments to the United States Constitution make up the *Bill of Rights*. These amendments were added after representatives of the ratifying states demanded guarantees protecting individuals from arbitrary and unreasonable acts of government. The Bill of Rights guarantees: freedom of religion (and bars the establishment of a national religion); freedom of speech and the press; the right to petition the government for redress of grievances; that no person will be deprived of life, liberty, or property without due process of law. Other guarantees, while not as far reaching as these, are extremely important in the field of criminal law and procedure; the right not to be twice placed in jeopardy; security from unreasonable searches and seizures; that no warrants can be issued except upon probable cause supported by oath or affirmation and specifically describing the persons, places, or things to be seized; that no person can be compelled to be a witness against himself; the right to confront accusers; the right to have compulsory process to secure witnesses; the right to a speedy and fair trial; the right to be represented by counsel of the person's own choosing, or if the accused cannot afford one, then to have the state provide one; the right to be protected against excessive bail, fines, and the imposition of cruel and unusual punishments.

In the United States, with its federal system of government, there is a dual system of law, that in effect at the national governmental level and that in effect in the states. Early in the development of the Constitution, an important question arose concerning whether the Bill of Rights posed a limitation on activities of the federal government only, or on activities of both the federal and state governments. In 1833, the United States Supreme Court declared that the entire Bill of Rights was directed not toward the states but solely toward actions of the federal government. (Barron v. Baltimore, 32 U.S. (7 Pet.) 243, 8 L.Ed. 672 (1833)).

The ratification of the Fourteenth Amendment following the Civil War ultimately led to sweeping changes in this doctrine. Among other things, this amendment provided that "No State shall make or enforce any law which shall abridge the privileges and immunities of citizens of the United States; nor shall any state deprive any person of life, liberty, or property without due process of law, nor deny any person within its jurisdiction the equal protection of the laws." While this amendment did not by its express terms make the guarantees of the Bill of Rights applicable in the states, subsequent Supreme Court interpretations established that the "liberty" and "due process" clauses did protect from state action those basic rights which were "implicit in the concept of ordered liberty." *(Palko v. Connecticut,* 302 U.S. 319, 58 S.Ct. 149, 82 L.Ed. 288 (1937)). For example, the Fourth Amendment protection against unreasonable search and seizure has been made applicable against intrusion by state officers (*Mapp v. Ohio,* 367 U.S. 643, 81 S.Ct. 1684 (1961)), as has the Fifth Amendment's right against self-incrimination (*Malloy v. Hogan,* 378 U.S. 1, 84 S.Ct. 1489 (1964)) and the Sixth Amendment's right of counsel (*Gideon v. Wainwright,* 372 U.S. 355, 83 S.Ct. 792 (1963)).

Thus, one can see that criminal procedure in the states operates within two legal systems—(1) specific state statutory or common law and (2) the Constitutional requirement of "due process of law". The nature of this dual legal system has posed some procedural problems in the states. But in a legal system dedicated to the principle that a person is innocent until proven guilty, and in which the government's powers are carefully circumscribed in the area of criminal processes, the procedural rules become a basic safeguard for the individual. As currently interpreted, the Bill of Rights expressly limits the powers of government officials and upholds the especially important principle that government at all levels is subordinate to the Constitution.

The Prosecution Chain

When we speak of "processing" an accused person through the criminal justice system, we reinforce the idea that there is machinery set up by a bureaucracy which moves an individual from one step in the process to another. This is true largely because the criminal justice system (a better word would be "complex") is one large bureaucracy geared, although not well, for handling or "processing" vast numbers of persons. To get an idea of the complexity of this process, let us follow a person accused of a serious crime (a felony) through the maze that makes up the system.

For the felony cases, one of two procedures may be used to initiate criminal prosecution: the *grand jury indictment*, or the *information* filed by the prosecutor charging a person with the commission of some offense. The two procedures are not radically different, and specific differences will be noted as our mythical defendant proceeds through the system.

First, let us analyze the system under which an information is the method of securing prosecution of a defendant. Theoretically, a case begins when a public investigator or police officer enters the prosecutor's office to present the facts. Often the officer has enough evidence to request that an arrest warrant be issued. The prosecutor examines the evidence, asks for any needed clarification and perhaps requests additional information and investigation. When the prosecutor decides that there is adequate information for possible future prosecution, he will draw up a *complaint*, (sometimes called the *charge*) that the suspect has committed a particular crime. At the same time, he will also execute a sworn *affidavit*, setting forth the evidence which causes the police officer and the prosecutor to believe that the defendant committed the crime. The officer and prosecutor then seek out a judge who reads the affidavit. The judge may ask some more questions to ascertain that the affidavit supports the level of assurance known as "*probable cause*," a reasonable belief that the person named in the affidavit is probably guilty and should undergo subsequent steps in the criminal process. If the judge agrees that probable cause is substantiated, he or she will accept the complaint and issue an arrest warrant. The officer who initially brought the evidence to the prosecutor or another officer will then execute the warrant by arresting the defendant. This completes the initial step in the criminal justice process.

In the vast majority of cases, however, this process is radically altered. Most often the criminal process commences with an arrest by an officer based on probable cause. An *arrest without a warrant based on probable cause* is legally permissible because it ensures that the apprehended offender will not have an opportunity to escape or alter evidence. Usually arrests do not result as the culmination of a detailed investigation after which a prosecutor is consulted for a determination of legal sufficiency. The suspect is taken into custody and transported to the police station where the formal paper work charging him with a crime must be obtained after the fact.

As soon as possible, an officer, not necessarily the arresting officer, visits the prosecutor's office, presents the evidence upon which the arrest was based, and asks if the state wishes to prosecute. It is here that police officers' knowledge of the law, their persuasive powers, and their knowledge of individual prosecutors have great importance. In borderline or vague situations, the officer can have impact on the decision to continue the process. For a number of reasons the prosecutor may decline prosecution. In this event the suspect is released from custody.

Should the prosecutor decide that there is adequate evidence, he will prepare a formal *complaint*. It should be noted that there is no need for an affidavit; a magistrate will not be asked to issue an arrest warrant, since the suspect is already in custody. In the next step, the prosecutor takes the complaint to a magistrate for a short hearing at which both the suspect and the arresting officers are present. The magistrate accepts the complaint, and the defendant is arraigned. The *arraignment* process is a critical phase in the legal process, not only because of the magistrate's review of the sufficiency of the complaint, but also because the defendant is furnished with certain important information. The accused is informed by the magistrate of the charges and advised of constitutional rights, in particular the right to remain silent. The magistrate tells the defendant of the right to a lawyer, and states that the court will appoint an attorney in the event that the accused is unable to afford one. The crucial part that the magistrate plays in this scene is obvious. During this initial appearance, the magistrate is often referred to as a "*committing*" *magistrate.*

Bail is considered after a lawyer is appointed. Bail is in essence an amount of money or an equivalent amount in property that a defendant must deposit with the court as a guarantee that after release he or she will appear for the various subsequent steps in the criminal process. Very frequently the defendant does not have the necessary funds so a professional bail bondsman, who furnishes the amount of bail is hired. In return, the defendant pays a percentage of the bail amount (usually 10-15%) to the bondsman as a fee.

Today, more and more use is being made of a technique for releasing defendants who cannot post monetary bail yet in all probability will return for their court appearance. "*Release on own recognizance*" indicates that the defendant is released without bond after the magistrate is satisfied that there is little chance of a non-return by the accused. If released, the defendant is told to return at a particular time to plead to the charges in the complaint.

If the accused is not able to make bail and is considered a poor risk for release on own recognizance, the magistrate signs a *commitment order* and the defendant is transferred to the jailer from police custody. Typically, the magistrate, as the last step in the initial arraignment, sets a future date at which the defendant will enter a plea. Sometimes the plea is made at the arraignment, but frequently the attorney for the defendant will want to review the charges and make a more detailed investigation to ascertain the strengths and weaknesses in the prosecution's evidence. Typically, the plea is entered a few days after the arraignment. At this time, the defendant, his or her attorney, and the prosecutor appear. Usually the defendant pleads not guilty. As a practical matter, the defendant frequently wishes to enter a guilty plea at a later proceeding. Many defense attorneys use this tactic hoping to persuade the prosecutor to reconsider the case and subsequently reduce the charges or seek dismissal of the complaint.

In any event, assuming that the plea is "not guilty", the magistrate next sets a date for a *preliminary hearing*, often scheduled to take place within a two-week period. Often it does not, even though the state law may mandate that it must take place within a specified number of days. If the time limit is exceeded, the complaint is dismissed and the defendant is released. Should this happen, the person can then be rearrested, a new complaint filed, and all of the preliminary steps taken again; double jeopardy does not protect a defendant from retrial until the commencement of the trial itself. If the defendant is out on bail, the old bail is extinguished, and a new bail usually must be secured when the second complaint is issued. If a bail bondsman was retained, the bondsman loses the fee for bail on the first complaint. Also, the prosecutor becomes concerned about such delays because the opposing side may argue that the defendant is being denied the right to a speedy trial. Successful argument could result in a dismissal of the charges. Furthermore, the publicity that may attend excessive delays also could be embarrassing to the prosecutor. Because of these concerns, the prosecutor and defense attorney get together and agree on a date for the preliminary hearing, which frequently is beyond the statutory maximum number of days. In short, the defendant waives the right to a preliminary hearing within the required number of days.

On the set day, the parties assemble in a courtroom, usually before a magistrate or some other inferior court judge, for the preliminary hearing. Here the prosecutor presents enough evidence of this case (*prima facie* case) for the judge to determine whether or not the defendant should be prosecuted in a court having jurisdiction over felonies. Usually, the court conducting a preliminary hearing does not have such jurisdiction. If the prosecutor presents enough evidence to convince the judge at the preliminary hearing that there is probable cause to believe that the defendant committed the offense, the defendant is held to answer the charges in the court of proper jurisdiction. In state systems, this felony court is often a superior or circuit court. Whatever the designation, it is the state trial court of general jurisdiction over felony cases.

Once held to answer, the judge certifies the case to the superior court (this term will be used to designate the felony trial court in the remainder of this section). In a few days the defendant, his or her attorney, and the prosecutor appear in the superior court where the prosecutor files an *information* which formally accuses the defendant of the charges that were initially contained in the complaint. This gives the superior court authority to hear the felony charge against the defendant.

The preliminary hearing serves to benefit both the prosecution and the defense. From the prosecutor's perspective, it is desirable to test the strength of the case by subpoenaing witnesses and questioning them under oath. The prosecutor can also note how well they are able to stand up under cross-examination by the defense. The defense, on the other hand, has the opportunity to determine the strength of the prosecution's case. This is especially important when gauging how far the defense can go in negotiating a plea or some other disposition with the prosecution. The opportunity for the defense to cross-examine prosecution witnesses is often crucial because it gives the defense attorney an excellent opportunity to pin down the witnesses.

At the preliminary hearing, the defense is in a position to *discover* evidence in the hands of the prosecutor. Either party can find out a great deal about the opposing party's case before going to trial: facts, deeds, documents, identity of witnesses, exculpatory evidence, and the like. However, the discovery of evidence by the prosecutor is limited by the defendant's privilege against self-incrimination. For this reason, many states today hold that, to the extent the defendant is allowed pretrial discovery, so is the prosecution. Nevertheless, each side attempts to keep the other in the dark as much as possible. In some instances, the rules of discovery work to the advantage of the prosecution, particularly when the prosecutor retains a very strong case against the accused. By actually letting the defense "discover" the weight of the evidence, the prosecutor is in a very strong plea-bargaining position and is more likely to gain a plea from the defense without the necessity of a trial.

The preliminary hearing additionally gives the defense the opportunity to challenge the legality of evidence in the hands of the prosecutor. In the area of search and seizure, a successful challenge to the admissibility of legal evidence at the preliminary hearing may all but destroy the case against a defendant. If, as a result of exclusion of such key evidence, the defendant is not "held to answer", the case ends.

In those states using the information system to begin criminal prosecutions, the prosecutor does not have to go this route; rather, he has the option of presenting the case to the grand jury which may return a "*true bill*" indicating that there is probable cause to charge the accused by grand jury indictment.

The *Grand Jury* is a body of people (generally 23 in number) drawn, selected, and summoned according to law to serve as a constituent part of a court of criminal jurisdiction. The purpose of the body is to investigate and inform on crimes committed within the court's jurisdiction and to accuse persons of (indict them for) crimes when it has discovered sufficient evidence to arrest and hold them for trial.

In theory the grand jury, like the preliminary hearing, provides protection against the excesses of overzealous government officials. It ensures that malicious arbitrary prosecutions by the state are stopped, thereby protecting the citizen from the expense of a trial and the embarrassment that often accompanies it. Some modern students of the grand jury question the validity of this theory. It is argued that the grand jury does exactly what the prosecutor desires, because the grand jurors usually have contact only with the prosecutor and prosecution witnesses in what is essentially a secret proceeding. The grand jury has no independent investigative staff and is dependent on the facts in a case as developed by the state. Thus, the grand jury essentially becomes a "rubber stamp" rather than the protective device envisioned by its designers.

It is common for the prosecutor to take certain kinds of cases before a grand jury even though he has the power to file an information. Cases involving important public personages or those involving political figures are usually taken to the grand jury. This is done in order to protect witnesses; the grand jury transacts its business in seclusion and can spare witnesses possible injury or death by allowing them to give testimony and evidence outside the glare of the news media.

In sex cases involving small children as victims, the prosecutor frequently goes to the grand jury. The sexual experience is a traumatic event for the child, as is the trial and its often unfeeling cross-examination. The prosecutor reasons that the grand jury route will spare the minor the ordeal of cross-examination, as none takes place in a grand jury hearing.

After either the preliminary hearing or the grand jury, should the defendant be held to answer the charge, the case will proceed on through the system. Let us now turn back to the general processes following a preliminary hearing.

If the defendant is held to answer the charges against him, the judge will insure that the defendant has an attorney. Then the defendant will be *arraigned on the charges in the information.* This arraignment is similar to the initial arraignment before the magistrate; if additional information or new charges turn up at the preliminary hearing, they will be read at the second arraignment along with the charges in the original complaint, if still relevant. Superior court will hear any motions made by the defense attorney. Almost always the defense counsel will move to set aside the initial findings of the magistrate or judge who made the finding of probable cause, usually on the basis that there is insufficient evidence.

Should this fail, the defense attorney will then move to exclude evidence, on the grounds that it was secured as a result of an illegal search and seizure. Often the defense attorney does not know positively whether the evidence was improperly seized, but will make the motion in order to preserve the objection in the court records. If the defense attorney does not excercise an objection at the proper time, a higher court may hold that the right to object was waived, even should it be proven later that the evidence was in fact illegally seized.

After the arraignment comes the plea, which is the defendant's response to the charges contained in the indictment or information. By far the most common pleas are *guilty* and *not guilty*. If the defendant pleads guilty it is an admission in open court that he or she in fact committed the crimes specified by the charging instrument. This, of course, is a very serious step since, in effect, the defendant is waiving the right to trial and accepting the sentence provided by the court without presenting a defense. Due to the obvious Fifth Amendment hazards involved in the process, the presiding judge will accept such a plea only if satisfied that it is made in a voluntary manner without coercion or deceit. Since most criminal cases are resolved through plea bargaining, in which the defendant is offered a reduced sentence or charge in return for a guilty plea, this process of insuring that undue influence has not affected the plea is somewhat of a charade. The judge may refuse to accept a plea of guilty if it seems that the plea was not voluntary; also, the law may forbid a guilty plea (for instance, many states will not permit a plea of guilty to a capital offense). In such cases a plea of not guilty is entered for the defendant. Should a not guilty plea be entered for the defendant by the judge, or if the defendant pleads not guilty, a date is set for the trial to commence, since the defendant is asserting that either he or she did not commit the crime specified or that there is an affirmative defense which nullifies the criminal intent (self defense, etc.).

Under certain circumstances, a defendant may enter a plea of *nolo contendere*. Although this plea has the same effect as a guilty plea, it offers protection from its use as an admission of guilt in civil suits arising from the same criminal act.

The plea of *not guilty by reason of insanity* is an affirmative defense which admits to the acts charged but indicates that the defendant was not sane and therefore not responsible for his or her actions when the crime was committed. This will usually lead the judge to order a psychiatric examination of the defendant before trial. This plea is normally used in conjunction with a plea of not guilty.

There are several technical pleas which can be entered. Probably the most common is a *plea of double jeopardy*, also called a plea of or previous conviction/acquittal. Here the defendant is claiming protection under the Fifth Amendment by arguing that he or she has previously been placed in jeopardy under the same accusation. A little used but possible defense tactic is to enter *a demurrer to the information* or indictment instead of making a plea. This alleges some technical defect in the instrument or process through which the defendant was charged. However, once such deficiencies are corrected, the defendant must enter a regular plea.

The pleading stage is often delayed so that the prosecution and defense attorney can negotiate over the plea to be entered. The prosecution attempts to gain a guilty plea in order to avoid the costly trial process, while the defense attorney protects the interests of the client by seeking the least severe punishment. If an agreement is not reached, then a plea of not guilty is entered while negotiations continue. During this period most criminal cases are settled by the entry of a negotiated guilty plea. If such an agreement cannot be concluded, the not guilty plea stands and a trial date is set.

Prior to the actual commencement of the trial, the prosecutor, defense attorney, and defendant, under supervision of the court, begin the *jury selection* process if the defenant has opted for a jury trial. If not, the case will be tried before a judge sitting as fact finder. Most felony cases are tried before a jury. The prosecutor presents the state's evidence first. The defendant then presents his or her case in refutation of the prosecution's case. When both parties have completed their case, the prosecution presents a closing argument, followed by the defense. The prosecution is then afforded a final opportunity to rebut the closing comments of the defense. Finally, the judge instructs the jury regarding the applicable law in the case, and the jury retires to deliberate and reach its verdict. The defendant can be acquitted or convicted, or a "*hung jury*" may result, which indicates that the jury was unable to reach a unanimous decision of guilt. If this occurs, the prosecutor may retry the case or drop the charges. Between 65 and 70 percent of all defendants are convicted, however.

When there is a conviction, the defense attorney makes a *motion for a new trial* because of some alleged errors. The motion is usually rejected and the judge sets a future date for sentencing—about two to three weeks, in order to have a pre-sentence investigation of the defendant completed.

The defendant next appears in court at the time set for *sentencing* when one of the following things may happen: the defendant can be given a prison sentence, can be sent to the county jail for a short period of time, can be placed on probation but sent to the county jail for a period of time as a condition of probation, or can be placed on probation for a specified period of time. When placed on probation, a defendant is not incarcerated. After reading the pre-sentence report and listening to arguments from the prosecution (for imposition of a strict sentence) and defense (for leniency), the judge pronounces the sentence. When this process is completed, the judgment can be appealed to a higher court. This appellate process will be considered next.

The Appellate Process

An *appeal to an appellate court* is designed for reviewing lower court decisions to determine if a substantial error has been committed. An appeal is usually taken by a defendant, but either or both of the parties may appeal, although the grounds upon which the state may appeal are much more restricted. Appeals are made to appellate courts, which are established specifically for the purpose of reviewing lower court decisions. However, in some states the primary felony trial court of general jurisdiction, for example, the superior court, is authorized by state law to serve as an appellate court for various kinds of actions taken by inferior courts. For example, the superior court may review misdemeanor convictions if the defendant appeals. Still, pressing this kind of appeal is the exception rather than the rule.

The appellate court is theoretically supposed to concern itself with deciding *questions of law* which arose during the trial. If there was an error that either potentially or actually led to an adverse judgment against the party which appeals (appellant), then the appellate court may take steps to correct the error. For instance, the appellate court may find that the trial court improperly instructed the jury on a point of law. In such a situation the error of the lower court is an error of law, and the appellate court may direct that the case be sent back to the trial court for a new trial. Or, the appellate court may issue other instructions regarding how the error may be corrected.

Review by an appellate court will not be made when the appellant claims that the jury made an error in finding questions of fact based on evidence presented during the trial. Findings of fact are usually matters thought best left within the province of the trial court. Consequently, appellate courts are reluctant to disturb such findings. Occasionally the record of the trial sent to the appellate court will be devoid of or sorely lacking in evidence to support the jury finding. In this situation the appellate court may revise the lower court decision or order a new trial, because it is considered an error of law to permit a finding where there is no evidence to support it.

Several important rules govern appeals. *An error first raised only on appeal will normally not be considered by the appellate court* unless it has resulted in a miscarriage of justice. For example, a defendant who may have been afforded no opportunity to object to final instructions to the jury may, on appeal, validly claim an error in the instructions even though he did not object to them at the initial trial. *An appellate court is guided by a presumption in favor of the validity of the finding or verdict of the trial court.* The court will sustain a conviction if there is sufficient evidence to uphold the conviction of guilt, even if there is evidence which might warrant acquittal or other evidence which is consistent with innocence.

Usually found in the law of a state is a provision stating that *no judgment shall be set aside unless, after an examination of the entire case including the evidence, the appellate court shall be of an opinion that the error complained about has resulted in a miscarriage of justice.* This rule basically implies that minor errors of criminal procedures, rulings on evidence that do not harm the defendant, or rulings on questions of court room processes which do not affect the findings or decision in the case are not a basis for a reversal by an appellate tribunal. This rule has resulted in the legally perplexing phenomenon of *non-reversible error.*

The following steps usually occur when an appeal is processed. The party wishing to appeal must complain to the appellate court that an error has been made in the lower court, and the party must then take the steps necessary to present the entire case to the reviewing tribunal. Specific grounds upon which the prosecution or defense may base an appeal are often set out in every state. The reasons for which a prosecutor can appeal are greatly restricted, and do not include acquittal as grounds.

Defendants usually may appeal in the following instances:

1. From a final judgment of conviction. In this situation a sentence or an order placing the defendant on probation is considered to be a final judgment for purposes of appeal. Also, when the court accepts this kind of appeal, it may review a lower court decision denying a motion for a new trial by the appellant.
2. From an adjudication of guilt when the defendant claims to fall within a special class of persons. In other words, the defendant is claiming to be insane, a narcotic addict, or a sexual psychopath who should thus be excused of criminal responsibility.
3. From an order made after judgment in which a substantial right of the defendant is affected.

The state may appeal as a general rule in the following situations:

1. From an order setting aside an indictment, information, or complaint.
2. From a judgment for the defendant on a demurrer to an indictment. A *demurrer* is a pleading by the defendant stating that the allegations contained in the pleadings are not sufficient for the case to proceed further. A demurrer merely tests the sufficiency of the complaint.
3. From an order in which the judge withholds judgment because some error appears on the face of the record. This procedure is called "arrest of judgment."

The hearing held by the appellate court permits the *appellant* (sometimes called the *petitioner* or *plaintiff in error*) and the *appellee* (also referred to as the *defendent in error* or *respondent*) the opportunity to argue the case before the court. Usually an appellate court is composed of three or more judges who listen to the arguments of counsel and then vote on the appeal. A majority vote carries the issue.

No new evidence is presented at the hearing. The court bases its decision on three grounds: the argument of counsel at the hearing; the transcript of the trial court proceedings, and the appellate court justices' interpretation of the applicable law.

Appellate court hearings are calm, lacking the verbal combat often found at the trial court level. In fact, an appellate hearing is essentially a discussion (between the attorney and the judges) of the applicable legal principles. Each party to the hearing also presents "*legal briefs*" which are basically the legal arguments supporting one side or the other. Once the judges decide which side will prevail, the appellate court will take steps to correct the trial court, if the error was substantial enough. Primarily the corrective action involves reversal of the judgment of the conviction, thus finding for the appellant, or remanding the case for a new trial in conformity with the appellate decision. The trial court is guided by the appellate court's written opinion of the defects in the trial court's actions, or by the proper interpretation of the law to be applied. The *written opinion* is provided by one of the justices.

Occasionally one or more of the justices do not agree with the *majority opinion* of the court. When this happens, those judges prepare a *dissenting opinion*, setting forth their reasons for disagreeing with the majority. Dissenting opinions are extremely important in cases where the vote of the justices is close, because a change in court personnel may mean that a new judge might readily adopt a well written, logical, and legally and socially acceptable dissent. In the area of constitutional law, dissents have often become the law of the land in later years because of changes in judicial philosophy, societal conditions, and the political leanings of judges. Frequently, several of the judges on an appellate court agree that the issue should be decided in a certain way, but for different reasons. When this occurs one or more judges may submit a *"concurring opinion"* setting forth reasons for agreeing with the decision. The reasons may be completely different from those in the opinion, or they may be based on slight differences in perspective.

In summary, the appellate process is provided to correct errors made by lower courts. However, not every error results in the reversal of a conviction. Errors must be substantial in nature and deprive the defendant of a fair and just hearing, thus amounting to a miscarriage of justice. The appellate court does not as a rule substitute its opinion for that of the jury where questions of fact are involved. The appellate court is concerned with whether or not the law was properly explained and utilized by the trial court. Very rarely will an appellate body reverse a verdict because of a complete lack of evidence, even though the tribunal may not have decided the issue the same way of as the jury.

Summary

Social order in the United States is based on the law, which serves to educate the citizens, encourage voluntary conformity through an understanding of its ramifications, and provide a means of settling disputes. In order to regulate the day-to-day conduct of our society, law has become extremely complex, especially the field of criminal law. For the police, the courts, and the defendant the process of ensuring justice has become almost overwhelming.

Criminal law is grounded upon the concept that society is sufficiently concerned about specific types of conduct to want to prohibit or change them. Laws have penalities attached which theoretically serve as a deterrent by informing individuals beforehand what will happen should they transgress a law considered necessary by the larger society. However, whether or not as it now operates actually serves as a deterrent has been seriously questioned.

Law in America is based upon the common law. However, in most states, statutory law has replaced the common law in the criminal law field, and the police officer is most involved with statutes. Even so, the common law is often consulted to ascertain the meaning of words and phrases, to interpret a statute as a whole, and to understand the basis for a statute based on a common law crime.

The United States Supreme Court has gone to great lengths to protect the civil liberties and rights of American citizens. The court has interpreted the United States Constitution as prohibiting states from infringing upon most of the individual rights set out in the Constitution. While there has been no blanket incorporation of the Bill of Rights into the due process clause of the Fourteenth Amendment, the Supreme Court, by its doctrine of selective incorporation, has mandated that many constitutional criminal protections are safeguarded from state infringement. Among these are the privilege against self-incrimination, the right to counsel, protection against double jeopardy, and the right to confront an accuser.

Crimes in the various states and at the federal level are generally classified as felonies and misdemeanors. Some states have now authorized another classification for minor offenses—traffic violations, for example—which are referred to as infractions or violations. The total system of laws in the United States is basically comprised of the two distinct systems, federal and state. The federal system primarily enforces federal laws; the state, the laws enacted within its own borders. Most of the criminal laws are found in the states. Consequently, law enforcement is concerened mostly with state laws, both statutory and common law.

Topics For Discussion

1. **What is law? Discuss the difficulty of defining law. What is the common law, and what are its origins? What purpose does the common law serve in your state? How and where is it found?**
2. **What are the three vital functions of law? Discuss each fully by showing how each is applicable in your state.**
3. **Discuss how law serves as an agent of social control both in civil and criminal matters.**

4. **Distinguish statutory from common law. how is the rule of *ejusdem generis* applied to statutes? What does the concept mean?**
5. **Discuss how the desire to prohibit certain conduct actually becomes a law. What processes and practical problems are involved?**
6. **Distinguish civil rights from civil liberties. Give examples of each.**
7. **What is meant by the doctrine of selective incorporation? due process under the law? fundamental right? Give examples of individual federal criminal constitutional protections which have been made applicable in state criminal trials.**
8. **What article in the United States Constitution discusses the judicial power of the federal courts? What are the provisions of the article?**
9. **Define the various ways of classifying crimes. What is meant by *malum prohibitia*? *Malum in se*? *mens rea*? criminal negligence?**
10. **What does "jurisdiction" mean? Discuss generally the kinds of matters over which the federal and state courts have jurisdiction.**
11. **What is the grand jury? How does it function and what are its purposes in your state? What is an "information"? If used in your state, explain how.**
12. **Discuss the doctrine of *stare decisis*. Why is it of practical importance in both civil and criminal law?**
13. **Discuss the appeal processes available to a defendant convicted of a felony in your state. Research and discuss the grounds for appeal by the defendant and the prosecutor in your state.**

Annotated Bibliography

Berman, Harold J. and Greiner, William R. *The Nature and Functions of Law.* Brooklyn: Foundation Press, 1966. The book was designed to fit into a liberal arts curriculum, but it fits well into graduate as well as undergraduate courses devoted to the nature and purposes of law. The four parts of the book stress law as a process of dispute resolution; law as a process of maintaining historical continuity; law as a process of protecting and facilitating voluntary arrangements; and law as a process of resolving acute social conflicts.

Dix, George E. and Sharlot, M. Michael. *Basic Criminal Law: Cases and Materials.* St. Paul: West Publishing Co., 1974. This text, written for the criminal justice student, covers the criminal law in a simple, straightforward manner. Topics covered include: the criminalization decision; principles of criminal liability; inchoate crimes; crimes against property; habitation and the person; and defenses.

Felkenes, George T. *Criminal Law and Procedure: Text and Cases.* Englewood Cliffs, New Jersey: Prentice-Hall, 1976. This unique text presents in case brief form those constitutional decisions that have an impact on the criminal law and procedures applicable at the federal and state levels. Each opinion is analyzed, especially to show how it relates to the overall constitutional protections afforded a person accused of a criminal offense.

Felkenes, George T. *Constitutional Law for Criminal Justice.* Englewood Cliffs, New Jersey: Prentice-Hall, 1978. This book is a constitutional text which covers the constitutional aspects of criminal law and procedure as well as the more traditional constitutional problems, i.e., commerce clause, speech, and religion.

Introductory materials for each chapter present a historical perspective and overview. Chapters on corrections and juvenile issues addressed by the United States Supreme Court are included, and cases of constitutional importance are extracted.

Kaplan, John. *Criminal Justice: Introductory Cases and Materials.* Mineola, New York: Foundation Press, 1973. This book, usable in graduate and undergraduate programs, is an attempt to fit a law school teaching approach, the casebook, to the needs of undergraduate programs. The book is comprised of cases, problems, and a large number of excerpts which are followed by questions or comments on the problems in the area. Included are such topics as: "Why Punish Crimes," "An Overview of the Criminal System," "The Police," "Constitutional Rights and the Exclusionary Rule," "The Trial," "Sentencing," and "The Extent and Causes of Crime."

Summers, Robert S. and Howard, Charles G. *Law: Its Nature, Functions and Limits.* Englewood Cliffs, New Jersey: Prentice-Hall, 1972. This text deals with law as it pertains to a general liberal arts education. It is written for the layperson who wishes to become familiar with law and the functions it serves in society. One unique and strong feature of this highly recommended book is its discussion of the limitations of the law.

5

POLICING THE COMMUNITY
Interaction and Reaction

Chapter Objectives

The study of this chapter should enable you to:

- ☑ List ten mental images triggered by the word "police".
- ☑ Define "community".
- ☑ Give an example of role conflict.
- ☑ Distinguish public relations from community relations.
- ☑ Explain why police should be concerned with community relations?
- ☑ List ten community relations programs.
- ☑ List five areas of concentration for improving police-community relations.
- ☑ Summarize the philosophy of humanism as applied to police work.
- ☑ List five future social trends and their impact on police.

Introduction

This chapter will deal with police and community reactions to each other and suggest ways and means for improving the police-community interaction.

The police stand at the threshold of the criminal justice system. They initiate and react to situations, conditions and circumstances suggesting violations of the law. They are the mechanism for dealing with threats against the established social order. Their functions of law enforcement and order maintenance tend to give them the appearance of being outside the very community they serve.

As a result, the police are vulnerable to misunderstanding, criticism, isolation, fear, and doubt. In order to counteract this vulnerability, they have made considerable efforts to close the gap between themselves and the community of which they are an integral part. This effort has been labeled *police-community relations,* and it's essential to the success of the police mission.

"Police"—A Trigger Word Any mention of the police causes a reaction, and this reaction is usually anything but neutral. History, politics, culture, and the media have contributed in various ways to the multiple images raised by the word police. Police officers, themselves, justice system observers and writers, and the public alike have almost exhausted the cliches and mental images: friend or foe, role model or bogeyman, overpowered authoritarian or handcuffed whipping-boy, defender of the faith or scourge of the earth, a victim of the condition known as the policeman's lot, damned if they do and damned if they don't, cop, philosopher, the fuzz, the bull, guide, smokey, friend, the man, pig.

Few consider that the target of this outpouring of sentiment is a human being who has the capacity to improve the human condition. It's hoped that the preceding chapters of this book have opened the door to a clearer understanding of the complexity that stands behind the term *police.*

The Community—An Ephemeral Concept

The fact that there's no clear way of arriving at a concept of what a community means creates an initial barrier to any meaningful treatment of how the police and a community are related. The definition of community is a source of considerable debate among sociologists, some of whom even suggest that the community is a dead and dying concept.[1]

In light of the alienated living conditions existing in some American urban centers—conditions in which neighbor is unknown to neighbor, and a stranger is viewed as either threat or prey—an idea of community is difficult to conceptualize. A secondary problem in assessing any one community is the fact that many special interest communities also exist. Together, they create a chorus of conflicting values which, at some point in time, become conflicting demands upon police resources. Much of the role conflict existing within the police profession is a result of the fragmented and frequently discordant voice of the community. The following story about "Bob", a new police officer, serves as an example of this type of role conflict.

> *In Bob's department, there was a general order which required that patrolmen check doors and windows in stores and businesses at irregular time intervals during evening hours. The chief wanted this done—so the trainers told the recruit. When Bob got in the field, he was told by his supervisor that he should check doors and windows—but it's unnecessary when the business is checked by a private watch service.*
>
> *Later, when Bob began to talk to more experienced patrolmen, they told him that "it's a waste of time to do these security checks." They suggested that he might shake a few doorknobs when a supervisor is around or there are citizens on the street—but that's all. The exception would be the merchant who was willing to pay a few dollars to a patrolman for a little extra attention to his building.*
>
> *Contrary to what he had been told in the field, our recruit knew from reading his role model's book,* Police Administraton, *by O. W. Wilson, that patrolmen should check the security of the doors and windows of commercial buildings even when private watch services are utilized.*
>
> *Because of a rise in commercial burglaries, the Chamber of Commerce expressed its strong opinion in a newspaper article that doors and windows should be checked by police patrolmen frequently and regularly whenever a business is closed—including daylight hours on Sundays.*
>
> *A community group of residents later reacted to the statement of the Chamber of Commerce and publicly voiced its opinion that the police should not perform security checks at all. In its view, the police should concentrate their patrol effort in residential areas—protecting citizens, not buildings. They added that businessmen should pay for private watchman service and not burden the police with it.*
>
> *A spokesman for the Association of Private Watchmen concurred with the community group and stated that the police should not be in the watchman business.*[2]

A third concern in assessing the concept of community is disparity between the *model* community and the *real* community, or between what the community *says* it is (or should be) as opposed to what it really is. An example of this disparity was found during a recent discussion in a class of college students who were studying the administration of justice. After spending several class sessions defining and assessing the crime problem and its impact on the community, the students expressed a fairly high level of frustration concerning the topic of how to deal with individuals who commit thefts. During a discussion in which the students voiced general disapproval of those who steal and made supportive statements about the desirability of taking some type of official law-enforcement action against the thieves, the practice of price switching (replacing price tags on merchandise with tags removed from lower-priced merchandise) was introduced. Surprisingly, an overwhelming number of the class members condoned this practice. Several students openly admitted that they themselves had engaged in price switching and would continue to do so in the future. They seemed to be able to make some subtle distinction between outright theft and the merchandise discounting and value theft which result from price switching. This group of students, a community of sorts, who simultaneously opposed theft and supported price switching exhibited a simplified form of disparity. Though this example is obviously ripe for some additional sociological examination and interpretation, it seems to illustrate the conflict we face when trying to understand what we mean and who we are speaking of when we use the word community.

Obviously, the concept of community transcends that of a mere collection of human beings who occupy some geographic space. Born in an era of small-town, rural, agricultural, and static environments, the concept of community needs updating. As a starting point, the term community when used in this chapter will refer to the collective essence of behavior types and mixed values held by people residing within a local political system. While this may at first shed more darkness than light, the ambiguity of this new concept of community may be a significant step toward understanding and structuring the police response.

Police-Community Relations—A Historical Review

It's difficult to trace a clear and precise path in the development of police-community relations. Obviously, Robert Peel had some feeling for it when he caused the establishment of the police of the Metropolis in London in 1829. While setting forth some basic principles of police operations, Peel advised the English Constable that "a perfect command of temper is superior to violent action." While not all-inclusive, this advice was at least a beginning response to an anticipated negative reaction on the part of the public to the establishment of a police force in a free country.

Other than this English aversion to police power and the early advice of Robert Peel, little evidence exists that police-community relations was considered an important topic of concern, training, or practice for quite some time afterward. The relationship between the police and the citizen wasn't totally ignored, of course, but most of the concern in this area centered on public relations, or image-building. The New York City Police Manual of 1914—in addition to providing technical advice to officers on patrol, physical conditioning, arrests, court procedure, fingerprinting, and investigation—featured a section on discipline and deportment with specific recommendations on the kinds of attitudes which police officers should extend toward civilians both on and off duty. It included a generalized appeal to the police to act in a courteous and gentlemanly fashion toward the public and to repress emotional reactions.

As the police profession grew in importance, however, and training and orientation received more emphasis, little attention was paid to the specific issue of community relations. Training approaches were primarily aimed at getting officers to behave themselves and to maintain and uphold the decorum and reputation of the police department, the term *community* relations was seldom used to identify the dynamics of police-community interaction. Most references to this issue were contained in a public relations context, suggesting some effort at image-building and maintenance. An early definition of law enforcement public relations indicates the image, impression, and reputation orientation of police thinking at that time.

> *Public relations in law enforcement involves the activities that the various law enforcement agencies undertake in carrying on their work with the public. These activities are planned and conducted so as to give the law enforcement service a good reputation with the public and establish the service as one that functions in the public interest. Public relations comprises the sum total of all the contacts, attitudes, impressions, activities, policies, and opinions that are involved in the relationships between the public and law enforcement agencies.*[3]

Considerable emphasis was also placed upon impartiality in the area of law enforcement, and officers were instructed to disregard race, color, creed, or national origin of violators when carrying out their law enforcement duties.

By 1955, the emphasis and direction of law enforcement public relations was a topic attracting some attention from major police administrators. William H. Parker, then Chief of the Los Angeles Police Department, talked of the gaps existing between theory and practice.

> *We find police departments which have accepted the necessity for good public relations, they have created public relations units, they talk it in staff conferences, and teach it in their training classes. And yet, having observed all the prescribed rituals, they find themselves and the citizenry encamped in familiar positions, lines drawn up for the old battle of criticism, resentment, and more criticism.*
>
> *All too often, then, we hear the familiar cry "public relations do not pay," and the old whine that "police work inevitably incurs resentment." The police administrator, disappointed and disillusioned, rationalizes that police work is an underprivileged, persecuted, and particularly distinct class of endeavor to which the basic rules of organization, management, and social psychology do not apply. In his disappointment, he becomes, as Shakespeare put it, "A wretched soul, bruised with adversity." Public relations, the great panacea—the one-shot cure-all—has failed to produce results.*[4]

A different sentiment was expressed in a training guide for peace officers issued by the California Attorney General in 1958. The guide gave the following answer to the rhetorical question, "Why are Community Relations of interest to the Peace Officer?"

> *Respect for the peace officer, and the law he represents, by the people of his community, and particularly by people of every ancestry, is probably the best insurance we have against the breakdown of law and order. This community respect is built up through physical contact and a good performance record. The key toward gaining community respect is to treat all individuals the same*

> *—with fairness, impartiality, honesty, courtesy and firmness. Differential treatment leads to a defiance and misunderstanding on the part of those who are discriminated against. People who have been on the receiving end of discrimination cannot help becoming sensitive to indications of prejudice. Some will even read prejudice into perfectly innocent remarks or gestures. To obtain the cooperation and trust of such a person, it helps to know some of the more obvious mistakes to avoid. This should all be of interest to the peace officer because: (a) In law enforcement we do not always work with tangible products, but rather in the complex field of human behavior. (b) Tensions between community groups are a constant threat to community peace and order. (c) When these tensions develop to a point of actual riot, no one wins. No matter what happens then, too often the peace officer gets the blame.*[5]

It's ironic that a California city was the site of a drunk driving arrest which triggered a 1965 incident known as the Watts Riot. This riot resulted in thirty-four deaths, 1,032 injuries, 3,438 adult arrests, and damage to over 600 buildings amounting to a loss of over $40 million. A special commission created by the state governor to study the causes and consequences of the riot concluded that:

> *Much can be done to correct the existing impressions and to promote an understanding between the police and the community, and this, we believe, is essential in the interest of crime prevention. The steps that have been taken apear to us to be insufficient. Further action is indicated.*[6]

The impact of the August rioting in the Los Angeles community was massive. The 1960's were characterized by the police as the years of the "long, hot summers." The fact that it took so long to rebuild damaged structures seemed to symbolize the difficulty of mending the relationships which had also been damaged during the riots. The shattered relationships of urban police and their communities coined a new phrase and a new concern: *Police-Community Relations.*

Police-Community Relations – A Dialogue

The present state of police-community relations raises varied questions and is sometimes a cause for dispute. This dialogue is an attempt to review a variety of opinions on community relations thought and strategies.

Why Police-Community Relations? It may seem unnecessary to ask the question *why*, particularly after reviewing the staggering statistics of Watts, but the question is one that's frequently asked. With the intense development of police-community relations activities following in the wake of urban city riots, police have been prone to see the community relations effort as a program meant to appease those hostile to the interests of law and order. Police have tended to view departmental community relations efforts as similar to the early public relations programs—a waste of time.

Some valid counter-arguments have been made supporting the integration of a community relations consciousness into police agencies. Proponents of these arguments see the community relations effort as a means of sustaining the organizational, physical, and mental health of police organizations and police officers themselves. A basic fact of life for police agencies is that the public is the source of their operational resources. From an organizational health perspective, the fact that the public is willing to bear the financial support for police operations is a critical inducement to the police to be responsive and attentive to community relations. In the highly competitive arena of municipal funding, the public support of law enforcement agencies may depend upon the amount of appreciation the people have for their police department.

Police-community relations are also crucial to the physical health of the officers themselves. Many community relations strategies are aimed at reducing and controlling emotions and violence. Despite laws declaring it a crime to assault a police officer, the rising incidence of such assaults suggest that there's a need to make even greater efforts to better police-community relations.

The third consideration—mental health—is perhaps the most important. Police work isn't easy; it's filled with stress, frustration, fear, and the unsettling condition of frequently having to deal with the unknown. The nature of the work can lead to a self-deprecating view and a consuming cynicism. The dedication of the police recruit is too often soured by the nightly street encounters. The persecution complex underlying the often-heard statements, "The courts don't back us up," or "We're a minority group," is partly responsible for the isolation of the police from other segments of the community. This in turn leads to intense misunderstanding and distrust. The issue of mental health becomes extremely critical in those rare instances when the police selection process has failed to screen the police candidate who's motivated by a desire to use the power of his or her office as an outlet for sadism or revenge. The array of mental aberrations held by the fictional officers known as the *Choirboys* in Joseph Wambaugh's novel give some clues as to why police-community relations is an important issue. Viewed from the perspectives of departmental, physical, and mental health, community relations has the potential of acting as preventive medicine.

What is Police-Community Relations? This question raises considerable controversy. Polling police agencies throughout the United States results in a laundry list of activities, all of which are termed community relations. These include:

Formalized citizen complaint procedures. Through open-door policies, citizens' advisory committees, and the establishment of internal affairs or internal investigation units, some police agencies have attempted to literally open up to the community in the sense of allowing, and in some cases encouraging, citizen scrutiny of and input into police operations. Many of these formalized procedures have been police responses to suggestions for establishing citizen review boards. Because they often think of themselves as semi-military organizations, many police agencies generally opposed control or review by "civilians." In response to public pressure, they initiated internal control systems which, in many cases, had been lacking or lax.

Ride-along programs. Based upon the desire to bridge the gaps between the police and the public and increase public empathy for the police, some agencies have developed "ride-along" programs as part of their police-community relations effort. These programs have been successful in varying degrees. They do provide members of the public with a first-hand look at what police officers refer to as being "out on the streets." The success of this type of approach is sometimes hampered by procedures requiring lengthy application forms, waiting lists, background checks, and insurance waivers, not to mention the fact that the public has to want to participate. In most cases, the participants are pro-police to begin with. While these programs have some merit, they seem to fall short in affecting the target population of the community which has negative opinions of the police.

School visitations. Considerable effort has been directed toward getting the police into the schools. Grammar school children are normally visited by "our friend the police-officer," who lectures them on traffic safety, the perils of accepting favors from strangers, and suggestions for dealing with home and school emergencies. At the secondary level, visitations may involve discussions on alcohol, drugs and narcotics, traffic laws, curfew ordinances, and sexual misconduct statutes. A limited number of agencies have actually placed officers in schools as law enforcement counselors.

Uniform modifications. Although this approach is generally considered to be a fad, some police agencies have switched from helmets to soft hats (or no hats at all) and from semi-military uniforms to casual blazer jackets with pocket insignia and name tags.

Speakers bureaus. Speakers bureaus and organized station-house tours have been cited by some agencies as the mainstays of their community relations efforts. Some have suggested that these efforts are non-productive since speeches are most frequently made to groups holding positive attitudes toward the police. There seems to be no acceptable measure of the success of such programs. This lack of measurement is serious since the police organization most often evaluates performance on the basis of objective measures such as citation, accident, and arrest rates.

Shows, events, and auxiliary activities. This category includes Police Athletic Leagues, bike rodeos, summer camps, community recreation centers, and other activities designed to bring police officers into nonofficial contact with community members. While highly visible, it is unknown if these activities have any tangible impact on improving police-community relations.

Crime prevention. This approach is usually supplemented by pamphlets containing suggestions for foiling the residential burglar, armed robber, purse snatcher, mugger, rapist, etc. In some agencies, this approach has graduated from a community relations strategy to a specialized activity. This type of approach is characterized by slogans such as "Neighborhood Watch," "Citizens Alert," "Crime Stopper," and "TIP - Turn In a Pusher."

Crisis intervention/management/referral. The essence of this approach is the development of a training program in intervention and communication techniques. The program is designed to identify the source of a problem resulting in a non-enforcement service call to the police agency. The crisis intervention approach is an alternative to responding to neighborhood and family disturbance calls with the threat of arrest of one or more of the parties involved. The primary approach is to diffuse the immediate confrontation, prevent violence, and gather information about the incident. As a secondary phase of this effort, participants are diverted to appropriate public or private agencies for assistance, information or treatment related to the cause of the original incident. In this way the police open the doors to social services without taking on the full responsibility of social workers.

Most of the community relations efforts mentioned here have been the work of specialized community relations units which have been created as additional "boxes" in the department organizational chart. Despite the existence of these specialized units and their programs of activities, police observers still point to the significant gap which exists between community relations philosophy and its incorporation into the day-to-day operational environment and character of the individual police officer.

> *Community relations is not a part-time task of the Police Department, or a mere postscript to its traditional work. It is an integral part of all police work. Improving community relations is a full-time assignment of each man on the force. Healthy community relations can only be achieved by inculcating an attitude—a tone—throughout the force that will help facilitate a creative rapport with the public.*[7]

Evidence exists to suggest that the issue of individual officer attitude—the "tone-setting" alluded to above—is the unachieved goal of the present. The challenge remains one of instilling a community relations consciousness in the minds of the police themselves. This necessitates long-term efforts involving the improvement of individual police skills and attitudes toward understanding, communication, involvement, service, and fairness. Throughout this process of improvement, it's extremely important to avoid placing the police in a defensive position by explicitly or implicitly suggesting that the police are insensitive brutes in need of extensive programming. An accusative, derogatory, or condemning approach to police behavior must be avoided. The real task should be one of searching, exploring, identifying, and facing the problems of maintaining law, order, safety, stability, and equilibrium in a society characterized by individual freedom, technological change, diversity, and a political philosophy which is largely based upon distrust and restriction of the powers of government.

Police-Community Relations— Who, Where, and When?

It should come as no surprise that the respective responses to who, where, and when are: (1) each individual police officer, (2) everywhere, and (3) all of the time.

The idea that each individual police officer should be responsible for police-community relations may meet with some resistance from those holding a "wait and see," "there's no problem here," or "I'll accept my responsibility as soon as the community accepts theirs" attitude. These attitudes must dissolve if the police are to be sincere in their efforts to improve community relations. The responsibility of the individual officer calls for development of a proactive attitude that doesn't wait and see, that recognizes the problem and seeks refinement of its subtleties, and that accepts the responsibility of initiating action as a condition of the police profession.

Successful police administrators and rank-and-file police officers are those who have learned, or are learning, in an on-going way, to understand change and to endeavor to cope with it. The not so successful police personnel, be they administrators or rank-and-file members, have relinquished the initiative and merely react to change. If today's and tomorrow's police administrators and rank-and-file police officers are to truly function as agents of change—which I submit that they must rather than just react to change—they must fully understand the critical changes occurring, their implications for police strategies, and then they must act. In a word, I would submit, gentlemen, what we must stop doing as police agencies and police officers is being merely reactive to change; we must be proactive. We should adopt that word as part of our vocabulary. We have to have a problem sensitivity, problem solving abilities and proact.[8]

Evidence that the police have to accept that a problem exists and needs to be overcome can be given by two examples. Charlotte Opstein's discussion problem involving a police locker room conversation provides the first one. In the problem a police supervisor overhears an officer saying, "Those damn niggers are more trouble than they're worth. We oughta treat 'em like they do in the South, and then maybe they'll stay in line."[9] When this problem was used in an inservice supervisory training class, several police participants refused to acknowledge that the statement was evidence of any internalized attitude which would be detrimental to police operations. In refusing to accept this incident as indicative of a problem, these supervisors effectively placed themselves in a reactive mode for the future. They closed themselves off from the possibility that the supervisor might need to discuss the incident with the overheard officer.

The second example is drawn from an informal interview with a police officer on the subject of community relations:

The public is going to have to make the first move in improving police-community relations. They (the public) should do this by following the orders of a police officer upon being stopped. If it's a mistake (the stop) you can go your way and excuse the hassle because the officer is only doing his job.[10]

Major segments of the community would argue that (1) the function of the police is not to "hassle" people, and that (2) the community should not lightly excuse police mistakes.

How To Approach the Improvement of Police-Community Relations

What's offered here is not intended as a "how-to" guide for resolving a contemporary police issue. The fact that many police department community relations units have been closed down may be partly the result of their being viewed as panaceas. Nothing suggested here is a cure-all or total remedy; no such thing exists. What is presented is a framework of topics which, if examined and integrated in a conscious effort, deserve attention as possible avenues toward improvement. A major assumption at work here is that each officer is a part of, and not apart from, the police-community relations effort.

Understanding "Understanding" is currently a very hot topic. The success of *Roots* as a novel and a television program has been credited with developing new levels of understanding. Colleges teach courses on differential perception, empathy, culture shock, self-development (not to mention self-awareness, self-disclosure, self-concept, etc.). Despite the abundance of materials and media directed toward understanding, substantial misunderstanding and prejudice continue to exist and adversely affect the police-community relationship. A. C. Germann suggests that police understanding may be hampered by the Neanderthal perspective anchored in traditional police "boot camp" training approaches.[11] Professor F. K. Heussenstamm performed an experiment which afforded specific examples of police ignorance, prejudice, and bigotry:

> *[I] recruited five black, five white, and five Mexican-American drivers with no traffic violations within a year and asked them to sign pledges that they would obey all the rules of the road as carefully as possible. Each then affixed a Black Panther Party sticker to his car bumper. Strangely, within 17 days all 15 experimental subjects had bad driving records—amounting to 33 summonses handed out by police, with fines totaling $500.*[12]

Further need for understanding is evidenced by two documents found recently posted in a police station muster room. One item was a one-page poem of sorts stereotyping "niggers" as non-working welfare recipients who alternately filled their time with fishing, Cadillac driving, and backwoods sex. The second item was organized as an application for membership in the N.A.A.C.P. ("niggers, apes, alligators, coons, and possums"). The application form included checkoff entries such as: (1) number of legitimate children (if any), (2) white schools you would like to attend, and (3) abilities as agitator, preacher, or tap dancer. The fact that this material was placed on a police bulletin board in an area restricted to police access only is appalling. It illustrates how much improvement is really needed.

Another gap in the area of understanding is the often different perceptions of citizens and police about the police role. A recent interview of a deputy sheriff on the subject of crime prevention produced the following comments:

> *The best thing the public can do is stay out of our (the police) hair and quit calling us for such trivial things as domestic fights. That takes up more of our time than anything else. (Laughing) You'd be surprised at how many women like their weekly ass-kicking. These people can always get a restraining order (or peace bond) but that's a civil problem, not a police problem. The community is a big rip off, everything's a rip off.*[13]

This response was anything but understanding. The demeanor of the officer was seen by the interviewer as bitter, unsympathetic, and crude. The comment itself was ill-informed. The behavior of the officer during the interview was aggressive and macho. As in many police interviews, the responses were couched in terms of "us" (the police) and "them" (the public).

Some police administrators have been reluctant to see the gap in understanding as an organizational concern. Some have shrugged their shoulders and adopted the view that "it's okay to hold prejudices as long as you don't show them." The difficulty of adhering to this simple statement continues to hamper understanding.

The road to improved understanding involves breaking out of the isolation of what some have called the *police culture.* The first phase of understanding may be self-directed at preventing the development of cynicism which is prevalent among police officers. Another interview illustrates the problem of self-understanding:

> *I hate my job. If I had to do it all over again, I would be something else. You wake up in the morning with a general good feeling, but by the time the day is over you feel like putting your head through the steering wheel of the patrol car. I'll give you an example. As I drove by the high school this morning these two girls standing on the corner turn around and start shouting, "Hey, Pig". I cruised around the block trying to catch them. If I could have caught them I would have liked to smack them a couple of times.*[14]

Several suggestions for increasing officer understanding have been made in the past. For example, education and training can be effective; however, these must be carefully designed to avoid mere intellectualizing. Examples of education and training programs of interest exist. The Police-Community Relations Leadership Training Program in California,[15] examined the responsibilities of law enforcement agencies by intensive ten and twelve hour training days spent in discussion and sometimes confrontation with community representatives of diverse political, legal, social and cultural points of view. Unstructured interaction with a welfare family during a food stamp-financed evening meal provided participants with a new perspective on poverty. Role playing exercises with video tape playback for evaluation purposes reinforced the understanding that social control is less a matter of police power and more a function of community support and participation. The Invitation to Understanding Training Program of the

New York Police Department[16] involved scheduled on-duty discussion sessions composed of six black officers and six white officers to explore emotion, perception, and prejudice. These sessions expanded to include participant interaction on such topics as career success, economic security, family, freedom, honor, humor, power, and social acceptance. Near the end of the program a "sham trial" role-playing exercise gave officers the experience of trying to defend themselves against accusations and perceptions unsupported by facts. The Operation Empathy Program[17] of the Covina Police Department involved sending officers through a 24-hour masquerade experience as a down-and-outer in a skid row section of Los Angeles. Without money or identification, officers experienced first-hand understanding. Some officers were actually taken into custody, handcuffed, and jailed. All of these programs required actual involvement and participation and brought meaning to approaches which, in many other cases, had included nothing but lectures. As suggested earlier, the true success of police-community relations rests upon the willingness of the individual officer to attempt to understand himself or herself and others; taking initiative in this area requires combating the isolation and cynicism of the police culture. Edwin Markham's short rhyme seems to set the necessary tone:

He drew a circle to shut me out,
Heretic, rebel, a thing to flout;
But I, with love, had the will to win,
I drew a circle that took him in.

Communication Although understanding and communication are closely related, the importance of communication in and of itself can't be overstressed or repeated too often. Basically:

1. Every police agency should immediately adopt policies and procedures which provide for effective communication with the public through agency employees. Those policies and procedures should:
   a. Ensure that every employee having duties which involve public contact has sufficient information with which to respond to questions regarding agency policies; and
   b. Ensure that information which he receives is transmitted through the chain of command and acted upon at the appropriate level.
2. Every police agency which has racial and ethnic minority groups of significant size within its jurisdiction should recognize their police needs and should, where appropriate, develop means to ensure effective communication with such groups.
3. Every police agency which has a substantial non-English-speaking minority within its jurisdiction should provide readily available bilingual employees to answer requests for police services. In addition, existing agency programs should be adapted to ensure adequate communication between such non-English-speaking minority groups and the police agency.

4. Every police agency having more than 400 personnel should establish a specialized unit responsible for maintaining communication with the community. In smaller agencies, this responsibility should be the chief executive's using whatever agency resources are necessary and appropriate to accomplish the task.
   a. The unit should open and keep open the lines of communication between the agency and recognized community leaders and should elicit information from the citizen on the street who may feel that he has little voice in government or in the provision of its services.
   b. The unit should be no more than one step removed from the chief executive in the chain of command.
   c. The unit should identify impediments to communication with the community, research and devise methods to overcome those impediments, and develop programs which facilitate communication between the agency and the community.
   d. The unit should conduct ongoing evaluations of all programs intended to improve communication and should recommend discontinuance of programs when their objectives have been achieved or when another program might more beneficially achieve the identified functional objective.[18]

Communication theory has generally outlined the elements of the communication process as involving an *idea*, a *sender*, a *setting*, and/or *environment*, a *process*, a *receiver*, and a *result*. Ideally, the internalized idea of a sender is transmitted through the environment by a process which provides the receiver with the same internalized idea of the sender. The theory sounds simple and is reinforced by Plato's words, "The light within meets the light without." Gordon Allport reminds us, however, that:

> *Nothing that strikes our eyes or ears conveys its message directly to us. We always select and interpret our impressions of the surrounding world. Some message is brought to us by the "light without" but the meaning and significance we give to it are largely added by the "light within."*[19]

A training film produced by the San Diego Police Department contains a short segment entitled "That's right, turn left" in which a new recruit officer suffers from the unclear messages transmitted by his training officer. This film and our day-to-day encounters reinforce the recognition of how far we are from this idealized theory. The direction of improved police-community relations must give due consideration to improving the communication process.

Again, part of the improvement must be directed through initiative and proaction by the police. The police need to take the time to talk to people. They need to explore the language of different cultures to avoid what's been referred to as "linguistic segregation."[20] The circulation of an item known as the "chitlins test"[21] in which questions were devised to test the understanding of Black argot provided graphic evidence of how "culturally deprived" the white middle-class population is. One question on the test asks the geographic origin of the "Hully Gully" and provides multiple choice answers of East Oakland, Filmore, Watts, Harlem, and Motor City. Responses by Blacks taking the 30 item test resulted in scores of 29 and 30 correct while whites completing the test scored between 6 and 15.

In addition to expanding linguistic understanding, the need exists for the police to utilize communication as a method of reducing fear and conflict which may erupt into violence. The process of being arrested, handcuffed, and carted off in the caged rear seat of a police vehicle in which the interior door handles have been removed is an experience which can easily lead to violent desperation. The first arrest in particular induces repeated questions of "What's going to happen to me?" Many experienced and effective officers have found that the potential for violence is reduced when the arrested person is leveled with in a forthright manner. For example, when the decision to arrest is made, the officer should advise the arrestee that he or she is under arrest. If handcuffing is appropriate, the officer should handcuff the arrestee and say, "I'm handcuffing you as part of the normal arrest procedure." On the way to the station, the officer should explain the obvious absence of the interior door handles and prepare the arrestee for the booking process by outlining the steps of the procedure which may include searching, fingerprinting, photographing, and an opportunity to make telephone calls to arrange bail.

This type of communication indicates an open, direct, straightforward, and honest approach to dealing with people. It's not the same as molly coddling. And, if this type of treatment is appropriate for the arrested offender, it's also appropriate for the person who's stopped or temporarily detained for investigative purposes. Perhaps the reluctance of many police to respond to the question, "Why did you stop me?" is due to the fact that they (the police) don't have an answer. Charlotte Epstein has suggested that one method of improving human interaction might be the development of *anecdotal records.*[22] Applied to the communication process, the keeping of an anecdotal record simply requires a brief notation of daily on-the-job communication followed by a careful analysis of what was said. This process was extended a step further by the Oakland Police Department, which assigned tape recorders to selected officers as a means of recording and analyzing on-job verbal communication. The anecdotal record can serve the same purpose as the director in a theatre production.[23]

> *THE COMPASSIONATE COP — Patrolman John Bodkin, 34, and his partner Charles Anderson, 43, are called to investigate a domestic spat on Manhattan's Upper West Side. Inside the apartment they find a young Negro couple. One look convinces Bodkin that the husband is coiled like a spring, ready for battle. Pointedly, Bodkin, who is white, detaches his nightstick and takes off his hat. "Do you mind if I smoke?" he asks, "I'm a cigar smoker, and some people don't like the smell of cigar smoke in the house." Stunned by this unexpected show of courtesy, the man nods assent. The fight drains out of him. "Eventually," said Bodkin, reporting on the outcome, "they shake our hands. We never had another call from them."*[24]

In evaluating how he or she comes across, today's police officer must start from a position of self-disclosure. Paul Brouwer has referred to this as the power to see ourselves and to grow by self-examination, self-expectation, self-direction, and self-examination.[25] John Gardner has called this quality one of self-renewal.[26] Carl Rogers has pointed to this exercise as part of becoming a fully functioning person by increasing openness to experience, by becoming a person who is no longer fixed but is in process, by trusting the human organism, and by continually searching for answers to such questions as: "What is my purpose in life?" "What am I striving for?" "What am I doing?" "How am I perceived by others?" and "How do I feel?"[27]

Thus, the experience of *self* is important in initiating improved police-community relations.

Involvement Understanding and communication overlap with involvement, which is the third prerequisite to effective community relations. Involvement begins with a sincere interest in the community. In the 1960's arguments were being advanced that police officers should live in the communities that they worked in. The arguments had little to do with where police officers lived; the real issue was a search for a method to increase police involvement and commitment to the community and to diminish the community perception of the police as a foreign army of occupation. This real issue remains today and requires concerted effort by each individual police officer. The officer must strive to avoid "kiss-off" tactics such as advising disputing landlords and tenants that their disagreement is a civil problem. While the answer may be legally correct, it's meaningless to the involved parties who are unsophisticated in the nuances of the law.

Anyone advocating involvement faces a hurdle in trying to overcome the emotional armor which an officer must possess in order to deal with the instances of cruelty, inhumanity, and death. There is a difference, however, between emotional armor and emotional death. It took considerable armor to unearth the thirty-six mass murder bodies in the Yuba County California pear orchard in what is now referred to as the Juan Corona case. It would be ridiculous to assume that the officers involved in this operation were completely insensitive to these deaths, even though the victims were predominately transient farm workers without strong community identities and ties.

When the derogatory term "pig" came into use, the police blithely translated the epithet into a symbol of pride, integrity, and guts. It's hoped that the police are willing to take pride in their community, that they're willing to maintain a relationship of integrity with it, and that they possess the "guts" to extend themselves into the community and onto the street corner. The fairly recent emphasis on police-initiated citizen involvement in crime prevention activities is one step in the direction of improving police and community involvement with one another. This type of activity requires a certain willingness to work together, however. For example, if one police officer urges citizens to call the police and report suspicious behavior, and he or she is followed by another officer who responds to the subsequent suspicious behavior calls and advises the caller that there was no need to call or that the police are too busy to get involved with these type of calls, then nothing is accomplished. When talking about involvement, it's important to caution people against overinvolvement. To paraphrase many police officers, a cop has to think on his or her feet. Part of this "thinking on your feet" must be directed toward knowing when to back off, withdraw, or disengage. The current slogans of the "war on crime" have tended to produce a do-or-die battlefront mentality which equates loss of a single "battle" with loss of the "war." The realities of police work call upon the individual police officer to be sufficiently involved in the life of the community to recognize when an individual decision or action must be deferred to forestall the sparking of a community civil war. The word *defer* as used here is synonymous with *postpone*, not *abandon*.

Without involvement, the police function becomes a situation in which strangers enforce the law upon other strangers.

Service The service orientation of the police has been treated by James G. Wilson in *The Varieties of Police Behavior* and by Elaine Cumming in *Policeman as Philosopher, Guide and Friend*. The often quoted statistic that eighty percent of all police activity is service-oriented has lead to institutional slogans such as "protect and serve" and "service with concern," which are often painted on the doors of police vehicles. The unfortunate circumstance which calls for added attention to the role of service as a community relations issue is that there's still a need for "service with concern" signs to be painted on the hearts and minds of individual police officers who insist on seeing themselves as Wyatt Earps—gun-slinging crook-catchers and nothing more. A means must be found to maintain the fairly high altruistic commitment of the police recruit throughout a career which may be marked by a thankless response to a heroic act.

One encouraging sign in this area of service orientation is the development of programs designed to assist victims in understanding their role in the prosecution of criminal cases. In many cases, the victim of crime suffers not only the initial loss resulting from the criminal act but also the subsequent losses of time, money, patience, and faith. He or she is required to serve as a witness and incur court delays as part of a process to convict a person about whose guilt the victim has no doubt. In response to this problem, the Sacramento Police Department, funded by the Police Foundation, developed a victim advocate program to provide liaison between the police and the court treatment of the crime victim. This program is a prime example of an agency reaching out beyond the traditional limits of the police function to provide community service. Family crisis intervention techniques which lead to meaningful referrals to other private or public agencies also are examples of the extension of police service beyond the bounds of police tradition. Care must be exercised in having the police act as referral agents, however. Adequate follow-up must be conducted to ensure that referrals result in problem resolution and supplemental service. Police-community relations may be damaged by "dead end" or ineffective referrals.

Service is what the public demands, and they're entitled to satisfaction. Police officers are generally loathe to be considered social workers, and perhaps with good cause, but their placement in the community on a twenty-four-hour-a-day basis makes them the primary providers of emergency social services and the chief referral agents for follow-up services. Any inconsistencies in statements or slogans and service can hinder community relations.

> *The Service Ideal is nothing more than dedication to the needs of one's clients or constituancy. Whenever there is a conflict between personal goals and that of the client's interests, it is the client who must prevail. Too often bureaucracy defeats the needs of the client because it conceives of its own purposes as being paramount over those of its clients. Development of a service ideal is especially difficult since so much of the time the client's needs are ignored.*

It will perhaps be somewhat easier in the short run to effect Role Redefinition than any of the other processes. Much police work is of the social worker, caretaker, counseling service kind of activity. Thus, the police function must be reviewed and at least its crime prevention function narrowed to the kind of real crime control activities that would make the occupation more reasonable in its scope. At present these varied activities have reduced the law enforcement crime control functions of the police to less than twenty percent of their total working time. When one is responsible for "everything," one is also vulnerable for the inevitable mistakes in carrying out the impossible. That is the heart of the Policeman's lot.[28]

This same philosophy is at the heart of the role training materials developed as part of Project S.T.A.R.[29]

Project Star

1. *Project Scope*
   Project STAR was a collaborative 39-month effort that began in May, 1971, involving four states (California, Michigan, New Jersey, and Texas), the U.S. Department of Justice Law Enforcement Assistance Administration, and numerous local criminal justice agencies. The American Justice Institute, with the assistance of the System Development Corporation and Field Research Corporation, designed and conducted the research and demonstration effort under contract to the California Commission on Peace Officer Standards and Training and with the guidance of Advisory Councils in participating states.

   Project STAR was concerned with increasing the effectiveness of the criminal justice system. The Project was based on the assumption that better identification of the role requirements of criminal justice system personnel, both now and in the future, will make possible the development and implementation of appropriate education and training programs. These programs will contribute to the improvement of performance of criminal justice system personnel in assigned roles and, as a result, to the effectiveness of the criminal justice system.

2. *Project Objectives*

   General project objectives are to:

   - *Identify and describe the various roles of operational criminal justice personnel.*
   - *Identify major tasks and formulate performance objectives for appropriate tasks.*
   - *Determine knowledge and skill requirements for operational criminal justice personnel, including police officers, caseworkers, correctional workers, prosecutors, defenders, and judges.*
   - *Formulate education recommendation for these criminal justice personnel and the public.*
   - *Develop training modules that address those performance objectives not satisfied by existing education and training programs.*
   - *Develop appropriate selection criteria and recruiting strategies.*
   - *Identify social trends that may affect the criminal justice system and develop measurable indicators.*
   - *Set forth implementation plans and procedures for a continuous assessment of knowledge and skill requirements, as well as changing job responsibilities, for operational criminal justice personnel.*

The S.T.A.R. training modules carry a consistent theme of considering and resolving problems to the benefit of the "prime beneficiary." The "prime benificiary" approach is strongly client-centered and calls upon the police officer to make decisions to bring maximum benefit to the public. A rather clear distinction is drawn between the kinds of decisions which are made to protect the reputation of the police department, and the kinds of decisions which are made to provide service and benefit to the community.

Fairness The final condition treated here is the need for total fairness to permeate the personality of each individual officer. The concept of fairness is presented as an alternative to the personal value system of the individual officer. John P. Kenney has found that the personal value system of the officer is frequently the key to action:

> *More revealing, however, of the role of the police in the processes of the administration of criminal justice are the yet unpublished studies made under my direction by graduate students at California State College, Long Beach. We took a rather unique approach by hypothesizing that the police set the parameters of law enforcement for our society. More specifically the hypothesis was that, collectively, the uniformed field officers establish the parameters and that their collective value systems predominantly influence who is and who is not arrested.*
>
> *Preliminary findings of the study show that the field officer's decision to arrest, that his personal value system is the key to this determination, that he is the least experienced in terms of time on the job, that he is young, approximately 25 years of age, (in the Southern California area) and has some college education. Limited influence is exercised by superiors, by the general attitude of the community, and by court decisions and by the legislatures.*[30]

Decisions which are laden with the personal value system of the officer are clearly contrary to an American theme of fairness. Americans subscribe to concepts of fair play, fair dealing, and fair treatment. This view is even extended into situations of combat with the call for a fair fight. Many a charge of police brutality has been based merely on the fact that one person has been taken into custody by two police officers—a circumstance which appears to violate a one-on-one fair fight ethic.

The fairness spoken of here is not an absolute, objective thing; it is a quality, however, that's generally recognized when it's experienced. And it's important to the mission of bridging the gap between the police and the community.

Humanism – A Police Philosophy

Thus far, this chapter has been an attempt to distill the volumes of material that have been written about community relations. The rather obvious emphasis has been on treating the improvement of police-community relations by urging the police to engage in perpetual self-renewal and to act as catalysts in striving for a more humanistic community. The emphasis has been purposeful in calling upon the police establishment to serve not only as agents of the law, but to serve as change agents in improving human development, human understanding, and the human condition. The credo of humanism offers a concise philosophy which incorporates much of the same intent:

1. I believe . . . in the essential dignity of every human being, no matter what their status in life. To those citizens having the most contact with the police, life has provided little opportunity and much disappointment. The test of this belief in human dignity depends upon my not becoming disillusioned or bitterly cynical toward people who exhibit weakness and inadequacy.
2. I believe . . . that people can change. They can change their attitudes, values, life styles, and philosophies. If I accept this assumption about human nature then I can avoid the fallacy of personality fixation which tends to classify people as "good" or "bad" and incapable of changing behavior once a certain age level is reached. If I believe people can change then rehabilitation replaces retribution as a solution to people problems.
3. I believe . . . that people change people. Humans change only through the help of other humans. All police officers can become a force for purposeful human change—a force prepared to help man cope more effectively with his limitations, inadequacies, and strengths. Every police contact becomes an opportunity for developing a sense of "peopleness" moving policing forward as a positive feature of a governmental system which always places people first.
4. I believe . . . in the essential goodness of all men, who, if given a chance, can attain that level of human potential with which they have been

endowed. The police are a vital part of the chance they need. By crossing their lives, the police can be, and often are, a source of hope, help, and opportunity.[31]

There are several realistic conditions which must be considered if the move toward a more humanistic society is to gain full operational acceptance by the police. Some means must be found to allow the police to see the damage they do themselves by self-isolation. It's ironic to discover the existence of a National Association of Police Community Relations Officers (NAPCRO), which sets forth laudable goals of improving community relations, promoting professionalism, and preparing comprehensive program materials—and which permits voting membership *only* to police officers.

> *Active Members ... Full time federal, state or local sworn and civilian employees actively engaged in Police Community Relations of any duly constituted public law enforcement agency or governmental agency meeting the requirements as defined herein. Any commissioned police officer who maintains an active interest in police community relations. Dues are $15.00 per person. Only active members have the right to vote.*[32]

In addition to reducing their isolation, the police may need to reassess the tradition-bound methods of gaining conformance to the law by raw authoritarianism. This encompasses the full range of current practices from outright unlawful procedures and physical abuse to the verbal argument of authority which is communicated as, "I'm the law, don't ask questions, just do what I say." There's no question that police work presents conditions calling for direct action and authoritative commands such as *Stop! Drop the gun! Open the door!* It's only being suggested here that the authoritative approach may be tempered a bit by being limited to appropriate emergencies and that, in the interest of his or her own safety, an officer might learn to recognize that compliance with unreasoned authority is shortlived.[33]

Reducing isolationism and authoritarianism will assist the development of humanization, as will the recognition of the weakness of propaganda. Many of the community relations efforts to date have been little more than efforts to propagandize.

In the late 1960s, the Black Panther Party distributed a document known as the "Black Panther Coloring Book." The police community was enraged over the content of the book, which depicted cartoon drawings of grossly abusive uniformed pig-like police officers being shot, stabbed, ambushed, and abused by Black adults and children. Cartoon captions included justifications for the depicted violence, such as "A black father defends his family against the Pigs." The most disturbing issue surrounding the coloring books was the report that copies were distributed to Black preschool children who were participating in free breakfast programs in ghetto areas of American cities. While police obviously did not object to hungry children receiving free breakfast they did view the operations as a brainwashing tactic for distribution of hate and violence propaganda.

The Black Panther Coloring Book was strict propaganda, a symptom of the deteriorating relationship between the Black community and a predominately white establishment which was most vividly represented on a twenty-four-hour basis by police. The police response to the Black Panther Coloring Book was to move swiftly into the captive audiences of the public schools to distribute "Officer Friendly" coloring books. Obviously, real police-community relations is, and must be, more than a coloring book propaganda war.

The humanistic principles presented in this chapter call for change. In short, the police officer must become an agent of change. In accepting this responsibility, the individual officer should understand that he or she is *an* agent of change, not *the* agent of change.

If police officers suppose that they are *the* agents of change, it will be difficult for them to see the obvious fact that if their task is to be the humanization of the community, those they work with must be something more to them than the objects of their action. They, too, must be perceived as agents of change. If the police can't see this, success will be limited to manipulating, directing, and tenuously maintaining the status quo. If, on the other hand, they recognize others as well as themselves as agents of change, they'll cease to think of themselves as the agents of change and enter into a subject-to-subject, or "win-win," relationship with the community. In this kind of relationship both police and community will recognize the need to strive for mutual benefit without violence, exploitation, and harm to each other. This mutually inclusive responsibility must serve as the philosophical base for sustaining police-community relationships.

The Future

In discussing the future of police-community relations we need to assess social trends, judge their impact, and plan for change alternatives. This assessment, judgment, and planning form the basis for success. "Success is more likely to come to those who work for and with a social trend than those who work against it."[34]

Futurists suggest that increased population, urbanization, diversity of opinion, growth of knowledge, and reduced resources will be only a few of the conditions which will persist into the future.[35] The challenges and dilemmas of the future may be more intense versions of problems which face the police today.

There seems to be no way to completely prevent hostility between the police and the community, but there are steps that can be taken to increase trust. Specific areas of attention may include greater citizen involvement in police policy making, greater visibility of internal discipline, an increase in minority participation in law enforcement careers, emphasis on human relations training, an initiation of studies of media impact on the public perception of the police, the development of grade school curricula to educate the community on the police mission and function, and the conducting of periodic surveys to determine police-community problems

. . . in this country we have tended to put PCR in too narrow a compartment, failing to understand fully that all the major issues in the police world today pose fundamental police-public dilemmas. What is involved are attitudes of the police toward themselves, toward the public, and toward their job—and on the other side, attitudes of community groups not always coinciding with those of the police. Indeed, a central complication is that there are sharp differences of opinion among individuals and factions on both sides.[36]

Summary

This chapter has been directed toward reviewing the topic of police-community relations. The title of this book is suggestive of the need for the police. Some may suggest that the police imperative is an imperative in the "necessary evil" sense; however, the intent of this chapter is to suggest that although the police are "necessary" they need not be "evil."

We have reviewed the development of police-community relations from its origins in rules of deportment for image maintenance to the development of a full menu of programs and slogans. The opinion has been advanced that there's considerable room for improvement, and that improvements will be the result of individual officers who strive for greater understanding, improved communication, increased involvement, a commitment to service, and a subscription to fairness.

An argument has been made for the integration of humanism into a philosophy for police functioning. A precondition for this integration will be the reduction of police isolation, a reduced reliance upon authoritarianism, and a recognition of the limits of propaganda.

It has been suggested that the police look to the future to prevent compartmentalization. Perhaps the greatest need of the future is a personnel evaluation system which stresses the assessment and improvement of individual officer efforts toward improving human understanding, communication, involvement, service, and fairness as a replacement for the mechanistic measures of arrests, convictions, field contacts, and citations. It's hoped that the police will move forward and address the future.

Topics For Discussion

1. **Discuss the causes of the strong mental images triggered by the word, "police." Suggest some methods for dealing with these causes.**
2. **Discuss the concept of community. Identify your community. Compare your community to an "ideal" community and discuss the differences.**
3. **Discuss the problem of a citizen who demands full enforcement of the law, but asks for special consideration when apprehended committing a minor offense.**
4. **Discuss how to measure the effectiveness of community relations efforts. Reduced crime? Reduced citizen complaints? Other measures?**

5. **Discuss how you do or will prevent yourself from becoming isolated, alienated, and cynical from exposure to police work.**
6. **Discuss your feelings and reactions when close friends, relatives, coworkers or peers make derogatory and/or racist remarks.**
7. **Discuss the concept of "prime beneficiary" as it applies to police service.**
8. **Discuss the credo for police humanism. Is it realistic? Why or why not? How would you change or modify it?**
9. **Discuss what policing might be like in 1990.**

References

1. Colin Bell and Howard Newby, Community Studies: *An Introduction to the Sociology of the Local Community,* New York: Praeger, 1971.
2. James W. Sterling, Changes in Role Concepts of Police Officers, Gaithersburg: 1972, p. 17. Reprinted with permission.
3. Elton Woolpert, *Municipal Public Relations: A Suggested Program for Improving Relations with the Public,* Chicago: International City Managers Association, 1940, p. 1.
4. William H. Parker, Roport on Lectures Presented to Peace Officer Administrative Institutes, Sacramento, California: Department of Education, 1956, pp. 213-232.
5. Edmund G. Brown, Guide to Community Relations for Peace Officers, Sacramento, Attorney General, 1958, p. 18.
6. John A. McCone, *Violence in the City – An End or a Beginning,* Sacramento: State of California, 1965.
7. Law Enforcement Task Force of New York City, *Report to Mayor-Elect John V. Lindsay:* New York, 1965.
8. Charles Gain, *Remarks to Community-Police Relations Leadership Training Program:* Lake Arrowhead, 1971.
9. Charlotte Epstein, Intergroup Relations for Police Officers, Darien, Conn.: Hafner, 1970, pp. 22, 29, 160.
10. Interviews, 1977. The quoted materials are the result of random interviews with uniformed law enforcement personnel on duty in the metropolitan area of Sacramento, California. Interviews were conducted by the administration of justice students at Sacramento City College under the supervision of the author.
11. A. C. Germann, "Changing the Police—The Impossible Dream?" *Journal of Criminal Law, Criminology and Police Science,* Northwestern University School of Law, Illinois: Vol. No. 3, 1971.
12. F. K. Heussenstamm, "Forum Newsletter," *Playboy,* 1971. pp. 58-59.
13. Interviews, 1976. The quoted materials are the result of random interviews with uniformed law enforcement personnel on duty in the metropolitan area of Sacramento, California. Interviews were conducted by administration of justice students at Sacramento City College under the supervision of the author.
14. Interviews, 1977. The quoted materials are the result of random interviews with uniformed law enforcement personnel on duty in the metropolitan area of Sacramento, California. Interviews were conducted by administration of justice students at Sacramento City College under the supervision of the author.

15. "Target – Improved Police Community Relations," *Police,* October, 1971, p. 62.
16. "Invitation to Understanding, An," *The Police Chief,* June, 1971, p. 20.
17. "Operation Empathy," *Newsweek,* December 15, 1969.
18. National Advisory Commission on Criminal Justice Standards and Goals, *Police,* Washington, D.C.: U. S. Government, 1973, pp. 29, 30.
19. Gordon W. Allport, *The Nature of Prejudice,* New York, N.Y.: Addison-Wesley, 1954, p. 161.
20. "How to Talk Black," *Newsweek,* February, 1972, p. 79.
21. "The Chitlin Test," *The Sacramento Bee,* April 21, 1970.
22. "The Chitlin Test," *The Sacramento Bee,* April 21, 1970.
23. Alan J. Schwartz, "Crisis-Communication and the Police Officer," *Police,* February, 1972.
24. Time, "The Compassionate Cop," March 23, 1970.
25. William Eddy, et. al, *Behavioral Science and the Manager's Role,* Washington, D.C.: NTL Institute, 1969.
26. John W. Gardner, *Self-Renewal,* New York: Harper and Row, 1968.
27. Carl R. Rogers, "Toward Becoming a Fully Functioning Person," *Perceiving, Behaving, Becoming: A New Focus for Education,* Washington, D. C. Association for Supervision and Curriculum Development, 1962, pp. 21-33.
28. Arthur Niederhoffer, Abraham S. Blumberg, "The Police in Social and Historical Perspective," *The Ambivalent Perspectives on the Police,* Waltham, Massachusetts: Ginn and Co., 1970, p. 15.
29. *"Impact of Social Trends on Crime and Criminal Justice, The,"* Cincinnati, Santa Cruz: Anderson/Davis, 1976.
30. John P. Kenney, *"The Unbalanced Scales of Criminal Justice,"* Convocation Address: Caldwell, Idaho, 1970.
31. Frank L. Manella, "Humanism in Police Training," *The Police Chief,* February, 1971, p. 26.
32. National Association Police Community Relations Officers, Washington, D.C., 1977.
33. Arthur Niederhoffer, *Behind the Shield: The Police in* Urban Society, New York: Doubleday, 1967.
34. William F. Osborne, *On Culture and Social Change,* Chicago: University of Chicago Press, 1964, p. 109.
35. "Impact of Social Trends on Crime and Criminal Justice, The," Cincinnati, Santa Cruz: Anderson/Davis, 1976.
36. Louis Radelet, "Police and Community Relations at This Point in Time," *The Police Chief,* March, 1974.

Annotated Bibliography

Allport, Gordon W., *The Nature of Prejudice,* New York: Addison-Wesley Publishing Co., 1954. A penetrating study of the origin and nature of prejudice. A social study of prejudgements which remain irreversible even in the light of contrary evidence. Material is directed at a major problem in human relations.

American Bar Association, *The Urban Police Function,* New York: American Bar Association, 1973. A word of standards and commentary developed by the American Bar Association on the police function. Includes several sections which are relevant to policing and the community.

Berkley, George E., *The Democratic Policeman,* Boston: Beacon Press, 1969. An overview of the police role in a democratic society. Compares the democratic police environment with European police practice. Includes an interesting treatment of policing the police.

Campbell, James S., and Sahid, Joseph R., and Stang, David P., *Law and Order Reconsidered,* Washington, D.C.: National Commission on the Causes and Prevention of Violence, 1969. This Commission staff report is recommended reading for all interested in a clear understanding of American law, political and social order and the agencies of law enforcement.

Cohn, Alvin W., and Viano, Emicilio C., Editors, *Police Community Relations: Images, Roles, Realities,* New York: J. B. Lippincott Co., 1976. A contemporary collection of addresses, essays and lectures dealing with the context of police-community relations. Includes section on the police role; community interaction; tension, conflict, improvement and change strategies.

Epstein, Charlotte, *Intergroup Relations for Police Officers,* Darien, Conn: Hafner Publishing Co., 1970. Written by a police department social scientist. Treats topics of group learning, prejudice, planning for change, rumor control, developing anecdotal records, the American tradition of law and equality. Contains role play and case study materials.

Kirkham, George L. and Smith, Eugene, Police: *The Human Dimension,* New York: Harper and Row Media, 1975. A collection of eight 16 mm films accompanied by detailed discussion guides containing objectives and questions. Topics include ethics, authority, stress, minorities and the community.

Niederhoffer, Arthur and Blumberg, Abraham S., *The Ambivalent Force: Perspectives on the Police,* Waltham, Mass: Ginn and Co., 1970. A broad collection of readings dealing with contemporary police/community relations. Treats issues of organizational pressures, values, police sub-culture, discretion, law enforcement, brutality and other aspects. An advanced reader.

Reiss, Albert J., *The Police and the Public,* New Haven: Yale University Press, 1971. A survey of the policeman's lot based on field observation experiences. Includes an examination of police manners and morals and a proposal for police reform.

Roberg, Roy, *The Changing Police Role,* New Dimensions and New Issues, San Jose: Justice Systems Development, 1976. A review and update on the police role in society. Recommended reading for police supervisors, managers, serious students of police and others.

Russel, Harold E., and Bergel, Allan, *Understanding Human Behavior for Effective Police Work,* New York: Basic Books Inc., 1976. This book treats the role of the police officer as practicing psychologist. In addition to a review of the variety and complexity of human behavior, there is extensive material on the assessment and management of abnormal behavior in the field.

Skellow, Robert and Bart, Morton, *Issues in Law Enforcement,* Virginia: Prentice-Hall, 1976. A collection of essays shedding light on issues of the police role, professionalism, crisis and conflict management. Includes extensive cases for evaluation and analysis.

Sterling, James W., *Changes in Role Concepts of Police Officers,* Gaithersburg, Md.: International Association of Chiefs of Police, 1970. A research project report by I.A.C.P. under a grant from the National Institute of Mental Health, Department of Health, Education and Welfare. An extensive review of police personality, role conflict, attitudinal orientation, perception of danger, self-understanding and other police behaviors.

Saltenberger, Otto H., and Allan, David Y., Coordinators, *The Impact of Social Trends on Crime and Criminal Justice,* Cincinnati/Santa Cruz: Anderson/Davis, 1976. A futuristic look at crime and an attempt to assess the consequences on criminal justice agents. Provides specific suggestions on future training and education of police and other criminal justice personnel. Served as one of the bases for development of role training materials for Project S.T.A.R.

Toch, Hans, and Grant, J. Douglas, and Galvin, Raymond, *Agents of Change: A Study in Role Reform,* New York: John Wiley and Sons, 1975. An extensive case study of a grant project involving the National Institute of Health, H.E.W., State University of New York and the Oakland Police Department directed toward reducing personal violence in police-citizen contacts.

Wilson, James Q., *Varieties of Police Behavior,* New York: Harvard University Press, 1968. A major work examining police discretion and the management of law and order in eight communities. Identifies law enforcement "styles" (watchman, legalistic, service). Discusses public and political impacts upon police operations.

6

POLICE AND YOUTH
The Challenge of Delinquency and Crime Prevention

Chapter Objectives

The study of this chapter should enable you to:

☑ Characterize the three major elements of the criminal justice system on which the repression and control of crime depend—punishment, rehabilitation, and prevention.

☑ Prepare an evaluation of the deterrent value of punishment as an instrument of crime control.

☑ Discuss the role and impact of reform and rehabilitation in the criminal justice system.

☑ Consider the validity of the statement that enforcement has been given a fair trial and that alone, it is not the answer to the problem of crime and the criminal.

☑ Evaluate the assumption that in the majority of cases, the adult criminal offender was well on his way to frustration and social disaster as a juvenile delinquent.

☑ Comment on the difficulties involved in approaching the problem at the age level of juvenile delinquency.

☑ Support, qualify or disagree with the concept that it is to beginning behavior deviations in the lower grade school levels that the police and community agencies must now turn their attention, in terms of identifying the pre-delinquent or potential delinquent and then addressing the clinical resources of the community to the problem.

☑ Discuss police organization and program for delinquency and crime prevention.

Introduction

A discouraged Egyptian priest, who lived when the pyramids were being built, observed that "Our earth is degenerate in these latter days. There are signs that the world is coming to an end. The youngsters show a disrespect for their elders and a contempt for authority in every form. Crime is rampant among our young people and vandalism is general."

The Egyptian priest would find little comfort upon taking a look at the massive crime rates that prevail today. Nor would he be inspired by the circumstance that in *all* categories of major crime—homicide, rape, robbery, aggravated assault, burglary, larceny, and automobile theft—the majority of arrests made by the police are of young people, eighteen years of age and under.

The Problem

The repression and prevention of crime in this country rest precariously on three major elements of the criminal justice system: (1) punishment, (2) reform or rehabilitation, and (3) the prevention of delinquency and crime.

Let us look closely at the first two. The debate on the deterrent value of punishment continues without interruption.[1] Bailey and Lott state that, according to current research, the threat of capital punishment doesn't stop criminals; therefore, punishment is not really an answer to juvenile delinquency or any other kind of crime.[2] They observe:

> *The presumed deterrent effect of punishment provides the cornerstone of our criminal justice system, but it would be a mistake to assume that deterrence is well established in theory and research. . . . In examining the literature, one repeatedly finds the assertion that the certainty of punishment is a more effective deterrent than its severity. While the evidence is clearly suggestive of certainty's greater deterrent value, some caution should be exercised in drawing any firm conclusion at this time. . . . Until recent years, most deterrence investigations have focused primarily upon homicide and the death penalty. These investigations have led most investigators to accept what Thorstin Sellin has termed the inevitable conclusion: " . . . the presence of the death penalty—in law or practice—does not influence homicide rates."*

The current sentiment among the states to abandon the electric chair and other forms of execution in favor of lethal injection, a less painful and less objectionable way of death, may serve indirectly to further lessen the deterrent value of capital punishment.

What then, about rehabilitation? The question immediately leads to an unpleasant word—*recidivism,* the tendency of offenders to continue their pattern of criminal behavior. The percentages on the wrong side of the ledger are known to everyone in the criminal justice system. At no point in the entire system has failure so dominated our effort to contain crime and the criminal.

Perhaps as a result of this dismal record, an important change is taking place in the field of criminology. Basically, reform and rehabilitation are being abandoned as working concepts, while punishment and protective confinement are again being seen as the only practical answers to criminal behavior. John Monahan summed it up precisely:[3]

> *The cycle of reform has come full circle. The cutting edge of criminological thought now argues for a return to punishing according to the crime rather than treating the offender. The* "Age of the Promise of Treatment" *gave way to the* "Age of Treatment Program Evaluation," *and the findings were so bleak that we are now back to the "Age of Punishment." Recent moves in Illinois and California restricting indeterminate sentences and de-emphasizing therapy leave little doubt that punishment is the wave of the foreseeable future.*

Similarly, Louis F. Carney observes:[4]

> *The firm conclusion of the Keldgord Report* (California Board of Corrections 1971, *p. ix,), which merely echoes the belief of authorities in the field, is based on what researchers call "hard data." Concrete statistical evidence exists to prove that imprisonment is a failure as a rehabilitative instrument. Studies have shown, notably in California and Washington, that the length of sentence has no effect on reformation. . . . Approximately 8,000 persons are sent to jails and prisons in the United States every day. Over 95 percent of them will return to the community, and more than 70 percent of that group will recidivate and get on the police blotter again. These figures can scarcely be called a tribute to the effectiveness of our correctional apparatus.*

While conceding that imprisonment is a failure as a rehabilitative instrument, Carney makes a strong case for community-based corrections as an alternative to imprisonment. He points out that the idea is not new, and that since probation and parole first came into practice, community-based corrections has been a progressively developing concept. He indicates that because approximately two-thirds of the correctional caseload of the country is already under supervision in the community, the challenge ahead is to develop still further the concept of community-based correctional effort.

The recidivism rate is even more frustrating when one considers the professional gains made by the police during the past half century in the area of criminal investigation alone. Important advances have been made in the application of scientific disciplines to investigative procedure. Prompt case solutions have become almost routine, thanks to the increased range of skills and information possessed by the officer and detective. The trained police officer and detective, supported as they are by the technical resources of the laboratory, make for a strong investigative team. From the records we are compelled to conclude that the American police have been doing a commendable job of law enforcement.

Even so, it is becoming obvious that investigation and enforcement have their limitations. Many people feel that the enforcement approach to crime control has been given a fair trial, and that it has not produced the desired results. Police administrators are aware that, despite their best efforts, there has been no appreciable reduction in crime in recent years. In fact, if we examine the annual criminal caseloads of police departments and the number of commitments to prison, and then use these statistics as a guide in measuring criminality in the United States, we are forced to conclude that crime has been increasing at a consistent rate far greater than that of the population.[5]

This discouraging fact has prompted the police to look in other directions for more effective means of crime control. In casting about for a solution, they have increasingly realized that the present system of arrest, prosecution, conviction, and punishment doesn't work. The criminal offender either escapes successful prosecution, or goes to prison to renew criminal contacts and eventually emerge with a grudge against society and a polished aptitude for new criminal activities.

How, then, can we go about bridging the gap between the crime rate and crime control? It would seem that a society with our technological expertise could make considerable progress in the approach to the problems of human behavior. In the face of demonstrated failure in the areas of punishment and reformation, no alternative remains but to focus the tools of scientific method on the prevention of delinquency and crime. It has been estimated that the resources expended in this country over the years on punishment and reformation represent an outlay of more than one hundred times the national debt.

The Formula of Prevention

Webster defines prevention as: *to come before, to anticipate, forestall, to meet or satisfy in advance, to act ahead of, to keep from happening, deal with beforehand, taking advance measures against something possible or probable, a getting ahead of, the use of forethought to avoid the necessity for unwelcome events or counteract threatening developments.* After thirty-two brilliant years as Chief of Police in Berkeley, California, August Vollmer stated, "I have spent my life enforcing the law. It is a stupid procedure and will never succeed until supplemented by preventive measures."[6] In order to appreciate the significance of this statement, it seems appropriate to comment briefly on the man who made it.

The author served his first eight years in a police uniform under Chief Vollmer in the Police Department of Berkeley, California. The chief's influence was pervasive in the lives of his officers, many of whom went on to become the nation's chiefs of police, while others became administrators of academic programs in police science and criminal justice in leading universities. The Vollmer system of police administration attracted national and international attention. The mention of his name anywhere in the world, as the author has found in London, Paris, Rome, Brussels, Amsterdam, Athens, Alexandria, Cairo, Bierut, Jerusalem, Taipei, Manila, Kuala Lumpur, Singapore, Bankok, Seoul, Tokyo, and the Virgins, commands attention. The name August Vollmer is universally linked with the concept of police service. Vollmer's proposals, meeting head-on the challenge—*to act ahead of, deal with beforehand*—set a precedent in the field of delinquency and crime prevention. They offer a scientific formula in a viable approach to the dilemma posed by crime and the criminal, second in magnitude only to war as a social problem.

Crime prevention is basically concerned with the *potential* offender, before institutionalization or other firm measures are necessary. Studies have shown that, in the majority of cases, the adult criminal offender was once known to the police as a juvenile delinquent. The fact that the young delinquent is the forerunner of the adult criminal offender has been proved by the analysis of thousands of criminal careers. Opinion now generally holds that it is much better to attempt to reform the juvenile delinquent than to wait until the individual reaches maturity as a confirmed adult offender. Juvenile personality, temperament, and behavior traits are still somewhat in the formative stages and, as a result, juveniles are more responsive to therapeutic measures than are adult criminal offenders.

The therapeutic approach may be implemented by means of "diversionary justice," or diversion of the case away from adjudication before the bar. This is a prejudicial disposition in which the extraordinary discretionary powers of the police are brought into play. The case bypasses the juvenile court and is carried into a "neutral zone" where the clinical resources of the community (social, psychological, psychiatric and medical) are brought into contact with the case.

An important factor in implementing this approach is the development of local Youth Service Centers or Youth Service Bureaus, which can be traced to the recommendations of the 1967 Report of the President's Commission on Law Enforcement and Criminal Justice Administration. In combination, these centers or bureaus attempt to determine the needs of the juvenile in a factual and diagnostic manner and then develop a treatment program using appropriate community resources.

Commendable as efforts like these are, the results of this approach at the age level of juvenile delinquency are far from impressive. With behavior patterns at the threshold of firming up and becoming a permanent life-style, an attempt at change is a formidable task. After the home has failed, and after the church, neighborhood, and community have failed, the police are called in to make an arrest and somehow effect a dramatic change in a juvenile's life pattern. When the enforcement process itself fails, the youngster becomes involved in more serious infractions and is sent to the reformatory, where society again expects a miracle. Here the young offender accumulates the credentials which eventually lead to the penitentiary. The record clearly shows the futility of depending upon a miraculous transformation of personality at this stage.

As early as 1937, Warden James A. Johnston of the Federal Penitentiary at Alcatraz, speaking on the functions of the modern prison, concluded, "Prisons have important work to perform. I want to see them bettered, improved, modernized and humanized. But, when all is said and done, the finest prison that we can build will stand as a monument to neglected youth."[7] Walter Dunbar, Director of the California State Department of Corrections, observed, "We are trying to help the offender after the criminal pattern has developed. This is almost like waiting until a youth is crippled by polio to give him vaccine."[8]

When behavior problems are permitted to develop unattended until a juvenile offender knocks on the door at police headquarters, the cause is virtually lost. In fact, the juvenile's presence in jail or a detention home for the first time is usually nothing but a formality, the most recent occurrence of a chain of events in a conditioning process which has led inevitably to the end result.

Chief Vollmer early perceived the futility of those trademarks of failure —the jail and the penitentiary, symbols of society's failure to control delinquency and crime—and became convinced that the police and community agencies should address themselves to early deviations in behavior patterns and the determining conditions which induce them. In the past, we have dealt with the end result rather than with the conditioning factors which produce the delinquent and criminal. Even today, crime control policy is reminiscent of the housewife who was so busy swatting the flies in the kitchen that she failed to notice the garbage can outside the window where they were breeding by the thousands. As Lowell J. Carr stated:[9]

> *It is not enough to treat. Inefficient as the actual procedures in the correctional cycle may be, there seems to be little prospect that they can ever be made efficient enough to do the whole job that is needed. Back behind the personality that has broken the law, there is always an earlier phase of that same personality that has just begun to deviate.*

The Hawthorne Study, the Bodin Study, and other research investigations have established that delinquency and crime usually stem from early life maladjustments and that delinquent juveniles and adult criminals display in almost every case a history of early behavior difficulties.[10] These studies reveal, among other things, that from two to three and one-half percent of the public school population in the average American community are children with problems sufficiently severe to warrant special attention. This vast array of children represents a major segment of the adult population with which the machinery of justice will spend its time and energies in the future. As a veteran jurist stated:[11]

> *Messrs. Police Officers, Sheriffs and State Patrolmen: Do you want to meet the young killers, rapists, stickups, automobile thieves, burglars, and others you will be chasing in a comparatively short time? If you do, go to the shools and look at the records that show the following information: chronic tardiness, persistent truancy, scholastic progress below mental ability, poor citizenship, unwillingness to accept correction, and lack of interest. These records, among others, are red-flag warning signals of delinquency and crime and will point you almost unerringly to your man.*

Addressing the teaching profession, he said:

> *Mr. and Mrs. Schoolteacher: Would you like to do something for the public health of your community in the field of sick conduct? Then, heed your records. Under your very eyes are developing the symptoms of infection that will*

develop into the ruptured appendix or organic collapse of good citizenship. The attendance record alone, is enough to put us all on guard.

The philosophy of crime prevention stems from the belief, confirmed by research, that the burglar, killer, prostitute, automobile thief, and thug do not develop suddenly. The records show that in the majority of cases, they display deviant characteristics in early childhood and progress by almost imperceptible degrees into confirmed criminal offenders. Early discovery and diagnosis of childhood problems—physical, mental, social, or a combination of these three—is gradually opening the door to opportunities for the prevention of delinquency and crime.

Chief Robert T. Williams of the Grandview Police Department, Grandview, Missouri, recently noted that the criminal system in this country does not attempt to treat criminality until *after* it has developed and has become a problem.[12] He notes that we make no effective effort to prevent the development of criminality, but instead take an after-the-fact approach. Deputy Chief John E. Winters of the Youth Aid Division in the Metropolitan Police Department of Washington, D. C., recently directed attention to "a widespread belief *that the early discovery of the pre-delinquent or potential delinquent is the key to the prevention program.*"

In 1936, Nathan Bodin, a graduate student at the University of California at Berkeley, became interested in the prevailing opinion among sociologists and others that the problem child, the child with difficulties—social, physical mental, or a combination of all three—was, in the majority of cases, the forerunner of the delinquent and the criminal. He chose as the topic for his master's thesis *Do Problem Children Become Delinquents and Criminals?*[13] From the *inactive* files of the Bureau of Research and Guidance in Berkeley, he selected 116 adults who fourteen years earlier had been considered problem children in the Berkeley Public Schools, because they "could not be satisfactorily managed in the regular school classroom."

When Bodin performed a follow-up study, he found that of the original 116, ninety-two and one-half percent had since become delinquents and criminals. This study as well as others brings into sharp relief the need for mechanisms which will assist in identifying potential pre-delinquents in the first, second, and third grades, and even at the nursery and kindergarten levels, so that the clinical resources of the community and other services can be used on behalf of these children.

The use of prediction as an evaluative tool is nothing new. Techniques for projecting the crime and traffic accident curves of yesterday into the future, aptitude tests, and the like have been around for years. Recently, though, prediction scales and techniques have been the subject of extensive research, and they have become increasingly sophisticated. There is now a large body of literature concerning attempts to predict human behavior.[14] The research efforts in this area by Eleanor and Sheldon Glueck, eminent sociologists at Harvard University, have attracted widespread interest and recognition. Similarly, the prodigious inquiry of the President's Commission on Law Enforcement and Administration of Justice commands the respect of workers throughout the field.

While no estimate of future behavior can be made with mathematical certainty, *a statement of degree of probability is conceded to be an appropriate prediction objective,* and is certainly acceptable for the job at hand. Research has made available prediction scales and techniques which substantially satisfy this objective. Eleanor and Sheldon Glueck, for example, present the following five factors as the basis for a prediction scale: Supervision of child by mother; discipline of child by mother; cohesiveness of family; nonsubmissiveness of child to parental authority; destructiveness of child.

Factors that have been developed as predictors by other researchers include: social assertion; social defiance; suspicion; degree of emotional stability; stubbornness; running away; stealing; temper tantrums; disobedience; sex play; gambling; use of vile language; begging; staying out late at night; lying; state of health; extrovert v. introvert tendencies; depression; complaining tendencies; results of psychological and psychiatric tests; reading ability; maladjustment; norm-violating behavior; objectionable personality traits; poor working habits; attitude toward schooling; attendance record and truancy; academic achievement level.

There is general agreement that the identification of potential delinquents before entrance in school or soon thereafter would allow the application of diagnostic and therapeutic measures in a program geared to a practicable philosophy of delinquency and crime prevention. To complacently wait for certain manifestations of delinquency is to almost literally ask for trouble.

The clinical approach to early behavior deviations is strengthened by the observations of Sheldon and Eleanor Glueck, who concluded that the external environment is less significant in generating delinquency and crime than the *biological endowments of the individual and parental influence during the formative years.* According to them, the general environment contributes relatively little to our understanding of an individual's maladjustment to the demands of accepted social standards. They add, however, that the pathology of the environment, including poverty, the slums, and other factors that retard social development demand our attention.

It is significant that the Gluecks and others are taking into account the biological endowment of the individual as a factor in the origins of delinquency and crime; it is increasingly recognized that human behavior is genetically as well as socially determined. However, little can be done at present in the area of genetic endowment because of the general attitude toward this subject and the need for additional data in the biological sciences. Still, some progress is being made. The increasing number of genetic counseling centers across the United States is of more than ordinary significance in this respect.

The police occupy a commanding position in these new approaches to the crime problem. Police administrations have the machinery and the methods to focus the community's attack on crime at the source—the formative years in the life of the individual when behavior patterns are taking form. They have mobile personnel who can move rapidly and routinely into areas where other agencies would find unhampered movement difficult. They have the power of the state behind them. Through the nature of their work, the police are more familiar than any other organized group with crime hazards in the community. They are in a position to understand the criminal and the forces which result in his or her development. They have in their files the basic data concerning crime and delinquency necessary for an intelligent approach to the problems of delinquency and crime.

Because the police and the schools are generally first to have official contact with problem youngsters, they have an opportunity that other branches of government lack. Cases of developing delinquency and the conditioning factors which produce them come under observation by the police and schools long before other social agencies are aware of them. Also, the police operate under a mandate from the people to achieve crime control and to preserve the public peace and order, a task which carries with it some of the obligations of leadership.

The prevention of crime is a fundamental responsibility of the patrol force. The preventive role of the individual beat patrol officer is a basic element of modern police service service. The mere presence of a properly organized and efficiently operating patrol force has traditionally been regarded as one of the greatest crime deterrents developed by organized society.

The preventive effectiveness of the individual beat patrol officer is largely reflected by the amount of crime and delinquency reported in the patrol area to which he or she is assigned. A point is reached in the growth of a community and its police department when, due to an increased juvenile caseload, the preventive role of the patrol officer must be supplemented by specialized assistance. The crime prevention division or unit has become a standard feature of American police organization and practice.

The establishment of a new service unit within a department involves either drawing upon the personnel resources of an existing unit, usually the patrol division, or recruiting from the outside. Police administrators generally recognize that a minimum of five percent of the departmental strength should be assigned exclusively to crime prevention work. This means that the police administrator with a force of twenty officers should assign at least one to work primarily on juvenile cases. In smaller departments, the responsibilities of the task must be assumed by a member or members of the patrol force.

The crime prevention or juvenile unit should have status in the organizational structure equal to that of other divisions, and as a line agency should be located under the direct control of the commanding officer in charge of line operations. The elementary functions of a police department and its crime prevention unit include discovery of cases and their investigation. Beyond this point, current practice involves two general types of operations. The distinction is determined largely by the procedural patterns employed in the disposition of juvenile cases. In the first type of operation, the police force functions primarily as an agency of discovery and referral. Juvenile cases are referred to the juvenile court, to the welfare department, or to some other social agency or agencies in the community, where disposition of the case rests. Wherever this type of operation prevails, the police have essentially abdicated their obligations and responsibilities with respect to delinquency and crime prevention.

In a more professional and enlightened approach, the police juvenile unit assumes responsibility for the disposition of a substantial number of juvenile offenders and cases of beginning behavior deviation which come to the attention of the department. Here, the law enforcement function is augmented by a clinical approach to the adjustment of behavior difficulties.

When Chief August Vollmer established the Crime Prevention Division in the Police Department of Berkeley, California on July 1, 1925, *the first of its kind* in police history, the division was given jurisdiction in all cases involving women and girls, and boys up to the age of twelve. The program was predicated upon the problem youngster's need for special study, care, and control. Its distinguishing features included a marked limitation on "case referrals" and a definite police thrust into the challenging realm of pre-delinquency.

The social case work approach to young behavior problems encountered by the police dominated the operation. This was indicated clearly by the qualifications Chief Vollmer required of the person (Mrs. E. G. Lossing) appointed as head of the new Division, as well as the members of her staff, who were to be trained social caseworkers. These qualifications included:

> *The woman police officer in charge of the Crime Prevention Division of the Berkeley Police Department, as well as each additional policewoman who may be appointed later, shall be a trained social worker, preferably with the stress laid on the psychological and psychiatric training, as evidenced by a certificate of recognition from a recognized Graduate School of Social Work, or the equivalent of such a certificate from a school of the first class, and she must have had some practical experience in work with delinquents.*
>
> *The policewoman's work in Berkeley will consist largely in dealing with predelinquency problems. Primarily, it is intended to harmonize the agencies that are here in an effort to concentrate these forces that deal with the health, education and morals of the children upon the problem child long before he reaches the police station.*[15]

In processing an individual case, the preliminary factual investigation was followed by diagnostic procedures which sought to identify those factors in the individual and his or her environment responsible for behavior deviations. The clinical resources of the community, including medical, psychological and psychiatric services, were used. These findings were integrated with the social case history of the youngster as developed through the investigations of the police case worker; together, they formed the basis for an "official" or "unofficial" disposition of the case.

If the circumstances warranted placing the youngster in a detention home and referral of the case to the juvenile court (which seldom occurred), the case was classified as "official" and no longer considered active in the files of the crime prevention division. However, division personnel cooperated with the court and probation officers by making available the factual and diagnostic data already assembled; in addition, they gave testimony if required and conducted follow-up work in connection with the case when requested to do so.

"Unofficial" action consisted of keeping the case within the department, official referral only as a last resort. In most cases, the factual investigation and diagnostic data did not warrant such referral, yet it was necessary to recognize the fact that the youngster required help to avoid later tragedy. Based upon the case diagnosis, the child was placed upon "unofficial" probation, and the police case worker brought the youngster into contact with those community resources which would be of the greatest therapeutic value.

The foregoing type of police operation is featured in the First, Second, Third, Fourth and Fifth Editions of the author's *Police Organization and Management,* now in its twenty-eighth year as a university text and police reference work.[16] Among others who, like Chief Vollmer, support the police use of the community's clinical resources to implement the diagnosis and treatment of developing behavior problems are the late O. W. Wilson, Superintendent of the Chicago Police Department and former Dean of the School of Criminology at the University of California, and Roy C. McLaren, former Director of Field Operations for the International Association of Chiefs of Police and now Chief of Police in Arlington, Virginia.[17]

The police field itself has yet to reach general agreement concerning the nature and scope of police operations in the crime prevention division. Richard W. Kobetz, for example, holds that the only appropriate alternatives open to the police in a juvenile case are referral to the juvenile court or referral to one or more social agencies in the community, while police participation in a casework or treatment approach is off-limits.[18] This view is probably influenced by the public's image of the police role, which even today is seen as being primarily punitive.

Future policy with respect to youth in the community who are nearing the threshold of trouble will be influenced by the capability, training, experience, and philosophy of the police administrator, as policy decisions are made at the level of top management. There has been a general failure to recognize the basic principle that the formulation of police policy, both the means and the method, is not a function of public opinion. The people can approve or disapprove. But average citizens have no time for an intensive study of police science and administration, and it would be unwise to expect of them an interest in government that would go to any such lengths. Administrative and managerial talent must therefore initiate those procedures which will produce results. Bruce Smith stated as early as 1933:[19]

> *Police service has become a complex and highly technical calling. The problems of law enforcement can be satisfactorily described and made real only to persons who have had some experience with public administration, or who have themselves known the complexities which surround the business of handling and directing large numbers of men.*
>
> *In other words, the task of law enforcement is now a problem of management, and lies beyond the comprehension of those who are not experienced in it.*

> *Such experience is possessed by relatively too few members of a popular electorate to provide a sufficient backlog of informed and understanding public opinion.*

It may be said, then, that the quality of American police service is a direct and inherent responsibility of administration and is not predetermined, as is generally assumed, by public opinion.

Thus, on July 1, 1925, Chief Vollmer broke with tradition, as he did on so many occasions in a brilliant career, to bring change to the field of crime prevention and control through an entirely new kind of police operation, supported by the findings of research and scientific method.

This writer became a uniformed officer in the Berkeley Police Department in December of 1925, six months after the establishment of the new crime prevention division. In the months and years ahead, he had a reserved seat at a performance, characterized by what seemed miracle after miracle, in the transformation and redirection of one youth's life pattern, at a point when temperament, attitudes and other values are flexible and behavior patterns are just beginning to emerge.

It was a typical case—that of a nine-year old girl who one day conferred her favors on five boys under a bridge in a remote section of Berkeley. The boys talked and the case came to the attention of the police. Preliminary investigation by social workers in the crime prevention division indicated that this pattern of behavior had prevailed for some time. Her school record was unsatisfactory, although she was of above average intelligence. Certain factors in the home and the neighborhood operated as a negative influence upon the girl and her two younger brothers, and serious emotional problems complicated the situation.

In the due course of time, through the efforts of sympathetic and trained personnel in the crime prevention division, and with the availability of appropriate resources in the community, she turned her life around. She graduated from high school and the university, appropriately enough with a major in sociology, and eventually married a young engineer.

Perhaps police administration in this country may take another look at its role in delinquency and crime prevention. The comments of the Honorable Seymour Gelber, Circuit Court Judge in Miami, Florida, speaking in 1976 before the 83rd Annual Conference of the International Association of Chiefs of Police in Miami, may be prophetic. Emphasizing a close police liaison with the public schools, he stated:

> *More and more police departments are involved in new programs concerning diversion, counseling, learning disabilities, and other rehabilitative techniques. The police officer now finds it difficult to say, as he once so frequently did, "I arrested the little thief, and some social worker had him back in the street before I could get back to the station house." For today, that social worker he refers to, may be a fellow officer in his own department.*
>
> *All in all, with the increasingly large number of police diversionary programs, and with a new focus on dealing with the schools, I see the police accepting and fulfilling a whole new area of responsibility in the juvenile field. You can view it as an awful nuisance to be avoided, or as a great opportunity to be sought.*

But notwithstanding your perception, this new role is here. It is upon you, and you'd best adjust yourself to its significance.

As an example of the new trend are the prototype programs that are operating in the Dallas Police Department and in the Los Angeles County Sheriff's Office. These appear to be organized, disciplined, structured diversionary and counseling programs that are funded, researched and equipped to perform. I recommend them to you for further study and consideration.

Like every other crisis that has ever imposed itself upon society, the public has learned to expect the police to provide the answers. So welcome aboard.

The Dallas Operation

Unique among police youth services or delinquency and crime prevention programs is the Dallas operation, which carries forward the Vollmer tradition of police involvement in the process of behavior modification among youth.

The Youth Services Program of the Dallas Police Department was funded by a federal grant through the Criminal Justice Division of Texas, for the period from December 1, 1973 through September 10, 1976. Since that time, the City of Dallas has continued funding the project in the regular police operating budget. The rationale for the development of the program was based on the excessive number of juveniles being referred to the Juvenile Department for conventional processing through the juvenile justice system. There was also an excessively high rate of recidivism.

Following an intensive orientation and training program for personnel assigned to the Youth Services Program, the operation was launched near the end of 1973.

Youth Section Programs The Youth Section of the Dallas Police Department has four major youth programs, all of which are designed to meet the needs of the department and the community in dealing with youthful offenders. The four programs are: The Youth Action Centers Program; The First Offender Program (FOP); The Counseling Unit (Youth Service Program); and the Fireman/Counselor Program.

Youth Action Centers There are seventeen police officers, two sergeants and one lieutenant assigned to the Youth Action Centers, located in the schools. School officials and probation and police officers work closely in the operation of these centers. The police officers maintain the basic liaison with Dallas area schools. Their duties include processing truants, conducting speaking engagements, handling offenses and disruptions committed in the schools, and conducting traffic safety education and enforcement. In addition to these duties, the officers mark and enter bicycles into the Police Department's computer identification system. The officers work closely with school administration officials and individual school principals, acting as police representatives in dealing with problems in and around the schools.

These officers handle a large number of incidents, and if they were not available youth taken into custody would have to be handled by patrol officers and Youth Section investigators. The only costs of the program are the salaries of the officers and the price of their supportive equipment.

Diversion Programs

In Dallas the First Offender Program, and Counseling Unit are used as diversionary alternatives to the standard juvenile justice system. The Firemen/Counselor Program is an extension of the Counseling Unit. At the first level after arrest, minor offenders are diverted into the First Offender Program. At the next level, more serious offenders who need more in-depth services are diverted to the Counseling Unit. At the final level the most serious repeat offenders are referred to the Juvenile Department.

The process begins when a youth is taken into custody for a law violation. The field unit officer takes the juvenile to the Youth Section and an investigator is assigned the case. The investigator explores the offense and arrest situation with both the youth and the parents, and then makes a determination of the youth's disposition. The investigator has four alternative dispositions:

1. release to parent, no action
2. release to parent and assign to Counseling Unit
3. release to parent and assign to First Offender Program
4. refer to the Juvenile Department.

In making the disposition the investigator takes into account the offense, prior record, needs of the juvenile, and the parents' and youth's attitude. If the youth is eligible for the FOP or Counseling Unit program the investigator obtains a voluntary commitment from the child and parents and enrolls them in the program. A computerized identification and tracking system, developed as part of the program, facilitates the police investigator's processing of the case.

First Offender Program The First Offender Program consists of lecture-presentations within an informal classroom setting, presented by Youth Section police officers. The goal of the program is to make first offenders more aware of the law and of the consequences of their behavior. Separate sessions are conducted for youths taken into custody for minor drug offenses and other offenses. The regular presentation for first offenders consists of a slide show and lectures covering various aspects of the law, with an emphasis on the juvenile justice system. There is a separate presentation for drug offenders, consisting of slide shows and lectures by medical personnel and ex-offenders which help make first offenders more aware of the health, psychological, and legal aspects of drug abuse. These programs are now conducted by on-duty Youth Section personnel. Two three hour non-drug sessions are conducted each week, while one drug related program is conducted over a two night period each week. Each child referred to the

F.O.P. is required to attend either one of the non-drug sessions or the two-night drug related programs.

The recidivism rate for the First Offender Program is 17.4%, compared to a control group rate of 24.6%. The program is being continued by on duty operations and counseling unit personnel. The only costs are the salaries of two persons for each session and the price of supplies and equipment.

Counseling Unit A youth enrolled in the Counseling Unit is assigned to a police youth counselor in the region in which the juvenile lives. The City of Dallas is divided into four regions, with three counselors assigned to each area. The youth and parents then proceed through a three stage process involving: 1) intake, 2) direct, and 3) follow up. During the intake stages the youth is evaluated with respect to home, school, and free time problem areas. Following this assessment, the counselor develops minimal goals for the youth and parents and shows them how skills training during the direct phase will help them reach the goals. The youth and parents next enter the direct phase of the program, during which they meet in a group for 16 hours over one month. Content for the youth includes: (1) physical fitness training to increase level of energy and involvement in recreational activities, (2) emotional-interpersonal skills training to facilitate more effective communication, and (3) training in classroom learning skills to facilitate better classroom behavior and to improve grades. While the youths receive their training, the parents are also receiving 16 hours of training on how to manage their child's behavior and how to improve their communication. Before each meeting is over, the parents and youth come together to practice what they have learned. They then receive homework assignments. Skills training for youth and parents is emphasized because the Texas Youth Council Needs Assessment in 1974 indicated that juvenile offenders' lack of critical skills contributed to their delinquency.

Following the direct phase of the program, a youth enters the follow-up phase. During this phase the youth and parents are placed on programs in which they apply their newly learned skills to problem areas assessed during intake. Examples of such problem areas are school attendance, obeying limits at home, getting involved in an activity, and improving communication. The youth and the parents meet with the counselor once a month for four months to review progress. The parents are encouraged during this process to begin on their own to develop management plans for their children and to use the counselors for feedback on overall progress. At the same time a youth may be assigned a fireman counselor at the nearest fire station. This fireman counselor (a volunteer with sixteen hours of training) meets with the youth once a week for the four month period to monitor the youth's programs, to tutor, to provide constructive recreation programs, and to provide strong male leadership.

Throughout the three stage process the parents and youth must achieve certain performance objectives before they are ready to go to the next level. During the intake stage they have to admit that there are problems and make a concrete commitment to complete the program (i.e. attend meetings, do homework assignments). During direct, both youth and parents have to make demonstrable improvements at participating in meetings, learning the skills, and applying the skills at home, school, and during free time behavior. Finally, during the follow-up and before termination is considered, the youth and parents have to achieve the minimal improvement goals outlined during the intake phase. If there are serious breakdowns during the process, the youth and parents are recycled through the direct phase.

If supplementary action is needed at any stage of the program, community agencies can be utilized to augment the program efforts. Various referral services such as recreation, special education services, welfare services, mental health services, and other clinical resources are brought into play as necessary.

The counselors prepare for the teaching delivery by developing systematic skills curricula for both parents and youth. These curricula serve as lesson plans and allow the counselor to maximize skill learning for the youth and parents. Each skill's module explains what the skill is, why learning it is important, when and where the skill can be used, and how to apply the skill at home, school, and in free time. The module also includes homework assignments. The skills are presented in a "tell, show, and do" format; the learners hear about the skill, see it used, and then practice it themselves. Thus, the curriculum ensures that the goal of skills acquisition and application are achieved. The Counseling Unit Program is designed to work with a child and the parents for a six month period.

For 2,833 juveniles who have completed the counseling program the recidivism rate is 10.7%, compared to a control group rate of 44.6%. The cost of continuing the program at the current level is approximately $225,000 annually.

Fireman/Counselor Program The Fireman/Counselor Program, a coordinated effort between the Police and Fire Departments, utilizes on-duty firemen in the stations to work with juvenile offenders referred to them from the follow-up phase of the counseling program. This meets the juvenile's need for extended contact and increases the number of juveniles who can be handled in the counseling program.

The primary objective of the Fireman Counselor Program is to provide for the child a friendly, teaching, caring, and supportive relationship. Firemen are uniquely suited to such a volunteer counseling role for a number of reasons. As a group, they possess a family and community-oriented outlook as well as stable, mature personalities. Additionally, the location of fire stations throughout the community makes these counseling services conveniently available to a large number of juveniles.

Counseling takes place in the fire station while the fireman is on duty. The YSP counselor will arrange an immediate orientation meeting with a counselor and the youth. After this first explanatory session, the juvenile and his counselor meet by themselves, normally on a weekly basis. Later they may decide to meet more or less frequently. The Fireman/Counselor Program is designed to last for a four month period. If the fire company has to respond to an emergency call before the juvenile arrives or during the meeting, the youth is to go home, to be contacted by the counselor who will reschedule another meeting. The counselors, who participate in the program on a voluntary basis, have found that the fire station, its equipment, and its activities are of great interest to most children.

The Fireman/Counselor Program operated under a $32,829.00 federal grant from March 1, 1976 through January 31, 1977. Sixty-six firemen volunteered and had been trained to work in the program. An application has been submitted to the Criminal Justice Division to expand the program to 300 volunteers and include all fire stations in the city. The project has received 70 referrals to date and has reduced the recidivism rate from 10.7% to 7.1% for those participating.

The implementation of the department's diversionary programs has brought about a significant reduction in the number of referrals (workload) to the Dallas County Juvenile Department. In 1973 the referral rate was 74% of all youth taken into custody. Since the diversionary programs have been operational, referral of cases to the juvenile court has dropped to 62%, a reduction of 12%. The recidivism rate for all youth taken into custody in 1976 was 50.3%. The recidivism rate in the Youth Services Program is 10.7%; in the First Offender Program, 17.4%. The Diversionary Programs are voluntary and may last from one night in the First Offender Program to approximately one year if a youngster goes into the Youth Services Program and then progresses to the Fireman/Counselor Program.

Figure 6.1
Juvenile Offenders Contacted or Taken into Custody by D.P.D. During 1975*

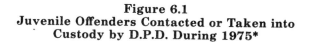

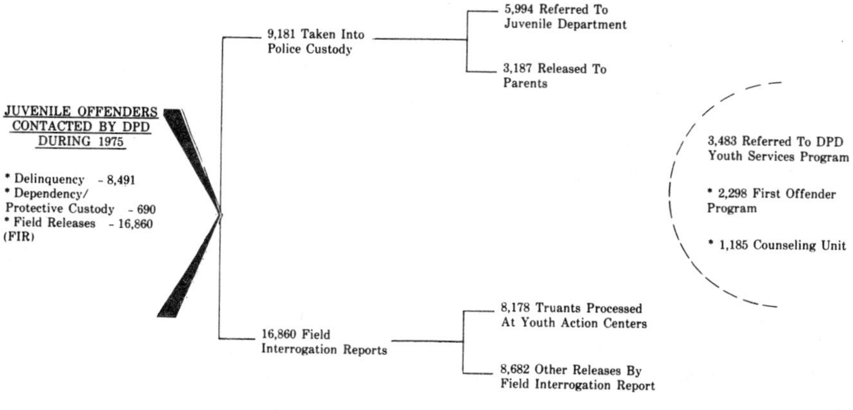

*Annual Report, Police Department, Dallas, Texas, 1975.

The Los Angeles County Sheriff's Diversion Approach

In 1970, the Los Angeles County Sheriff's Department launched one of the country's most ambitious delinquency and crime prevention projects. Known as the Juvenile Referral and Resource Program, it is geared to the diversion of selected first time or minor offenders away from judicial disposition in the juvenile justice system to community-based organizations which have the resources, clinical and social, to help the youngster with beginning behavior deviation problems. In addition, a concerted effort is made to reach "hard core" delinquents, including burglary and narcotics violators, through the diversionary process.[20]

Well known for the strictly professional calibre of its operations, the Los Angeles County Sheriff's Department is involved with thirteen diversion projects, and actively administers three of them—*Cerritos Corridor, Positive Alternatives for Youth, and Southeast Early Diversion.* These three are essentially the same operation, divided geographically. The department defines *DIVERSION* as *The strategy of providing dispositional alternatives which will prevent young people with behavior problems from getting "locked into" the formal juvenile justice and corrections system.* Typical criteria for diversion, applied by one juvenile sergeant who is a graduate of the Delinquency Control Institute at the University of Southern California with sixteen years of experience in the department as well as three years in the field of juvenile investigation, include:

1. Mutual agreement of both parent and child that referral to a community agency would be beneficial.
2. Safety of both the community and the child, which must not be jeopardized. For example, is it safe to divert a youth back to the community after a violent child molestation incident?
3. Prior referrals, if any. Have they been beneficial to the youth and/or family?
4. Prior police contacts, if any.
5. Timing of offenses by age. What is the chronological pattern of offenses? For example, are offenses linked into a discrete time period? (i.e., 13 to 15½ yrs.—no offenses; 15½ to 16 yrs.—four offenses; 16 to 17 yrs.—no offenses.)
6. Quality of prior offenses.
7. Quantity of offenses—unless very numerous (which could possible indicate pathology), quantity would be considered least in importance.
8. Family relationships.
9. Present offense.
   a. Here again, the safety of the community and the child are heavily involved.

b. The severity of the crime is carefully considered, and crimes of extreme violence generally are excluded from the list of divertable cases.

Crime Countermeasures

In addition to using a case work approach to individual behavior problems, an efficient police force seeks to lower the crime rate by encouraging merchants, banks, jewelry stores, and other high hazard locations to install burglary and hold-up alarm systems wired directly to police headquarters. The installation of improved locking devices to promote greater building security, increased illumination of buildings from within and without, proper handling of cash and high-value merchandise, and the education of the public in self-protection against criminal attack all constitute activities intended to repress crime by eliminating the opportunity for it. The modification or elimination of environmental hazards which threaten the community's youth also falls in this category.

Within this frame of reference, science and technology have not been slow in addressing their resources to two important objectives —a reduction in the opportunity for delinquent and criminal behavior, and an increase in police apprehension capability. Most notable in this connection are the Annual Carnahan Conferences on Crime Countermeasures and the Annual International Conferences devoted to the same cause, the latter sponsored by the Department of Electrical Engineering, College of Engineering, and Office of Continuing Education of the University of Kentucky. The following page, which reproduces a *Call for Papers* for the 1977 Conference, indicates the scope and content of these programs.

In a closely related area, there is an expanding and promising development in various areas of the country. Police personnel join with members of the faculty from universities and colleges to teach mini-courses at the high school level on various aspects of the criminal justice system. Wherever these programs have been initiated, they have met with an enthusiastic response from both students and school personnel. Instructors are selected on the basis of demonstrated audience appeal, a working knowledge of the subject matter, and teaching ability. Instruction is provided on a volunteer basis at no cost to the public school system.

It is a relatively simple matter to determine when most students are scheduled for a free period, in order to provide the maximum opportunity for attendance at course sessions, which are usually one hour each week for a period of from five to seven weeks. It is quite easy to determine when the most students have a free period during the day. Then the course may be offered during that time. Such courses usually last one class period and are offered for five to six weeks. It is generally conceded that the initial course should be 'non-credit' and should not include any exams or papers. Generally, handouts at each lecture outline important points and explain terminology where necessary. Usually, about one-third of the hour is left open as a question and answer period.

Call for Papers

1978 Carnahan Conference
on Crime Countermeasures
May 17-19, 1978

CARNAHAN HOUSE, LEXINGTON, KENTUCKY

Papers are invited for the 1978 Carnahan Conference on Crime Countermeasures. Principal emphasis will be placed on engineering developments as applied to law enforcement, security and crime prevention.

Related papers are solicited which describe recent developments in the following fields:

- Police Systems
- Command, control and communication systems
- Alarm devices and systems
- Computer systems security
- Automatic vehicle monitoring
- Automatic identification and authentication of voice, handwriting, fingerprints, and other signatures
- Entry control systems
- Searching aids: x-ray, sonic, magnetic, microwave
- Electromagnetic spectrum conservation
- Communication privacy and security including advanced modulation techniques
- Pollution detection
- Related areas of basic science and novel applications

This conference will provide a forum for users, developers, and manufacturers to review state-of-the-art techniques in this specialized area. Conference Proceedings will be published and distributed to each attendee as well as selected libraries throughout the world.

Deadlines:

Abstract (200 words) . . . September 19, 1977
Notification of acceptance . . November 8, 1977
Paper deadline . . . . January 16, 1978

Mail Abstracts to:

John S. Jackson, Proceedings Editor
Dept. of Electrical Engineering
University of Kentucky
Lexington, Kentucky 40506
Telephone: (606) 257-3926 or 258-5949

EXECUTIVE COMMITTEE

William D. Barkhau Consultant	John S. Jackson University of Kentucky	Lawrence D. Sanson General Telephone Company of Ky.
David K. Blythe University of Kentucky	Thomas P. Kabaservice The MITRE Corporation	Earl L. Steele University of Kentucky
George C. Byrne Stanford Research Institute	Walter S. Konar Stanford University	Ralph J. Summers GTE Sylvania, Inc.
James C. Daly Aerospace Corporation	Sanford A. Mullings Jamaica Constabulary Office	Louis L. Taylor Bernard Johnson, Inc.
Werner Heinl Bundeskriminalamt	Fred Nichols IEEE EMC Group	Carmen J. Tona Consultant
Kenneth D. Hopper Bell Telephone Laboratories	Alan N. Rapsey United Kingdom Home Office	Joseph H. Wegstein National Bureau of Standards

Sponsored by the University of Kentucky and Institute of Electrical and Electronics Engineers

In most high school libraries, there are relevant supporting materials which the instructor can refer the students to in connection with the lectures. In one community, a senior citizen provided the high school sufficient funds to augment existing library resources with a complete collection of current texts covering all aspects of the criminal justice system.

All agree that breaking down the barriers between the police and the students is a constructive step forward. Such positive contact can influence attitudes concerning the qualities and responsibilities of good citizenship. Orientation toward professionalization in this branch of the public service, and the likelihood of encouraging some youngsters to consider the career opportunities that await them in this professional field, are additional gains not to be overlooked.

Summary

Crime and the criminal continue as an increasing threat to organized society; as a social problem, crime is second only to war in magnitude. With respect to the available instruments of social control, the repression and prevention of crime in this country rest precariously on three major elements of the criminal justice system—punishment, reform or rehabilitation, and prevention.

Informed observers agree that the impotence of punishment as a deterrent factor, and the demonstrated limitations of reform or rehabilitation, now bring into clear focus one of the greatest challenges ever to confront an organized society—a viable approach to the prevention of delinquency and crime, in which the behavioral sciences must play a commanding role.

The project of crime prevention is concerned with the offender and potential offender before the need for institutionalization or other firm measures appears. Studies have shown that, in the majority of cases, the adult criminal offender was once known to the police as a juvenile delinquent. That the young delinquent is the forerunner of the adult criminal has been proven by the analysis of thousands of criminal careers. We now generally accept the idea that it is much better to attempt reform of the juvenile delinquent than to postpone action until the individual reaches maturity as a confirmed criminal offender. Moreover, at the age of juvenile delinquency, personality, temperament, and behavior traits may still be in the formative stages, and may be more responsive to therapeutic measures than are the fixed behavior patterns of the adult criminal offender.

Figuring largely on the juvenile offender's agenda is a procedure that has come to be known as *diversionary justice,* which simply means diversion of the case away from formal legal adjudication. It is a prejudicial disposition carrying the case around the judicial process into a neutral zone, in which other resources of the community may be brought into play toward the adjustment and re-direction of a life pattern.

The philosophy of crime prevention stems from the conviction, now confirmed by research, that the burglar, prostitute, automobile thief, thug, and others in the "twilight zone" of human behavior do not become that way suddenly. The records show that in the majority of cases, they start their abortive development in early childhood and then progress by almost imperceptible degrees into confirmed criminal offenders. The juvenile delinquent and subsequent adult criminal offender of today was once a child with beginning behavior deviations which were permitted to develop largely undetected and without receiving appropriate clinical attention.

Early discovery and diagnosis of the physically, mentally, and socially different child is gradually opening the door to opportunities for the prevention of delinquency and crime, which now overshadow the man-hunt and the sequence of events thereafter. Genius that he was, Chief August Vollmer of the Police Department in Berkeley, California early perceived the futility of the jail and the penitentiary, and became convinced that the police and community agencies must address their attention to beginning deviations and the conditions which induce them.

The foregoing brings into sharp relief the need for prediction mechanisms which will assist in identifying potential pre-delinquents in the first, second, and third grades, and perhaps even younger. In this manner, the clinical resources of the community can be brought into play on behalf of the youngster. Prediction scales and techniques, increasingly sophisticated, have been and continue to be the subject of extensive research. A large body of literature is now available concerning attempts to predict human behavior. While it is true that as of yet no estimate of future behavior, arrived at by any means, can be made with mathematical certainty, a statement of degree of probability is conceded to be an appropriate prediction objective.

The police occupy a commanding position in these new approaches to the crime problem. Police administration has the machinery and the methods to focus the community's attack on crime. The police conduct an around-the-clock operation. They have rapidly mobile personnel who can move routinely into areas where other agencies would find unhampered movement difficult. They have the power of the state behind them. Also, the police operate under a mandate from the people for security and law and order.

In the early 1920s, Chief Vollmer set the pace through the establishment of a Crime Prevention Division in the Berkeley Police Department, the first of its kind in police history. The social casework approach was to dominate the operation, as indicated by Vollmer's charge that:

> *The woman police officer in charge of the Crime Prevention Division in the Berkeley Police Department, as well as each additional policewoman who may be appointed later, shall be a trained social worker with stress laid on psychiatric and psychological training.*

The brilliant success of the new Crime Prevention Division is a matter of record. As of 1978, growing evidence of a re-birth of the Vollmer tradition holds an important promise for the years ahead.

In addition to the casework approach to individual behavior problems, an efficient police force seeks to depress the crime rate by encouraging merchants, banks, jewelry stores and other high hazard locations to install burglary and hold-up alarm systems wired directly to police headquarters. The police may also educate the public in other activities intended to repress crime by reducing the opportunity. The modification or elimination of environmental hazards to youth in the community may also be part of the police effort to drive down the crime rate.

Topics For Discussion

1. **Discuss the deterrent value of punishment. On what would you base your opinion that it is successful, or that it has apparently failed, as an instrument of crime repression and control?**

2. **Analyze rehabilitation as an alternative to punishment. Has it failed or succeeded? If the former, should it be abandoned altogether, or given further trial? If the latter, what recommendations would you make?**
3. **Why would an all-out attack on the problem of crime and the criminal at the age level of juvenile delinquency probably be limited in its results?**
4. **Discuss some of the factors that have contributed to a rapid improvement in police apprehension capability during the past quarter century.**
5. **What effect does enforcement pressure have in terms of crime rates? Explain your answer.**
6. **Do you agree with the Vollmer thesis, which focuses on beginning behavior deviations in the early years of the youngster's life, even kindergarten, and brings the clinical resources (social, psychological, psychiatric and medical) of the community into contact with the problem? Why or why not?**
7. **Discuss the police role within the above frame of reference.**
8. **Draw an organizational diagram of the police juvenile unit in a department with a personnel strength of 150 officers. Indicate its location in the organizational structure.**
9. **What would you consider to be the desirable qualifications of a police juvenile officer?**
10. **How would you determine or measure the efficiency or effectiveness of the police juvenile unit?**
11. **It has been stated by one observer that no crime at all would lead to social stagnation, since social change and social progress involve conflict and violation of existing mores. Prepare a comment of about 150 words responding to this statement.**

References

1. M. Ehrligh, "The Deterrent Effect of Criminal Law Enforcement," *Journal of Legal Issues* 1, 1972, 259; J. Gibbs, "Crime, Punishment and Deterrence," *Social Sciences Quarterly* 48, 1968, 515; L. Ball, "Why Punishment Fails," *American Journal of Corrections* 31, 1969, 19; Llad Phillips and Harold L. Votey, "An Economic Analysis of the Deterrent Effect of Law Enforcement on Criminal Activity," *Journal of Criminal Law, Criminology and Police Science* 63, 1972.
2. William C. Bailey and Ruth P. Lott, "Crime, Punishment and Personality: An Examination of the Deterrence Question," *Journal of Criminal Law and Criminology* 99, 1976.
3. John Monohan, A review of *The Future of Imprisonment,* by Nerval Morris, Chicago Press, 1974.
4. Louis F. Carney, *Introduction to Correctional Science,* New York: McGraw-Hill, 1974, p. 388.

5. See *Statistical Abstract of the United States* and *Uniform Crime Reports.* U.S. Government Printing Office, Washington, D.C.
6. August Vollmer, *Community Coordination,* Coordinating Councils Inc., March-April 1939.
7. Warden James A. Johnston, Federal Penitentiary at Alcatraz; *Functions of the Modern Prison,* quoted in an address delivered by Henry W. Wiehofen, U. S. Assistant Attorney General, *The Police and Crime Prevention,* at the University of Illinois, June 17, 1937.
8. Walter Dunbar, *California Youth Authority Quarterly,* Vol. 16 No. 1, 1963.
9. Lowell J. Carr, *Delinquency Control,* New York: Harper Bros., 1938.
10. August Vollmer, *Pre-delinquency,* Journal of Criminal Law and Criminology, XIV, 2, Aug. 1923, pp. 279-283.

    Nathan Bodin, *Do Problem Children Become Delinquents and Criminals?* Condensed from a Master of Arts Thesis, University of California, Journal of Criminal Law and Criminology, November-December, 1936, pp. 545-559.
11. William G. Long, *The Relation of Juvenile Courts to Other Agencies,* Pullman, Proceedings of the Fifth Pacific Northwest Law Enforcement Conference, 1944, p. 26; E. K. Wickman, *Children's Behavior and Teacher Attitudes,* New York: Commonwealth Fund, Division of Publications, 1928, pp. 232-33.
12. Robert T. Williams, "On Prevention: After the Fact—Before the Fact," *The Police Chief,* June 1973, P. 20.
13. Bodin, *op cit.*
14. See Eleanor and Sheldon Glueck, *Predicting Delinquency and Crime,* Cambridge: Harvard Univ. Press, 1959; Eleanor and Sheldon Glueck, *Unraveling Juvenile Delinquency,* Cambridge: Harvard Univ. Press, 1951, pp. 15, 257-71, 284, 288; Eleanor and Sheldon Glueck, *Delinquents and Non-delinquents in Perspective,* Cambridge: Harvard Univ. Press, 1968, p. 184; William C. Kvaraceus et al., *Delinquent Behavior, Principles and Practices,* Washington: National Education Association, 1959, pp. 32-51; Robert M. MacIver, *The Prevention and Control of Delinquency,* New York: Atherton, 1967, pp. 104-123; President's Commission on Law Enforcement and Administration of Justice, *The Challenge of Crime in a Free Society,* U.S. Govt. Printing Office, 1967, p. 71; President's Commission on Law Enforcement and Administration of Justice, *Task Force Report: Juvenile Delinquency,* U.S. Govt. Printing Office, 1967, p. 18.
15. *Departmental Rules and Regulations,* Police Department, Berkeley, California, 1925.
16. V. A. Leonard and Harry W. More, *Police Organization and Management,* Mineola, N. Y.: Foundation Press 1978.
17. O. W. Wilson and Roy C. McLaren, *Police Administration,* New York: McGraw-Hill 1972.
18. Richard W. Kobetz, *The Police Role and Juvenile Delinquency,* Gaithersburg, Md.: International Association of Chiefs of Police, p. 264.
19. Bruce Smith, "Politics and Law Enforcement," The Annals of the American Academy of Political and Social Science, Vol. 169, September 1933, p. 72.
20. Information made available through the courtesy of the Los Angeles County Sheriff's Department.

Annotated Bibliography

Carney, Louis P., *Introduction to Correctional Science,* McGraw-Hill, New York, 1974. With its constructive approach to the problems and the future of correctional administration, this work recognizes the "critical and relentless" need for trained and committed professionals. While conceding that imprisonment is a failure as an instrument of rehabilitation, the author lays a strong foundation for community-based corrections. He points out that the idea is not new, and that since the time probation and parole began, community-based corrections has been a progressively developing concept. The author indicates, among other things, that approximately two-thirds of the correctional case load of the country is already under supervision in the community and that the challenge ahead is to expand existing practice.

Edgar, J. M., *Juvenile Delinquency Prevention,* National Institute of Law Enforcement and Criminal Justice, Law Enforcement Assistance Administration, Washington, D. C., released May 11, 1977. An important and carefully prepared compilation of data concerning delinquency prevention programs and related projects.

Kenney, John P., and Pursuit, Dan G., *Police Work With Juveniles and the Administration of Juvenile Justice,* Fourth Edition, Charles C. Thomas, Publisher, 1970. Professors Kenney and Pursuit have provided a well-written, authoritative and practical procedural manual for a police juvenile unit and its personnel. They cover, among other things, the selection and training of juvenile officers, community coordination for delinquency prevention and control, youth gangs, the problems of narcotics and sex crimes, and juvenile unit operations. The authors go beyond a basic description of police services for youth and provide resource material and guidelines not otherwise accessible to the officer working with young people.

Kobetz, Richard W., *The Police Role and Juvenile Delinquency,* International Association of Chiefs of Police, Washington, D.C. 1971. Well known for his contributions to the field, the author's presentation includes analyses of the nature and extent of the problem, contemporary police juvenile operations, police action in juvenile cases, guidelines for policy formulation, and the administration of juvenile units.

Kobetz, Richard W., and Bosarge, Betty B., *Juvenile Justice Administration,* International Association of Chiefs of Police, 1973. This comprehensive volume represents a successful effort to bring "the state of the art" into contemporary perspective and develop recommendations to improve the operation of the entire system. The authors take a dim view of police efforts at extending the range of activity in the prevention cycle beyond the referral function.

Leonard, V. A., *Police Crime Prevention,* Charles C. Thomas, Springfield, 1972. Written for the smaller police departments with a personnel strength of from one to seventy-five officers, this volume portrays the futility of depending on enforcement alone in the strategy of crime suppression and control, and presents a viable police program for the prevention of delinquency and crime.

Leonard, V. A., and More, Harry W., Jr., *Police Organization and Management,* Fifth Edition, Foundation Press, Inc., Mineola, New York, 1978. Designed both as a working manual for police organizations and as a text at the university and college level, the volume draws the blueprints for best practice and procedure in the organization and management of the police enterprise, including small, medium-size and larger police departments, sheriff's departments and the state police, as well as commercial and industrial security forces.

More, Harry W., Jr., *Principles and Procedures in the Administration of Justice*, John Wiley & Sons, Inc., New York, 1975. The primary purpose of this textbook is to provide a comprehensive analysis of the principles and procedures of the justice system. This current concise and unified treatment of the subject is written for pre-service and in-service personnel and provides the reader with an understanding of the foundations of the justice system. Three of the chapters deal with the major components of the system —law enforcement, the judiciary, and corrections. The remainder of the chapters focus on the traditional elements of the criminal process, including the justice process, legal foundations, the prosecutorial process, bail, the judicial process, and prosecuting and defense attorneys.

Munro, Jim L., *Administrative Behavior and Police Organization*, W. H. Anderson, Cincinnati, 1974. This book will prove useful to research-oriented workers interested in a theoretical approach to the phenomenon of organization. Addressed specifically to the second and third year undergraduate student, it deals with the findings of research in the behavioral sciences.

Exception must be taken to the author's expressed hope (Preface) "that curriculum changes in the next decade will render police administration texts obsolete and that the general focus will be upon the administration of the criminal justice system as a coherent whole." An elementary requirement of scientific method in the approach to any major inquiry involves dividing the problem into its component parts or disciplines and addressing the analysis to each one individually, without the loss of synthesis and perspective.

Steinberg, J. Leonard and McEvoy, Donald W., *The Police and the Behavioral Sciences*, Charles C. Thomas, Publisher, Springfield, 1974. The authors view the evolution of a practical working relationship between the police and the behavioral sciences, particularly in the areas of human relations, recruitment, selection, and organizational development.

Wilson, O. W., and McLaren, Roy C., *Police Administration*, McGraw-Hill Book Company, New York, 1972. One of the mainstays in the expanding literature of the police field, this comprehensive volume is addressed primarily to the police executive and command personnel. The authors point out, however, that establishing administration as the primary audience also makes the book more useful to the critical student of police management.

7

POLICE ORGANIZATION AND ADMINISTRATION
Change or Status-Quo

Chapter Objectives

The study of this chapter should enable you to:

☑ Provide an overall perspective of police administrative organization and management.

☑ Describe the Vollmer-Wilson legacy to police administrative organization.

☑ Present the organizational models adopted by the police.

☑ Identify the impact of contemporary organizational theory upon police administrative organization.

☑ Describe a methodology for managing for results.

☑ Present styles of leadership for the police manager.

☑ Discuss methods of developing managerial skills.

☑ Present concepts of organizational development.

☑ Present a projection of what may be the future of the police.

Introduction

The work life of Americans in the police service has begun to reach a level of complexity, intensity, and challenge never before experienced. This has come about because of a general movement in society toward a fuller realization of human potential, the march of automation and administrative technology, and the need to accommodate both within the context of declining budgets and increased public scrutiny of governmental programs and institutions. The police are also faced with increasing legal constraints imposed by legislative acts and court decisions, and by administrative and citizen demands for more attention to individual and group civil rights and increased services to a variety of clients, i.e., the aged, youth, persons in custody, demonstrators and ordinary citizens. In order to meet the changing needs and demands the police are becoming more professional, are adopting new administrative and management technology and are introducing changes in methods of operation. However, change is taking place slowly and only in the more progressive departments.

As the size and complexity of any function increases, effective organization becomes more and more important. The challenge for the police today is to create an organizational framework which can respond to the demands made on it. The multiplicity of police agencies in America, ranging in size from a few officers to some thirty thousand serving diverse communities, makes it difficult to come up with universally applicable administrative organizational concepts and principles. However, there are administrative and organizational models, ways in which police departments are structured and administered, with features which when applied with imagination, may serve many needs of almost all police agencies.

The character and nature of the management of police agencies is as diverse and complex as their organizations. Management has to do with the processes which bridge the gap between the institutional requirements imposed by the community, the political and administrative environment, the legislatures and the courts, and the behavior or persons both within and outside the police agencies which influence the policing of communities. Whether there is to be effective management or not depends largely on the police executive and his ability to provide leadership for an agency. He has many ways by which he manages. He may be a "loner" or he may work closely with and through subordinates. He may be a maintainer of the status quo or he may provide dynamic leadership using the latest management techniques including management by objectives and organization development. In any event he deals with people with an organizational setting, and how he does this determines to a great extent the character and nature of policing in a community.

Projections into the future are not easy but the administrative environment for police agencies is changing. Rapid changes are taking place in our society as a whole with the development of great megalopolises, urban sprawl, and phenomonal advances in the technology for communication, transportation, and medical care. Peoples' views of themselves and others are rapidly changing. Whether they want to be or not the police are caught up in the changes and are a part of them. How they address the changes will shape the future of policing in America.

This chapter deals with some key features of the administration, management and organization of police agencies from historical, theoretical and practical perspectives.

The Vollmer-Wilson Legacy

The late August Vollmer, Chief of Police in Berkeley, California (1905-1932) was the first to perceive the need for precision and professionalism in the police service. Vollmer contributed much to the improvement of standards for selection and training of police officers. He was instrumental in initiating many of the present-day police academic programs in universities and colleges, introduced modern concepts for record keeping, adapted the radio to police communications, and introduced scientific technology as an investigative aid. He also formalized programs of citizen involvement for policing communities—the model for present-day police-community relations programs—and initiated a social service approach to aid the police in dealing with juvenile delinquency in the local community. Vollmer also attached great importance to making the beat officers responsible and accountable for most police activities on their assigned beats, including full investigation of cases, thus establishing the basic elements of the current emphasis on team policing. (For a comprehensive overview of Vollmer's contribution see Carte, Kenney, Leonard and More listed in the bibliography.)

Vollmer successfully demonstrated that a modern police operation requires community involvement, a balanced program, an administrative organization which emphasizes the role of the field officer, and the incorporation of the best of science and technology into the fight against crime. His approach to police administration put the issue of crime and criminality in perspective with the service and problem-solving needs of the public.

Building upon Vollmer's work, the late O. W. Wilson introduced the police services of America to the modern concepts of organization and management, primarily through his editing of the early editions of *Municipal Police Administration* and by his own manuscript, *Police Administration.* He adapted for police use many of the organizational concepts and principles which theoreticians had developed for use by businesses and other public agencies. He is particularly known for his operationalizing for police use the public administration model of organization which provided a theoretical yet practical way to structure and administer public agencies.

Wilson's approach to police administration put in perspective the multitude of considerations which are so essential for a full-service police operation. His work provided prescriptive guidelines for the police executive to follow in establishing relationships with mayors and city councils, and also furnished guidelines for beat layouts, space planning, records management, and traffic control, among other areas. His publications are considered handbooks on police administration, organization, management, and operations, and have been for over three decades.

Contemporary Administrative Organization Theory

Most police services are modeled on a military-bureaucratic style of organization. They are characterized by military ranks, a well defined hierarchy of relationships, unity of command, limited span of control and a delineation of staff-line relationships. The military features were first introduced by the London Metropolitan Police Department when it was organized in 1829. Introduced in the 1930's, the public administration organizational model formalized the key features of a bureaucracy which had developed over the previous century, and which O. W. Wilson introduced for use by the police in the late 1930's.

The military-bureaucratic style of organization does not, however, fit the operational nature of police work. Police work is principally a "one-on-one" operation, wherein one officer deals with an individual who has a problem, whereas military operations usually involve group action. The individual police officer exercises considerable discretion in the decisions he makes as contrasted with his military counterpart. Furthermore, most police agencies are small, thus the formal nature of relationships called for in a military-bureaucratic type organization just does not apply.

Despite the fact that it may not be the best suited for police organization, the military-bureaucratic model still remains the most popular form of organization regardless of the size of the agency. The use of military ranks as position designators and a perceived need on the part of police managers and supervisors to "command and control" have been factors limiting adoption of new approaches to organization. This has certainly limited recognition of the impact of the socio-psychological behavior of persons in the police agency on organization, a key feature of informal organization theory.

The identifying characteristic of the military-bureaucratic model is formal structure. Emphasis is placed on different job functions and different levels of superior-subordinate status. At the top of the police agency is the chief of police. The administrative support units in staff positions are just below the chief, and three major sub-units—referred to either as divisions or bureaus with sub-units—complete the structure. (see Figure 7.1) This structural approach was introduced with adoption of the public administration organizational model in the late 1930's and has several characteristics. The structure reflects grouping of similar tasks, organization by function, time, levels of authority, and occasionally place—i.e., beat or precinct station. It also reflects specialization. The administrative support units of planning, personnel and training, budget and accounts, public information, community relations, intelligence, internal affairs, and inspections perform the staff activities essential for administration and management of the agency. The major units for field operations, technical services, and investigations perform the essential line and auxiliary activities directly related to fulfilling the purposes for which the agency has been organized. Usually, the field operations unit is responsible for the patrol and traffic control activities; technical services is responsible for communications, records, jail and property control; and investigations is responsible for follow-up crime investigations, youth services, specialized investigations such as fraud and arson, and vice and narcotics control.

Figure 7.1
Traditional Police Department Organization

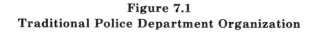

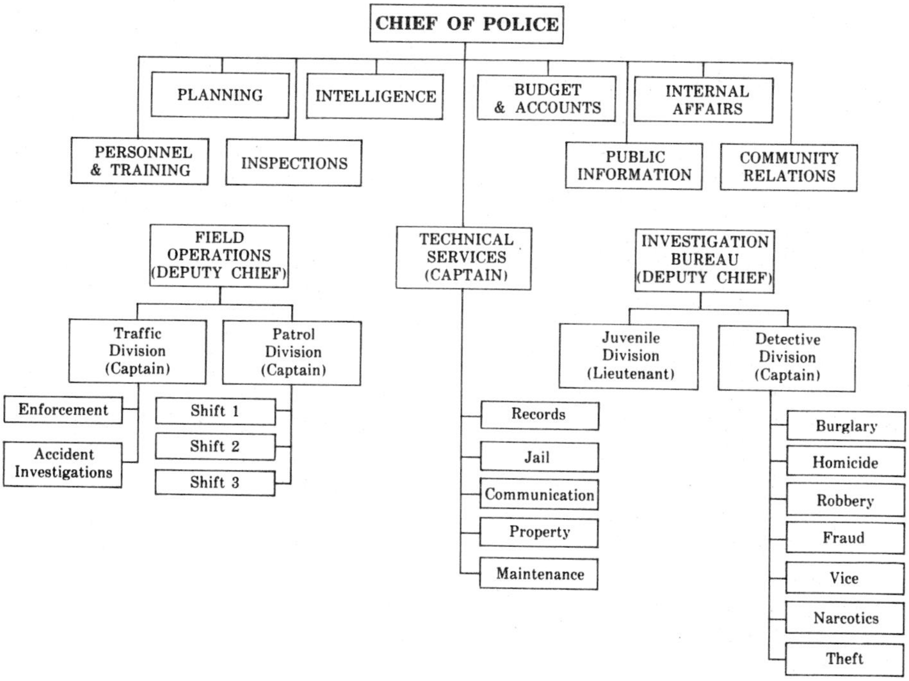

The uniformed patrol unit is limited in its responsibilities to responding to calls for services, making preliminary case investigations, patrolling (which may or may not require facilities and hazard inspections), and initiating investigations of incidents or offenses observed. The traffic unit has primary responsibility for traffic law enforcement and accident investigations. The detective unit is responsible for almost all follow-up case investigations and specialized investigations such as vice, narcotics, forged documents, arson, and frauds, and the preparation and presentation of cases for prosecution. The juvenile unit is responsible for investigations of cases which are peculiar to juveniles, such as child beating, bicycle thefts, school vandalism, and runaways, and for the final disposition of the juveniles which are involved in most cases which come to the attention of the police.

The military-bureaucratic model has advantages and disadvantages. Each individual has a job that is clearly defined. This is an advantage. There is, however, a tendency for each organizational unit to become an entity unto itself, more interested in maintaining its own status than in the organization as a whole. The structure by its very nature, tends to limit personnel development. Jobs become rountine, and morale becomes low. A sterile administrative environment is often the outcome. However, this model or any other structure can be viable with good leadership, high quality personnel, and a desire on the part of all employees to provide quality service.

Some Modifications of the Model The basic model presented here has been and is being modified. New theories of organization and management are being adopted. Police administrators are recognizing that there are organizational mixes other than the traditional which facilitate the managment processes and lead to more effective operations. Higher quality personnel with greater individual capabilities are forcing realignment of relationships and modification of numerous operations. The introduction of new technological advances, such as the computer, are having a dramatic and often traumatic effect upon both administrative and operational practices.

One major change is the expansion of the police chief's power by creation of an *office of chief of police*. This is done by incorporating into that office the administrative functions of planning, training, finance, inspections, personnel, community and public relations, internal affairs, and intelligence—the vital staff support activities so essential to administration of the agency. By assuming direct control over these functions, the chief is able to reduce friction between operational and staff personnel, since staff personnel perform their duties in the "name of the chief" as the chief's direct representatives. The chief is also placed in an improved position to direct and control line activities.

Another major change is the utilization of non-peace officer employees and administrative assistants. This eliminates the need to train officers for staff work relieving them for general police duties. In larger agencies, a combination of peace officer and non-peace officer personnel may be desirable to ensure continuous operational experience input into completed staff work.

Agencies are also combining different functions under a single head. An operational division will combine the patrol, traffic and investigative functions. The administrative and technical services functions may be placed in an administrative services division. This reorganization approach is based upon the thesis that the span of control for the chief of police is reduced, freeing the chief for increased community involvement and more time to devote to major policy decision-making efforts. It is also alleged that integration of the field operational functions provides for a more effective and efficient approach to crime control with improved direction and coordination. Similarly, integration of the administrative and technical services functions presumably assures more effective guidance of and control over support activities.

Use of computers by the medium-sized and large police forces is bringing change in organizational relationships and some facets of operations. There has been improvement in the command and control function with better communications between headquarters and field units resulting in more effective deployment, faster response time to calls for services, and generation of more complete data on field activities which facilitates administrative control over field operations. The computer has revolutionized the records storage and retrieval programs by the generation of more data on a timely basis for use in the policy-decision making processes and other staff activities.

In the future, the application of a digital classification fingerprint system will have a major impact. This will make it possible to reduce the numbers of agency identification personnel and shift the classification and storage of prints to regional, state and national repositories. The computer systems have already increased reliance upon state and national repositories for storage and retrieval of information on wanted persons, stolen property, stolen vehicles, and on a large number of the more notorious or dangerous criminals.

Community Oriented Policing (C.O.P.) is being adopted by an increasing number of agencies. In C.O.P., individual field officers or teams of field officers are responsible for all police agency field activities. Simply stated, C.O.P. means that all field officers will continuously interact with citizens on an informal and formal basis to facilitate crime prevention as well as law enforcement. It usually includes officer participation in community meetings, informal visits to new residents, checking with merchants on security and other problems, and friendly visits to bars and places of entertainment.

An organizational model called *team policing* has given rise to many new administrative ideas. Team policing formalizes organizational relationships in a manner which maximizes the input of all departmental personnel in the decision making processes in order to make all operations more effective. A key feature is that staff and line personnel are expected to work together as a team focusing upon agency goal achievement rather than upon satisfying unit or personal needs—a common feature of the more traditional organizations. This simply means that a department's program activities—crime prevention, crime repression, law enforcement, crime investigations, traffic control and juvenile control—become the focus of departmental efforts. Administrative staff activities truly become supportive of program endeavors. A suitable characteristic of the model is the concept of concensus about alternation of roles between staff and line personnel. Team policing de-emphasizes superior-subordinate relationships. Emphasis is on work to be done rather than on bureaucratic relationships of "who is responsible to whom". Personnel work as a team in dealing with problems and situations rather than being primarily concerned with the chain of command and prescribed responsibilities for each officer, supervisor and manager.

Few departments have completely adopted the team policing model of organization. To date, most departments which have introduced team policing have limited it to the field operations. Field teams have been organized each to police a sector or area of a city, eliminating the traditional beat. All other units of the department operate in a traditional manner. However, some few departments have incorporated the traffic and investigative functions into the team operations, drastically changing the performance of program activities and operational and management roles of personnel involved in field activities. Few departments have made any attempt to change administrative staff roles and functions, primarily because police executives seem to feel a need to maintain support activities under their direct command and control or are unable to comprehend the need for integration of program and support activities.

A change to a full-fledged team policing organization comes only with a thorough understanding of the relationship between program and sustaining activities (see Figure 7.2). Programs develop from the establishment of goals and objectives. Sustaining activities, on the other hand, are concerned with the development of methods, skills and techniques. With the development of goals and objectives departmental programs follow logically. For example, an investigative program is essential for achievement of law enforcement goals and objectives; a traffic program, to achieve traffic safety and control; and a community relations program to achieve crime prevention and participation in the development of an environment of order and stability. Sustaining activities are just that; they aid and support achievement of program goals and objectives. For example, the personnel and training sustaining activities have as their only purpose facilitating and sustaining program activities. Records management is directly related to aiding and assisting getting the program requirements accomplished. The key to integrating program and sustaining activities is planning, a responsibility of the top management team.

The top management team in essence sits as a "board of directors" for the department. The chief assumes the position of the chairman and each member then brings to the team an area of expertise and competency. It is the major responsibility of the team to resolve substantive issues, that is to develop programs and necessary sustaining activities and to plan for their implementation. Each team member inputs his program plans and expectations which are then evaluated by the team as a whole with a view to having an overall well-balanced operation when all program inputs have been evaluated and put in perspective. Once all program activities have been agreed upon and the necessary sustaining activities provided for, then the top management team turns them over to operational teams for implementation. The top management team then monitors, and evaluates implementation on a continuous basis to assure that guidelines are being followed. It also assesses changing needs and requirement and plans for changes in program elements and for new programs.

Operational teams are responsible for the resolution of technical issues necessary for program implementation and for providing the sustaining activities which facilitate program implementation. Such teams may be generalist in nature in that each has a full service program responsibility or there may be a combination of generalist teams and specialty teams, the latter assuming program responsibility over activities not easily performed by generalist teams.

Operational teams are headed by a team manager who has overall responsibility for program implementation which includes command of personnel. Supervisors and workers within each team must assume a group responsibility for achievement of program goals and objectives. The latter also assume considerable supervisory responsibilities exercised in the form of peer pressure since all are collectively held accountable for program achievement.

For the model to be effectively implemented there must be a full commitment from almost all personnel to make it work. The chief, above all, must be committed and he must be an effective leader to bring synthesis and integration to a wide variety of inputs into the police decision-making

Figure 7.2
Illustrative Team Policing Organization

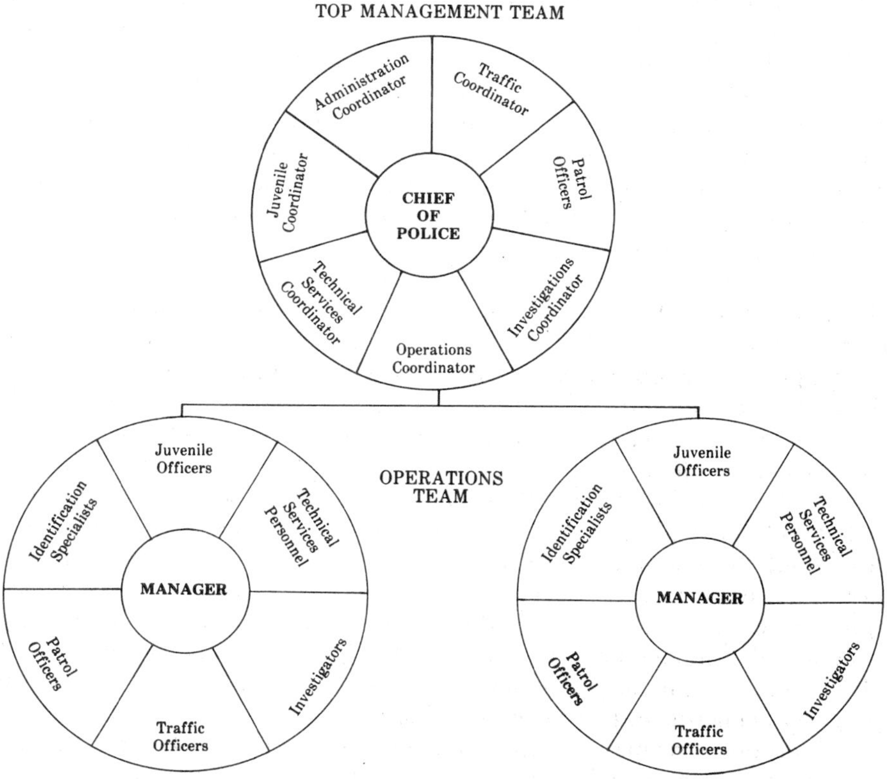

process. Top management team members must become sophisticated planners, program monitors and coordinators who are as keenly aware of all programs as of the ones they each develop. Planning which includes involvement of all affected personnel at every stage is the key to success. An adequate time frame of from three to five years for full implementation is deemed advisable.

Administrative Management

The police administrator operates in a complex world with pressures from the community, the legislative body, city management, and from within his department. The major thrust of his efforts is dealing with people and their behavior in the organizational setting in which he works. However, he must cope with the institutional environment which imposes sanctions upon him and formally defines the context within which he must work. He must deal with a host of processes which are the major tasks of management by which he bridges the gap between the institutional requirements and the behavior of the numerous individuals or group with whom he has face to face relationships.[1]

The institutional environment is reasonably fixed. It includes the legal framework—constitutions, charters and statutes—within which the department must operate, the city or county governmental organization and the character of the community. The administrator has only relative influence over the sanctions, requirements and expectations emanating from these institutions, but must be constantly cognizant of the restraints they impose upon him in carrying out his administrative functions.

The police administrator is confronted with two major sets of behavioral relationships. On the one hand he interacts almost continuously with people outside of the department. He regularly has meetings with other department heads, city management, city councilmen or members of the board of supervisors, community leaders, dissident elements of the community and with professional colleagues. Within the department he has almost daily face to face interaction with his management personnel and periodic meetings with various and sundry other members of the department. In these interactions both with people from within as well as outside of the department, he is concerned with power relationships, struggles for position or favor, perceptions of individuals and groups about their roles, personal intrigue and a host of other behavioral manifestations.

The administrator's tasks of management, which include communicating, coordinating, directing, motivating and controlling, are the processes by which he integrates and synthesizes the operations of the department. He utilizes his administrative staff, key management personnel and the departmental organization to assist him in the integration and synthesis processes and in accomplishing the mission of the department.

Organizational structure aids the administrator in the performance of his administrative functions in that it provides a stabilizing influence within the department for establishing relationships, for performance of program and sustaining activities and for direction, coordination and control of operations. Changes in the formal organizational structure come slowly and are dependant upon concurrence from top management including the city council or board of supervisors. Within the context of the previous discussion of organizations, the administrative management functions of the police administrator and his key management personnel will follow.

Collegial Management Collegial management is an approach to management which involves participation of key departmental personnel in the policy decision-making processes. It replaces unilateral decision-making by the chief administrator but does not relieve him of the ultimate responsibility for decisions which are made. Basically, it provides for a maximum of input from key personnel who are most affected by the administrative decisions which are to be made. Its purpose is to accomodate to cliques which may offer resistance to administrative decisions, to improve the flow of communications, and to alleviate real or imagined misunderstandings of the intent or motives for the decisions. Motivation to accomplish stated goals and for objectives increases as subordinates are given opportunities to participate in decisions which they must carry out.

Collegial decision-making may be utilized for a number of different purposes and in numerous ways. It may be reserved primarily for top policy decisions to be made by the chief administrator and his top staff serving as a collegial body or it may permeate all levels of an organization for the making of major policy decisions and for the making of decisions affecting one or more segments or units at the operational level of need. A top management body may include representation from detectives, from sergeants or from patrolmen depending upon the subject matter under discussion. At lower levels, operational decisions may be made by a lead officer and patrol officers working as a team.

In team policing, the emphasis is on collegial decision making. In the models previously described the group decision-making may be limited to a squad or basic car unit or it may involve all personnel as in the approach which establishes a top management team and operational teams.[2]

The task force approach to planning is a good example by which affected personnel are intimately involved in the decision-making process. As need for study and analysis of a particular management problem arises, a task force headed by a lieutenant, working in the area of concern and staffed by selected personnel also working in or affected by the problem is assembled. The task force then thoroughly researches the problem, prepares a report including recommendations and then participates in the ultimate decision-making process.

The key to collegial management is the willingness of the principal manager, be he the chief administrator or the lead man of squad, to permit full participation of all personnel involved. This requires that the leader perceive his role as a controller/moderator who demonstrates considerable personal security which facilitates discussion and openness. Participating members must assume a positive position based upon thorough preparation and understanding of the issues to be resolved. There must be a recognition that the leader must retain the prerogative of making the final decision since he is accountable; however, if he does override his colleagues his reasons for doing so must be clearly stated.

Styles of Leadership Leadership is one of the most essential yet complex requirements for effective administrative management. Often regarded as *the* important modifier of organization behavior, leadership has to do with the ability of a leader to motivate and influence people in an organizational setting. Leadership represents a choice of power instruments but is not synonymous with power. In brief, it has to do with the establishment of meaningful relationships between the leader and followers for the purpose of accomplishing the mission or purposes of an organization. Leadership, basically involves the capacity to influence, but it cannot necessarily be endowed by position in the hierarchy.[3]

In police departments there exists confusion over the concepts of command versus leadership, particularly in agencies with traditional organizations. Command is seen as an exercise of power granted by the formal hierarchy. It is continuous and regular and is usually sufficient to insure adequate performance because participants expect and accept such behavior. Most police personnel simply do not care to challenge commands. In contrast as greater involvement of all personnel in the decision-making processes takes place and changes occur in organizational relationships leadership occurs as personnel care enough to challenge commands and do so. Thus, changes which have been described as taking place in police organizations place a higher demand upon the police administrator to deal with the non-routine matters and not to waste himself trying to lead in matters where personnel are quite willing to accept routine orders.

The functions of leadership may be briefly described as the working toward unity and cohesiveness in the organization to see that membership is a pleasant and satisfying experience, that the goals and objectives for the organization are achieved, and group interaction is facilitated among organization members. These functions are general enough to apply to all organizational levels and may apply to both individuals and groups.

Increasing emphasis is placed upon the modern manager to be "democratic" in his relationships with subordinates and at the same time maintain the necessary authority and control in the organization for which he is responsible. This is most difficult in a police department with its military-bureaucratic approach to organization. However, the need is present for police managers to become more "democratic". Thus, how can a police manager choose a reasonable leadership pattern?[4]

Without going into detail the police manager has a continuum or range of possible leadership styles available to choose from. Based upon use of authority by the manager he may adopt an authoritarian style which is boss-centered and is based upon the manager making decisions in a more or less unilateral manner. The style becomes more democratic as the manager encourages greater participation in the decision making process by subordinates, thus achieving a greater subordinate-centered style. To avoid a completely laissez-faire style as more areas of freedom are granted subordinates, a manager sets limits within which subordinates may function.[5]

Since the police manager is not wholly the "master of his own destiny" in choosing a leadership style or type, he must take into consideration the forces within himself, the forces in subordinates and the forces in the situation. Each manager has his own value system, has a confidence in subordinates, his own leadership inclinations and his feelings of security in uncertain situations which limit and influence the style or type to be adopted. Likewise forces in the subordinates such as their willingness and capabilities to assume responsibilities, their tolerances for ambiguity, their abilities to identify and work toward goals, their experience and knowledge backgrounds which prepare them to deal with problems and their perceptions of the leader, all influence what style or leadership type the manager may adopt. Forces of the situation including the type of organization, group effectiveness, problems inherent in the situation, the pressure of time and the political environment may be strong influences upon the manager. These then are the principal forces which limit and circumscribe the leadership style and role of a manager in any given instance and tend to determine his tactical behavior in relation to his subordinates. In each case his behavior will be such that goal attainment is reasonably feasible within the limits imposed.[6]

In summary leadership is a factor in administrative management which influences the effectiveness of an organization in goal and objective achievement. There is no singular blueprint or model and each manager must develop his own style based upon the forces inherent in himself, his subordinates and the situation. The general trend is toward more "democratic" leadership which involves an increasing involvement of subordinates in the decision-making processes.

Developing Managerial Skills Management development continues to be one of the most difficult problems facing the police service. Only within the past decade have management training programs been introduced and their content is so varied that there is little or no agreement as to what should be taught nor how it should be taught and result evaluations are nonexistent. Career development programs have been introduced in a few departments with limited results. The one conclusion that can be drawn is that effective management development is inseparable from broader programs of organizational change and improvement.

Development of management skills appears to revolve around a combination of formal academic educational exposure, participation in management training programs, planned career development experiences and general experiences. The relative importance of each is unknown and the impact of each on managers or prospective managers will vary depending on individuals general background, academic preparation, overall job experiences and experiences within their own agencies. What is known is that there is a very complex set of relationships which exists between supervisors, middle managers and top managers in each agency which suggests that programs for developing managerial skills should be carefully developed by each department based upon a very careful organizational and management analysis of departmental expectations and needs and of individual backgrounds and needs. Without such analysis and establishment of need, management improvement efforts may lead to considerable conflict.

Without the planning of an overall management development program for a department, improvement in certain management skills for particular individuals may be achieved. Academic courses are available which deal with broad management subjects such as personnel and financial management, organizational and management theory and general administration. Academic courses may improve proficiency in communications, statistics and accounting. Training programs are usually available in most communities or regions, either general in nature or police oriented, which deal with planning, data processing, group leadership, budget preparation and aspects of personnel management. Departments may develop their own or join with other agencies in developing training programs dealing with such subject matter areas as the managing of criminal investigations, patrol operations and juvenile or traffic control.

Perhaps the major area in which a department can make a contribution to its own management development is in the planning of a series of management experiences for its officers within its own department. Commonly referred to as management career development such a program can provide for movement of management personnel from one assignment to another which include the assumption of new management duties and responsibilities, some at higher levels. Such a program enhances the overall management skills of a number of managers and prepares individuals for assumption of higher managerial responibilities as vacancies occur or new management positions are created.

Managing for Results Managing for results refers to a systematic approach to management based upon achievement of established objectives for any number of identifiable programs or activities within a department. The basic elements of the approach is that objectives are achievable and measurable. The approach is best understood as a total philosophy of management permeating every element of a department but more often is limited in its application to easily identified programs or activities which have achievable and measurable attributes. It is a method of maximizing the utilization of personnel within the department and of enhancing the communication process, both key features of the changing organizational and management approaches to the administration of police agencies.[7]

An illustrative example of an application of management by objectives (M.B.O.) sets the stage for a more detailed discussion of the approach. A department decides to reduce crime by five percent within the next year in the city, an objective both achievable and measurable. Careful planning is required in order to determine the deployment of personnel and their assignments. The first need may be to reduce response time to calls for service with crimes in process. The first step will be to reduce communication processing time of the telephone calls reporting incidents and the dispatching of calls to the field unit by X amount of time. A second step will be to reduce travel time of unit(s) assigned to respond to the call by Y amount of time. A careful analysis may be necessary of the types of offenses which can be reduced. For example robberies may be reduced by reducing response times but an overall reduction in burglaries, assaults and thefts may not be affected to any measurable extent by improved response time. Field officer participation in the decision making process may determine that assaults cannot be reduced because the "Saturday night fights" at local bars and in homes are just a part of citizens' "recreation", but that concentration upon burglary and theft prevention techniques involving citizen participation may lead to substantial reductions in those offenses. The latter may involve expanded participation of the community relations unit in its crime prevention efforts. Continuous monitoring of departmental efforts may determine at the end of six months that a seven percent reduction in thefts and burglaries has been achieved but only a two percent or no reduction in victimless crimes, thus identifying a need to concentrate during the second six month period on victimless crimes.

In our illustrative example the stage is set for a more detailed discusion of MBO as a management system. Planning for implementation of the system is absolutely essential. Often employment of an outside consultant for this phase is important to acquaint management personnel with the system including all of the nuances inherent in the processes. Operational personnel should be consulted and should actively participate in the decision-making process, particularly in decisions related to the types of crime and operational activities which may be required to reduce the number of each. Once the plan for the program is developed and implementation takes place then a continuous monitoring process follows. The monitoring process should not be limited to the collection of data but should include inputs from middle managers, supervisors and operational personnel relative to their perceptions about what changes may be needed in operational requirements as well as their perceptions about changes which may be taking place in criminal activities. Program modifications should take place as needed at all organizational levels. At the end of the year a comprehensive evaluation of the program should take place as to results and what happened and why.

If a department opts for application of MBO for all facets of its operations a comprehensive planning for program and activity monitoring with provisions for modifications is necessary and evaluation must take place for each program and activity. It is a time consuming process but the results should be more meaningful service to the public served and to all personnel of the department. The system of MBO theoretically brings spirit and life to an organization with creation of an atmosphere which emphasizes a balanced management style.

Organizational Development[8]

Organizational development (OD) is a long range, planned and managed organization-wide effort to improve organizational effectiveness by either coping with or controlling change with the use of applied behavioral sciences including action research. Basically it is oriented around problem solving processes as a means by which an organization goes about diagnosing and making decisions about opportunities and challenges in its environmental setting for an extended period of time, five to ten years or longer. It is dealing with the process of organizational renewal essential for introducing changes which inevitably influence operations and which are essential if an organization is to remain a viable entity.

As has been discussed previously, police administrators and managers tend to perceive their roles as maintainers of the status quo and have developed administrative organizations and management styles which limit perceptions of the future. Even with the adoption of contemporary theories of organization and management a myopic approach to the future tends to prevail. Few departments are making any planned approach to OD and few have even recognized that substantial changes are rapidly taking place in our society with major impact upon the administration of the police function.

OD does not just happen. There must be an awareness of the need for change which is shared by key management personnel. There must be an awareness that changes which are taking place are more all encompassing in a community than may be recognized as taking place within the department only and that such community changes impact the department in many ways. An informal community "cultural" change system is at work at all times which has long range implications for the department. These changes must be examined.

Strongly recommended by most experts for OD activities is the creation of an ongoing work team which includes both superiors and subordinates. In comprehensive OD, temporary work teams, overlapping team memberships and intergroup relationships should be a principal focus. In order to avoid myopia which usually results from using only in-house personnel for a do-it-yourself approach, OD experts generally recommend use of an outside consultant to serve as a change agent or catalyst. The outside consultant often sees the "big picture" more easily than agency personnel and is in a position to aid in overcoming individual or group protectionism of the status quo.

Goal setting and planning toward management for their achievement is another key feature of OD. This involves not only focus upon departmental goals but upon the setting of individual and small group or organizational unit goals and planning for their achievement. Again the purpose is to revitalize and to energize the department as a whole.

Another important feature of OD is education and skill development for all personnel. Long term planning should take place beginning with a careful review of the skills, experiences and educational backgrounds of all personnel followed with development of a comprehensive training and educational program to meet the needs of each individual vis-a-vis departmental needs. Such an approach makes possible, over a long period of time, the bringing of the capabilities of all personnel up to departmental expectations.

Briefly, in summary, OD is a reorientation of departmental personnel's thinking and behavior toward the department and its organization. It focuses upon departmental work and the solving of work problems. It is not limited to structural improvement but focuses upon all aspects of an organization. It is concerned as well with individuals in the organization.

A Projection Into Tomorrow

Change is the most threatening issue confronting the police of America today. The concentration of our population in large megalopolises with their attendant urban sprawls and a people whose roots have largely been cut makes for a society quite in turmoil. Although there are increases in crime and violence and there are the "mad bombers", the terrorists, and the militant activists all of which are impacting the administration of the police function, their primary influence is on tactics and strategies rather than upon the police as an institution. The changes which are having the greatest impact are societal in nature. They include increase in personal and social mobility, the rise in urbanization, the spread of secularization, decline in the family, civil rights movements, equal rights for women, and the rise in education. These changes and others are having and will continue to have the greatest impact upon our police.

How are the police to address these multitude of societal changes? What impact is there upon the administration of the police function and upon police organizations? If what we've seen in the past three decades of societal change is any measure of how the police will react, the scene for the future is rather glum. If the police continue to remain the rather closed institution of the past there is little hope. However, there appears some light at the end of the tunnel. There is a new "breed" of police administrators and managers being infused into more and more agencies. They are individuals who are well educated, individuals who are developing a social conscience with understanding of the societal changes which are taking place and individuals who are trying hard to break out of the mold of the past. They are beginning to see that maintenance of the status quo, both organization and operation-wise, is not adequate for coping with the changing times.

Administrators will become more humanistic in their outlook toward society and will focus their efforts upon the development of organizations staffed with personnel who share their views. This will bring about greater concern for human relations values within police organizations manifested in greater participation of all personnel in the policy making and decision-making processes. Group efforts will replace individual decision-making; however, the importance of the individual will be elevated. This will lend some emphasis to acceptance and adoption of the team policing model for police organizations with considerable expansion in the role of the individual officer.

There will be increasing involvement of concerned citizens and civic groups in the policy making and decision-making processes and in policing operations. This will come about due to an increasing recognition that policing is a community responsibility as well as a responsibility of the police department. Organizational and operational changes must take place in order to accomodate to greater citizen involvement.

Administrative organization and management changes will be enhanced by introduction of organizational development programs and a greater emphasis upon improvement of managerial skills. This will be accompanied by more research in the area of police organization and management with a significant attempt to operationalize contemporary general theories of organization, management and administration for police applications. Educational and training programs will become more available to all police agencies and will be significantly more oriented toward meeting the changing police needs. Thus, a much closer relationship between the academic and police communities will result.

Increasing unionization of the police imposes a new dimension upon the management of police organizations. There are indications that some unions are becoming quite militant, reflecting a philosophy of maintenance of the status quo organizationally and operationally. However, other unions are showing a willingness to share with management in the acceptance of change and management is learning how to deal effectively with unions and their demands which assures progress.

If the police do not begin to make the changes suggested there are indications that city management—city managers, mayors and city councils—will become more active in influencing the administration of the police function. Shrinking financial resources has already signalled that city management can no longer tolerate inefficient police operations or support fringe programs, thus forcing a reevaluation of police organizations and operations by police department management. Likewise, city managements are becoming increasingly attuned to public demands for modification of the delivery of police service to meet more humanistic expectations.

Summary

Police departments have generally been organized on the basis of the military-bureaucratic and public administration organizational models. August Vollmer and O.W. Wilson did much to operationalize these models for police application and introduced many modern concepts of management to the police service which have only been slowly assimilated. The police have generally been satisfied to maintain a status quo posture in their approaches to administrative organization and management and only recently have any marked changes begun to take place.

Modifications in police organizations are appearing through the creation of an office of chief of police which consolidates the traditional staff functions including personnel, budget, inspections, planning and training under the direct management of the chief and give personnel performing them greater stature vis-a-vis the line personnel and expands the chief's management capabilities. There is a trend toward consolidation of the line functions of patrol, traffic and investigations under a single command officer and to consolidate technical services and administrative staff functions, if the latter are not incorporated in an office of chief of police, under a single command officer, reducing the chief's span of control and relieving him from considerable detailed management which makes possible his greater attention to broad policy and operational issues.

Introduction of team policing approaches to organization has placed increasing emphasis upon community involvement in the policing processes and has generally expanded the role and functions of the uniformed field officer in community relations activities and the investigative processes. Detective responsibilities have been dramatically altered in that the central or headquarters investigation unit deals primarily with major complex crime investigations and monitors the other investigations for coordination and quality control purposes. The policy and operational decision-making process under the approach involves increased participation of personnel at all levels and replaces decision-making by administrative fiat.

The police administrator operates in a complex world of pressures from the community, legislative bodies, city management and from within the department. The institutional environment which includes the governmental organization, the legal framework of the constitutions, charters, and statutes is relatively fixed while the behavioral setting of continuous interactions with numerous individuals and groups is relatively fluid. His tasks of management, which include communicating, coordinating, directing, motivating and controlling, provide him with the tools and techniques by which he integrates and synthesizes departmental operations and fulfills his adminstrative responsibilities.

The chief approaches his administrative management tasks based upon the leadership style he has adopted which may be "democratic" or authoritarian in nature. In the "democratic" approach to leadership, there is a greater involvement of subordinates in the decision-making process referred to as collegial management. Management skills which he uses are developed through a mix of background education and experience, on-the-job training and planned experiences.

An emerging approach to management is the utilization of a methodology of managing for results. Often referred to as management by objectives, a program approach is developed which breaks departmental operations into specific programs for which measurable and achievable objectives may be established; thus, every aspect of departmental operations is oriented toward mission and goal achievement. The approach is all encompassing in that it involves all personnel in program planning and implementation on a continuous basis, since there is continuous evaluation of achievements.

Organizational development is a long range planned and managed organization-wide effort to improve organizational effectiveness by either coping with or controlling change with the use of applied behavioral sciences, including action research. Basically, it is long range planning which is oriented toward problem solving and touches on every facet of administration, organization and management of a department. It emphasizes full involvement of all personnel at whatever level of input they have a concern and are capable of making inputs into the decision-making process.

Looking to the future there appears to be an increasing need for a more humanistic approach to providing police services. This requires greater community involvement both in operations and the policy decision-making process by police administrators and, in fact, all personnel of a department. Such involvement has a major consequence of changing departments' organizations, their management processes and their operations.

Topics For Discussion

1. **Discuss the Vollmer-Wilson legacy to police administration.**
2. **How have the military-bureaucractic and the public administration organizational models influenced police organizations?**
3. **How does the creation of an office of chief of police modify staff-line unit relationships?**
4. **Discuss the modifications which are changing the traditional police organizational structures.**
5. **What is community oriented policing?**
6. **Describe the various approaches to team policing and their impact upon police organizations.**
7. **Discuss the effect of collegial management upon the decision-making processes.**
8. **Discuss leadership styles and the forces which shape them.**
9. **Review the various approaches to developing managerial skills.**
10. **How does managing for results or management by objectives change a department's approach to administrative management?**
11. **How does a more humanistic approach to policing affect the administration of a police department?**

References

1. John P. Kenney, *Police Administration* (Springfield: Charles C. Thomas, 3rd. Rev. Edition, 1975), p. 8.
2. Ibid; Chapter 7.
3. John M. Pfiffner and Frank P. Sherwood, *Administrative Organization* (Englewood Cliffs, N.J.: Prentice Hall, 1960), Chapter 19.
4. Harry W. More Jr., *Effective Police Administration* (San Jose, Cal.: Justice Systems Development, Inc., 1975), p. 350.

5. Ibid., p. 346.
6. Ibid., p. 350.
7. Ibid., Chapter 6.
8. Ibid., p. 225; Paul M. Whisenand and R. Fred Ferguson, *The Managing Police Organizations* (Englewood Cliffs, N. J.: Prentice Hall, 1973), p. 415.

Annotated Bibliography

Carte, Gene E. and Elaine H., *Police Reform in the United States*, Berkeley; The University of California Press, 1975. This monograph is a history of the era of August Vollmer and his contributions to the police service.

Kenney, John P., *Police Administration*, Springfield: Charles C. Thomas, Publisher. 3rd. Rev. Edition, 1975. This text has a broad social science approach for the presentation of police administrative, organizational and management concepts. It emphasizes concepts rather than techniques.

More, Harry W. Jr., Editor., *Effective Police Administration*, San Jose, Ca.; Justice Systems Development, Inc., 1975. This book is a collection of selected articles by outstanding authors which deals in a comprehensive manner with the key concepts of management as they are applied to the police field.

Toch, Hans; Grant, J. Douglas; and Galvin, Raymond T.; *Agents of Change: A Study of Police Reform*, New York: John Wiley and Sons, 1975. This book is a case study of change in the Oakland, California Police Department made cooperatively by the School of Criminal Justice, State University at Albany, New York and the Oakland Police Department. It presents a detailed analysis of changes introduced and methods used to affect change.

Whisenand, Paul M. and Ferguson, R. Fred, *The Managing Police Organizations*, Englewood Cliffs, N. J : Prentice Hall, 1973. This text deals in considerable depth with the key management concepts essential for administering a police department.

Wilson, O. W., and McLaren, Roy C., *Police Administration*, New York: McGraw Hill Book Co., 1972. This text is a comprehensive and detailed presentation of administrative, organizational and management concepts and practices for administration of the police function.

____________. Law Enforcement Assistance Administration, National Institute for Law Enforcement and Criminal Justice, *Neighborhood Team Policing*, by Peter B. Bloch and David Spect, Washington, D. C.; U.S. Government Printing Office, 1973. This monograph presents a rather comprehensive coverage of team policing and its applications.

____________. Law Enforcement Assistance Adminstration, National Institute for Law Enforcement and Criminal Justice, *Managing Criminal Investigations; Prescriptive Package*, By Peter B. Bloch and Donal R. Weidman, Washington, D. C., U. S. Government Printing Office, 1975. This monograph presents the current research and management approaches to the managing of criminal investigations.

8

PRODUCTIVITY AND THE QUALITY OF WORKING LIFE IN THE POLICE FIELD

Chapter Objectives

The study of this chapter should enable you to:

☑ Define productivity.

☑ Recognize the correlation between productivity increases and improvements in the quality of working life.

☑ Explain how to increase police productivity.

☑ Develop a methods improvement/work simplification plan.

☑ Identify weaknesses in a non-systems approach to productivity improvement.

☑ Refute some objections to the introduction of the productivity concept.

☑ Be familiar with at least six contemporary police areas where improvements in productivity and the quality of working life are major considerations.

☑ List four challenges to traditional thinking in the police field.

Introduction

In March of 1973, the National Commission on Productivity established a Law Enforcement Advisory Group for the purpose of exploring methods of improving productivity in the police field.[1] Their report, *Opportunities For Improving Productivity in Police Services,* and subsequent police articles on the subject have emphasized both the quantitative and qualitative aspects of productivity. Some writers have addressed peripheral areas, such as the impact of unions and the feelings of the individual employee, but most have concentrated on the mechanical process of improving productivity in the police field.

The National Commission experienced many changes during its existence. At the outset its major task was to focus attention on the importance of productivity to the nation's economic health. In legislation signed by the President on June 8, 1974 (Public Law 93 - 311), the Commission's name was changed to the National Commission on Productivity and Work Quality and its mandate was expanded to include efforts to help improve the morale and quality of work of the American worker. The following discussion will attempt to follow this broader approach while dealing specifically with police productivity.

Productivity Improvement

Productivity growth is a goal that the police should try to achieve in a variety of ways because, in the long run, it can help to alleviate the problems of cutbacks and increasing demands that face many departments today. The "Proposition 13" syndrome is likely to affect police departments for many years.

Broadly speaking, productivity can be defined as the relationship of the volume of goods and services produced to the physical inputs used in its production. (Naturally, the police "business" is mostly concerned with services.) Productivity can therefore be measured in terms of the ratio of outputs (arrests, calls answered, response time, etc.) to inputs of labor, capital, materials, or a combination of these. The most widely used measure relates output to the input of labor time, which includes the time of both employees and managers. Outputs must be quality controlled by establishing standards against which accomplishments can be measured. Without such controls you would only have a work measure—an output per unit of input.

Output per hour simply indicates how much labor time is associated with the volume of output. The concept of output per hour or per man-day does not imply sole or even primary responsibility on the part of the work force for productivity improvement, since worker skill and effort are clearly only two of many interrelated sources of improvement.

Productivity growth is influenced by a number of factors—the education and skill of the work force, technological innovations, utilization of capital and capacity, quality of management, and the state of labor relations, among others. These vary in relative importance, but none may be ignored.

There are two basic ways to improve productivity: by obtaining more outputs utilizing the same inputs, or by maintaining the same outputs with reduced inputs.

For example, if ten officers (input) assigned to a particular area or unit made 100 arrests a year (output), resulting in 80 convictions (standard), the productivity of this operation could be increased if these same officers made 120 arrests over a similar period and maintained their 80% conviction rate, or if eight officers working the same area or unit made 100 arrests during the course of the year with an 80% conviction rate. (Productivity would be further increased if the other two officers no longer used in this operation were made responsible for outputs in another assignment.)

Thus productivity can be considered as doing a job better with the same or less resources. How can this be accomplished in the delivery of police services?[2]

Increasing Police Productivity

The report of the Advisory Group acknowledged the difficulty of transferring the concept of productivity in its rare form from the economics of production to the operation of law enforcement agency. Increasing productivity can, however, be considered in the following four ways.[3]

First, increasing police productivity means improving current police practices to the best level known, to get better performance without a proportionate increase in cost. In its simplest form, this means doing the things that are considered to be a necessary part of good police work, but doing them as well or efficiently as the best current practices permit. For example, officers assigned to patrol spend a great deal of time on such activities as filling out unnecessary long reports, or on activities that are important but that would require less time if better coordinated, such as the long hours spent waiting to testify at a trial. These activities could be minimized through better administrative procedures, thus increasing the time available for more important assignments.

Of course, freeing up more police officer time—or improving upon other practices—won't guarantee that the force will be more effective in deterring crime, apprehending criminal offenders, or providing non-crime-related services. But it is a first step in making the force more effective, and can be accomplished at little or no cost to the department.

Second, increasing police productivity means allocating resources to activities which give the highest return for each additional dollar spent. A police department carries out a range of activities, many of which are non-crime-related and most of which are necessary to its overall capability and its responsibility to the public. Beyond a given scale, however, expanding certain activities will give the force less value than initiating or expanding others. For example, would a 500-man force get more value from adding a few more officers than from providing the existing 500 men with mobile radios? These are the kinds of decisions—rarely so simple in reality—that continually confront police managers, but that are often made with insufficient understanding of the options available or of their true costs and potential values. They require asking not just whether the force is doing things right, but also whether it is doing the right things.

Third, given the uncertainties of police work, increasing productivity means increasing the probability that a given objective will be met. The professional police officer—from the chief to the patrol officer—must deal constantly with many unknown or ambiguous factors. He or she is continually assessing the likelihood that this or that may happen, and as a result, the more skillful he or she becomes at increasing the probability that each activity will result in a useful accomplishment, the more productive the overall operation will be.

The best way of increasing the probability of achieving intended impact is by assigning personnel when and where crime is highest or calls for service are heaviest. Simple observation can indicate the "when and where" in general terms; careful analysis of available data can more accurately pinpoint likely times and places of crime occurrence and significantly increase the probability of officers being where they're most needed.

Fourth, increasing productivity in police work means making the most of the talents of police personnel. Sworn officers are better trained and more expensive than ever before. This means that they are capable of higher performance; that economy requires that they be used more effectively; and that they expect to be treated with greater respect. Too often the individual talents of sworn officers are overlooked or suffocated by rigid organizational procedures. This both squanders public resources and stifles human potential. Our system should not—and increasingly will not—tolerate either.

Examples of better human resource development and management abound and can be expected to become increasingly important to police managers. They may include making patrol officers responsible for following through on investigations; permitting senior patrolmen to refuse promotion but receive a higher salary and prestige as a patrolman; and developing alternative career paths for professional police officers.

Effectiveness and Efficiency

The ability to get a job done, including meeting the standards set for quality control, indicates the effectiveness of an operation. A special arrest unit which sets out to make 100 felony arrests and have an 85 per cent conviction rate during the course of a year is effective if they accomplish such statistics, presuming that such figures will impact on crime conditions in their jurisdiction. If their output was achieved with 10 officers (average arrest per officer - 10) rather than 50, then it is an efficient operation since the average felony arrests per officer per year is normally two. This conclusion is based on the fact that efficiency is determined by how much or how little resources (input) are expended in producing outputs. Effectiveness and efficiency must both be present if there is to be a real productivity improvement. Measurement such as arrests, response time, man-hours, etc. are essential to monitor effectiveness and efficiency. Since such measurements are developed in-house, they serve as a very legitimate management tool. Perhaps some day they can replace the Uniform Crime Report as an indicator of just how a department is doing in its attempt to deliver quality service at the lowest cost.

It makes more sense for chiefs to compare their departments' response-time figures from one year against what was expected another year (since they control the allocation of their departments' resources), rather than attempting to compare the crime rates for their cities with those of other cities of comparable size but more resources.

Methods Improvement/Work Simplification[4]

Before standards can be set, present levels of service must be determined. Are they satisfactory, or are there opportunities for improvement? These determinations can best be made by applying proven work simplification techniques to analyze operations and identify ways for increasing employee output and at the same time improving the quality of their working life.

Before discussing specific techniques, it would be useful to define the terminology of how employee hours are expended:

- *Productive work time* is time spent on work tasks which contribute directly to the desired outputs (e.g., directed patrol, selective traffic enforcement, etc.)
- *Nonproductive work time* is time spent on work tasks which are either unnecessary or marginally useful in achieving the desired outputs (e.g., filling out detailed daily activities reports.)
- *Idle time,* sometimes referred to as "down time", is concerned with the time during which employees are not engaged in assigned work tasks. Idle time may either be self imposed or refer to periods when the employee is prevented from performing assignments because of circumstances beyond his control (e.g., means of transportation during inclement weather.)

Work simplification is concerned with maximizing the output during productive work time and minimizing time expended in other, less productive ways. It requires factual knowledge of the present level of productivity. This can be determined by analyzing ways in which labor time is spent; the operating methods used; the output level which could be achieved; the reasons for nonproductive, nonwork, and idle time; and ways to correct deficiences.

Review of Organizational Relationships

Upon undertaking a work simplification study, analysts must understand what services the agency provides and how it is structured to deliver those services. The first step, then, is to review the agency's organization charts and staffing levels. The charts should show the agency's formal structure and list personnel assigned to each work activity, and should also include a functional structure identifying all the work processes performed. If these charts don't provide adequate details, or if they are obsolete, new ones should be prepared (this is, of course, also true if none exist at all). While this initial step is undertaken to become familiar with the agency's activities, procedural improvements often involve restructuring an agency's organization. Therefore, the organizational charts should be reviewed again during the course of the work simplification study.

Analysts may find that organizational shifts are required. For example, detectives may be assigned to decentralized locations; staff functions such as record-keeping may be centralized; or a clerical pool or new unit, such as planning and development, may be created.

Since statistical records, performance reports, and other record-keeping files are useful in examining historical trends and may be integrated into a new control system, the analyst should become familiar with these reporting systems in the course of reviewing the agency's organizational and functional relationships.

Work Distribution Analysis

The next step is a detailed review of work processes and individual employee tasks. A work process is defined as a series of tasks required to complete a single responsibility. Each individual task, or operation, contains a series of uninterrupted steps, or work motions, performed at a single work station. For example, in a Traffic Division, *issuing delinquent citation notices* is a work task or operation, and *stuffing* notices in an envelope is a single step, or work motion.

The best way to begin is to construct a work distribution chart which identifies all significant work processes, delineates the tasks performed by each employee, and approximates the amount of time spent by the employees on each task.

The analyst then estimates the time spent each week by each employee performing the work processes and tasks and records this on a work distribution chart (See Table 8.1). The chart will have to be updated later in the study, as new data becomes available, to reflect the time requirements more accurately.

The analyst determines from the completed work distribution chart the major work processes; that is, those that consume the greatest percent of each employee's total hours. Generally the greatest potential for productivity improvement lies with these procedures and thus they warrant the most analytical attention.

A sound understanding of the job classification structure and specific job descriptions is also essential, since improvement opportunities are often found through restructuring work assignments; for example, by not using highly skilled personnel to perform routine clerical tasks.

Typical shortcomings in work assignments often found through work distribution analysis (see the sample work distribution chart, Table 8.1) are:

- *Misguided Effort.* Work priorities may be misdirected or lacking altogether, as when too much time is spent on relatively unimportant tasks rather than on work associated with the principal objective.
- *Inefficient Use of Skills.* In police work, overqualified personnel are sometimes assigned jobs which lesser-skilled employees could perform; or employees are assigned to do work for which they lack the proper training. In such cases of employee misuse, the price is paid in lost productivity. That six people are involved in purchasing parts suggests at least two possibilities: an additional buyer may need to be hired or a partsman position should perhaps be allocated to that of a buyer. Of course, a sound recommendation would be based on further analysis.
- *Unrelated Tasks.* When employees are assigned to several unrelated tasks, problems can arise because more errors tend to occur when people are interrupted frequently or when they must switch to another, unrelated activity. The analyst should identify potential problems associated with work assignments lacking continuity. Stores Clerk #3 may be prevented from performing all of the many different assigned tasks proficiently.
- *Overspecialization.* Employees assigned too few tasks may become bored, lose interest, and perform poorly. Moreover, it may be difficult to find satisfactory substitutes when those employees are on vacation or sick leave. Partsman #4, whose job consists solely of rebuilding parts, may be overspecialized. The analyst should determine if it would be beneficial if the Partsman assignments were more varied and whether other employees are also trained in this specialized task.
- *Too Many Actors.* Assigning the same task to a number of employees can lead to problems, since individual styles differ and tend to result in

Table 8.1

Work Distribution Chart
Police Vehicle Maintenance Parts Room

Process/Task Description	Total Man-Hours	% Total	Parts Manager	Partsman # 1	Partsman # 2	Partsman # 3	Partsman # 4	Stores Clerk # 1	Stores Clerk # 2	Stores Clerk # 3	Buyer # 1	Buyer # 2
NEW VEHICLE PARTS PURCHASES												
Reviews orders, specifications	38	10	10		3						10	18
Compares vendor prices	49	12		5	2	4					25	16
Selects vendor, places order	22	6		5								6
NEW VEHICLE PARTS DISTRIBUTION												
Receives and stocks parts	69	17			5			23	29	12		
Distributes parts to mechanics	97	24			30	31				11		
TIRE CONTROL												
Receives and stocks tires	12	3						5	4	3		
Distributes tires to mechanics	7	2						3		4		
Discards old tires	6	2						2	2	2		
INVENTORY MAINTENANCE												
Updates computer records	23	5		4		4		7	5	3		
Orders new parts	8	2	5	1		1				1		
REBUILT PARTS CONTROL												
Receives and stocks parts	12	3					12					
Distributes parts	28	7					28					
ADMINISTRATION AND MISCELLANEOUS	9	2	5							4		
SUPERVISION	20	5	20									
Total Man-Hours Per Week	400	100%	40	40	40	40	40	40	40	40	40	40

inconsistencies in work procedures. This breeds excessive cross-checking of work assignments and, unless guidelines and quality controls are enforced, leads to inconsistent results. The analyst should make certain that the best procedures are being followed by all employees. In Table 8.1 too many employees may be assigned part-time to inventory control. The analyst might want either to reduce the number of employees assigned to this function or reallocate an existing position to inventory control full time.

Work Flow Analysis

Flow charts are used to record the progress of work from the time an agency first assumes responsibility for an action until its final disposition in the agency, or until it is passed on to another agency (e.g., the courts). In a detailed flow chart, each step of, for example, transporting a prisoner is identified: 1. "handcuffs prisoner"; 2. "places prisoner in vehicle for transportation to police station." For relatively minor processes, a simplified flow chart may show several individual steps combined as a single item; for example, "transports prisoner to police station."

While each task identified on the work distribution chart should be subjected to flow chart analysis, the level of detail may vary depending on the size, complexity, or degree of difficulty of the task. Particular care should be taken in flow-charting all jobs which 1. take more than 15 percent of the agency's total employee-hours, 2. require the services of several different employees to complete, 3. need close coordination with other agencies, or 4. are identified in the work distribution analysis as troublesome tasks.

Some flow-charting procedures are complex, particularly those used in computer systems analysis, while others are relatively unsophisticated. The analyst constructing a flow chart should always be sure that the chart shows *actual* work procedures as opposed to "approved" or "recommended" methods shown in a procedures manual but which may not be practiced. A procedural manual should be consulted if available but it should never be accepted as the primary information source for a flow chart without on-site inspection and validation. The reasons for any variations in actual as opposed to approved methods should also be investigated as a possible explanation of why procedural problems have developed.

The analyst should review the flow charts with agency supervisors and individual employees, a process which provides an opportunity to establish rapport while discussing possible alternative procedures with those who will be affected by proposed changes. For their part, the employees, with their special knowledge of the job, can often contribute meaningful ideas on how to simplify their work. In fact, it's particularly important that agency personnel work with the analyst during the study; the extent of such cooperation usually determines the degree of success in implementing improvement ideas.

The analyst reviews each task in the completed flow charts to spot identifiable problems and improvement opportunities. This is approached in much the same way as a news reporter evaluates the validity of a story, asking the traditional who, what, when, how, where, and why questions. Common faults which may be found in this way include:

- *Excessive Detail.* Work procedures often include steps which are duplicated elsewhere, or are needlessly complex, or that serve no useful purpose. Some procedures that were established years before may no longer be needed (such as an accident report to the Motor Vehicle Bureau that they no longer require, since it involves damage of less than $200).
- *Poor Coordination.* Failure to coordinate work or to become familiar with related work among agencies commonly causes the efficient handling of a work process to break down. An apparently streamlined method for one agency may create additional work for another (this is further discussed in the section on SYSTEMS APROACH) and an apparently necessary work function may be unnecessary because another agency already performs the task. Thus a police court liaison detail which prepares a listing of court times for officers may be needlessly duplicating information already available in the court's administration office. A simple programming change in a computerized court scheduling system could remedy this by providing an additional listing for the police department.
- *Outmoded Equipment.* Staff and other costs of performing a task can often be reduced by replacing antiquated equipment. However, care must be taken that the cost of new machinery, equipment, hardware, and software does not exceed the anticipated dollar savings.
- *Inadequate Forms Control.* Misuse of the numerous forms used by every agency in the completion of assigned tasks and for reporting purposes can have serious adverse effects on productivity. A poorly designed form may require too much time to record information; or forms may be routed unnecessarily to individuals not directly involved in the work; or they may seek unnecessary data or not seek vital information; or they may be difficult to read; or they may have to be combined with other forms requiring similar information.
- *Incorrect Work Assignments.* Just as the analyst looks at skills use in the work distribution chart, he or she also needs to review the flow chart for incorrect work assignments, particularly in terms of over- or underqualified employees performing tasks more appropriately assigned to others.

The Systems Approach

Knowledge of specific methods of increasing productivity cannot be employed without the realization that, when implemented at one level, productivity improvement will have agency-wide implications. In some cases this could be counter-productive and even extremely costly to the entire agency, especially if one particular operation becomes too productive.

The installation of burglar alarms in the majority of commercial establishments might increase the number of arrests at such locations, and probably the number of convictions also, since the apprehension of the perpetrator might take place at or near the scene of the crime. Thus, an anti-burglary operation could be very successful. However, would this operation be achieved at the expense of time and effort expended by the police in answering a large number of false alarms? One could expect this to happen due to an increase in the presence of equipment subject to human and mechanical errors. The effects of a program on the entire mission of a police agency must be evaluated before a legitimate claim of increased productivity can be made.

Thus, it becomes very important to consider productivity improvement as a philosophy for the entire agency. It shouldn't be the sole responsibility of any one unit, nor should it be limited to any one or two activities. Naturally, each entity within an organization can and should identify specific areas where productivity improvements are possible. However, the various interrelationships within an agency should be examined to ensure that overall goals, rather than just unit objects, are being achieved as a result of the introduction of a new procedure or program. The recognition of the importance of a systems approach shouldn't be limited to internal organization considertions alone.

Although the time an officer spends in court could technically be considered *Productive Work Time,* the many hours of waiting in court might well be considered *Idle Time.* When one considers the overtime costs of this procedure, it becomes apparent that some type of interagency agreement is necessary between the courts and the police. This situation becomes even more critical when the quality of working life is considered. One complaint that's frequently heard from police officers has to do with the amount of time they spend in court. Although some of their resentment has been tempered by overtime pay, it's still quite common.

Financially troubled New York City decided to do something about this situation.[5] Under an agreement which involved the Police Department, the office of the District Attorney, and the city's administrative judges, arresting officers may be excused from appearing at a defendant's arraignment, or first court appearance, after giving a statement concerning the circumstances of the arrest to the assistant district attorney assigned to the case. The decision to release an officer will be made by the prosecutor only when it's virtually certain that no disposition will be made at the arraignment and that the case will be sent to a grand jury for possible indictment.

This plan, which will reduce "down time," will primarily involve the more serious felonies such as murder, rape, and robbery. Misdemeanors and lesser felonies, which can be and often are resolved at arraignment, will not be covered under this arrangement.

It's estimated that this plan will reduce employee-hours (inputs) by 50,000 hours per year and result in a saving of at least $400,000. It will also allow officers and detectives involved in approximately 13,000 arrests of the type affected by the plan to carry on their patrol or other duties instead of waiting in courtrooms for their cases to be called.

Carrying the systems approach one step further, we must also consider the defendant. The Legal Aid Society, which provides council to indigents in New York, will be monitoring the new plan to make sure that the constitutional rights of the accused aren't adversely affected by this procedure.

Coordination and Consolidation

Coordination and consolidation are two concepts that usually find their way into productivity discussions. Both describe processes that can produce productivity improvements by reducing inputs and/or increasing outputs. These concepts are included in the discussion on the system-wide implications of productivity programs since, if not considered in their complete context, they might not produce the desired results.

Coordination (sometimes preceded by cooperation and finalized by consolidation) can take place when an agency seeks to bring together the efforts of two or more of its units into a smoothly functioning team (e.g., team policing, when patrol, traffic, and detective units are united). It can also take place when several agencies with related programs seek to coordinate their efforts to achieve a common goal (e.g., Strike or Task Forces of federal, state, and local officers coordinating their efforts against specific targets—narcotics, organized crime, and, most recently, fences.)

In addressing the issue of coordination as it related to Research and Development (R&D) programs, the National Advisory Committee on Criminal Justice Standards and Goals made several points concerning the limits of this process:

> *First, some of the most effective coordination occurs as a result of officials informally talking to each other or casually reviewing each other's reports. When this type of informal communication is absent, formal, administrative mechanisms may not be effective substitutes. Second, the costs of noncoordination are often assumed to be higher than the costs of coordination. This is not always the case. For example, duplication of effort by R&D-funding agencies is often assumed to be undesirable and something to be eliminated. This view, however, overlooks the value of independent replication of results and may actually be cost-ineffective overall. Furthermore, the costs of coordination can be high. Transaction costs alone, measured in time spent by officials in a coordinating activity, can interrupt other agency work and should be weighed against the presumed benefits of coordination. Third, coordination is a poor substitute for the deficiencies of gaps, omissions, and oversights with respect to the adequacy of a given R&D program. There is no persuasive evidence, however, that the weakness of the planning and decision making processes that gave rise to any inadequacies can be overcome by coordinating mechanisms. These inadequacies are better resolved in the context in which they arose.*[6]

It can thus be seen that coordination has the potential for bringing about productivity improvements; however, positive results aren't always achieved, and even when they are, they aren't automatic. This observation is also true when considering consolidation. Large agencies aren't necessarily better agencies. Arguments could be presented for partial consolidation of support functions such as record-keeping, forensic services, planning, training, and possibly communications, but there's little evidence to support the premise that large police departments are more effective or efficient than smaller ones. If the proportion of an agency's officers assigned to patrol, and the ratio of citizens to patrol officers, are used as criteria for evaluating the effectiveness and efficiency of a police department, at least one study indicates that smaller agencies are outperforming bigger ones.

The Workshop in Political Theory and Police Analysis at Indiana University, and the Center for Regional and Urban Studies at the University of North Carolina at Chapel Hill performed a Police Services Study funded by the RANN Division of the National Science Foundation. During this study, 80 Standard Metropolitan Statistical Areas (SMSA) located in 31 states were examined. The conclusions concerning the possible effects of consolidation on street patrol were quite interesting and a commentary on that portion of the report follows.[7]

One finding was that larger police agencies generally assign a lower proportion of their officers to patrol duties (patrol deployment). There are several reasons for this phenomenon. One reason is that larger departments tend to assign more officers to *specific non-patrol* direct service duties, such as traffic control or criminal investigation. Larger departments are also more likely to produce their own auxiliary services and to assign officers to these non-patrol duties. Training of recruits, radio communications, and adult pre-trial detention are auxiliary services produced more often in larger departments than in smaller ones.

Table 8.2

Patrol Deployment and Density:
Municipal Police Departments

Number of Sworn Officers in Municipal Police Departments		Number of Agencies Reporting	ON-STREET PATROL FORCE (10 P.M.)	
			Median Number of Officers on the Street	Median Number of Inhabitants per Officer on the Street
Full time:	1 to 4	209	1	1,623
	5 to 10	209	2	2,383
	11 to 20	124	3	2,877
	21 to 50	121	5	3,244
	51 to 150	77	13	3,985
	Over 150	45	30	4,256
Part time only:		48	1	1,107

Adapted from p. 36 *Policing Metropolitan America*, Ostrom, Elinor, Parks and Whitacker, (U.S. Government Printing Office, Washington, D.C.) 1977

For the municipal patrol agencies, variations in proportions of departmental sworn personnel actually deployed for street duty (patrol density) have a direct bearing on the ratio of citizens to patrol officers (Table 8.2). A patrol officer in the median municipal department of from five to ten sworn officers serves slightly fewer than 2,400 citizens, while a patrol officer in the median department with more than 150 full-time sworn officers serves more than 4,200 citizens. One should remember when considering these figures that the larger departments generally tend to have more sworn officers per 1,000 residents than do the smaller. But the larger departments haven't translated this relative personnel advantage into an on-street presence as well as the small to medium size agencies have.

The finding that smaller municipal departments usually deploy more officers per thousand citizens suggests that consolidation of police agenices without changes in traditional organizational structures and/or service philosophlies might increase rather than decrease costs. This could occur since more officers would have to be employed if the ratio of citizens to officers on patrol existing prior to consolidation was to be maintained.

Having taken a closer look at the coordination and consolidation issues, let's now turn our attention to some questions that are raised challenging productivity improvements.

Concerns About Productivity

The announcement of a drive for productivity improvements can create concern within the rank and file. Although it's true that in industry a technological or systems change—often referred to as a productivity improvement—may eliminate some jobs, this only takes place when productivity isn't increased enough to offset job loses. In reality, as productivity has risen in the United States, the production of goods and services has also expanded and, as such, new job opportunities have become available.

In the police field, productivity improvements aren't aimed at eliminating jobs but rather, in many cases, they're necesary as a result of layoffs caused by budget cuts. Even when positions aren't eliminated, freezes and increases in calls for service have necessitated the better use of available police resources. It makes good administrative sense to seek out productivity improvements before an emergency arises. Proactive approaches should replace reactive productivity programs stimulated by economic crises.

Will organized labor automatically oppose productivity improvements? This is a legitimate concern in view of the rise of the union movement in the police field.

Almost any program enacted unilaterally by management will meet some opposition from organized labor. Productivity improvements that affect labor, if not developed in a participatory atmosphere, will receive the same treatment. It's not that unions oppose productivity improvements *per se*, but rather that they're protective of their members and, as such, ask questions about any changes that affect employees.

Productivity presents an ideal arena for labor-management consensus. Police management should develop the analytic capacity to improve and monitor the delivery of services, while the union develops positions on productivity that are acceptable to their membership.

Labor-management committees, working outside of contract provisions, can be more effective in facilitating cooperation in productivity improvement than meetings at the bargaining table itself, where specific inputs and outputs can become subject to lengthy and time-consuming negotiations and, if placed in the contract, can become subject to grievance procedures.

Productivity improvements are a concern to organized labor, and labor can be very helpful if they choose to become involved in the process. This is especially true when the element of improving the quality of working life is introduced on an equal basis with drives for increases in productivity.

One of the more serious misconceptions prevalent in any discussion concerning productivity improvement in the police field is the belief that outputs can't be measured and, as such, measurements are impossible. For whatever they're worth to any one agency, it's possible to quantify areas such as arrests, convictions, calls for service, and response time. (Because of intervening variables, some of these figures might not be meaningful.)

The input aspect of productivity measurement is normally quantifiable. If an agency utilizes a program budget, they need only extract the cost figures for the program being examined. A line item budget will require some computations in order to arrive at the total cost of all the resources devoted to the program. Regardless of the type of budget used, cost figures can be determined. The Advisory Group to the National Commission (previously mentioned) discovered for instance that Detroit implemented a closed-circuit television system for stationhouse security. The cost was $1.1 million to install and staff the system (police trainees monitored the consoles). This replaced 130 sworn officers who cost $2.6 million. These officers then became available for return to regular patrol duties where their services were needed. The net reduction in resources (inputs) was $1.5 million and the results (outputs) were the same, or possibly even better, since television cameras don't take unauthorized breaks and can be positioned so that all four sides of the stationhouse can be viewed at the same time.

There are some occasions when exact measurements aren't possible. For example, it's impossible to measure the number of crimes which didn't take place because a police officer spent time working in a Police Athletic League (PAL) program for inner-city youth. In such cases, indicators can be used which demonstrate relationships between fiscal resources spent on specific activities (e.g., crime prevention) and the total department budget, or the extent to which the community is involved in department programs.

Measurements are possible in the police field. Inputs and many outputs are quantifiable, and when precision isn't available, indicators can be used as a department attempts to measure its productivity improvements.

The many concerns which surround the concept of productivity in the police field are stimulated, in most cases, by misconceptions (e.g. labor will resist it; measurement is impossible). Correct information and favorable experiences will address these concerns. Unfortunately examples of the latter in the police field are few, isolated, and just beginning to circulate. Therefore, the successful efforts in the private sector, and to some degree in the public sector (e.g., solid waste disposal), will remain for the present the prime examples of what can be achieved in improving productivity and the quality of working life.

Contemporary Considerations

The assumptions that are being challenged today in the police field, coupled with other changes, have created an opportunity to develop a more productive and pleasant work environment. However, this favorable atmosphere is accompanied by confusion, doubt, and many unanswered questions.

In response to pressures for upgrading police personnel, many agencies have attempted to attract college-educated men and women into the police field. Federal guidelines and local policies have, however, resulted in the alteration of many standards and requirements for entry into police work. Mandated minority quotas, residency requirements, elimation of entrance tests, etc. are considered by many as being in direct conflict with the mandate to upgrade police work.

Since it's fairly well-recognized that a police department can better serve a community if it understands the population, it stands to reason that members of the community should be represented within the department. Therefore, which action—recruitment of college educated personnel, or recruitment of members of the local comunity—results in better law enforcement? Obviously, a college graduate from the community would appear to be the ideal answer. The solution is not quite that simple because of conflicting performance standards for police officers. In other words, what constitutes a "good cop" isn't easily determined—nor is the value of the college cop.

Difficulties In Demonstrating Better Performance[8]

More difficult than one might initially realize are problems of establishing the appropriate criteria to be applied in measuring performance. One must clearly define the ways in which performance is expected to improve as a result of college education. For instance, in a police department with extremely low productivity in terms of arrest rates, clearance rates, and the like one might very well expect that the infusion of officers with a collegiate background would lead to increased productivity, as measured by these standards. If this were definitely one of the goals of recruiting collegiate officers, and the behavior of the officers was directed to these ends, then certainly higher arrest and clearance rates would indicate the success of the imposition of higher educational requirements. On the other hand, however, arrest and clearance rates are often highly inflated and, in fact, counter-productive. That is, arrests are made in many situations which would lend themselves to alternative solutions, or arrests are made with insufficient evidence, or crimes are reported cleared upon dubious criteria.

If this situation is attributed to the competence of agency personnel, and it often can be, then the infusion, of collegiate officers might very well be directed toward the goal of reducing arrest and clearance rates, although reductions in these rates are usually thought of as indicating poorer performance. Similarly, one might desire the crime rate to go up or down, depending upon the perceived ability of officers to establish community rapport which, in turn, affects the extent of reporting, thus causing rates to rise in some instances and fall in others. In short, determining the success of any police program, including higher personnel productivity measure is dependent upon individual agency and situational characteristics. Hence, efforts at establishing the credibility of higher educational standards for the police are plagued by an inability to define appropriate variables to differentiate "good" performance from "bad" performance.

The problem of determining enhanced productivity is further complicated by inappropriate expectations. What we've unfortunately failed to recognize in both police training and educational programming is that most of the specific tasks of patrol officers can only really be learned through experience. The police role involves knowledge of dozens of formulas, dozens of forms, and scores of "ways of doing things." No amount of formal instruction given in the classroom will, for instance, prevent a police recruit from being "had" a few times by con artists on the street. Sociologists like McNamara, Skolnik, and Wilson have all observed that there is a significant body of knowledge in the police service characterized by the term "street wisdom." It's unfortunate that far too many administrators, and even a number of educators, have looked to formal educational programs to enhance a student's ability to apply and use street wisdom. It will simply not happen. As a matter of fact, we could probably expect certain deficiencies in this regard on the part of college graduates. One aspect of street wisdom is knowledge of the value of systems, jargon, and the like of lower socioeconomic classes, and the recruitment of college graduates will diminish rather than increase the possession of such knowledge on the part of police forces. A college-educated officer will not necessarily be a better officer in every possible way. Some hard decisions have to be made regarding the attributes one is willing to give up in any personnel selection process in order to gain others.

Another serious methodological problem plaguing efforts to justify higher educational standards for the police is establishing precisely what level of improved performance justifies the impositon of higher standards. That is, it's not merely enough to establish that collegiate police officers do perform more adequately, however defined, than non-collegiate officers. It must be established that the increase in productivity justifies the increased expense and the difficulties thus created for minority recruitment. Such a determination would be difficult enough to make if police productivity was easily measured, or if the goals of the police service were universally agreed upon by those in the field. However this is not the case.

The problem of determining "significant" productivity differences is compounded by the fact that the nature of the police patrol officer's task is generally far more constrained than is wise. If we conceive of the task as merely writing traffic tickets and shining a spotlight in windows to ascertain whether they're broken, then certainly arguments for higher educational standards are weak. However, if the task is made what it ought to be, then any standard less than a baccalaureate degree is inappropriate.

One can't expect to place college graduates in a job that involved only routine and mundane tasks and have them perform significantly better. In fact, a college education can increase expectations such that if college graduates are delegated nothing but routine or mundane tasks, the motivational level among them as a group will be lower than the motivational level which might be expected from those without a college background. We will only realize the full potential of raising police educational standards whenever the police task is adjusted to complement the educational background of the recruit. Efforts to substantiate or justify the need for a college background among police officers suffer from the fact that in many if not most agencies the police task isn't what it ought to be.

Preventive Patrol

The Police Foundation's 1973 study of patrol activities in one section of Kansas City challenged the longstanding assumption that a percentage of a patrol officer's time should be devoted to undirected preventive patrol because such an activity impacts on the incidence of crime and the public's fear of crime.[9]

Under its National Evaluation Program, the National Institute of Law Enforcement and Criminal Justice studied traditional preventive patrol and issued a report which substantiates the basic findings of the Police Foundation experiment, namely, that routine preventive patrol could be altered substantially without noticeably affecting crime patterns.

> *The Preventive Patrol Experiment suggests the possibility of change in patrol practices and manipulation of patrol resources and, by inference, directs attention to the question of how patrol time can be most effectively spent. In light of the steadily increasing demands being placed on the police, overtaxed municipal budgets, and rising operating costs, tremedous pressure has been mounting for improvement of the effectiveness and productivity of existing departmental resources in lieu of expansion. Given the pressing nature of these concerns, it is clearly important to determine whether patrol officers' time is being fully and efficiently utilized. According to information currently available, general patrol activities may not necessarily be the most productive use of an officer's time. Consequently, even at present levels of staffing, there may be a very substantial number of patrol hours available for experimenting with a wide range of potentially useful strategies and tactics such as directed patrol and increased involvement in the community. It may also be possible to staff special units from within department personnel without the addition of new staff.*[10]

Whether a patrol officer is college educated, from the community, or interested in challenging work, the substitution of meaningful assignments for routine tasks should enhance the quality of his or her working life. A follow-up investigation, for example, would normally prove more stimulating than taking a dog bite report at a hospital. If individual officers have some input into their job enrichment, both personal and organizational rewards will be even greater.

Before leaving the subject of preventive patrol, it should be acknowledged that some highly motivated officers use their routine preventive patrol time to carry out personally directed assignments including crime prevention and community relations activities. The increase in their individual productivity because of directed assignments would probably be marginal and might even decrease unless they participated in identifying the times and places for such assignments.

The Role of the Detective

If preventive patrol activities are considered a less than productive use of a patrol officer's time, then what about the role of the detective in some police departments? After a crime is committed and reported, and after a patrol officer has conducted a preliminary investigation, two detectives arrive at the scene (sometimes assisted by an evidence technician) and ask the same questions already asked, answered, and recorded by the officer who called in the case in the first place.

Although the situation might not be as drastic as this in many departments, there is room for productivity improvements in the investigative process. A starting point might be the acknowledgement by police professionals that every crime committed need not be investigated by a detective. And, when an investigation is carried out, there might be no need to go beyond the preliminary stage if a substantial amount of time has lapsed between the commission of the crime and its discovery, or if there are no leads as to the perpetrator.

The Rand Corporation, in their study of the criminal investigation process, disclosed some of the ways cases are solved:

> *The single most important determinant of whether or not a case will be solved is the information the victim supplies to the immediately responding patrol officer. If information that uniquely identifies the perpetrator is not presented at the time the crime is reported, the perpetrator, by and large, will not be subsequently identified.*
>
> *Of those cases that are ultimately cleared but in which the perpetrator is not identifiable at the time of the initial report, almost all are cleared as a result of routine police procedures.*[11]

It might be possible to decrease the size of detective divisions and limit their investigations to major cases. Although some individuals might be inconvenienced or even embarrassed by a transfer to patrol, especially if the transfer involves a reduction in pay, those remaining should be able to devote additional time to the more important and difficult cases. This should improve the quality of their working life.

The previously mentioned National Evaluation Program dealing with traditional preventive patrol developed information on how the investigative function might be handled more productively:

> *Two other approaches for the better utilization of patrol officers' time have been suggested. In the very early stages of exploration is the possibility that by assigning investigative responsibilities to patrol officers, the size of the detective bureau can be drastically reduced, releasing officers assigned to that division for patrol activities. Recent experiences in Rochester, New York (in a Police Foundation-funded effort) seem to indicate that the traditional organizational split between the detective and patrol divisions may result in the underutilization of personnel. The work in Rochester seems to suggest that patrol officers may quite effectively become more involved in investigative activities, and that detectives may appropriately be assigned to street duty. In Cleveland Heights, Ohio, the actions of the department were far less tentative. The size of the detective bureau was drastically reduced, and the size of the patrol force increased along with reassignment of many traditional detective functions to the patrol officers who had received the requisite training. Both programs seem to present promising ways of increasing the effective utilization of manpower and, as such, they are appropriate topics for detailed evaluation.*[12]

Improved Utilization of Personnel

If the transferring of some investigative responsibilities from detective to patrol officers can result in improvements in productivity and the quality of working life, serious consideration should then be given to the use of civilians to handle certain calls for service currently handled by patrol officers. Such non-sworn personnel could respond to non-crime or non-emergency calls for service such as: lost/found property; notification messages; dangerous obstructions in the street; minor vehicle accidents, etc. The key to this process is the identification, on an agency-by-agency basis, of appropriate jobs—a task which should involve labor and management collaboration.

Where civilians can equal the outputs previously accomplished by sworn officers, then the savings in salary, overhead, and training reduces the cost of resources (inputs), resulting in productivity improvement. In some clerical tasks such as typing, there might even be an improvement in the quality and quantity of the output. The quality of working life is also improved for the sworn officer who is no longer required to perform menial tasks. Care must be exercised in assessing the cost and benefit tradeoffs in any civilianization program to ensure a continuation of the level of service expected by the community.

Additional improvements can be affected by combining some jobs (arrest processing officer and cell attendant, armorer and range instructor, etc.), transferring some services (parking meter enforcement to Finance Department, detention responsibilities to Corrections Department, etc.) and reducing time-consuming procedures (issuing summonses in lieu of arrest in some cases, early arrest screening to weed out non-prosecutable cases, etc.).

Two of the most obvious ways that the effectiveness and efficiency of personnel utilization can be improved are also the most difficult to implement in some agencies because of laws, contracts, and emotions.

It makes sense to deploy available personnel when and where they will be needed. Why, then, do some police agencies divide their patrol force equally among three shifts? This would seem to indicate that there are as many calls for service between midnight and 8 a.m. as there are between 4 p.m. and midnight. Few if any police administrators could support such a position, but some are forced to live with such a situation by reason of labor contracts, ordinances, or statutes. It required some eight years of negotiations and a 1969 State Law to change a 1911 State Law that prohibited the New York City Police Department from introducing a "fourth platoon" to work from 6 p.m. to 2 a.m.[13] By taking some officers from other shifts, New York City was finally able to place officers on the street during the hours when they were most needed.

When there are no restrictions against differential manning, including the "fourth platoon" approach, police agencies can improve their potential for increasing productivity by having more patrol officers on duty during those times when calls for service are the heaviest. Couple this relatively obvious maneuver with deployment to locations where crimes are most likely to occur, and you should be able to increase outputs with the same resources due to the fact that they're being better utilized.

Although acknowledging the moral and legal restrictions to such an approach, some police officials have suggested both unofficially and informally one other method for deployment. Since it is acknowledged, even by ardent supporters of rehabilitative programs, that most crimes are committed by those who have already been through the criminal justic system more than once why not assign personnel based on the geographic concentration of such recidivists? There are presently enough officers available in many communities to provide around-the clock surveillance to individuals or groups of known recidivists. This procedure has been implemented, on a limited basis, in the case of major criminals. The prospect of expanding it are remote, but the fact that some officials are talking about such an approach demonstrates their openmindedness to alternatives.

The other available method for improving personnel utilization concerns the option of placing one or two officers in a patrol car. Barring any labor contract that prohibits such discretion on the part of police management, or an emotional climate generated by the killing of an officer riding solo (regardless of other more contributing variables than the absence of a partner) a police agency which makes extensive use of two-officer units could effectively increase the amount and variety of their patrol activities by shifting to the deployment of some one-officer cars. The synthesis of available evidence drawn from various studies suggest that, except in extremely hazardous areas, the assignment of two officers to a patrol unit car is an inefficient use of personnel. Unit performance, unit efficiency, officer safety, and officer attitudes were all examined in a study of patrol staffing in San Diego with the conclusion that two-officer regular patrol units were not justified in that city.[14]

Unfortunately, it's difficult to isolate the emotional effects of this type of approach on an officer who finds himself or herself suddenly riding alone without a partner. If a feeling of increased danger results because of this change, it could influence some decisions on the part of the officer—with positive or negative results in the areas of productivity and quality of working life.

Even without the presence of prohibiting legislation or labor contracts, it's difficult in some cases for police administrators to introduce resources that have the potential for improving personnel utilization. The initial outlay and the cost of operating a helicopter makes the justification for such a resource more difficult than, say, the addition of five extra beat officers. Although its surveillance, detection, and improved response capabilities, in addition to its use as an alternative to high speed ground chases, might be more effective than the five beat officers in the long run, most communities and their elected officials would probably support the option of the five additional officers. Thus, the police administrator who wishes to introduce alternatives to traditional patrol resources should be prepared to build a strong, factual, and perhaps even emotional case for his or her position.

Probably the most effective and efficient type of resource available to a cost-conscious, personnel-short police agency is also the most controversial. Electronic surveillance as a proactive tool can normally reduce considerably the amount of traditional resources needed to prevent crimes or arrest perpetrators. Although the time and effort involved in obtaining authorization for a telephone tap and then properly maintaining it is significant (one reason why this technique is not used indiscriminately), if a plan to plant explosives at some location is recorded and then prevented, the savings (output) could be quite substantial.

When electronic surveillance methods are used properly, the rights of the suspects are ensured, the protection of lives and property is enhanced, and police agencies are able to make maximum use of their officers and their equipment.

Training

In response to the increasing clamor for the professionalization of the police, many agencies have not only attempted to recruit college graduates, but have also sent more of their officers to training programs (other than recruit training) offered by different institutions and organizations at various locations around the country. The availability, in some cases, of Law Enforcement Assistance Administration (LEAA) training funds has accelerated this process. Just as the value of education to the police officer is being questioned, so too must be the millions of dollars expended on out-of-house training be carefully considered. What has been the return for the dollars spent? Here again, it becomes difficult to develop exact measurements concerning the value to the individual and the agency, but there are three types of information that will at least indicate the seriousness with which these programs are approached.

First of all, one must consider how the programs and their sponsoring organizations are chosen and evaluated. Normally, a program is chosen because of its reputation, location, or facilities (not necessarily in that order). Although these are legitimate considerations, they don't answer enough questions to justify issuing a $1,000 check to an officer for travel expenses and tuition. Just because a Lietenant from the agency attended a similarly named program two years before, and thought it was great, doesn't mean that another program will be. An examination of the topics scheduled and the speakers for the *current* program might make the Lieutenant's recommendations irrelevant. It is possible that a similar program is available locally (consider the savings on travel alone), and the decision to choose the program conducted in a resort area in the south during the winter was based on creature comfort rather than potential return for the dollar spent. Of course, if the latter is the case, and it is agency policy to grant an unofficial sabbatical with training funds, then an increase in functional skills on the part of the attendees shouldn't be the primary objective of the "trip," but rather it should focus on an attempt to evaluate improvements in attitude, morale, and so on.

Regardless of how a program is chosen, there should be a formalized evaluation of this training effort when the participant returns in order to see if the objective established for sending a representative was achieved. The results of this process can then be used to determine if the agency will participate in future programs offered by the institution or organization evaluated. A critique of speakers might also be catalogued by the training division to further assist in the process that should precede any decision to send an employee to a non-mandated course.

Another void that should be replaced by written policy concerns the selection of individuals to attend these out-of-house programs. When one moves away from the very functional, skills-oriented courses (e.g., homicide investigation, data processing etc.) into broader areas (e.g., management development, community relations, productivity, etc.) attendees seem to come from various divisions within a department and represent different ranks. There's nothing wrong with such a heterogenous audience *per se*. The cross-fertilization alone creates a learning process in and of itself. From a productivity point of view, however, a problem arises when the $1,000 expended to send the employee has little or no chance of producing dividends because the attendee doesn't have the opportunity, ability, or desire to use the information obtained.

A sergeant who "supervises" a K-9 dog has no immediate use for information available in a supervision course and therefore wouldn't be too motivated to absorb the material presented; the captain who has two months of service remaining before retirement and is selected to attend a two-week management course will have little time (or desire) to practice newly acquired knowledge in his or her current organization; and the bright young lieutenant with both undergraduate and graduate degrees in administration will probably receive less than a $1,000 worth of new information at a short course in principles of management. In all cases the bottom line should still center around the return expected from sending officers away to non-mandatory programs.

Sometimes the sponsoring agency attempts to assist in the selection process by spelling out who should attend (e.g., Institute on Organized Crime: "the highly specialized nature of the course requires that personnel selected to attend be limited to those who have assignments or planned assignments in the organized crime investigative field"—(NCJ-99876-). The Police Executive Institute, funded by the Police Foundation and LEAA, also suggests criteria for those who participate in their executive development workshops.

Even if an agency finds it difficult or restrictive to establish criteria for selecting officers to attend such programs, there should at least be some type of policy which indicates who should *not* attend.

Another indication of an awareness on the part of an agency that out-of-house training is expensive and, as such, the outputs should be maximized can be determined by examining post-program procedures back at the agency. One officer has acquired X amount of information at the cost of $1,000. Does he or she now become the sole custodian of the knowledge acquired, or is there an attempt to disseminate this information? If the information obtained can be passed on to nine additional officers, the *per capita* cost of the training can technically, or at least philosophically, be reduced from $1,000 per person to $100 per officer.

A debriefing should take place on the first work day following the return of an officer from a course, not only for evaluation purposes but also in order to determine what information should be disseminated, who should receive it, and how it should be passed on. (One criteria for attendance at programs where information received must be passed on to other officers might be the potential attendee's ability to accomplish the dissemination task.) The decisions on what, who, and how can be made by management personnel, representatives from training and, where the training involves skill development, officers who are working in the functional area covered during the program. The process will increase the return from training funds expended and assist officers in the performance of their work.

Data Collection

Before improvement in productivity and the quality of working life can be documented, data must be collected to identify current baseline levels. A search for such information might reveal deficiencies in the present system of collecting data. It's difficult to improve response time if figures aren't available, for example, on dispatch, queue, and travel time. If a decision is made to arrange personnel hours according to calls for service, and there's no system of recording calls for service according to the time they're received, it will be impossible to proceed any futher until such data are developed.

Ideally, the identification, collection, and analysis of pertinent information should be a collaborative venture involving knowledgeable police practitioners and technicians familiar with the use of techniques commonly employed by industrial engineers, professional planners, programmers, system analysts, and accountants. Although there's really no excuse for the absence of knowledgeable police personnel who can identify the types of information they need, and it might be a little difficult to locate a skilled analyst, it's not an impossible task. If such talent isn't already available within the police agency, other agencies within the larger governmental structure more than likely will have at least some type of analyst on the payroll who can be called on for assistance. A local college or university might have such talent available in the form of faculty or a graduate student looking for some part-time work. Even if data collection involves the expenditure of some funds that might have purchased one or two more officers, the potential return from a better utilization of existing resources through analysis of needs and demands would normally far exceed the expected "output" from one or two more officers.

There has even been a major productivity improvement in one form of data collection—namely, surveys. A recent report disclosed that telephone victimization surveys can be as effective as the more expensive face-to-face studies.[15] Although this study was aimed at gathering victimization information, there's no readily available reason that random digit dialing (a telephone survey technique that utilizes a mathematical formula to randomly select subjects, thus avoiding at least one sampling bias—the exclusion of households with unlisted numbers) couldn't be used for other types of survey. This low-cost alternative to personal interviews definitely reduces inputs and, if the quality of responses (outputs) can be maintained, then it offers the opportunity for those charged with the responsibility for this type of data collection to increase their productivity.

Team Policing

When Chief Constable James McConnach of Aberdeen, Scotland, introduced his version of team policing in 1948, the police world, as well as most of the public sector wasn't using the term *productivity*. However, most of the techniques which have previously been suggested in this chapter as vehicles for improvements in productivity and the quality of work are contained in the general concept of team policing.

Guidelines for a team policing model were developed in conjunction with the selection of this concept for replication by the Officer of Technology Transfer of the U.S. Department of Justice, LEAA, National Institute of Law Enforcement and Criminal Justice. Acknowledging that each agency should develop its own model, the following parameters appear in a manual prepared for the replication program:

- The department establishes teams of police officers ranging in number from twenty to forty.
- Decentralization of operations to a neighborhood or geographic area, with stability provided by permanent assignment of officers to that team and geographic area.
- Each team, under the direction of a team commander, is given the necessary authority and responsibility for providing police services for that geographic area. These services include patrol operations, investigations, planning, evaluation, resource allocation and training.
- The team commander, whose rank and title will be established at the outset, has his authority and responsibility clearly spelled out and is provided with a communication channel that allows access to the Chief of Police.
- There exists a rational decision making process within each team whereby objectives are set, plans developed and implemented, and the overall activities of the team evaluated.
- Positive interaction between the police and community they serve (the neighborhood geographical area).
- Maximum interaction among team members.[16]

If these parameters are followed, an increase in productivty and the quality of working life should result, since the actions and activities of a team should proceed along the following pattern:

With decision-making placed at a very low level and personnel limited to between 20 and 40 officers, random preventive patrol is quickly replaced by directed preventive patrol, usually suggested by officers who are familiar with the crime problem of "their" community. The "two-platoon" system for investigations (patrol does preliminary and detectives do follow-up investigations) is replaced by the generalist concept in which patrol officers are responsible for all aspects of crime control. There is also a marked increase in diversionary actions for petty crimes as evidenced by a reduction in misdemeanor arrests. However, felony arrests increase as the community assumes more and more responsibility for crime control by providing information before, during, and after the commission of a serious crime. Because of this community cooperation there's almost no need for two officer cars. Since a large portion of the training is dictated by local needs, it's conducted *in* the community, sometimes *with* the community, and in some instances *by* the community. Analysis of problems and suggested solutions is conducted at not only the team level, but even at the beat level.

The job enrichment potential in team policing should be obvious—but so should some of the problems. The new role for the veteran officers who perceive themselves as "tough cops" rather than as part of the community (although, if they think back long enough, they were probably thought of as both if they previously walked a steady beat) can be traumatic, especially if these officers are now evaluated, according to their ability to keep the peace without resorting to violence or arrest. Another problem area concerns the reduction in workload and size of detective units as patrol officers assume investigative reponsibilities. This sometimes creates a power struggle within the agency. Since team policing results in a "flatter" organization, the need for some ranks might disappear and even those that are retained might be thinned out. The Lieutenants, Captains, and Majors who have helped to build a department aren't going to be overly receptive to a concept that could cause them to lose their jobs. The key to these and more subtle problems lies in the administrator's ability to juggle existing resources with an eye towards the future (e.g., retirements, annexation, and expansion of the agency, etc.).

Even if the introduction of team policing improves the productivity of a large percentage of the agency and enables an equally high percentage of employees to enjoy their work more, it could still have the opposite effect on the remaining members of the department. Although the dissatisfied officers might be few in number, they could still cause some problems. Rebellions and revolutions have been started, and won, by only a small percentage of the populace. The potential sabotaging of team policing, or any new program, should remain a concern of the vigilant police administrator interested in improving productivity and the quality of working life.

Miscellaneous Challenges

All of the considerations discussed up to this point should be fairly familiar to students and practitioners interested in police administration—although perhaps not in the context of productivity and quality of working life. There are several other approaches that could be considered challenges to the *status quo*, only one of which will probably be readily recognized.

Public Safety. Over the years, there have been various attempts to better utilize the public safety resources of a city by recognizing that both police and fire services have a certain degree of "down time." In the case of the latter, it's easily calculated and, as such, it's usually the police that gain personnel in a consolidated public safety arrangement.

Thus, in some locations, the traditional methods of delivering these public safety services by two separate agencies have been replaced by various forms of consolidation. Some attempts have been successful while others have failed.[17]

Generally speaking, the successful attempts have been characterized by careful study and planning, and have been voluntary insofar as employee participation is concerned. Few failures can be attributed solely to technical problems, while many are the results of political difficulties stimulated by outside opposition.

From a productivity point of view, the potential gains and losses for each agency should be the key consideration. Thus, the public safety approach to the delivery of police and fire services should be determined on an individual basis and one which considers facts, not emotions stimulated by generalities, and isolated and exagerated examples of failures.

The other challenges to traditional thinking in the police field have to do with contracting, consulting, and pensions. The suggestions dealing with these areas all have potential for improvements in productivity and the quality of working life. There are also problems associated with each approach. All are just concepts that merit testing and refinement.

Contracting. For years Scottsdale, Arizona, has contracted with a private fire company. Many firms contract with private guard services. Some smaller localities contract with larger police agencies to provide police protection. Would it be possible for police agencies, or their larger governmental body, to contract with private firms for some police services? If some quality controls can be exercised over the outputs, might it be possible for private police to handle traffic control, provide certain types of escorts, maintain security over some institutions and buildings, and perform other functions? What about requiring insurance investigators to handle routine larcenies involving insurable items? Or mandating that alarm companies respond to the alarms they install?

The concept of contracting has limitless applications. Some contracting arrangements can be instituted by policies, or ordinances, that require the private sector to assume additional responsibilities for the areas in which they earn large sums of money (e.g. alarm systems). Certainly there are potential problems, but the police must expand beyond their current thinking on how to best deliver services with dwindling or scarce resources.

Consulting. At some time or another, most police agencies have been studied by one or more consultants. Recommendations generated from such studies are contained in voluminous reports that unfortunately in many cases are put to rest in bookcases and shelves throughout the agency. By and large, recommendations are good, and they cost a great deal to assemble, but they're useless if the desire or ability to implement them isn't present within the police agency. The concept of implementation consulting has been proposed[18] and would replace a consultant's report with a team of professionals who, on a temporary basis, would assume not only the responsibility for problem identification and resolutions, but also the authority for implementing solutions and change. By substituting employee-days for permanent positions, an environment conducive to change can be developed (there are no "friends" to consider) and the work can be accomplished better and more quickly because staff specialists are concentrating their efforts in their area of expertise.

Naturally, the size of the agency, the nature of the change desired, and legal restrictions must all be examined before any decision is reached to utilize the concept of implementation consulting. When compared to what is accomplished from a $25,000 study, implementation consulting might be the alternative that local government has been searching for, especially in view of the economic crunch that most cities face today.

Pension

One of the sacred cows in the police field is the pension that accompanies the job. This is due to the fact that in many cases the security needs it fulfills are instrumental in attracting and then keeping men and women in the police field. This same pension can, however, be considered an albatross for the individual officer as well as the police agency. If officers feel that they can't leave a particular police department because they don't want to "lose their pension," they can easily become less productive. They might feel compelled to just put in their time ("play it safe," "don't make waves," etc.) so they can collect their pensions. This isn't the type of motivation that produces happy workers, nor is it the type of climate in which organizational goals are easily met.

Police officers shouldn't be locked into jobs they don't like. On the other hand, management shouldn't be required to retain a non-productive employee, after only a short probation, until he or she is eligible for a pension.

The Institute for Local Self-Government in Berkley, California, and others are currently exploring the feasibilty of replacing a pension, at least in the early years of employment, with a contractual arrangement. Under the latter approach, the employer and employee would both get to take a longer look at each other before making any commitments. At the conclusion of a two, three, or four year contract, the employer and employee would both have the option to review the contract with "re-enlistment" bonuses available upon renewal. If either of the parties didn't agree to a renewal (the employer would maintain the ultimate right to such an option) then appropriate severance payments would be made. And, since both parties wouldn't be required to contribute to a costly pension plan, extra dollars would be available for salaries, re-enlistment bonuses, and severance pay.

The net result of this dramatic departure from traditional personnel practices in the police field should be the presence of more productive workers in a police agency. Once again, it's acknowledged that there could be some problems with this approach, but the assumption that pension practices should never be changed can and should be challenged.

Summary

Although the word "productivity" was seldom used in the police field until recently, the objectives for the concept—namely, the delivery of quality service with a minimum expenditure of resources—have been pursued for many years by some progressive police agencies. Now, as resources are dwindling and service requirements are increasing, few police agencies can afford not to pursue productivity improvements. At the same time, the labor force has become more educated, better trained, and, in many cases, organized. Thus, police administrators must become more sensitive to the needs of their officers and the quality of their working lives.

A participatory approach to the identification of potential areas for productivity improvements, and in the implementation of appropriate programs to accomplish such improvements, will, in most cases, also result in a better quality of working life for police employees.

The integration of the needs of police officers with the goals of their agency should result in maximum utilization of resources while the community they serve becomes the recipient of better police services.

Topics For Discussion

1. **Discuss some differences between current methods of evaluating a police agency and the use of productivity measurements.**
2. **Discuss the importance of productivity improvements for today's police agencies.**
3. **Discuss some shortcomings that might be found in work assignments for police officers.**
4. **Discuss the systems approach to productivity improvements.**
5. **Discuss potential problem areas in introducing programs aimed at improving productivity and the quality of working life.**

References

1. The Advisory Group and their 1973 positions were: J.P. Morgan, Jr., Chairman, Director of Public Safety, St. Petersburg, Florida; Dr. W. Edward Cushen, Chief, Technical Analysis Division, National Bureau of Standards; Carl V. Goodin, Chief of Police, Cincinnati, Ohio; Peter R. Gray, Judicial Conference of the State of New York, New York, New York; Cole Hendrix, City Manager, Charlottesville, Virginia; Clarence M. Kelley, Director, Federal Bureau of Investigation, Edward J. Kiernan, President, International Conference of Police Associations, Washington, DC; Prof. Richard C. Larson, Department of Urban Studies and Planning, Massachusetts Institute of Technology; Joseph H. Lewis, Police Foundation, Washington, DC; Thomas J. Madden, Law Enforcement Assistance Administration, Washington, DC; Dr. Jay Merrill, National Institute of Law Enforcement and Criminal Justice, Washington, DC; Prof. Gordon E. Misner, Director, Administration of Justice, University of Missouri, St. Louis; Patrick V. Murphy, President, Police Foundation, Washington, DC; James R. Newman, Lt. Col., Police Department, Kansas City, Missouri; Peter J. Pitchess, Sheriff of Los Angeles County, Los Angeles, California; John R. Plants, Director, Michigan State Police; Rocky Pomerance, Chief of Police, Miami Beach, Florida; Prof. Thomas Repetto, John Jay College of Criminal Justice, City University of New York; Paul J. Watson, Special Agent, Federal Bureau of Investigation; Jerry V. Wilson, Chief, Metropolitan Police Department, Washington, DC.

2. Legislation establishing a National Center for Productivity and Quality of Working Life was signed into law by the President on November 28, 1975, as Public Law 94-136. This legislation transferred the staff and functions of the National Commission On Productivity and Work Quality to the Center and resulted in its current title.
3. *Opportunities For Improving Productivity In Police Service,* National Commission on Productivity, Washington, DC. 1973, pp. 2-3.
4. *Improving Municipal Productivity: Work Measurement For Better Management,* November 1975, The National Commission on Productivity and Work Quality, Washington, DC 20036 (pp. 3-12). (Adapted for *police* productivity programs.)
5. *Court Systems Digest,* Washington Crime News Services, January, 1977, p. 7.
6. *Criminal Justice Research and Development,*National Advisory Committee on Criminal Justice Standards and Goals, Washington, DC, 1976, pp. 17–26.
7. *Workshop Reports, On Street Patrol,* Workshop in Political Theory and Policy Analysis, Indiana University, November 1976, pp. 1–3.
8. *Police Education Characteristics and Curricular,* National Institute of Law Enforcement and Criminal Justice, Washington, DC, July 1975, pp. 3–5.
9. *The Kansas City Preventive Patrol Experiment,* Police Foundation, Washington, DC, 1974.
10. *Traditional Preventive Patrol,* National Institute of Law Enforcement and Criminal Justice, Washington, DC, 1976, p. 78.
11. *The Criminal Investigation Process: Summary and Police Implications,* The Rand Corporation, Santa Monica, California, October, 1975, p. 7.
12. *Traditional Preventive Patrol,* National Institute of Law Enforcement and Criminal Justice, Washington, DC, 1976, p. 80.
13. *And the Beat Goes On: Patrolmen's Unionism in New York City,* NSF/RANN Grant GI 39004, August, 1974.
14. *Patrol Staffing in San Diego, One-On Two-Officer Units,* Police Foundation, Washington, DC, 1977.
15. *Random Digit Dialing: Lowering the Cost of Victimization Surveys,* Police Foundation, Washington, DC, 1976.
16. *Full Service Neighborhood Team Policing: Planning For Implementation,* Public Safety Research Institute, Inc., St. Petersburg, Florida, 1975.
17. For readers interested in a summary of results of consolidated agencies see: *Management Information Service Report,* International City Management Association, Washington, DC, Vol. 8, No. 7. July, 1976.
18. *Implementation Consulting,* Public Safety Research Institute, Inc., St. Petersburg, Florida, 1976.

Annotated Bibliography

Bernstein, Samuel J., and Reinharth, Leon. "Management, The Public Organization and Productivity: Some Factors To Consider." *Public Personnel Management 2* (July-August 1973), 261–66. ". . . Increased individual and organizational productivity. . . is a function of the level of integration of the four basic organizational components; the individual, the group, the organizational system and the public

International City Management Association. *Jurisdictional Guide To Productivity Improvement Projects.* Washington, DC, The National Commission on Productivity and Work Quality, 1975. The need for a means of disseminating information on the various ways in which different jurisdictions are solving their productivity problems led the Commission to publish this Guide, which lists descriptions of productivity projects initiated by local governments throughout the United States. The descriptions are grouped by functional areas, such as General Administration, Public Health, and Public Works, and are sub-divided into specific topics. They include brief statements of the problem addressed by the project, the project design, the results, and the name of the individual or office to contact for further information.

Morgan, J. M. (P.) Jr., "Police Productivity," *The Police Chief,* Vol. XLI, No. 7, July, 1974, pp. 28–30. Reviews the activities of the advisory group on productivity in law enforcement in terms of the concept of productivity and a consideration of means of measurement.

"Police Productivity," *Local Government Police Management,* Chapter 7, International City Management Association, Washington, DC, 1977. Discusses productivity as a philosophy and methodology for management. Identifies target areas for productivity improvements and the impact of labor relations on the process.

National Commission on Productivity. *Employee Incentives To Improve State & Local Government Productivity.* Washington, DC,: National Commission on Productivity and Work Quality, 1975. In an effort to provide more efficient municipal services, many state and local governments have initiated employee incentive programs. These programs involve, for example, attendance, performance, and job enlargement incentives, and offer monetary and nonmonetary rewards to the participants. The Guide lists examples of these programs from throughout the United States and groups them according to the type of incentive used. Guidelines for the development, use, and evaluation of incentive programs are also presented. Indexes of the examples by function and geographical area are included.

Newland, Chester A., ed. "Symposium: Productivity in Government." *Public Administration Review 32* (November-December 1972): 739–850. This special issue of the Review presents a variety of articles dealing with different aspects of the problem of government productivity. Included are articles examining productivity in relation to the economy, definitions and measures of productivity, and the federal government's productivity programs. State and local government are discussed in articles which present case studies of productivity programs in New York, Wisconsin, and California. Other articles consider trends in public capital expenditure, public personnel concerns in relation to productivity enhancement programs, and certain aspects of public employment trends.

Ross, John P., and Burkhead, Jesse I. *Productivity in the Local Government Sector.* Massachusetts: D. C. Heath and Company, 1974. Productivity as a concept and attempts to measure it, especially in the public sector, have continually engendered misunderstanding. To clarify this confusion, primarily as it relates to local government, Ross and Burkhead examine the concept of productivity, the different means employed in attempting to measure it, its relation to the public and private sectors, and the problems, both theoretical and practical, which it gives rise to. A critical review of the empirical studies which have investigated productivity in different areas of federal, state, and local government aids in highlighting their concerns. The end result of their study is the development and application of a methodology which they feel will provide a viable means for measuring local government productivity and, in turn, furnish answers to the growing number of questions which citizens are asking about the performance of local government.

Wolfle, Joan L. (Ed.), *Reading On Productivity In Policing*, Police Foundation, Washington, DC, 1975. Six articles on productivity covering: The national view; the perspective from city hall; police accountability; unions and productivity; measurements; planning and implementing a productivity program.

9

POLICE POLICY

Chapter Objectives

☑ List the three factors affecting the formulation and execution of laws.
☑ Discuss the fallacy of assuming that policy-making is the exclusive responsibility of the legislative branch of government.
☑ Define policy at the operational and executive level of police agencies.
☑ Discuss how operational policy is formulated through individual police officer decision making.
☑ Describe the problems associated with a policy of full enforcement.
☑ Describe and discuss means for guiding and controlling the discretionary decisions of police officers.
☑ Describe the differences between the National Advisory Commission's and the American Bar Association's recommendations for guiding discretionary decision making.
☑ List the steps of the policy making process.
☑ Write a police policy statement.

Introduction

Police policies are the statements and/or actions through which the police become accountable to the democratic process. While the police must be subordinate to the legitimate political process, they are also one of the major participants within that process. Decisions and/or actions that create police policy may have an effect upon broader public policy. The degree and extent of enforcement of federal, state, or local laws can have a major impact upon society.

A classic example of this impact was seen in the 1933 decision to rigidly enforce traffic regulations in the city of Palo Alto, California. The Palo Alto Board of Public Safety's policy statement ordered that "*All* traffic laws *must* be enforced *immediately and continuously* within the city."[1] Initial reaction was overwhelmingly negative. Even the Chief of Police lamented, "The laws cannot be enforced beyond the willingness of the people to have them enforced, and the public won't stand for this." The merchants claimed that the speed cops would drive trade out of town. Visitors to the city were outraged when handed a traffic citation by "these small-town cops."

The attitude of the Palo Alto Police Court in 1933 toward the traffic law enforcement policy is best illustrated by Rollin Perkins, who discusses the incident in detail in his book, *Elements of Police Science*:

> *Visitors receiving tags for traffic violations ... [embarked] on a fruitless search when starting out to find some "citizen of influence" to get the tag fixed. There simply are not any such influential people in the city whose police department operates on the principle of "neither fear nor favor."*[2]

The personal attitude of Judge John E. Springer, who presided over the court, was clearly transmitted by a placard kept on his desk that read:

Things That We Know Without Being Told:

1. *You were not going that fast.*
2. *You are a careful driver.*
3. *The cop did not pace you.*
4. *The fast ones got away.*
5. *You favor law enforcement, but...*
   So tell us again. We love it.[3]

After eight months of "outbursts of indignation," the *Palo Alto Times* conducted a poll of its readers in order to determine how the citizens actually felt about traffic enforcement. The results were fourteen to one in favor of the enforcement policy. Evidence, although inconclusive, seemed to indicate that the enforcement policy was actually bringing trade into town rather than driving it away.

Implicit within the above example is the idea that laws should be enforced upon all the people all the time under all circumstances; however, such enforcement is not possible. Thus, the need for flexibility in executing the laws arises.

The need for flexibility in executing the laws results from at least three factors which affect the formulation and execution of legislative mandates. First, it is simply impossible to formulate a statute or ordinance which will encompass all of the conditions and circumstances which must be addressed.[4] For example, it is seldom possible to enumerate all of the various activities that would constitute breaches of the peace, or the conditions under which some prohibited activity would not necessarily be a breach. California state law defines an unlawful assembly as: "Whenever two or more persons assemble together to do an unlawful act, or do a lawful act in a violent, boisterous, or tumultuous manner, such assembly is an unlawful assembly".[5] If this is the case, then boisterous fans at a wrestling match constitute an unlawful assembly. If so, when? If not, why not?

The second factor arises from changes which occur after the passage of legislation, or as a result of the legislation itself. California's "Consenting Adults" law, passed in 1975, which permits consenting adults freedom in their personal sexual lives, was used shortly after its passage as a defense against charges of prostitution even though the laws pertaining to prostitution were not changed by the "Consenting Adults" act. The full implication of new law is often not known for years.

The third factor concerns the complexity and technical nature of matters confronting lawmakers. This is especially critical in the area of "scientific technology" (i.e., nuclear energy, environment, etc.), but is becoming increasingly important in the social and behavioral areas. What are the effects of long term discrimination? How do long prison terms affect criminal behavior? Will decriminalization of marijuana lead to greater usage? What are the effects of marijuana usage on society? Questions of this type are both complex and technical, and are seldom solved by the "one correct answer" approach.

The historic assumption that the legislative branch is solely responsible for the formulation of public policy is only partially correct. In his book, *Policy and Administration*, Paul Appleby discusses several problems associated with the fallacy of assuming that policy-making is the exclusive responsibility of the legislature:

> *A clearer understanding of the present reality with respect to policy-making and administration is needed by many. . . practitioners of public administration. . . Most of all, a clearer understanding is needed by citizens, confused by the complexity of government in complex society; they need to know how to fix responsibility, how to protect popular government, how to make democratic citizen concern central to that government.*[6]

Appleby concludes that administrators make policy, too. Decision-making in government is inevitable. And, in creating policy, government employees are subject to the same political constraints as other public officials are, including legislators and judges. Appleby maintains that these external political constraints provide us with the greatest protection against a public service that would otherwise become arbitrary, undemocratic, and zealously efficient.

For every policy decision made by lawmakers in the legislative branch, thousands more are made by administrators in the executive branch. Administrators make rules, determine what the law is, determine the rights of citizens with reference to the law, and make specific legislative policy out of vague legislative mandates. No one, Appleby concludes, has identified any boundary between policy-making and administration that could stand up under the test of reality.[7]

Only in theory, then, is it possible to distinguish between policy formulated by the legislative branch and policy formulated by the executive branch. As social issues become more complex, as the demand for faster solutions to social problems increases, and as the resources for responding to these complexities and problems become scarcer, the policy decisions made by public administrators will become increasingly critical. A majority of these policy decisions will have overt political implications. The term *political*, in this context, refers to who gets what resources, when, and how.[8]

Policy Defined

The term *policy* has several meanings for managers and employees of public agencies. At the operational level, policy is generally conceived in a narrow or restrictive sense. That is, policy is viewed as "a set of guidelines designed to standardize the behavior of personnel."[9] At this level, policy can be thought of as an authoritative declaration or prescription consisting of a statute, a rule, a general order, or a judicial decision.

Some of the common policy definitions for the operational level are provided below:

- Policies represent the totality of standards or norms that govern the conduct of people in the organization.[10]
- Policy is the broad general plan or principle underlying methods of procedure or the conduct of the department's affairs . . . [T]he policy statement will say what is to be done but not how it is to be done.[11]
- Policy consists of principles and values which guide the performance of a Department activity. Policy is not a statement of what must be done in a particular situation, rather, it is a statement of guiding principles which should be followed in activities which are directed toward the attainment of department objectives.[12]
- Policy embodies the philosophies, principles, attitudes, values, and intentions of management. It can be expressed orally or in writing, or it can be implied as a result of long-standing practices.[13]
- . . . [Policy] can be defined to mean a guideline for carrying out even the most detailed action, [but] the term usually refers to the broad statement of principle.[14]

At the middle-management and executive level, policy is generally conceived in a broad, encompassing sense. At this level, policy is often synonymous with the organization's objectives, and may be viewed as a general pattern of decisions and actions by departmental authorities that are united by a common and general objective toward which all of the decisions and actions are directed. Policy definitions for the administrative level of departmental hierarchies include:

- . . . [P]olicies are guides to thinking in decision-making. They reflect and interpret objectives, channel decisions to contribute to objectives, and thereby establish the framework for planning programs.[15]
- [Policy outputs are]. . . the authoritative allocation of values for society. . . .[16]
- A policy. . . is a declaration of intent on the part of government to do something.[17]
- [P]olicy is a broad statement of purpose or intent. Policies form the guidelines against which we measure our progress toward particular objectives.[18]

Policy at the top management level probably conforms more with the conventional usage of the word in socio-political literature, such as in the terms "foreign policy," "energy policy," and "social welfare policy." The underlying assumption about policy is that a formalized procedure exists for prioritizing and determining a course of action which will direct an organization toward the goals and objectives to be accomplished.

Therefore, policy developed at the executive level will, in most instances, guide and determine policy at the operational level. For example, a decision by the chief executive in a police department to limit resource allocations to the narcotics division may determine the extent of enforcement activities within that specialized unit. One would have to assume that the decision to limit enforcement activities was arrived at following an analysis of the overall enforcement effort of the department. What would result if no conscious effort was made ahead of time to evaluate the impact of this type of decision? Or, to approach this sort of situation from a different perspective, what happens when inaction on the part of authoritative decision-makers forces individuals to act *without* having defined policy guidelines to refer to?

Operational Police Policy-Making

A substantial body of literature already exists which discusses public policy. Until recently, however, the subject of *police* policy has been discussed primarily as it relates to departmental rules and regulations. There is a certain feeling of apprehension that goes hand-in-hand with writing about police policy, since no two people seem to define it in the same way; and, as yet, not enough is known about it to be able to say with confidence whether and how it may be differentiated from all other areas of public policy. The study of police policy is still in a primitive theoretical stage. As Einstein once pointed out, "The formulation of a problem is far more often essential than its solution."[19] The same may be true for police policy.

The management of police organizations is a very responsible task, perhaps the most responsible of any management position in any organization. The

> *continued success of democratic government will depend, in large measure, on the competent and conscientious behavior of police organization managers.*[20]

At no other time in the history of civilization has this responsibility been more acute. The relationship that is established between the need for effective, aggressive police action and the requirements of law and propriety will determine the future of democratic society. Today, the parity relationship between these two competing forces is determined not by police leaders but, more often than not, by individual police officers.

In his book *Police Systems in the United States*, Bruce Smith deals systematically with the manner in which democratic ideals are transformed into day-to-day realities by the individual guardians of society:

> *. . . [W]hen we equip a public servant with a gun, a club, a uniform, and a badge of ill-defined authority, we endow him in effect with informal powers and duties which are akin to those of prosecutors, judges, juries, jailers, and executioners.*
>
> *Thus, all the devices for popular and administrative control—the enactments of legislative bodies, the aims of governmental executives, the hierarchies of structural organization, and the expenditure of great sums of public money upon men and equipment—all converge at last upon one focal point: the policeman . . .*
>
> *The policemen's art, then, consists in applying and enforcing a multitude of laws and ordinances in such degree or proportion and in such manner that the greatest degree of social protection will be secured. The degree of enforcement and the method of application will vary with each neighborhood and community. There are not set rules, nor even general guides to policy, in this regard. Each policeman must, in a sense, determine the standard which is to be set in the area for which he is responsible. Immediate superiors may be able to impress upon him some of the lessons of experience, but for the most part such experience must be his own. . . . Thus he is a policy-forming administrator in miniature, who operates beyond the scope of the usual devices for popular control. He makes and unmakes the fortunes of governmental executives and administrators though rarely falling under the direct influences of the popular will. . . .*[21]

Although Smith perhaps articulates the police officer's dilemma better than anyone, the problems associated with ambiguous, unenforceable laws and the lack of official policy guidelines were recognized as early as the turn of the century by Leonhard Fuld, among others. In his book, *Police Administration*, Fuld comments on these issues:

> *Statutes are frequently enacted by the legislature of the state . . . and ordinances are sometimes passed . . . imposing upon the citizen petty restrictions in the conduct of their business which are almost impossible to enforce.*[22]

According to Fuld, many police executives neglect to direct the enforcement actions of police officers, resulting in the enforcement of unpopular laws and ordinances. Other executives attempt to require the enforcement of "laws obnoxious to a majority of the citizens."[23] Thus, lacking rational and responsible leadership, the individual officer is often alone in confronting dilemmas which arise on the job. Discussing the pragmatics of street enforcement, Fuld goes on to say:

> *It is the officer's ambition to learn all the statutes and ordinances in order that he may not through ignorance fail to enforce a single one. In so far as it is both impracticable and impossible for the policeman to enforce all the laws on the statute books, from the most insignificant to the most important, the experienced officer performs a valuable service in pointing this out to the young probationer. Yet the ambition to enforce all the laws is a very desirable ideal for a policeman to have before him and when by his instruction the older policeman not only ridicules this ideal but actually instructs him to neglect the enforcement of some very important statutes, he seriously impairs the efficiency of the young patrolman.*[24]

The ideal and publically stereotyped role of the police conflicts with the views of both Smith and Fuld. In the broadest sense, the police are assumed to be ministerial agents of the law whose only functions are those of investigating crimes, arresting offenders, and bringing them before the courts. Viewed in this manner, police are expected to be without discretion in their dealings with the individuals they have identified as being outside the law. For example, Section 82, Chapter 125 of the 1971 Revised Statutes of Illinois states:

> *It shall be the duty of every sheriff, coroner, and every marshal, policeman, or other officer of any incorporated city, town, or village having the power of sheriff, when any criminal offense or breach of the peace is committed or attempted in his presence, forthwith to apprehend the offender and bring him before some judge or magistrate to be dealt with according to law.*

The ideal ministerial role, therefore, imposes upon the policeman an obligation of "full enforcement." According to Herman Goldstein:

> *A policy of "full enforcement" implies that the police are required and expected to enforce all criminal statutes and city ordinances at all times against all offenders. It suggests that the police are without authority to ignore violations, to warn offenders when a violation has in fact occurred, or to do anything short of arresting the offender and placing a charge against him for the specific crime committed. It views the police function to be that of relating the provisions of law to a fine measure of the quantum of evidence. Out of this cold and somewhat mechanical calculation evolves an answer which provides the basis for police action.*[25]

This conceptualization of the police as neutral administrators of the criminal law has evolved, to a large extent, from the meaning of *rule of law* characterized by the phrases "supremacy of law" and "a government of laws and not of men." Restricted in this manner, the rule of law forms an ideal paradigm of legal authority in which government by rules takes precedence over government by the discretionary acts of those holding official power.

A. J. Dicey, writing in 1885, formulated two fundamental meanings of the rule of law. First, it means "the absolute supremacy or predominance of regular law as opposed to the influence of arbitrary power [excluding] the existence of arbitrariness, of prerogative, or even of wide discretionary authority on the part of government." Second, it means "the equal subjection of all classes to the ordinary law of the land administered by the ordinary law courts [and] excludes the idea of any exemption of officials or others from the duty of obedience to the law which governs other citizens or from the jurisdiction of the ordinary tribunals."[26] A more recent writer, F. A. Hayek, states that the rule of law means:

> *. . . government in all its action is bound by rules fixed and announced beforehand—rules which make it possible to foresee with fair certainty how the authority will use its coercive powers in given circumstances and to plan one's individual affairs on the basis of this knowledge.*[27]

Kenneth C. Davis labels these definitions as an "extravagant version of the rule of law" and states that they "express an emotion, an aspiration, an ideal, but none is based upon a down-to-earth analysis of the practical problems with which modern governments are confronted."[28] Davis maintains that the "extravagant version" of the rule of law has been universally rejected in practice, but only rarely in legal philosophy. At least one state, New Mexico, appears to have statutorily rejected the idea of mechanically applying the criminal law. Section 1, Article 1, Chapter 39, New Mexico State Statutes, 1970, states:

> *It is hereby declared to be the duty of every sheriff, deputy sheriff, constable, and every other peace officer to investigate all violations of the criminal laws of the state of New Mexico which are called to the attention of any such officer or of which he is aware, and it is also declared the duty of every such officer to diligently file a complaint or information, if the circumstances are such as to indicate to a reasonably prudent person that such action should be taken.*

By officially recognizing that the enforcement of criminal law requires judgment, the State of New Mexico has attempted to bridge the gap between the ideal state and the work-a-day world of policing. Yet, merely to recognize that law enforcement officers can and should use discretion in enforcing the law is inadquate.

That police officers must and do exercise discretion and judgment in enforcing the law is clear, but executives of police agencies have been exceedingly reluctant to officially acknowledge the informal and secretive practice of *selective* enforcement. "To acknowledge that law enforcement officials do exercise discretion requires an overt act—the articulation of a position—an action which is rare among those in the police field."[29] Davis, reporting on policy-making within the Chicago Police Department, states, that the written directives from the superintendent's office to others within the department seldom mention enforcement policy, "and nearly all of them studiously avoid any acknowledgement that any statute or ordinance may be properly left unenforced on any occasion."[30]

Even if police executives should have the urge to discuss the problems of attaining full enforcement, the typical executive would be reluctant to do so in public. "To acknowledge the exercise of discretion belies the very image in which the police administrator takes such pride and which the executive strives so hard to achieve. This is the image of total objectivity—of impartiality—and of enforcement without fear or favor."[31] Yet, time and again, studies have shown that the individual officer, left on his or her own to determine when, how, and against whom to enforce the law, applies and uses the law in a discriminatory manner.[32]

While the overwhelming majority of actions taken by police officers are firmly within the parameters established by due process decisions, many are clearly unethical and/or illegal. In the President's Commission of Law Enforcement and Administration of Justice *Task Force Report: The Courts*, it was noted that police discretion in many enforcement areas goes beyond the limits of due process:

> *The looseness of the laws constitutes a charter of authority on the street whenever the police deem it necessary. The practical costs of this departure from principle are significant. One of its consequences is to communicate to the people who tend to be the object of these laws [i.e., disorderly conduct, vagrancy, drunkenness, gambling] the idea that law enforcement is not a regularized, authoritative procedure, but largely a matter of arbitrary behavior by the authorities. The application of these laws often tends to discriminate against the poor and subculture groups in the population. It is unjust to structure law enforcement in such a way that poverty becomes a crime. And it is costly for society when the law arouses the feelings associated with these laws in the ghetto, a sense of persecution and helplessness before official power and hosility to police and other authority that may tend to generate the very conditions of criminality society is seeking to extirpate.*[33]

The use of the criminal law to intentionally harass some individuals may involve an abuse of power by the arresting officer. Davis reported that most of the officers interviewed during the Chicago study readily acknowledged that "most arrests for disorderly conduct involved an abuse of power."[34] In addition, Davis states:

> *The various harassment policies are made almost entirely by patrolmen, sometimes with the knowledge of their superiors but generally without the superiors' disapproval. Yet the superiors often assert in interviews that they disagree. The system of harassing by arresting for disorderly conduct those who have in no sense been disorderly is strongly disapproved by some supervisors—verbally in interviews, but not in firm orders issued to subordinates. The policy of harassing "known" criminals by frequently stopping and questioning them is usually approved and encouraged by superiors, but the policy stems from patrolmen, who give it their own twist.*[35]

The present situation of permitting—indeed, of requiring—the individual police officer to formulate policy on a day-to-day or case-by-case basis is not a healthy one. Over a decade ago, the *Task Force Report: The*

Police concluded that there were two alternative ways in which the police could respond to the policy problem confronting them:

1. *The first is to continue, as has been true in the past, with police making important decisions, but doing so by a process which can fairly be described as "unarticulated improvisation." This is a comfortable approach, requiring neither the police nor the community to face squarely the difficult social issues which are involved, at least until a crisis—like the current "social revolution"—necessitates drastic change.*
2. *The second alternative is to recognize the importance of the administrative policy-making functions of police and to take appropriate steps to make this a process which is systematic, intelligent, articulate, and responsive to external controls appropriate in a democratic society; a process which anticipates social problems and adapts to meet them before a crisis situation arises.*
   Of the two, the latter is not only preferable; it is essential if major progress in policing is to be made. . . .[36]

Adopting the second suggestion for resolving the police officers' dilemma rests primarily upon two factors: first, official acknowledgement of discretion; and second, development of written policy guidelines. This approach has been specifically recommended by the National Advisory Commission on Criminal Justice Standards and Goals and the American Bar Association.[37]

Concerning police discretion, the National Advisory Commission on Criminal Justice Standards and Goals: *Report on Police* states in Standard 1.3:

Every police agency should acknowledge the existence of the broad range of administrative and operational discretion that is exercised by all police agencies and individual officers. That acknowledgement should take the form of comprehensive policy statements that publicly establish the limits of discretion, that provide guidelines for its exercise within those limits, and that eliminate discriminatory enforcement of the law.

1. *Every police chief executive should have the authority to establish his agency's fundamental objectives and priorities and to implement them through discretionary allocation and control of agency resources. In the exercise of his authority, every chief executive:*

a. *Should seek legislation that grants him the authority to exercise his discretion in allocating police resources and in establishing his agency's fundamental objectives and priorities;*

b. *Should review all existing criminal statutes, determine the ability of the agency to enforce these statutes effectively, and advise the legislature of the statutes' practicality from an enforcement standpoint; and*

c. *Should advise the legislature of the practicality of each proposed criminal statute from an enforcement standpoint, and the impact of such proposed statutes on the ability of the agency to maintain the existing level of police services.*

2. *Every policy chief executive should establish policy that guides the exercise of discretion by police personnel in using arrest alternatives. This policy:*
   a. *Should establish the limits of discretion by specifically identifying, insofar as possible, situations calling for the use of alternatives to continued physical custody;*
   b. *Should establish criteria for the selection of appropriate enforcement alternatives;*
   c. *Should require enforcement action to be taken in all situations where all elements of a crime are present and all policy criteria are satisfied;*
   d. *Should be jurisdiction-wide in both scope and application; and*
   e. *Specifically should exclude offender lack of cooperation, or disrespect toward police personnel, as a factor in arrest determination unless such conduct constitutes a separate crime.*
3. *Every police chief executive should establish policy that limits the exercise of discretion by police personnel in conducting investigations, and that provides guidelines for the exercise of discretion within those limits. This policy:*
   a. *Should be based on codified laws, judicial decisions, public policy, and police experience in investigating criminal conduct;*
   b. *Should identify situations where there can be no investigative discretion; and*
   c. *Should establish guidelines for situations requiring the exercise of investigative discretion.*
4. *Every police chief executive should establish policy that governs the exercise of discretion by police personnel in providing routine peacekeeping and other police services that, because of their frequent recurrence, lend themselves to the development of a uniform agency response.*
5. *Every police chief executive immediately should adopt inspection and control procedures to insure that officers exercise their discretion in a manner consistent with agency policy.*[38]

In 1973, the American Bar Association approved its published *Standards Relating to the Urban Police Functions.* Their standards concerning police discretion are as follows:

4.1 *Exercise of discretion by police. The nature of the responsibilities currently placed upon the police requires that the police exercise a great deal of discretion—a situation that has long existed, but is not always recognized.*

4.2 *Need for structure and control. Since individual police officers may make important decisions affecting police operations without direction, with limited accountability, and without any uniformity within a department, police discretion should be structured and controlled.*[39]

Concerning the establishment of policy, *Report on Police* Standard 2.2 states:

Every police chief executive immediately should establish written policies in those areas of operations in which guidance is needed to direct agency employees toward the attainment of agency goals and objectives.

1. *Every police chief executive should promulgate policy that provides clear direction without necessarily limiting employees' exercise of discretion.*
2. *Every police chief executive should provide for maximum participation in the policy formulating process. This participation should include at least:*

a. *Input from all levels within the agency—from the level of execution to that of management—through informal meetings between the police chief executive and members of the basic rank, idea incentive programs, and other methods that will promote the upward flow of communication; and*

b. *Input from outside the agency as appropriate—from other government agenices, community organizations, and the specific community affected.*

3. *Every police chief executive should provide written policies in those areas in which direction is needed, including:*

a. *General goals and objectives of the agency;*

b. *Administrative matters;*

c. *Community relations;*

d. *Public and press relations;*

e. *Personnel procedures and relations;*

f. *Personal conduct of employees;*

g. *Specific law enforcement operations with emphasis on such sensitive areas as the use of force, the use of lethal and nonlethal weapons, and the arrest and custody; and*

h. *Use of support services.*[40]

The American Bar Association concludes:

> *Police discretion can best be structured and controlled through the process of administrative rule-making by police agencies. Police administrators should, therefore, give the highest priority to the formulation of administrative rules governing the exercise of discretion, particularly in the areas of selective enforcement, investigation techniques, and enforcement methods.*[41]

In Standards 4.4 and 4.5, the American Bar Association makes general recommendations for including the legislatures, courts and citizens in the administrative rule-making process.

As pointed out in the recommendations, the need for definitive police policy extends across the entire spectrum of police operations and practices. Two of the more critical areas are the handling of complaints against the police, and the equality of enforcement.

Handling of Complaints Against the Police.

The administration of justice in the United States is, to a large extent, justice without trial[42] because the decision not to invoke the criminal process is one of "extremely low visibility" and "seldom the subject of review."[43] In addition, formal and informal bureaucratic expectations work to insure that information which may be damaging or embarrassing to the agency is excluded from intentional public disclosure:

Secrecy among the police stands as a shield against the attack of the outside world; against bad newspaper publicity, which would make police lose respect; against public criticism, from which they feel they suffer too much. . . .[44]

While the emphasis on secrecy has been an important bureaucractic norm, several factors are beginning to work against its continuation. First is the growing concept of professionalism, coupled with a strong sense of personal ethics; this has been especially true since Watergate. Second, there appears to be a greater willingness on the part of many public employees to disclose questionable practices that they perceive to be unethical or illegal. Two of the most widely publicized cases have been those of Daniel Ellsberg, *The Pentagon Papers*, and Frank Serpico, (Corruption in the New York Police Department). The third and final factor has been the Freedom of Information Act, which requires public organizations to release information upon request (with a few exceptions).

Since the operations of most police departments are directed by a nearly autonomous administrator,[45] the receipt and processing of complaints is especially critical. The public's trust or mistrust of the 'police policing the police' will be in direct proportion to the openness and willingness of police executives to fairly administer the complaint process. Figure 9.1 is an example of how the Sunnyvale Department of Public Safety has addressed citizen concern through written policy.

Equality of Enforcement

The decision to arrest or not to arrest an indiviual is often based largely upon factors such as sex, age, race, dress, attitude, social or economic class, and personal or ideological values of the police officer—seldom, if ever, appropriate decision-making criteria. Selective enforcement of criminal and traffic laws and ordinances based solely upon these irrelevant criteria are not uncommon, and are partially responsible for much of the public's alienation from and antagonism toward the police.[46] Alienation and antagonism may eventually lead people to stop supporting the police, as well as government in general, and possibly resort to violence to achieve more equitable enforcement.

In discussing some of the sources of ineffectiveness in policy application, Michael Cohen makes the following point:

. . . When sizeable numbers of people, either through their own experiences or through learning of the experiences of others, perceive that authoritatively determined policies are not being applied effectively, they may question the good faith of those charged with the application, or they may question the ability of democratic mechanisms to produce results. In either case, the resulting suspicion and disaffection lend themselves first to sporadic, then to organized violence and protest[47] . . . .

To date, most citizen action has centered around making the police more responsive to local community control. This, in turn, has lead to both negative and positive reactions from the police.

Figure 9.1

CITY OF SUNNYVALE
CALIFORNIA

COMPLAINTS AGAINST THE POLICIES, PROCEDURES OR EMPLOYEES OF THE SUNNYVALE DEPARTMENT OF PUBLIC SAFETY

POLICY:

Any person who expresses dissatisfaction with the operation of the Sunnyvale Public Safety Department or with the conduct of its employees is entitled to a prompt acknowledgement and investigation of their complaint.

PROCEDURE:

Any person may make a complaint to any employee of the Department.

The complaint may be made by letter, telephone or in person.

The employee who initially receives a complaint may attempt to resolve it by offering an explanation if it seems likely that the complaint is based upon a misunderstanding of policies, procedures or legal requirements.

If the employee is uncertain of his ability or authority to provide accurate information or the complainant is not satisfied with the explanation, and feels that remedial action should be taken by the Department, the complainant is to be referred to the Commanding Officer* of the Division of the employee (or operation) complained of. (*Team Commander after hours).

The Commanding Officer (Team Commander) will accept the complaint and direct an investigation.

The investigation shall be conducted according to Department General Orders, Section 6.9.04 Discipline, Citizen's Complaints Against Personnel (or) 6.9.05 Discipline, Citizen's Complaints Against Departmental Procedures.

Upon conclusion of an investigation, the complainant shall be informed as to the findings of the investigation as well as any remedial action which may have been taken or planned.

Anyone who wants more information on this subject is invited to direct their inquiries to my office.

Reprinted by permission of the Sunnyvale Department of Public Safety, Sunnyvale, California

The negative reactions have been primarily concentrated at the patrol officer level, and are perhaps best demonstrated by the growing militancy and strength of police officer associations.[18] Positive reactions have ranged from special training programs in community relations, interpersonal sensitivity, and crisis intervention to specific police policies directed at equality of enforcement. The Los Angeles Police Department Policy Manual, section 340, "Equality of Enforcement," states in part:

> *. . . In order to respond to varying law enforcement needs in the different parts of the City, the Department must have flexibilty in deployment and methods of enforcement; however, enforcement policies should be formulated on a City-wide basis, and applied uniformly in all areas.*
>
> *Implicit in uniform enforcement of law is the element of evenhandedness in its application. The amount of force used or the method employed to secure compliance with the law or to make arrests is governed by the particular situation. Similar circumstances require similar treatment in all areas of the City and for all groups and individuals. To insure equal treatment in similar circumstances, an officer must be alert to situations where because of a language barrier or for some other reason, [the officer] may be called upon to display additional patience and understanding in dealing with what might otherwise appear to be a lack of response.*[49]

This policy guides police performance toward situational consistency and suggests that discretion is a function of the totality of circumstances related to a police-citizen encounter; e.g., seriousness of violation, time of day, type of area, number of persons involved, knowledge of person(s) involved, etc. Being situationally consistent means that police behavior and decisions should be consistent when they are confronted with *like situations*, and that their behavior should not change, even when one or more factors change unless a different alternative is *directly related* to obtaining a legally, or organizationally, defined desirable outcome.

For example, a patrol officer observes an unknown black male adult exceeding the speed limit by 10 m.p.h. at 11:00 a.m. in a business area with moderate traffic. The officer decides to stop the vehicle to give the driver a verbal warning. Assuming that a white driver does the same thing, under similar circumstances, the officer's behavior should be the same *unless* there is a valid reason, or causal connection, between one driver being black or the other white and the officer's using a different method—such as issuing a citation. (The object in any case, of course, should be that of influencing the driver to change his behavior.) In other words, if a verbal warning has a high positive correlation with changed driver behavior for white citizens, but not for black citizens, or vice-versa, then differences in treatment—a verbal warning for one, a ticket for the other—would be appropriate. However, in the absence of such a correlation, treating one differently than the other is situationally inconsistent.[50]

The Policy Process

For ease of conceptualization and discussion, the policy process can be divided into a series of interlocking, or overlapping, but distinct steps or phases. One of the simplest means of visualizing the policy process is to view it within a systems framework. The important elements and relationships are characterized as: environment, input, conversion process, output and feedback. The systems model focuses on: (a) an 'environment' that both energizes decision-makers and receives the output of their efforts; (b) the 'inputs' that carry stimuli from the environment to the decision-maker; (c) a 'conversion process' that converts (transforms) inputs into outputs; (d) the 'outputs' that carry the results of decision activity to the environment; and (e) 'feedback' that transmits the outputs of one period, as they interact with elements in the environment, back to the conversion process as the inputs of a later time. All of these elements interact with one another. Together they form the policy process system as it is outlined in Figure 9.2.

The police policy model could be energized from any point within the system. For example, suppose that the police officers' association had just received a favorable verdict from a suit filed against the department and the city under the Occupational Safety and Health Act regarding the failure to provide personal protective equipment. The outcome of this (environment) decision would serve as a demand (input) on the agency. This demand would require the department to address several issues: What is the department's responsibility in relation to the city's responsibility? Should the decision be appealed? What is the potential impact on the budget? What changes will be required in the current Health and Safety policy? Regardless of the decision made, the outcome of the process (conversion) will become the systems output into the environment. Once there is an output, feedback results, and the procedure begins again.

Figure 9.2

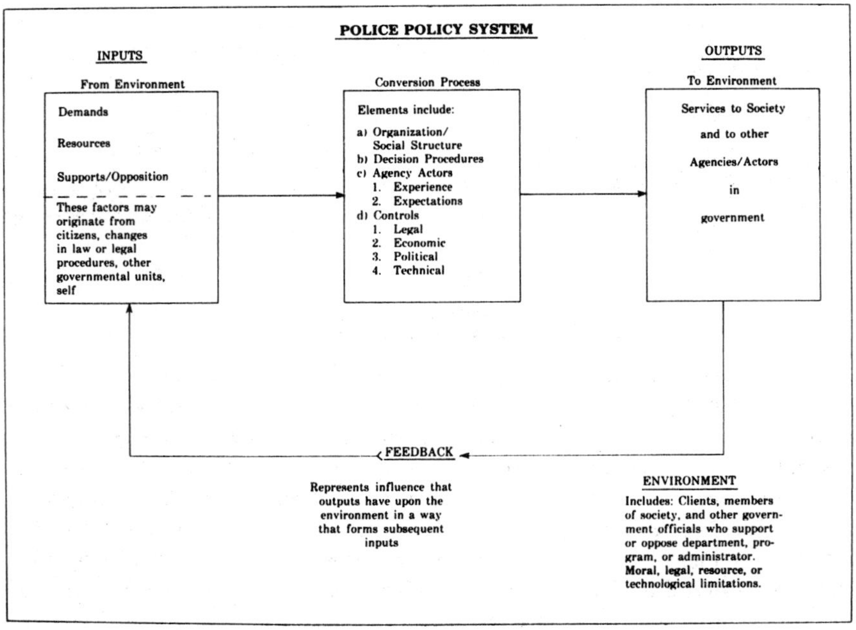

An expanded version of the basic systems model (see Figure 9.3) was utilized in the *Task Force Report: The Police.* This report identified the following steps: (a) identification, (b) referral—study and research, (c) consultation (internal and external); (d) formulation of policy; (e) promulgation of policy—articulation, publication and dissemination, and training; (f) evaluation—feedback.

Figure 9.3

Formulation and Execution of Police Policy

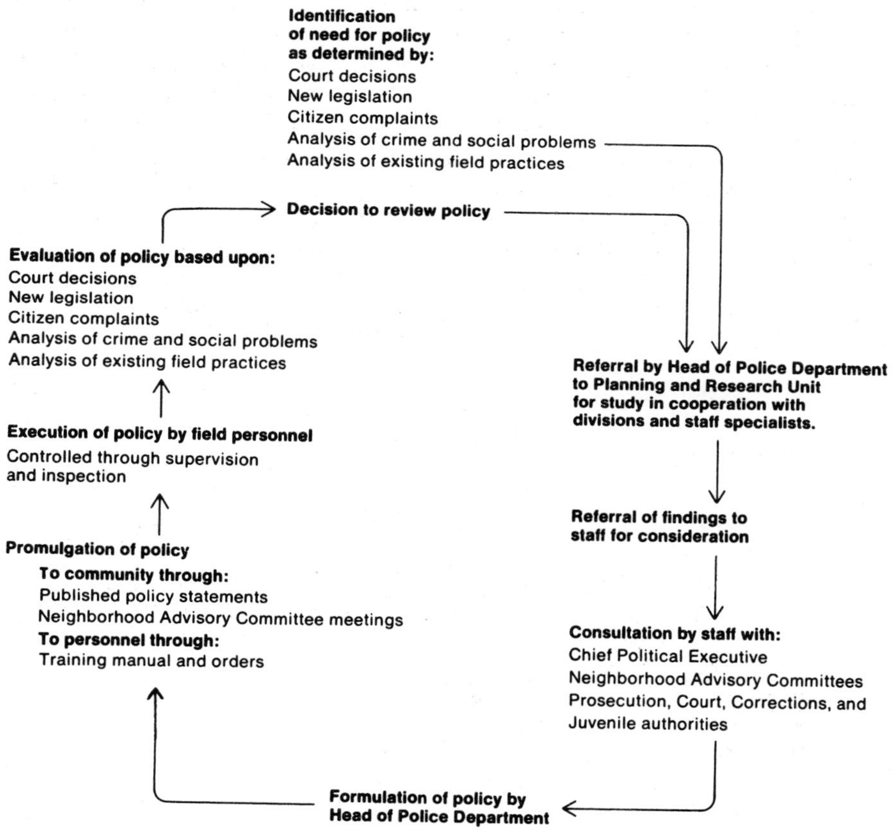

Policy-making is similar to the processes of budgeting and decision-making in that it is continuous and ongoing. By combining several steps, it is possible to reduce the overall policy-making process into four basic steps—formulating, consulting, implementing, and evaluating and reviewing.

Formulating policy consists of determining what is going on now, estimating alternative futures, and assessing needs. Data (facts and opinions) must be collected and subjected to analysis. Alternatives must be identified and evaluated. Questions must be asked and answered. Are existing policies effective? If not, how can they be improved? New policy statements may be drafted and circulated to interested individuals and groups that are both inside and outside the agency. Staff and public meetings should be held to discuss proposed policy. After public review, discussion, and evaluation, a statement of policy should be disseminated in written form to minimize or eliminate any misunderstanding concerning the intent of the policy. Although it is not easy to articulate exact expressions of intent, every effort should be made. The statements should be written in a clear and concise manner, free of police argot, and free of racist and/or sexist words. Policy statements must include sufficient detail to ensure that the action it directs will produce the desired results, but not so much detail that it unnecessarily limits the exercise of discretion.[51]

An example of a clear and concise policy statement is that of the Los Angeles Police Department regarding the conduct of undercover officers:

> **Conduct of Undercover Officers.** *In order to obtain information and evidence regarding criminal activities, it may be necessary that the department utilize undercover operators. Such operators shall not become "Agent Provocateurs" or engage in entrapment. The officers shall not commit any act or omit to perform any duty imposed by law which constitutes a crime.*[52]

Implementing or installing new policy, or substantially modifying existing policy, can be an exceedingly difficult part of the entire policy process. Efforts spent during the formulating stage to ensure that all interested parties had an opportunity to review and discuss the policy may be the key factor during the implementing stage. Acquiring support for a new policy will more than justify the effort expended. Whenever possible, a period of adjustment should be allowed before attempting to assess the policy's impact. In some cases, of course, a period of adjustment may be unfeasible. Changes in search and seizure laws caused by a supreme court decision may require immediate modification of existing policy.

The final step in the policy making process is *evaluating and reviewing.* This phase is needed to ensure that all policies are subjected to periodic evaluation "to determine the degree of conformity to policy norms and the quality of execution."[53] Since policies are designed to guide the exercise of discretion, they should not be unnecessarily restrictive, nor should they be so broad as to encourage or allow for arbitrary decision-making. Only through reviewing current conditions and practices can the proper balances be maintained.

If the evaluation and review step of policy-making is to be effective, the evaluator must have the authority and resources needed to conduct a systematic study. Without the authority to inquire into all facets of the policy under examination, its effectiveness or ineffectiveness will never be determined. A generalized internal review is not sufficient; however, questions must be asked and answered. Is the policy accomplishing its intended purpose? How extensive are deviations from policy norms? Political scientists label the process of answering these questions *policy analysis.* To facilitate policy analysis, policy is divided into three elements: policy output, policy action, and policy outcome.

A *policy output,* or *policy statement,* is defined as an authoritative statement of intent by a police agency to do something or refrain from doing something. For instance, the Los Angeles Police Department's policy concerning undercover officers states that the police *will* conduct undercover investigations, but the officers *will not* commit illegal acts. The function of a policy statement is explicit in its attempt to order the responses or the activities of a police agency. Accordingly, the policy output always implies that some choice among alternatives has been made.[54]

Policy action is what the policy agency actually does "as distinguished from what it says it is going to do (sometimes with many and conflicting voices) in its policy statement."[55] A policy output in the form of an affirmative action statement would lead one to assume that an individual would be employed regardless of sex, race, color, national origin, etc. provided that the person fulfilled all other valid criteria for employment. But what if research shows that zero females out of two thousand applicants were employed? What is the actual policy? It is reasonable to assume that the agency is discriminating against women? What other information would be needed before one could draw a conclusion?

If further investigation uncovered a pattern of actions which resulted in women being systematically excluded, then it would be obvious that the actual policy is not the policy *statement*, but in fact the policy *action.* The department's policy output is: Women Not Allowed.

A *policy outcome* is what happens in society as a result of the police department's policy outputs and actions. A policy outcome is predicated upon the prior existences of both a policy output and a policy action.[56]

Looking at the policy process as a series of steps or phase may be useful for some purposes, "but it tends to view policy-making as though it were the product of one governing mind, which is clearly not the case."[57] Looking at policy as a series of sequential events obscures the complexity, apparent disorder, and inherently political aspects of policy-making:

> *A policy is sometimes the outcome of a political compromise among policy makers, none of whom had in mind quite the problem to which the agreed policy is the solution. Sometimes policies spring from new opportunities, not from "problems" at all. And sometimes policies are not decided upon but nevertheless "happen."*[58]

Summary

Police policy-making is the response of police agencies to the supports, demands, and policies coming from both the external and internal environment. In order to understand the nature and impact of the police in its policy-making role, police policy-making must be viewed in the context of its external and internal environments.

The primary reasons for the existences of the police in a democratic society are: (a) to safeguard freedom, to preserve life and property, to protect the constitutional rights of citizens and maintain respect for the rule of law by proper enforcement thereof, and to preserve democratic processes; and (b) to maintain that degree of public order which is consistent with freedom and which is essential if our urban and diverse society is to be maintained.[59] In order to accomplish these tasks, the citizens through governmental bodies—have delegated to the police broad, yet limited, authority. The extent to and the manner in which any or all of these functions will be performed will vary from community to community. Choices about what tasks the police will or won't perform, what tasks will be performed by other sectors of the government, or what will be left for the private sector to handle, and how police authority is exercised are made over time in any given community and are normally in a process of at least slow change.

Although voluntary compliance with the law and the need for order are the general norms of behavior, a certain degree of disorder and lawlessness exists in every society. Therefore, in order to ensure harmony, government is coercive. Thus, the police, as an instrument of the government, are responsible for repressing disorder and lawless behavior. This does not mean that the police are continuously coercing involuntary citizen actions; rather, it means that the authority to repress is present and can, when necessary, be used.[60] Therefore, the essential issues to be resolved in a democratic society are: Who should use the police? What should the police be used for? When should the police be used? And, How should the police be controlled?

In the United States, the police are subjected to executive, legislative, judicial, and public scrutiny to ensure that they are accountable and responsive to the needs of citizens. "Community police agencies, as public organizations, have a dual accountability. Not only are they accountable to the rule of law in a democratic society, but they are also accountable to the 'public interest' in their own communities."[61] The private citizen can have an impact on police policies in a variety of ways. Constraints on police activities may result from direct complaints to police executives or to other policy-making bodies which have control over police authority. Indirectly, citizens can have an impact on the police by electing candidates to political office whose positions are based upon a platform of expanding or limiting the police exercise of authority. Additionally, citizens have access to the courts, both Civil and Criminal, whose decisions can halt or mandate specific actions by police agencies.

Actions by city councils, county boards of supervisors, and state and federal legislatures impact upon police policies by allocating or withholding resources, changing jurisdictions, or passing new laws. For example, a decision by the Department of Health, Education and Welfare to fund eighty percent of an experimental alcohol treatment program if the municipal governments will fund the remaining twenty percent may have a direct influence upon budgetary allocation to police agencies, as well as police and jail operations. In this instance, the city administrators may elect to use a portion of the police operating budget to fund the city's part of the program, based upon an anticipation that the alcohol treatment program will reduce by a certain percentage the need for police expenditures for handling alcoholics.

The greatest impact upon the police policies and actions have come from the courts, but, the courts are rarely concerned about the effects their decisions will have on police authority, they are rarely structured to provide significant guidance to officers in the infinite variety of complex situations that might in some way be affected by a particular court decision.[62]

To resolve, as much as possible, the dilemma for police officers, police agencies should develop policy guidelines. Policy should be designed, implemented, and enforced by authority of the chief executive officer, rather than by the systematic actions of the newest recruit. Policy designed in this manner will ensure that all segments of the community, and all personnel within the department, will have an opportunity to voice their opinion. When the "courts recognize that police agencies are preventing violations of constitutional rights by enforcing policies internally, the courts may decide that an effective alternative to the exclusionary rule exists."[63]

Topics for Discussion

1. **Discuss why police officers must exercise discretion when enforcing criminal statutes.**
2. **Discuss the need for police involvement when legislators are formulating laws.**
3. **Discuss why the police cannot separate themselves from legitimate political processes.**
4. **Discuss the advantages and disadvantages of formulating written policy.**
5. **Discuss why the public should be involved when police policy is being formulated.**
6. **Discuss how the public could be involved in the formulation of police policy.**
7. **Discuss the problems associated with developing police policy.**
8. **Discuss why some police executives are reluctant to acknowledge or officially direct the discretionary acts of policy officers.**
9. **Discuss why policy statements and policy actions should be congruent.**
10. **Discuss the advantages and disadvantages of situationally consistent law enforcement.**
11. **Discuss the advantages and disadvantages of viewing the police policy process from a systems perspective.**
12. **Discuss how police policy could be analyzed.**

References

1. Rollin M. Perkins, *Elements of Police Science*, Chicago, The Foundation Press, Inc., 1942, p. 334.

2. Rollin M. Perkins, *op. cit.* p. 337.
3. Rollin M. Perkins, *ibid.*, p. 337
4. Leonard D. White, *Introduction to the Study of Public Administration*, New York, The MacMillan Company, 1926.
5. California Penal Code, Section 407, *Unlawful Assembly*, 1976.
6. Paul H. Appleby, *Policy and Administration*, University, Alabama, University of Alabama Press, 4-5, 1949, p. 5.
7. Paul H. Appleby, op. cit., 1949.
8. Harold D. Lassell, *Politics: Who Gets What, When, How*, New York, World Publishing Company, 1958.
9. Jack L. Kuykendall and Peter C. Unsinger, *Community Police Adminstration*, Chicago, Nelson-Hall, 1975, p. 135.
10. Henry H. Albers, *Organized Executive Action*, New York, John Wiley and Sons, 1961.
11. O. W. Wilson, *Police Adminstration*, Second Edition, New York, McGraw-Hill, 1963.
12. Los Angeles Police Department, *Policy Manual*, in National Advisory Commission on Criminal Justice Standards and Goals, *Report Police*, Washington, D. C., U.S. Government Printing Office, 1973.
13. National Advisory Commission on Criminal Justice Standards and Goals, op. cit., 1973.
14. O. W. Wilson and Roy C. McLaren, *Police Adminstration*, Fourth Edition, New York, McGraw-Hill Book Company, 1977.
15. Harold Koontz and Cyril O'Donnell, *Principles of Management: An Analysis of Managerial Functions*, New York, McGraw-Hill Book Company, 1964.
16. David, *A Systems Analysis of Political Life*, New York, John Wiley and Sons, 1965.
17. Randall B. Ripley, *American National Government and Public Policy*, New York, The Free Press, 1974.
18. Charles D. Hale, *Fundamentals of Police Administration*, Boston, Holbrook Press, 1977.
19. Albert Einstein and L. Infield, *The Evolution of Physics* (1938) in Stephen Isaac, *Handbook in Research and Evaluation*, San Diego, Edits Publishers, 1971, p. 1.
20. Jack L. Kuykendall and Peter C. Unsinger, op. cit., p. 3.
21. Bruce Smith, *Police Systems in the United States*. New York, Harper and brothers, 1940, pp. 20-21.
22. Leonhard F. Fuld, *Police Administration: A Critical Study of Police Organizations in the United States and Abroad*, New York, G. P. Putnam's Sons, 1909, p. vi.
23. Leonhard F. Fuld, op. cit., p. vi.
24. Leonhard F. Fuld, ibid., p. 110.
25. Herman Goldstein, *Police Discretions: The Ideal versus the Real*, Public Adminstration Review, XXIII-XXIV, September 1963, p. 140.
26. A. V. Dicey. *The Law of the Constitution*, 8th Edition, in Kenneth *Discretionary Justice: A Preliminary Inquiry*, Baton Rouge, Louisiana University Press, 1969, p. 198.

27. Friedrich A. Hayek. *The Road to Serfdom*, 1944, in Kenneth C. Davis *Discretionary Justice: A Preliminary Inquiry*, Baton Rouge, Louisiana University Press, 1969, p. 72

28. Kenneth C. Davis, op. cit., p. 33.

29. Herman Goldstein, op. cit., p. 144.

30. Kenneth C. Davis, *Police Discretion*, St. Paul, Minnesota, West Publishing Company, 1973, p. 32.

31. Herman Goldstein, op. cit., p. 144.

32. Jerome Skolnick, *Justice Without Trial: Law Enforcement in Democratic Society*, 2nd edition, New York, John Wiley and Sons, 1975. James Q. Wilson, *Varieties of Police Behavior: The Management of Law and Order in Eight Communities*, Cambridge, Harvard University Press, 1968. Kenneth Davis, *Police Discretion*, St. Paul, West Publishing Company, 1975.

33. President's Commission on Law Enforcement and Administration of Justice, *Task Force Report: The Courts*, Washington, D. C., U. S. Government Printing Office, 1967, pp. 103-104.

34. Kenneth C. Davis, op. cit., p. 15.

35. Kenneth C. Daivs, ibid., p. 40.

36. President's Commission on Law Enforcement and Administration of Justice, Washington, U.S. Government Printing Office, 1967, pp. 103-104.

37. National Advisory Commission on Criminal Justice Standards and Goals, *Report on Police*, Washington, U.S. Government Printing Office, 1973, American Bar Association Project on Standards for Criminal Justice, the Urban Police Function, New York, American Bar Association, 1973.

38. National Advisory Commission on Criminal Justice Standards and Goals, ibid., pp. 21-22.

39. American Bar Association, op. cit., pp. 7-8.

40. National Advisory Commission on Criminal Justice Standards and Goals, ibid., p. 53.

41. American Bar Association ibid., p. 8.

42. Jerome H. Skolnick, op. cit., 1975.

43. Joseph Goldstein, *Police Discretion Not to Invoke the Criminal Process: Low Visibility Decisions in the Administration of Justice*, Yale Law Journal LXIX, March 1960.

44. William A. Westley, *Violence and the Police: A Sociological Study of Law, Custom and Morality*, Cambridge, M. I. T. Press, 1970, p. 111.

45. President's Commission on Law Enforcement and Administration of Justice, *Task Force Report: The Police*, Washington, D. C., U. S. Government Printing Office, 1967, P. 30.

46. David J. Brodna, editor, *The Police: Six Sociological Essays*, New York, John Wiley and Sons, 1967. James Q. Wilson, op. cit; David M. Peterson, *The Police, Discretion and the Decision to Arrest*. Ann Arbor, University Microfilms, 1969; Richard L. Palmer, *Toward Police Professionalism: The Elusive Path to an Ambiguous Goal*, Ann Arbor, University Microfilms, 1973; Jerome H. Skolnick, ibid., 1975.

47. Michael Cohen, *Sources of Ineffectiveness in Policy Application*, Midwest Review of Public Adminstration, Vol. 2 #2, August, 1968, pp. 78-79.

48. William C. Kronholm, *Blue Power: The Threat of the Militant Policeman,* Journal of Criminal Law, Criminology and Police Science, Vol. 63, No. 2, June 1972.
49. National Advisory Commission on Criminal Justice Standards and Goals, ibid., 1973, p. 602.
50. Jack L. Kuykendall, op. cit., 1977.
51. National Advisory Commission on Criminal Justice Standards Goals, ibid., 1973.
52. National Advisory Commission on Criminal Justice Standards and Goals, ibid., p. 607.
53. Harold D. Lasswell, *Research in Policy Analysis: The Intelligence and Appraisal Functions*, in Fred L. Greenstein and Nelson W. Polsky (eds), *Policies and Policy-Making,* Reading, Mass., Addison-Wesley Publishing Company, 1975 pp. 8-9.
54. Randall B. Ripley, *American National Government and Public Policy,* New York, The Free Press, 1974 p. 8.
55. Randall B. Ripley, op. cit., p. 8
56. Randall B. Ripley, ibid, p. 8.
57. Charles E. Lindblom, *The Policy-Making Process*, Englewood Cliffs, N. J., Prentice-Hall, Inc., 1968, p. 4.
58. Charles E. Lindblom, op. cit., p. 4.
59. American Bar Association, op. cit., pp. 4-5.
60. Otto Butz, *Of Man and Police: An Introduction to Political Science*, New York, Holt, Rinehart and Winston, 1960.
61. Jack L. Kuykendall and Peter C. Unsinger, ibid., p. 2.
62. National Advisory Commission on Criminal Justice Standards and Goals, ibid., pp. 22-23.
63. National Advisory Commission on Criminal Justice Standards and Goals, ibid., p. 25.

Annotated Bibliography

Davis, Kenneth Culp, *Discretionary Justice: A Preliminary Inquiry*. Baton Rouge: Louisiana State University Press, 1969. Discusses why there is discretion in the justice system and recommends ways for structuring and controlling discretionary decision making through administration law procedures.

Davis, Kenneth Culp, *Police Discretion*. St. Paul, Minnesota: West Publishing Company, 1975. A study of police discretion in selective enforcement based upon research at the Chicago Police Department. Reinforces and supports the preliminary discussions in *Discretionary Justice*.

Greenstein, Fred I. and Nelson W. Polsky, (editors), *Policies and Policymaking*. Reading, Massachusetts: Addison-Wesley Publishing Company, 1975. A collection of articles dealing with all aspects of policy. Excellent source of information on the subject of policy analysis.

Ripley, Randall B., *American National Government and Public and Public Policy*. New York: The Free Press, 1974. An overview of policy making by the federal government with an analysis of the relationships between congress, and the bureaucracy, the presidency, the courts, and the pluralistic publics.

Sharkansky, Ira, *Public Administration: Policy-Making in Government Agencies*. (second edition), Chicago: Markham Publishing Company, 1972. A discussion of governmental policy making from a systems perspective. Especially, the aspects of politics and policy decisions.

Smith, Bruce. *Police Systems in the United States*. New York: Harper and Brothers, 1940. Discusses the problems confronting society and the police in a democratic environment. Argues that many of the organizational weaknesses of police agencies stem from poorly selected and qualified police executives.

10

POLICE UNIONS

Chapter Objectives

The study of this chapter should enable you to:

☑ Describe the processes leading to the formation of a Police Union.

☑ Identify the conflicts and consequences that develop between police management and police unionization.

☑ Summarize the importance of the Boston Police Strike as applied to contemporary police unionization.

☑ List the causes and factors of police labor militancy.

☑ List the types of police job actions.

☑ Describe the organizational characteristics of union, fraternal, and benevolent police alliances.

☑ Identify the comparative elements between private-public labor sectors and police labor relations.

☑ Write a summarization of the controversiality associated with police unionization.

*Unions cannot be above government.
When one tries to organize the police
and the firemen of a big city,
one comes closer to usurping
the powers of government.*
Eleanor Roosevelt

Introduction

Police labor union activity is an issue of concern to municipal governments. Law enforcement personnel are increasingly more active in the area of labor relations. Yet, as the above quotation reveals, there is sometimes bitter controversy over the concept of police labor unions. Both today and in the past, police unionization has met resistance from management and the general public. While unions are an accepted and legitimate part of life in private industry, police management has considered unions as being almost treasonous. Unions and other police employee associations have been blamed for departmental inefficiency and for violating a sacred public trust. Some officials express amazement that individuals who perform such a vital governmental function can even consider organizing into a collective bargaining unit.

Union supporters, on the other hand, perceive official opposition as further evidence of management's unfair treatment. For them, union organization is a necessary safeguard of police employee interests and security. They consider unions as part of democracy, a method of insuring employee input into management's policy.

Out of these two positions comes the debate on police unionization. It involves the differing philosophies, goals and needs of police labor, police management and the public. This chapter examines the character of police unions. It traces the history of the movement, describes the different types of police labor organizations, and examines the case for and against unionization. Finally it suggests some principles that can be used in a framework for discussing the future of police unionization.

History of Police Unionization

Although references to police organizations were made as early as the Civil War, the current systems of police unions were not developed until after merit programs had been introduced into police services. Many of the early organizations were formed to provide protection from political intervention and to furnish what are now referred to as fringe benefits to the police employee. The police association also filled an important void by providing a social/fraternal function.

In 1889, the five-man police force of Ithaca, New York declared a strike of services after the mayor reduced their wages by three dollars. The strike only ended after the mayor agreed to pay the policemen their original wage of twelve dollars a week. Later, in 1918, a police strike occurred in Cincinnati, Ohio. A total of 450 police officers walked off the job in retaliation against the City because the administration had discharged several police officers. The policemen who were dismissed had been organizing for the purpose of bargaining for wage increases. The striking policemen returned to their duties after management agreed to reconsider the dismissals.

One of the first major police departments to seek affiliation with an organized labor union and to consider job action was the Boston Police. In 1919, members of that department applied for a charter with the American Federation of Labor. Previous to this time, the AFL had rejected the idea of police memberships. The Boston Police application caused a modification of original AFL charter policy and the petitioning police agency became unionized. The Police Commissioner of Boston immediately issued an order prohibiting any member of the police department from affiliating with any nondepartmental organization, except for certain specified police-veteran organizations; obviously, the AFL was not one of them. In retaliation, the unionized police members elected to withhold services from the City of Boston. The Boston Police Strike lasted approximately four days, during which criminal activity in that city increased.

At the height of the strike, President Woodrow Wilson issued this statement:

> *The strike of the policemen of this great city, leaving the city at the mercy of an army of thugs, is a crime against civilization. In my direct judgment, the obligation of a policeman is as sacred and direct as that of a soldier. He is a public servant, not a private employee, and the whole honor and safety of the community are in his hands.*[1]

The Boston Police Strike was less than successful, and the militant venture resulted in the dismissal of nearly eleven hundred police officers. The City of Boston then proceeded to recruit an almost new police department. In response to the President's statement and public alarm, the AFL revoked the Boston Police charter and stated that future attempts to organize police departments as unionized locals would get no support from that organization.

During this same time period, the Fraternal Order of Police was beginning to develop in Pittsburgh. The goal of this Order was to establish a social-benevolent association for police officers. The new Order was reviewed with suspicion and failed to make substantial gains in membership and acceptance until the 1930s.

The events of the Boston Police Strike had long-lasting effects on police labor relations. Municipal administrators continued to view with suspicion any police employee organization which seemed to suggest programs of self-interest.

Police Unionization In The 1960s

During the 1960s, police labor organizations began to emerge from what had been a long period of dormancy. Together with the renewed interest in unionization came a movement toward militancy in order to achieve employee demands.

Numerous reasons may be cited for the recurrence of police labor activity. One in particular was the growing awareness on the part of individual police officers to the changes which were taking place in private and public labor sectors at the time. Previous to 1945, workers in the public service sector fared slightly better in wages and conditions than laborers in private industrial sectors. Not until the end of World War II did employees in public service begin to recognize that private labor was rapidly advancing in economic benefits through organized labor. In order to remain in public service, the employee had to accept the uneven balance of benefits between public and private labor. Public managers attempted to promote tolerance for the imbalance by reminding their employees that governmental occupations stress job security, and the implied social status of being a social servant. The level of public employee acceptance began to erode with the growing awareness of continued increased incomes and benefits afforded the members of private labor, the rewards resulting from militant actions of organized labor associations.

In an attempt to discover ways of balancing conditions between public and private employees, the public worker sought to participate in formalized unionization and even began to duplicate the militant tactics of organized industrial labor. They were encouraged in their efforts when union leaders emphasized that government isn't a benign employer but rather an exploiter that must be fought and forced to yield to the union's demands.[2] Subsequently, public employee labor unions expanded to include nearly every aspect of labor in governmental work forces.

During the early 1960s, public employee dissatisfaction was augmented by the many changes which were starting to take place internally in governmental bureaucratic structures. Special departments were created to handle increasing demands for adequate social services, to explore new systems of moving masses of people, and to respond to community concerns related to elevated crime rates, poverty and racial strife. Due to the growth of serious social dilemmas, public administrators began to search for public employees who possessed the capabilities to seek solutions to these social problems. The governmental managers modified traditional hiring practices to achieve their personnel goals, lowering the age range of government employees and attempting to attract academically inclined individuals. This modified hiring program had certain inevitable consequences; the younger, educated employee brought to government a sense of initiative and vigor in decision-making and problem solving, and the same energy was used in demanding improved working conditions and salary adjustments comparable to those found in private industry.

The predicaments of the 1960s stimulated the rise in interest in public employee labor associations. These associations, in turn, provided group stimulation for the development of movements directed at producing changes in public administration. Public labor began to realize the power of employee militancy. Organized public labor, utilizing the withdrawal of services as the ultimate weapon against management presented a challenge to the traditional authorities of government. Public labor demanded that public administration recognize employee organizations and participate in collective bargaining, and public administrations soon learned that their powers of control and supervision would be limited.

The labor relation situation was further aggravated by the fact that administration lacked knowledge of reasonable or acceptable means to counter the challenge of labor. Public administration was inadequately prepared to confront the demands of public labor and lacked a way to identify the specific issues unique to public labor. Basically, public employees insisted that governmental management no longer regard them as public servants but as public government service employees with the same rights as employees in all other labor sectors. They demanded improved employment conditions, more fair personnel practices, and more benefits, in addition to other considerations.

While public service workers, labor associations, and administration gradually matured in their approach to labor relations, one segment of public service still lacked the achievements enjoyed by the majority of public sector laborers—the police employee.

Paralleling the movements in nonpolice labor sectors, internal factors in the police occupation itself caused its members to seek affiliations with labor organizations. First, this era saw the rise of numerous social and economic issues which directly affected the duties of the police officer. Student protests, racial demonstrations, and various U.S. Supreme Court decisions which were seen by the police as limiting their authority and power to enforce the law were among these issues. Along with increased public hostility and greater judicial restrictions, additional demands were placed upon law enforcement personnel. Police employees were told to control and counteract these social dilemmas and do their part to reduce the rising crime rates.

The police felt pressured by political and public demands and saw no promise of either compensation or reward. In an attempt to lessen what they perceived as occupational hardships, police employees began to look closely at the labor tactics of nonpolice employment sectors. One of the tactics they chose to use was militancy.

Organized militance among police officers has evolved in several forms. The most visible has been the establishment of new employee organizations or the transformation of existing organizations. For example, The Boston Police Department's more militant employee group formed the Boston Police Patrolman's Association (BPPA) even though four active police employee labor units already existed in the department. After being confronted with management resistance, the BPPA was able to defeat the federation of the other organizations and emerge as the bargaining agent for the Boston Police members. It's also interesting to note that various pressure groups were formed with existing employee organizations for the purpose of inducing modifications in organizational activities which didn't pertain to the organization at large; for example, Afro-American police groups sought satisfaction concerning the Black officers' grievances.

Organizational Characteristics of Police Unions

The late 1960s were formative years for organizations at the national level. The International Brotherhood of Police Officers, which was meant to represent police at all levels across the nation, was founded at this time; however, the IBPO failed to successfully compete against the well-established Fraternal Order of Police. By and large, national and state labor organizations have failed in their attempts to play major roles in police employee relations. This is probably due to the fact that police services, police employment, police productivity, and police economics are all confined to specific or local jurisdictional/governmental levels. In contrast to private sector labor, the hiring and recruiting of public personnel has geographical limitations.

Traditionally, public administration has attempted to curtail the movement of police personnel and avoid competitive situations. The lack of mobility within the police service contributes to the fact that public law enforcement is monopolistic in nature. This is usually seen as the primary reason why nationalized labor organizations have failed to gain a foothold in police employee organization leadership. Local economics, combined with the need of funds for individual benevolent, social, and community needs, have retarded the growth of nationalized police unions. The police associations who aligned with a national labor organization for leadership and direction would drain their own treasuries and force local police to interact with nonpolice labor leaders. The Fraternal Order of Police and the International Conference of Police Associations have probably been successful because they've emphasized local autonomy rather than national commitment.

In viewing the development of police employee organizations (unions) and current trends, it's necessary to keep in mind the role expectations of the police officer in our democratic society. The police officer's role is one of assuring the citizen that his or her property will be protected and that he or she will remain unmolested in his or her everyday life under constitutional "guarantees." In essence, the police officer affects the lives of all citizens in a manner unequalled by members of any other profession. Consequently, the citizenry expects certain types of behavior from its police officers, and it is unlikely that those expectations will ever change. It is this attitude which leads to public disappointment in police unionizing efforts and strike considerations and contributes to the complicated history of police-labor movement relations.

Issues surrounding the developments of police employee unions have appeared in various forms, in addition, the balance between the provisions of public safety and the welfare interest of the police officer is a delicate one. Legislative or management attempts to ignore or place restrictions on the implementation of collective employee-employer negotiations have failed. The traditional police management concept of equating all methods of collective bargaining specifically as an organized labor union, in the purest sense of the words, is in error. A group of workers can band together to bargain for wages and conditions with management without national union affiliation. Localized collective employee bargaining may be done in police departments in absence of an official alliance with a multi-member, strike endorsing, national labor organization.

In fact, the localized police membership may take several forms of representative collective action, as an example:

1. a purely localized organization;
2. a statewide organization;
3. and a nationwide organization, with limited local participation.

The three basic models can be subdivided into several smaller ones. The localized organization, for example, may fall into the fraternal order, the benevolent association, a police club, or some other employee group which has been developed for social and fraternal benefits. The state wide organization is generally divided into state affiliated police employee groups or a police group banded together for the purposes of sharing with various police members common occupational interests. The nationalized organization is usually a bonafide police order of some type, having interest in all phases of police occupational conditions.

The local organization is found in the majority of police agencies. This is usually a private association which can range from a formalized structure fulfilling only periodic needs for officer-member socialization to a full-fledged organization which engages in employee collective bargaining. It should be emphasized that the names of police organizations don't necessarily represent or describe their actual functions. The most conservatively named associations often tend to become militant employee labor groups.

Local organizations are often characterized by a lack of structural continuity. Selected or elected officers usually change on a yearly basis, and the plans and intentions of a group may vacillate with the desires of its membership.

One type of local organization is the *fraternal order*. This can either be an independent police group designed to satisfy locally based needs, or an employee group possessing a charter affiliation with a prominent police officer organization. One example of the latter type is the local chapter lodge of the Fraternal Order of Police. The FOP is described as a local, state, and national police employee association. The local lodge, with chartered state and national affiliation, is composed of a membership open to all law enforcement members regardless of rank, status, or type of public governmental police agency. The local lodge also has an option to open membership ranks to nonpolice persons. The nonpolice member, referred to as an associate member, may not vote in lodge elections of officers, may not set policy for the lodge operation, and may not attend the business meetings of the police members; however, he or she may utilize the physical facilities provided by the local chapter. The associate member provides social and economic support for the local lodge. It's not unusual for the local chapter to vote a "lifetime associate membership" to a deserving citizen as a result of service or contributions to the local chapter. Lodge structure may also provide for auxiliary memberships. Auxiliaries, normally composed of police wives, also provide social and economic benefits to the local chapter.

Although the local chapter is affiliated with a state and national order, it is in essence autonomous. While decentralized national order establishes universal policies and regulations, it avoids intervening into the local chapters' operations.

The Fraternal Order of Police has probably achieved more success than any other police employee associations of its type. The prosperity of the National Order is usually attributed to the fact that it allows the local lodge its operational independence.

The police benevolent association, or PBA, is a local police group without a state or national lodge relationship. This organization may serve its membership by providing community-service functions and acting as a protective instrument for its members in situations of confrontation with municipal administration. The PBA has shown a historical trend of militancy in order to achieve grievance demands concerning salaries and conditions of employment. It isn't unusual for a PBA to limit actual membership to nonsupervisory members of the department—demonstrating that the initials may well stand for *Patrol Officer's* Benevolent Association rather than *Police* Benevolent Association.

Subgroups referred to as *police clubs* or *police officer associations* usually originate to perform social functions for their membership. Club membership is restricted to local departmental officers and their immediate families, and this restriction provides a common denominator for group composition in social gatherings. These types of groups may be well suited for membership in a national police union, since they tend to be flexible enough to change from social service to militant employee leagues depending on the immediate needs of their memberships, and they're not usually obligated to state or national police organizations.

The second model of police employee associations includes the *statewide groups*. These state organizations, not including state organized and chartered fraternal associations, have only recently begun to exhibit a militant emphasis to achieve membership demands. Such groups are usually composed of law enforcement officers appointed and employed at the state level of government, such as State Police Officers, Highway Patrol Officers, and police agents of other state departments responsible for enforcing state statutes. Because past endeavors of state associations have failed to make an impact on the powerful state government structures, the state membership bodies have exerted *tactical militant methods*, active legislative lobbying, to achieve member demands.

Rather than suffer the frustrations of developing internal and external organizational controls, the state employee association may choose to identify with a parent state or national police employee organization. Such affiliations include State Police Lodges chartered by the Fraternal Order of Police. The police employee association retains a certain autonomy while having access to the influence of a state and national police association.

The *state common cause* or *mutual interest association* is the final suborganization of state employee associations. This type of group typically contains police members from several local employee associations who work together to share information on matters of interest to the individual police employee. The state mutual interest police association has the potential for becoming a powerful influence on effective employee labor relations. This is due, at least in part, to the fact that it's statewide and has strength in numbers. For example, the Police Officers' Research Association of California has a reported membership of several thousand municipal police employees.

Finally, the third model of police employee association is the *nationalized organization*. Two major independent police organizations deserve mention here: The Fraternal Order of Police (FOP), and the International Conference of Police Associations (ICPA).

The Fraternal Order of Police, as previously mentioned, is the oldest national league of affiliated police members. It possesses a great deal of power and influence in both employee relations and governmental legislation. Originally, the FOP was designed to serve as a fraternal, benevolent, and professional organization; in recent years, however, it's paid attention to the economic and employment conditions of its members. This change in emphasis has taken place without noticeably modifying the original objectives of the Order.

The National Order's meetings include one delegate per fifty members of a local chartered lodge and three delegates from each of the state lodges. During these conferences, the National President and Officers, National Board of Trustees, and selected delegates sustain or modify National Lodge policy.

Although each local chapter of the FOP is essentially autonomous, the National Order assesses a fee for each local police member. In return for the assessment, the National Order supplies its local lodge members with support during conflicts resulting from the member's employment and provides the lodge with several national publications so that the police member can keep up with current events in occupational developments, including labor relations data.

One of the more viable functions of the National Order is political involvement and formal lobbying conducted by the National representatives to gain positions of advantage for the individual police officer.

The International Conference of Police Associations consists of member-representatives from individual police employee organizations, rather than individual members.

The original concept of the ICPA, formed in 1953, was to create an organization with a membership composed of individuals from local police employee associations, with the advantages of affiliation in a large, national organization.

The conference sought to emphasize an organizational philosophy of progressive "professionalization" in public policing by establishing operational functions for the organization; the Conference would become a clearing house for the collection, analysis and dissemination of informational data pertaining to police employees and conditions of employment.

This beginning, and successful, emphasis served as a useful vehicle for the development and growth of the ICPA. The Conference demonstrated a capability to form an image acceptable to public governmental administrator by appearing as a "professional" association, rather than a police union.

The ICPA supplies the member/representatives with several vital and informative publications: "The Law Officer," a periodical providing updated material on collective bargaining and legislative reports affecting law enforcement, "Model Contracts and Clauses," a soft-bound guide for reference in forming contractual labor agreements, "Pension Benefits" and "Wage and Benefits Survey," two annual reports available for comparison and analysis.

One visible contrast to Fraternal Order of Police affiliations and inclusion of a police representation in the International Conference of Police Associations is the local FOP lodge; it is clearly identified in affiliation by lodge title, while an ICPA affiliate bears no local recognization.

One additional police employee association of national status may be mentioned, the National Union of Police Officers (NUPO). The description of this police union is concise because of the present diminutive impact on organized police labor relations.

Apart from the recruited union membership in mid-1970, numbering approximately 10,000 police officers, the subsequent initiations of membership have been less than successful. The lack of activity may well demonstrate the suggested lack of a nationalized interest by law enforcement personnel in aligning with a centralized national union organization.

Aspects of Police Association Membership

The status of memberships in police employee associations has been demonstrated, on a limited basis, by a 1969 research study compiled by a committee of the International Association of Chiefs of Police.[3] The Study Committee submitted a research instrument to police departments of the nation's one hundred largest cities, with a responding total of eighty departments. The collection of data showed the largest municipal police agencies employees chose local affiliations:

TABLE 10.1

NUMBER OF RESPONDENTS	TYPE OF EMPLOYEE AFFILIATION
15	Union
29	Fraternal Order of Police
34	Non-union, with varying degrees of collective bargaining activity

Accordingly, the Committee discovered the data indicated that while some police officer organizations have formed an affiliation with organized labor, the majority have remained independent, local affiliates of a police employee association. In utilizing the Committee's statistical information one must be aware of the responding population size; as reported, the study surveyed the largest one-hundred police agencies. This departmental size which employs the greatest number of officers may be pictured as a minority among the nation's police departments. This study is void of data for activity of police labor relations in the lesser populated jurisdictions that constitute an impact on police labor activity, taking into account the associational activity of police agencies employing twenty personnel or less, which is the size of the majority of police departments in the United States. However, if consideration is given to the presented study's population group, the data reflects the tendency for police employee associations to retain a position of autonomy from organized labor unions.

There is one additional study that deserves mention with consideration to the types and activities of police employee associations. The authors of the research project submitted an inquiry to the police chief, the police employee association and to the chief labor/relations officer in the thirty largest cities and supplemented the study with the same inquiry being submitted to thirty-five lesser populated police agencies known to be participating in collective bargaining. From the sixty-five cities responding, a total of twenty-one were selected for a field study, with the results of the research as follows in Table 10.2:[4]

TABLE 10.2

City	Population	Affiliation	Number of Members
Baltimore	985,759	AFSCME (1,416)	FOP (977)
Boston	641,071	BPPA	2,300
Buffalo	462,768	PBA	1,365
Cincinnati	452,524	FOP	960
Cleveland	758,759	FOP (2,257)	ICPA (1,750)
Cranston, RI	74,287	IBPO (70)	FOP (30)
Dayton	243,601	FOP	426
Detroit	1,513,601	DPOA, ICPA	4,801
Hartford	158,017	IBPO	437
Los Angeles	2,816,061	ICPA	6,877
Milwaukee	717,372	ICPA	2,042
New Haven	137,077	AFSCME	380
New York City	7,985,563	PBA	24,000
Oakland	361,561	OPOA	710
Omaha	346,929	Police Union	500
Philadelphia	1,948,609	FOP	7,154
Pittsburgh	520,117	FOP	1,400
Providence	179,213	FOP	395
Rochester, NY	296,233	ICPA	665
San Francisco	715,654	ICPA	1,700
Seattle	530,831	ICPA	1,111

The statistical results derived from this study support the police employee association's adherence to selective independence in affiliations with national police organizations. The trend of police labor relations is to remain within the boundaries of the respective police agency, in conjunction with an affiliated charter or alliance in a police organization of national status. There is evidence of little expectancy for the decentralized, local police agency members to align their employee associations with a formal and centralized police officer union.

Description of Police Labor Relationships

The active/aggressive police employee associations fall into one of four styles of relationships in labor-management functions.

1. *The Informal Relationship.* Individual officers make their desires known through normal department channels. The police employee organization does not necessarily represent the officers of the department on questions of salaries and working conditions. However, there may be occasional informal meetings between the police officers and the chief of police for the purpose of discussing matters of mutual interest.

2. *The Lobbying Relationship.* The police employee organization actively undertakes to present views on questions of salaries and working conditions through personal appearances at city council meetings. Appearances before the city council may be supplemented by occasional meetings between the chief of police and organization representatives, but these meetings are not for the purpose of negotiating, instead are generally exploratory in nature.

3. *The Consulting Relationship.* Representatives of the police employee organization initially meet with the police chief or his representative for the express purpose of developing mutually acceptable proposals on salaries or working conditions for submission to the city council. The council acts on such proposals, reserving the right to accept or reject. When the police chief and employee representatives fail to reach agreement on an issue, the parties may appear and present their positions directly before the council.

4. *The Bargaining Relationship.* Representatives of the employee organization meet directly from the onset of negotiations with a committee that represents the city council and/or the mayor's office. The purpose of the meeting is to develop a mutual policy on wages and conditions. Provisions may or may not exist for negotiation review by persons outside the department.

When employee groups and governmental agents are unable to compromise or reach satisfactory agreements, the police tend to seek other paths of protest to achieve their goals. These paths of protest are directed to gain public awareness, which at times, may be either positive or negative influences. Examples of these forms of protest are:

- The work slowdown—the police officers make fewer or no arrests for minor violations, such as parking and traffic tickets.
- The work speedup—the police start to write an inordinate number of tickets for all violations, regardless of the degree of the incident.
- The work stoppage—the police simply walk off the job assignments and refuse to comply with departmental orders.

- Mass resignation—rather than merely walk off the job, the officers involved resign from the department in mass.

There are other methods utilized as forms of protest, such as the sick call, known as the "blue flu" or a rather unique form of work stoppage whereby the officers fail to comply with orders due to their voluntary attendance at professional seminars to provide them with additional professional knowledge.

Lastly, and significantly, the most militant of police job action is the police strike.

The situation of a strike threat or a police employee work stoppage vote is the influencing weapon in most union-collective bargaining dilemmas. In nonpublic labor, the strike is the dominating example of labor union methods applied to management in attempting to force achievement of employee demands during negotiation procedures. Labor strike activity experienced in private industry is a mechanism generally acceptable to the working society as an effective means of manipulating management. For example, when management evaluates this manipulative technique as an effective pressure, the administration may select to correct certain occupational imperfections in working conditions demanded by the employee or reconsider the wages of their employees. The management may select the alternative of compromise rather than suffer the potential damaging effects of an employee strike which affects company productivity.

In conjunction with the labor society's acceptance of strikes in private sectors as a useful labor relations tool, the working population will usually tolerate the reduction of adequate services during an employee work stoppage in the semi-private labor sector, such as: home utility services, mass transit vehicle operators and nonemergency medical personnel. The lack of opposition to semi-private or private labor stoppages is because the community usually has alternative means of overcoming service shortages. For example, the management of utility corporations will take over positions of labor to maintain the service required to supply home with heat, power and telephone; community members may form car pools for transportation and the people have some form of emergency medical care available upon demand.

This prevailing attitude of toleration for work stoppages in private and semi-private labor curiously subsides when the suggestion of similar methods of labor militancy be applied for those employees in the public labor sector. The affected population often registers a display of amazement, together with a lack of understanding, for the public servant's desire to ignore their occupational obligations. One common perception is that the public employee(s) appear to disregard their duties which results in depriving the community of fundamental governmental services, those services granted and purchased through various forms of taxation. Most supporters of the view that public employee strikes should be prohibited do so on one or both of the following grounds: the indispensability of many governmental services and the strike is an economic weapon inappropriate in public employment.

Issues In Police Job Actions

The issue of public employee strike activity gains a noted intensity when labor militancy is focused on one particular segment of governmental employment—*law enforcement*. It is doubtful that any private or public employee militancy causes more of an arousal of furor among members of a community than either a reduction of public safety services by dissatisfied police officers or members of the community being subjected to the various job actions devised by militant police personnel.

There is at least one related reason for the attitudes of the community in their viewing of police personnel—the historical and prevailing idea that police officers are guardians of the community and the primary line of defense against criminal acts against life and property. Consequently, since this perception remains, it is doubtful the public's concept of policing will totally change. There is a suggestion that for any incident of police militancy, or the probability of a police job action taking place, there will be the presence of some community alarm to a measurable degree.

One other community reaction to police job action is described as the assumption that militant police officers fail to show regard for the people they swore to protect through ignoring responsibilities, a lack of consideration for the safety and welfare of the community. The community member holding this opinion seems to be oblivious to the fact that law enforcement personnel are also members of the same community; they are taxpayers providing support for the same community; and they maintain residences in or near the same community affected by the police labor action. These facts might lead to a belief that the police officer's militant behaviors are directed toward benefits, salary and work conditions rather than a collective vindictiveness or an example of retaliation against the community.

A description of attitude perceptions regarding police and labor relations can be provided from an analysis of reports developed by the Law Enforcement Assistance Administration, U.S. Department of Justice. The LEAA appointed a panel of police administrators and educators to serve on the National Advisory Commission on Criminal Justice Standards and Goals for the intended purpose of producing various task force research reports, with one report having a focus on the administration of policing. As an inclusion in the task force report on policing, the Commission presented an awareness to collective bargaining in law enforcement labor sectors.

Listed for purposes of discussion are several of the Commission's conclusions:

1. Every police agency, including all police employees, should be permitted to engage in collective negotiations to arrive at agreements in terms and conditions of employment that will insure service effectiveness and equitable representation for both labor and management.
2. Provide enactments of State legislation establishing police collective bargaining and protection for both bargaining units.
3. Provide provisions for local jurisdictions to create collective negotiations regulations specific to the local laws.
4. Develop procedures in retaining unrestricted management rights.

5. Prohibit job actions.
6. All police administrators should designate a representative to be present in all negotiations, with the stipulation the appointee continually provide protection for the community and the agency.
7. Enforcement agencies should afford educational opportunities to develop labor-management relations effectiveness.
8. Police administrators should establish procedures regarding operational features of the collective processes.
9. Administrators in policing should develop a recognition for employee groups, organize negotiation procedures and develop impasse solution methods.

To search for a rationalization to the Commission's statements, it is necessary to review the composition of the investigatory panel. The makeup of the Commission is clearly seen as management dominated; consequently, it may be difficult to consider the reflections of police management now encouraging collective negotiations in law enforcement when, historically, police administrators have denounced police employee collectivity and the formation of police associations. The important point derived from this report is that a management-dominated national commission has considered a concept of police collective bargaining.

Again, the police employee association designed to serve as a collective bargaining unit is seen as a threatening force to police management and as a negative effect on law enforcement service.

Once someone interested in police labor relations realizes the ever-present social and administrative oppositions to police employee collectivity, it becomes easier to consider the character of collective bargaining and the subsequent correlations to police labor activity.

Police and Labor And Collective Bargaining

The diverse character of collective bargaining, primarily focused on law enforcement, deserves a presentation of certain concepts and structural frameworks.

To express in a simplified manner, collective bargaining is a method of joint decision making, within agreed upon limitations, between labor and management. The ultimate objective is a design to reach mutually satisfactory goals for both parties comprising the bargaining process.

Additional to the definition of the phenomenon of collective bargaining, an interpretation may be related by labor viewing collective bargaining as a procedural method to achieve personal benefits and instill departmental changes, while management may view the collective bargaining as a labor peace-making apparatus to assure a continuance of protective services for the community.

The Taft-Hartley Act provides a legalized conception of collective bargaining: To bargain collectively is the performance of the mutual obligation of the employer and the representatives of the employees to meet and confer in good faith with respect to wages, hours, and other terms and conditions of employment—and the execution of a written contract incorporating any written agreement reached.

If a focus is set on the aspects of the Taft-Hartley definition, attention would be drawn to the words "in good faith"—an absolute requirement for effective bargaining on a mutual foundation.

The admitting on non-management persons into organizational decison-making processes, through unionization, causes management to narrow or surrender the traditional "closed-door-formulation" for departmental policy. For management to concede any portion of internal policy making and the enforcement of actions is an intervention into "management rights"—an essence of collective bargaining. Accordingly, management attempts to retain and protect maximum authority in the forming or agency policy in business operations and standards of employee performance.

"Management rights," also referred to as "management prerogatives," are held sacred by the administration during bargaining—there is the fear that expansion of employee influence may produce a synthesis for the reduction of management power, plus the employee induced restrictions regarding operational functions would reduce the overall effectiveness of the agency.

In an attempt to protect the administration from these restrictions, management may insist on a "management prerogative" clause being included in the contractual agreement. Such a clause may specify that management has exclusive rights of scheduling and assigning employees, hiring and promoting the labor staff and enforcing rules regulating the conduct of the agency's employees.

Although the national labor law may stipulate certain topics for discussion at the private labor sector bargaining table, there is no mandate to agree. The local bargaining parties develop their own system to monitor the labor agreement terms.

In the private sector collective bargaining agreements grievance systems with arbitration to resolve impasse are fundamental to the collective bargaining process. They are systematic devices designed and administered by both parties. Actually court and national labor relations board decisions have recognized and reinforced the voluntary roles of the private sector collective bargaining parties in respect to grievances and arbitration.

In contrast, public sector bargaining has not been permitted to develop the same procedures. Impasse resolution of interest issues is frequently a function of state law, which may lack provisions for arbitration.

In collective bargaining are *Interest* issues—those the two parties present at the bargaining table—and *Rights* issues—those conferred upon the parties by the collective agreement.

Arbitration of interest issues have been rare in private sector bargaining, but are more frequent in the public sector.

Although a private sector labor agreement may call for binding arbitration as the final step in a grievance process, such an agreement is still voluntarily entered into by both bargaining factions. This differs substantially in kind by a law mandating compulsory mediation, fact finding or arbitration (either advisory or binding) in a public sector collective bargaining interest dispute.

And whereas binding arbitration is normally the terminal point for private sector grievance processes, it is much less likely so in public sector rights disputes, partly because of the existence of civil service systems and partly because of a traditional management attitude towards the protected sovereignty of decision making.

We lack clarity of policy in police labor sector bargaining. Public unionization-collective bargaining has borrowed much from the private sector labor concepts. The issue of how to manage impasses that immediately and directly involve a variety of persons not an actual party to the bargaining relationship causes a retardation to the growth for public sector unionized bargaining. Other problems in public sectors such as coexistence with civil service systems may be equally difficult to effectively join with public sector and police collective bargaining.

Police sector bargaining may be described as more involved in recognition and early negotiation phases struggling to operate under local or state guidelines. Contrastingly, private sector collective bargaining concentrates upon negotiation and administration phases.

To provide auxiliary viewpoints to police unionization and collective bargaining, the attempt is made to exhibit impressions relative to collective employee activity.

- Collective bargaining may be seen as a device to contract the purchase of labor.
- Collective bargaining may be viewed as a formulation of democratic government between employer and employee.
- Collective bargaining may be demonstrated as a method of employee relations.

The union-collective labor agreement is basically a statement of conditions for which the employees agree to perform certain tasks, and assures that if the service is given, the provider shall be rewarded according to terms of agreement.

The thought of implementing a labor relations program, including collective bargaining by police employees, demands a period of planning prior to effecting or suggesting to administration the desire for police employee participation in labor negotiation.

For police employees announcing their labor demands in a collective method before police or municipal management, it is imperative the employees make certain decisions and formulate certain policies prior to any statement of intent.

First, there must be a selection of the bargaining unit—the employee organization selected by majority ballot to represent the police employees during labor negotiations. Several issues are unique and inherent to police bargaining unit formulation. A determination has to be made as to the acceptable rank level for membership in the association. Usually, the collective employee group will be composed of patrol officers, excluding the police personnel having supervisory rank. This affords an opportunity of all employee members sharing common interest, with a mutual concern regarding employment conditions.

Upon determination of the qualified unit, the selection of those members to serve as negotiating representatives requires attention be placed on the capabilities and qualfications of the membership body. A critical assessment of the association's personnel is necessary in order to select those who will be active participants in actual labor negotiations. It's desirable for those selected members to possess a functional knowledge of labor negotiating methodologies and techniques, keeping in mind the bargaining participants represent the entire association membership.

Generally, the negotiating team is composed of four to six units: the chief negotiator, an assistant to the chief negotiator and team recorder, and team researchers.

From the labor's viewpoint, it is wise to consider the makeup of the opposing bargaining team; for example, if the management has gathered a "professional" labor negotiating group, it then becomes tactful for the association to likewise employ individuals having the training and experience in labor relations to serve as the negotiating team.

The next step in the logical order of bargaining preparation is for the team units to begin drafting the claims and demands from the association membership. The drafted demands will eventually be presented to the opposing bargaining group in a more formalized proposition, referred to as the "contractual proposal."

At the completion of the bargaining process, and all labor-management arrangements are in an agreed state, the bargained results are reduced to a formal, structured document called the "labor contract" or the "memorandum of agreement." The final contract document contains all of the bargained for criteria in definite contractual language.

Legislation and Police Union Activity

There are approximately thirty-six states that entail legislation pertaining to bargaining by public employees—police employees have recognition and rights to bargain in twenty-nine of these states. The state governments, in some cases, retain certain rights and control over police pensions and work conditions, but others provide allowances to the local governmental sector to establish criteria for respective police operations.

There are fourteen states absent of collective bargaining for public employees: Arizona, Arkansas, California, Indiana, Louisiana, Mississippi, New Mexico, North Carolina, Ohio, South Carolina, Tennessee, Utah, Virginia, and West Virginia. It is interesting to note there are two states providing permission for strike actions by police employees: Montana and Vermont. The Montana State Supreme Court, in 1974, ruled in favor of police strikes by reason of the state legislation failing to specifically state the prohibiting of strike action, a void that may be fulfilled in future legislation.

Within the Vermont State legislation, the law allows for police strikes if the action is in accordance with established guidelines. The Vermont law allows for police to strike once an appraisal is made of guideline content:

there is a call for a thirty day pause of action, in effect after the factfinding conclusion report is presented to labor and managememt; the employee dispute may not be one that has previously been settled by arbitration; and, *the police strike must not affect the welfare, health or safety of the public.* It would seem nearly impossible to initiate a police strike action without in some manner affecting the welfare, health and safety of the public.

Other governmental proposals pertaining to public employee collective bargaining include the State of Illinois. The governor of the state provided an Executive Order regulating bargaining among the state employees; however, police employees were excluded in the order.

The legislators of the State of Indiana enacted in 1975 and again in 1977 provisions for collective bargaining among state employees, again with the exception of police officers and firemen; however, the Governor effectively vetoed the legislated bill. Consequently, the State of Indiana stands without public employee collective bargaining regulations.

The Appearance of Police Unions

The advent of governmental awareness to the police employee's work situation lends slight anticipation to a consciousness to the actual job conditions of the police. It is a maxim of politics that whoever controls the army also controls the nation. Is not the police the army of the municipality? The question that arises relates to the loyalty of the police during times of conflict between demands of the union and those of the community, and is who will take precedence? It is a contention that the very presence of a police union represents an incompatibility with police responsibility—the essence of divided loyalty and divided authority.

The most compelling and potent arguments against the unionization of police officers is the strike—organized labor's most effective weapon. It is foolish to believe that no-strike clauses and other relative union limitations will hinder or prevent the police union from striking against the administration. As the point has been well pictured by the Boston Police strike, the effects of strikes by police officers has greater far-reaching results compared to strikes by another occupational union.

On the other hand, advocates state that unionism supports a democratic state to reflect democratic practices. Those in favor of police unions furnish employee representation which serves as the necessary internal control against bureaucratic power in the police system.

As we have seen, the history of the trade union movement is filled with attempts to organize the police employee and the police system in one aspect or another. The center of success exists with the fraternal/social benefits in almost every case, together with benefits derived from the fraternal organizations acting as bargaining agents for its member-employees.

Police employee organizations or police unions appear no different than any other trade union in their desires for increased wages and benefits. For all the recent discussion of police professionalism, the police union member is indistinguishable from a trade or industrial union worker. Consequently, the call for increases of wages and benefits has in fact increased the costs of police services. This is not to say the unions are the direct cause of the increases in costs, only that they created the pace in which the costs began to rise, by serving as an avenue for increased economics. The cost factors probably would have increased according to the political, economic, and social pressures, but may have increases at a slower pace.

Police unions have opposed public managerial procedures for utilizing manpower within the police department; for example, the use of civilians for clerical and technical endeavors and for effecting specific arrest procedures in parking violations and traffic enforcement. This is an obvious reduction of managerial flexibility in the deployment of personnel and hampers the delivery of effective police services to the community.

Police union organizations have also had an impact on the disciplinary practices of the police agencies. The preliminary impact has been achieved by the union in their attempts to provide the accused officer with assistance or "rights" and "due process" and the requirement of management to be more equitable in disposition. In most cases of compensation, the overall effects of the union have been to center disciplinary methods in line with the rights enjoyed by the private sector employee.

The union organizations have also had a decided impact on the recruitment and selection of police employees. The areas most noticed have been lateral entry, educational standards and minority employment. The unions appear in opposition to lateral entry into the police department to provide some job security and allowance for job promotion in the respective department.

Some union opinions on educational standards for police officers do not form a continuum. Various organizations view advanced education as a means for the increasing of standards, while others regard education as a wage benefit which violates the standard of equal pay for equal work.

And, of course, due to present social plights, there are police unions interested in the minority hiring practices of police agencies. They have caused the agencies to review their standards and requirements and the testing instruments used for hiring and recruiting new police officers to staff the departments.

There is a purpose here to focus on an aspect that has been avoided by the union organizations—police performance. Many labor reports relate that only economic issues should be negotiated leaving the function of management rights or management prerogatives to the administration of police performance standards. A contrasting argument is the union desires for wage gains without the correlation of increased job performance. However, there is a generalization prevalent regarding valid criteria or data to evaluate police service, leading police negotiators to ambiguity and a moot point for both parties.

The only contrast in describing the police labor movement, past and present, is its diversity. Information reveals a wide variety of organizational arrangements among police groups and that national affiliations are not necessarily consistent in any observation of police system behavior.

Proposals For Police Union Relationships

There is a necessity for police employees and municipal administration to collect valid criteria relating to police unionization and means for employee grievance satisifaction. Additionally, attentions of police labor and management should be focused on alternatives to police militancy and restrict political persuasion.

An employee or manager contemplating the potential of a national federation of police should be aware that a nationalized police union does not appear to serve as a panacea for police labor ills, plus it seems unlikely that the police labor movement will merge with the traditional union labor movement. Since the bargaining and leverages are maintained on the local level, it would not seem feasible for police departments on a large scale to affiliate with an international nonpolice union, at least in an economic sense. Economically, a state or local police lobbying organization of police-only membership would eliminate draining local revenues to support activities of the majority (nonpolice) of a large scale national union. There is a stable consistency to police employee associational activity remaining at the localized level of collective negotiations. In the absence of a "police state," the administration and operations of providing safety and protection lies within the respective community jurisdiction and purchased through jurisdictional taxation; one exception is that an organized police federation might serve in a resource and advisory capacity to the local law enforcement personnel in the preparation and administration of labor negotiations.

Finally, the primary goals of a police employee association, with or without national affiliation, could stand in establishing ways and means of improving the individualized conditions of the members, and be sensitive to the overall quality of police service and performance.

A residual effect found in successful associational activity is the promotion of solidarity between employees. The solidarity results from a sense of belonging within a group having commanality in needs. The managerial acceptance of the police employee association provides grounds for continual interactions between officer-member and administration—participatory management. This not only allows labor to voice suggestions and recommendations in decision-making, but also affords a psychological value of recognizing personal contributions to service and performance.

Summary

Public views on police unionization are influenced by personal experiences, interests and administrative philosophies. And the issues are too human related and complex for answers categorically. The supporters of a logical approach to a controversy will view barriers created by traditionally established principles of police management, the rebellious nature of some police unions and the inadequate legislation for procedural unionization.

The police administrator has a tendency to surround the union matter with ideas of patriotism, management rights, community safety and law and order. In contrast, the police union member calls for employee security, adequate working conditions, compensation for occupational dangers and a constitution of human rights.

The systems of law enforcement operate in a complex statutory context which includes laws regulating the participation and performance of every police officer. Of concern is the controversy between police labor and police management supplementing or increasing the complexity without responsible, progressive achievements in the systems of criminal justice.

The modern police officer is seemingly void of the ultra-conservative casting applicable to the police officer of the past; instead, traditional attitudes are eroding through constant exposure to other public employee associational-occupational groups announcing their achievements as a result of employee unity in unionization. So it appears that a "trial by ordeal" remains to be the order of the day for present police unionization.

In any event, employee labor unity in its diverse organizational characteristics has become acceptable to the futurist police officer.

Topics For Discussion

1. **Discuss the historical developments of police unionization.**
2. **Discuss the basic organizational characteristics of a police union.**
3. **Discuss the impact of police unionization on management of police operations and services.**
4. **Discuss the concept "unions provide a democratic work environment for the police officer."**
5. **Discuss the possible consequences of a police strike or other related job action.**

References

1. Harry F. Bolinger, "Police Officer Views on Collective Bargaining and Use of Sanctions", *Critical Issues in Law Enforcement*, Harry W. More, Editor, Cincinnati; W. H. Anderson, 1972.
2. Lee C. Shaw and R. T. Clark, "The Practical Differences Between Public and Private Sector Collective Bargaining", *UCLA Law Review*, University of California, Volume 19, 1972.
3. International Association of Chiefs of Police, Special Committee on Police Employee Associations, Report to the 76th Annual Conference, Miami, 1969.
4. Hervey Juris and Kay Hutchison, "The Legal Status of Municipal Police Employee Organizations", *Industrial Labor Relations*, Volume 23, 1970.
5. Hervey Juris and Peter Feuille, *Police Unions*, Lexington; Lexington Books, 1973.
6. Jack Stieber, "Collective Bargaining in the Public Sector", *Challenges to Collective Bargaining*, Englewood Clifs; Prentice-Hall, 1967.

Annotated Bibliography

Albert, Robert Judd, *A Time for Reform: A Case Study of the Interaction Between the Commissioner of the Boston Police Department and the Boston Police*

Patrolman's Association (Cambridge: Massachusetts Institute of Technology, Publishers, 1975). The author examines the conflicts and consequences of labor negotiations between the administration and employees of the Boston Police Department. Emphasis is placed on a police employee association serving as a de facto police union.

Bopp, William J., *The Police Rebellion: A Quest for Blue Power* (Springfield: Charles C. Thomas, Publishers, 1971). This text relates the militant job activity of police in a labor union environment. The author denotes pressure forces for organizational and political interventions on police management.

Halpern, S. C., *Police Association and Department Leaders — The Politics of Cooptation* (Lexington: Heath-Lexington Books, Publishers, 1974). A case study of associational activity in three major police agencies. The analysis of data resulting from the inquiry shows comparative abilities in labor-management relations between police associations and police administration.

Heustis, Carl E., "Police Unions," *Journal of Criminal Law, Criminology, and Police Science*, Volume 48, No. 6, March — April, 1958, pp. 643–650. A historical perspective of police unions, including the question of the legality of unionized police agencies.

Kronholm, Wiliam C., "Blue Power: The Threat of the Militant Policeman," *Journal of Criminal Law*, Volume 6, June, 1972, pp. 294-299. The author's view of police militancy becoming potentially progressive into a police state. The exhibition of militant political and ideological concepts by police pose a negative factor to effective leadership, unless counteracted by a strong management approach.

Mielke, D. R., "Labor Negotiations with Police Unions," *Public Management*, Volume 55, April, 1973, pp. 10-12. The important elements, as mentioned by the author, regarding collective bargaining methods in police labor, with recommendations for operational employee-employer labor agreements.

National Symposium on Police Labor Relations — Guidelines and Papers, International Association of Chiefs of Policce, Washington, D. C., June 9–12, 1974. A publication of recommendations regarding labor-management relations in policing. The book represents a consensus of opinions from practitioners in the field of police labor relations.

Neel, S. M., "Collective Bargaining — A Problem for the Civil Service System," *Police Chief*, Volume 38, No. 4, 1971, pp. 72-77. An author suggests the removal of the civil service commission from involvement in labor relations and instead function as a review board of the police department. There are additional proposals for the commission to focus on police employee recruitment and establish educational standards.

Steffanic, M. D., "Professionalization in Law Enforcement," *Police Chief*, Volume 41, No. 7, July, 1974, pp. 62-63. The writer discounts the achievements of police unions providing a path professionalizing police officers.

11

POLITICS AND THE POLICE
Reality and the Problem

Chapter Objectives

The study of this chapter should enable you to:

☑ Understand the nature and dynamics of power as it exists within the police agency as well as external to the agency.

☑ Be familiar with the techniques in the appropriate use of power as an executive tool for insuring compliance.

☑ Understand the political influences, appropriate and inappropriate, which are exercised by and upon the police department as well as within its own ranks.

☑ Know the history of how the criminal justice system has been utilized throughout history as a tool against the unpopular in our society.

☑ Understand that police corruption does exist in some of our police agencies, but that corruption varies in degrees and according to geographical location.

☑ Recognize that affirmative action is a controversial political topic which involves many issues related to personnel quality, morale, and constitutional issues.

☑ Gain an understanding of the less than perfect quality of our police leadership, know their deficiencies and what needs to be changed in the future.

☑ Know the definition of "profession" and be able to evaluate to what extent police officers today are or are not professionals.

Introduction

Politics touch on American policing, and the police touch on politics. No longer can we view the police as a separate entity; instead, we must begin to recognize the American police service from the standpoint of the systems approach. Law enforcement is a part of the whole of society, and each segment of society is interdependent with other segments. The role and functions of one part affect all the others.

Not only do many relationships exist between police and politics, but many of the processes which occur within the police agency are themselves political in nature. The exercise of power is one such example of this. In addition, law enforcement has occupied a special place throughout American history as the force which serves those in political, legal, and cultural power.

More recently, certain special issues have developed in the arena of police and politics. In an era of post-Watergate morality, police corruption has become a major concern. The new commitment to the elimination of racial and sex discrimination has raised fundamental questions about affirmative action, its morality and constitutionality, and its effect upon police personnel administration. In addition, a commitment to higher education for police officers of all ranks has brought into focus the question of the quality of police leadership and the issue of professionalization of the American police service.

Power in a Democratic Society

In a democratic society, consensus of the governed is essential. In a *pure* democracy, each citizen has a direct voice in each societal and governmental issue. Such a system may sound ideal, but it's totally unworkable in a large, complex, fast-moving nation such as the United States, where pure democracy no longer exists outside a few small towns in New England which cling to tradition. If each citizen were to vote on each political decision, very little governmental business would be accomplished.

A *representative* democracy is a modified form of democracy in which citizens elect representatives to speak, act, and vote on their behalf. These include city council members, county supervisors, state representatives, and members of the U.S. House and Senate. Although each citizen no longer has the opportunity to participate in each legislative act, the advantage lies in greater efficiency and a more workable governmental system.

Since our elected representatives can't personally carry out all the responsibilities of government, however, still others are appointed to function in executive capacities. As Charles D. Hale, police administration expert, observes:

> *The concept of pure democracy is further weakened when elected officials select and appoint others to carry out the administrative affairs of government. While this further diminishes popular control over governmental activities, it increases efficiency. Appointed officials, insulated from political*

> *pressures and granted broad administrative powers, are able to devote their specialized skills to the complex problems of government. Usually, due to their technical training and experience, they are much more qualified to manage the administrative affairs of government, allowing elected officials to devote their time to more general policy matters.*[1]

The public's influence over governmental operations is further watered down when appointed officials employ subordinates who have delegated authority to carry out the daily duties. In a complex society, however, the system probably couldn't function in any other way.

The police service in American has been democratically created and funded, although it doesn't answer directly to the people. Typically, in a city, the people elect a mayor and members of a city council. The council usually appoints the chief of police, who then delegates authority to the various members of police force. In counties, a more direct link between the electorate and law enforcement exists in that the voters elect the sheriff directly. The sheriff is then answerable to the people rather than to the county board of supervisors with one exception: the board allocates funds for the operation of the sheriff's department.

The law enforcement function within total government has been described as follows:

> *The modern police service is a part of the governmental process that provides public safety in its broadest ramifications: protection of persons and property; crime prevention; firefighting and fire prevention; structural safety of buildings through codes and other means; traffic engineering; educational programs; and, in recent years, a range of environmental protection measures related to public health and other forms of control. Thus, law enforcement is only one part of the police service and the police service is only one part of the governmental process which makes community life possible in both rural and urban areas.*[2]

Government in the United States on local, state, and federal levels is divided into three branches: the legislative (to pass laws), the executive (to administer according to law), and the judicial (to review). Law enforcement, whether on a township, city, county, state, or federal level, is a part of the executive branch of government. The administration of any law enforcement agency—be it a city police department, a county sheriff's department, a state police agency, or a federal enforcement agency—is very much a matter involving politics.

Politics can be defined in a traditional manner as *the policies, affairs, or goals of a government or of the groups or parties within it.* Or, it can be defined more lightly as *the issue of who gets what and how.* Regardless of how politics is defined, though, it's clear that the American police agency is a political animal.

The police force is created by legislation; is funded annually by an elected body; is charged with enforcing laws which are passed by the legislature; is forced to compete with other departments for funds, recognition, and status; must be concerned with its public image; must maintain appropriate relations with the public and various governmental agencies; and is greatly affected in its work by social, economic, racial, demographic, and other factors. In other words, to deny that police administration is a political function is to deny the way things are.

Or, in other words:

Police-community relations (some of which are tension-filled) are heavily influenced by the complex nature of the environment within which policing occurs today. The political process within each community obviously varies with local priorities and needs. Even in the smallest communities, economic and social variables produce varying service expectations.

Municipal government itself is the common link between these often diverse and sometimes competing pressures in providing such common services as sewers, water, police, fire, and streets. Priorities must be set for each of these services by budget year, area (neighborhood), and similar measures.

Municipalities, communities, and even neighborhoods do not agree on what police priorities or actions should be. Just as many communities have experienced major disagreements about school location, school curricula, provision of welfare benefits, or protection of housing patterns, so there have been major disagreements about what the police should be doing and how it should be done. The increasing reliance on techniques of confrontation as a means for social change makes the police role even more visible and potentially controversial, since police action is frequently required in what can often be heated community conflicts.[3]

Since police is a political function, the political importance of power must also be recognized. Power has been defined as "the ability to effect obedience."[4] Commenting on that particular definition, management experts observe:

It can be defined in less harsh terms as the capacity to win compliance, to obtain followership, or to impose the will. Regardless of the niceties of definition, power is absolutely essential to achieve coordinated results. Unless power is lodged in the hands of some, and not all, within the enterprise, only disaster can follow. Individual differences are so great that spontaneous and comprehensive cooperation toward a common goal will rarely, if ever, take place. This is a truism.[5]

The exercise of power in a policy agency has great impact upon society, and the manner in which it is exercised is determined by the administrators who hold the power positions.

As one political scientist notes:

1. *Governmental decisions and behavior have tremendous influence upon the nature and development of our society, our economy, and our policy;*
2. *The great bulk of decisions and actions taken by governments are determined or heavily influenced by administrative officials, most of whom are appointed, not elected;*
3. *The kinds of decisions and actions these officials take depend upon their capabilities, their orientations, and their values; and*

4. *These attributes depend heavily upon their backgrounds, their training and education, and their current associations.*[6]

One of the first steps in the exercise of power lies in planning. Planning cannot be separated from budgeting and modern budgeting cannot be separated from the concept of *management by objectives.*

Traditional budgeting involves a superficial review of the past year's budget and a rather mindless but routine request for a certain percentage of increase in funds; for example, a ten percent increase in personnel, equipment, salaries, etc. It's a "business as usual" approach. Too often, little thought goes into what specific programs or goals will be related to the future budget.

Management by objectives is radically different. First of all, it calls for an analysis of the problems police are expected to deal with. In a city, for example, major problems may include robberies, homicides, narcotics, traffic injuries and deaths, and larceny. Since the city may not be able to deal fully and effectively with all of its problems, a judgment must be made regarding the issues which warrant special efforts. Rather than giving equal attention to all the city's problems, a decision must be made to select a small number of particularly important issues on which the police can hope to have an actual impact.

The police chief may decide, for example, that among the critical issues mentioned above, armed robberies, narcotics, and traffic injuries warrant particular police attention. Armed robberies involve a preventable threat to human life; narcotics may be filtering into the school system, presenting a serious health threat to young people; and traffic accidents have long been recognized as being the greatest threat to human safety and lives. On the other hand, larceny is not a crime which threatens human life, and, while homicides do involve the loss of life, they're generally not preventable by police because they tend to occur in homes and among families and friends; thus, these two types of crime may be excluded from the chief's list of priorities.

After selecting robbery, narcotics, and traffic as main targets, the police administrator, using management by objectives, must next decide what programs to implement to combat those three particular problems. He or she may, for example, select a prevention approach combined with a stakeout program for the robbery problem. For the narcotics problem, he or she may decide on a combination of an increased undercover operation and a school educational program. To reduce traffic accidents, the chief may choose to add more motorcycle officers and radar units.

Next, the administrator must decide how to staff and equip those operations. This decision must then be translated into specific goals (reducing armed robberies by 25 percent, reducing heavy narcotics sales in schools by 50 percent, and cutting injury accidents by 30 percent). Describing the programs intended to achieve those specific goals, the police administrator must then request in the budget specific personnel and other resources to accomplish tasks. Rather than blindly requesting additional funds for general use, the chief shows that he or she has analyzed goals, established priorities, planned programs toward goal achievement, and made budget requests which are tied to all those steps and issues.

To exercise responsible power, the police chief must monitor operations regularly and carefully. This type of feedback, or "cybernetics," involves regular analysis of the success rate of the operation, combined with appropriate action depending on the results. Such action could result in discontinuing a program, continuing it, or making appropriate modifications in it, depending on the circumstances. "Feedback," says Criminal Justice Professor Paul Whisenand and Police Chief Fred Ferguson, "is defined . . . as a means for controlling an organization by reinserting into it the results of its past performance."[7]

It can also be said that the results of police operations—whether positive, negative, or a combination—constitute *information.* Information, then, becomes a resource which is fed into the operational system just like any other resources (such as funds, equipment, personnel, etc.). The use of information as a resource is essential to the police administrator who wishes to properly exercise power according to the best management principles.

Just as the police administrator who wishes to utilize power to maximize the department's operational efficiency can't rely on traditional, routine, mindless budgeting, so also is it imperative that the administrator be aware of the concept of *exploitation of opportunity.*

In the words of Hardwick and Landuyt, business administration experts:

> *. . . the truth remains that much of the competitive advantage enjoyed by an administrator, his department, or company flows from his attitude toward and utilization of opportunities. The strategic leader is well aware of this fact. He knows that the "extra something" which may be gained by the judicious investigation and use of situations may make him or his a winner. He tends to seek out and to view opportunities in a positive light; he may even be so sensitive to their possibilities to attempt to create them.*[8]

The life of any organization—private or public—can be described as a *series of situations,* and it's reasonable to expect that in any series of situations there'll be some that can be used to advantage. The alert police administrator, using his or her power and authority to recognize, seize and exploit opportunities—fortuitous or created—enhances his or her power base and thereby acquires greater power and influence in future situations. This type then enjoys greater stature among his or her superiors, subordinates, and the public.

Some police administrators shy away from any management activity not absolutely necessary for the daily routine operation of the department. They do this either out of ignorance or fear. Their fears are present because they see innovative methods as too risky. True, risk is always present when action is taken; what these administrators overlook, however, is that inaction also carries a risk.

Before the administrator can exploit an opportunity, he or she must be able to recognize it. Hardwick and Landuyt observe:

Most ordinary administrators whose continuing mediocrity stems from their failure to see chances to improve and expand the operation really have some desire to be more successful. Much of their weakness lies in the fact that they do not know an opportunity when they see it. This deficiency may be due to one or more circumstances. It may involve the individual's inclination to favor personal safety, his natural laziness, his lack of intellectual attributes or imagination or perhaps he has been steeped in the philosophy of conservatism and conformity.[9]

The right opportunity consists of five elements, all of which must be understood by the manager. One is *critical moment*—the exact time in the development of a situation at which the other necessary elements can be synthesized. *Possession of power,* or the capacity to take action, is a second element. A third factor is *availability of means of exploitation.* If certain resources are required, they must of course be present. A fourth component is *absence of effective resistance and interference.* Freedom to decide and act without disabling obstacles is important. Finally, the *possibility of gain* must be present. An opportunity obviously doesn't exist if there isn't a situation present which can be used to advantage.[10]

The following list of hints on how to achieve, maintain, and increase executive power through the exploitation of opportunities was intended for business leaders but, as in the case of most administration theories, they can be applied to both the private and the public sectors:

1. Remember that the exploitation of an opportunity will involve moral values, and that the truly strategic leader will take the ethical course.
2. Be the first to seize good opportunities.
3. Examine dubious opportunities and, if they look too uncertain, let someone else take the first steps in their cultivation.
4. Remember that others may be attempting to use the same situation; there may be advantage in "taking them over" or joining them at some point, as far as fair play will permit.
5. Live dangerously with good sense; take risks in proportion to expected gains.
6. Remain flexible; compromise and redirect when feasible and ethical.
7. Manipulate fairly before you fight, but fight if the stakes are high enough.
8. Be willing to progress by steps and build sub-opportunities into a whole.
9. Leave an avenue of retreat; it may make possible an effective and interim tactic or provide a way of saving something if things go wrong.
10. While pursuing the main chance, be alert for new openings; the moment may reveal by-products in the form of other opportunities.
11. Get as much publicity for your intentions and efforts as will further them.[11]

Two courses are available to the police administrator: the *routine,* and the *dynamic.* He or she cannot choose the latter without a thorough understanding of the functions of power in relation to the issue of opportunities.

Power is sometimes seen as being synonymous with authority. In fact, however, there are distinctions. Authority rests in *position.* A chief of police or a sergeant of police has authority because of his or her official rank. Supervisory personnel in police departments often tend to rely on their rank to carry out their tasks. While this may be expeditious, it runs contrary to professional custom. For example, co-professionals (physicians in a hospital, partners in a law firm, or professors in a university) don't invoke rank to bring about change, but rather allow a free exchange of ideas before mutual decisions are made. This is not to suggest that rank has no place in a police agency, which is often involved in emergency field situations; the reliance on rank in police departments may have been overemphasized, though, because it affords individuals protection regardless of their level of competency.

If authority means the right to command, it must be recognized that "the right to command does not necessarily connote the capacity to command."[12] Power, however, as distinguished from authority, suggests the *capacity* to command, and therefore rests in the person rather than in the rank.

Regarding power, public administration specialists have observed that: "It may or may not coincide with the official structure of authority. Power in itself is not institutionalized in the sense that one can look to the organizational manual and find out where it resides."[13] Finally, on the subject of power, Whisenand and Ferguson write:

> *At this late point the police manager should recognize the political facts of life and change his style, utilizing the organizational power-politics to its best advantage. In many cases where the unswerving managerial style prevails, however, the manager is eventually demoted, retired, fired, or elevated to a state of limbo where he no longer has any influence. There are, of course, those few who have acquired considerable personal power through outside-of-the-organization politics. They seem to remain almost indefinitely, surrounded by a kind of bureaucratic moat, blindly impeding the organization and its individual elements from reaching optimum goals.*
>
> *We are in general agreement with contemporaries in the field that authority is an essential component of power, while power itself is not necessarily synonymous with authority. Power and authority are, however, legitimately a part of control.*[14]

Due to the internal and external relationships which the police administrator must face, it's necessary that he or she understand that his or her office and its functions are political ones. Once this fact is clear, the further fact that power is the key to achievement of police goals must not only be accepted but must be mastered in terms of technique.

Political Influences on Law Enforcement

Since law enforcement is not only a governmental agency function but also a part of the political system, it's important to understand the various political influences which affect law enforcement.

Political influences are both external and internal in nature. They are external in that the police department is subject to influences from the outside as well as to the department's own influence upon its environment. Internal political influences move down the hierarchy and, to a lesser extent, up the chain of command. Certain influences are also horizontal; i.e. they function on only one level and are peer-group oriented. Finally, politics are at work when decisions must be made as to who should get hired, retained, and even promoted.

External Influences External influences rarely flow in one direction. For example, relations between the police department and the community or the prosecutor consist of both incoming and outgoing communications, pressures, threats, games, demands, power plays, etc.

The groups or organizations with which the police exchange influences and the nature of those contacts—strong, weak, honest, dishonest, cooperative, disruptive—vary, of course, in detail from city to city and from state to state.

Herman Goldstein, author of *Policing A Free Society,* emphasized the political nature of policing as follows:

> *A further common misconception accounting for present difficulties is that the police function is apolitical. But city government is political and, of necessity, police functioning is political. The wide range of discretionary decisions . . . that involve the setting of policies are political decisions.*[15]

Some of the contacts between police and the environment are of an official nature. They include relations with the city council, the prosecutor, the courts, the probation and parole system, and other law enforcement agencies on local, state, and federal levels. Even in these official relationships, however, politics plays a part. Not every transaction is clear-cut but rather involves some use of pressure, trade-offs, or use of the "norm of reciprocity" ("do this for me, and I'll do that for you"). Such tactics are means to an end which suggests that they can be, but aren't necessarily, evil. Like tools, they aren't bad in and of themselves; rather, it depends on how they're used.

The state legislature has great impact upon the American police service and is one body upon which the police don't have an equal amount of influence. It affects law enforcement by passing laws which it expects local police agencies to enforce. Thus, without having direct authority over local law enforcement, state legislators exercise great influence over local policing policies, workloads, budget, prisoner loads, etc.

Some critics maintain that the legislators take the easy way out every time a problem arises and simply pass a law to deal with it, making a particular conduct unlawful. They feel that legislators usually don't concern themselves with the impact of such laws upon the local police departments. To combat this problem, and to free police to deal with serious crime, the prominent criminologists, Morris and Hawkins suggest the following legislative relief:

1. *Drunkenness.* Public drunkenness shall cease to be a criminal offense.
2. *Narcotics and drug abuse.* Neither the acquisition, purchase, possession, nor the use of any drug will be a criminal offense. The sale of some drugs other than by a licensed chemist (druggist) and on prescription will be criminally proscribed; proof of possession of excessive quantities may be evidence of a sale or of intent to sell.
3. *Gambling.* No form of gambling will be prohibited by the criminal law; certain fraudulent and cheating gambling practices will remain criminal.
4. *Disorderly conduct and vagrancy.* Disorderly conduct and vagrancy laws will be replaced by laws precisely stipulating the conduct proscribed and defining the circumstances in which the police should intervene.
5. *Abortion.* Abortion performed by a qualified medical practitioner in a registered hospital shall cease to be a criminal offense.
6. *Sexual behavior.* Sexual activities between consenting adults in private will not be subject to the criminal law.

   Adultery, fornication, illicit cohabitation, statutory rape and carnal knowledge, bigamy, incest, sodomy, bestiality, homosexuality, prostitution, pornography, and obscenity; in all of these the role of the criminal law is excessive.
7. *Juvenile delinquency.* The juvenile court should retain jurisdiction only over conduct by children which would be criminal were they adults.
8. *A Standing Law Revision Committee.* Every legislature must establish a Standing Criminal Law Revision Committee charged with the task of constant consideration of the fitness and adequacy of the criminal law sanctions to social needs.[16]

The authors explain their position as follows:

> *Politicians rely heavily on the criminal law and like to invoke criminal sanctions in connection with most social problems, if only to indicate their moral fervor and political virture. They take little interest in the consequences of the invocation.*[17]

Whether such legislative reforms will ever come about is questionable. While they would profoundly change the police responsibilities, it's doubtful that police generally favor major decriminalization or legalization. And, further, even if they did, police usually don't have the political apparatus to bring about such reforms by excercising influence over the state legislatures.

Various connections between police and those with political influence differ in intensity, frequency, and degrees of honesty from city to city and from state to state. Generally, the western United States have enjoyed a greater freedom from corruption than have the eastern, more established cities.

James Ahern, former chief of police in New Haven, Connecticut, describes his experience:

> *Every cop who wanted to get ahead had his "hook"—or, as they say in New York, his "rabbi." Everyone owed his success to a politician—from the Town Chairman on down—or to an influential underworld figure. Needless to say, in a situation like this there was no chance whatever of the department functioning in the public interest.*[18]

Ahern discloses one action he took to prevent political interference:

> *A day after I had taken office, I closed the second-story back door to the Mayor's office and issued a renewal of a long-standing and long-ignored departmental order prohibiting any police officer from seeing the Mayor without the authorization of the chief.*
>
> *Given the incredible tangle of grimy politics that still existed in the lower levels of government and in the structures of the city's political parties, this action was largely symbolic. But as a gesture it was necessary. It would be immediately evident to everyone in the police department that if I would not permit the Mayor who had appointed me to influence departmental promotions or assignments, I certainly would allow no other politicians to influence them.*[19]

But many police chiefs can't afford to be so courageous:

> *Police chiefs are politically vulnerable, and especially so if they serve at the discretion of their mayors. Since they do not have control over promotions in their departments, and since they are isolated from the command structure below them, they can offer no rewards to good cops. Any experimental steps they wish to make place their careers in jeopardy. Unlike people in other professions, unemployed police chiefs have few places to go. This leads to personal insecurity, which makes chiefs even less willing to take risks.*
>
> *Most police chiefs, however, having come up through the ranks of their own departments, alleviate their insecurity—as much as possible—years before they become chiefs. They protect their own, they play politics, and they survive. If they serve in cities where crime machines hold the real power and lubricate police departments with illicit funds, the chiefs function in ways that perpetuate machine power and cut off police from broad democratic controls. It is only when they are threatened by ghetto riots or student unrest, or when gambling and narcotics activities become so widespread as to incite a public reaction, that they stand a chance of being exposed; and even when they are exposed, the staying power of the crime machine is usually far greater than the power of those political leaders who are borne upward by brief surges of public indignation. Consequently, the years come, and the years go, and nothing changes.*[20]

A major concern of the police administrator is relations with "the community." "The community" is a term which can refer to any element ranging from the general public to militant minority groups. Many police departments have established police-community relations (PCR) units, often in response to the riots of the 1960s. Whether such units have done any good is an unsettled matter. Some police agencies have PCR units which give speeches before already approving audiences such as the PTA, the Lions Club, the Rotary Club, veterans associations, etc., telling the members what they want to hear. Rarely do PCR officers engage in dialogue with members of the public who are angry, frustrated, or militant. But, in defense of such police agencies, one can legitimately ask whether there's anything to be gained from exchanging views with the Black Panthers, the Weathermen, the Ku Klux Klan, and other fanatical groups. Perhaps there are groups in our society who are beyond open communication.

One recurring community issue concerns community control of the police. A key question is whether police should function uniformly throughout the jurisdiction (most often the city) or whether they should be responsive to particular community standards, values, and needs. On one hand, one can argue that certain cultural manifestations exist in certain areas which should be left undisturbed even though they may be in violation of law—for example, gambling and drinking in the street. Some will say that these are cultural traits which shouldn't be interfered with by "the outside army of occupation," meaning the police. On the other hand, the person who might be arested for the same act in a neighborhood where such conduct isn't a part of the culture could validly argue that he or she is the victim of discriminatory enforcement. On balance, therefore, it would seem that we are better able to justify equal enforcement of the law in all the city's neighborhoods.

Community control has become a most current topic. James Q. Wilson, Professor of Government at Harvard University, weighs the issues:

> *The issue of "community control" of the police has of late come to dominate any discussion of police-community relations, just as a few years ago such a discussion focused largely on "civilian review boards." The argument is that both better police protection and better police conduct can only be insured by giving neighborhoods control over their own police. In this way, the police will be responsive to the needs of the local citizens—the community will develop both policies for the exercise of police discretion and methods for the restraint or correction of police misconduct.*
>
> *It is difficult to evaluate this policy since, to a great extent, it is a slogan rather than a program. Its adherents believe fervently in it without being able to offer a very clear understanding of what might be involved. And since shifting authority over the police from city hall to the neighborhoods is perhaps the most far-reaching change that could be made in police practice, it is especially important that one examine it closely. "Community control" could vary from having neighborhood groups choose, or consent to the choice of, the police captain assigned to their precincts, to the creation of neighborhood police policy boards that would exercise day-to-day supervision over the policies and actions of officers assigned to a particular locale, and beyond even to organizing the neighborhood so that it could hire, train, and deploy its own independent police force. And the range of control could vary from control over local beat patrolmen (leaving specialized units, such as traffic or even the detectives, centrally managed) to control over all aspects of police work in the area.*[21]

Herman Goldstein favors a modified form of community control:

What decisions can be left to a neighborhood or some other subdivision of a larger municipality? It is unlikely that anyone would seriously suggest that state statutes prohibiting homicide or rape should be enforced differently in different areas of a city or even in different sections of a state. But a strong case could be made for adopting different operating policies for resolving conflict in order to acknowledge different cultural practices and preferences.[22]

Whatever one's position is on community control of police, it must be recognized that:

This changing environment, then, places great demands on both the police administrator and the municipal or county chief executive. No longer is it acceptable for police chiefs to remain isolated from the dynamics of their communities. Today, police administrators must assume a number of important duties, including interacting constructively with the political structure in the community. And city administrators must understand fully the complexities of policing so that they can serve as the link between the police agency and the political structure, as the latter is represented formally by the council or similar body.[23]

Internal Influences The American police department functions as a semi-military organization with a hierarchy, a chain of command, ranks, communications moving down the organizational ladder (mostly orders, policies, and directives), communications moving up it (mostly requests, inquiries, and reports). Such interactions almost always involved the exercise of influence or potential influence. But influences are also exerted *horizontally*, or on the same level—among captains, among sergeants, and among patrol officers. All such influences can either be helpful or destructive, benevolent or malicious, benign or evil. They can either move through the chain of command or informally bypass it.

Conformity is particularly valued in police departments. Conformity in police practices, attitudes, biases, enforcement emphases, personal and religious values, on- and off-duty behavior, and political leanings are but some of the areas in which the police officer is expected to conform to the status quo of the "the fraternity." The majority of police officers come from upper-lower- and lower-middle-class backgrounds where becoming a police officer is often a symbol of upward social mobility. Consequently, the cultures of those classes are predominant in the police service. At the danger of generalizing, then, a typical police officer is patriotic, religious, ethonocentric, not overly well-educated, traditional, and tends to follow a political philosophy of a conservative nature.

Police researcher George Berkley confirms this point:

In the United Sates, Jerome Skonik concludes after lengthy interviews with members of two police departments: ". . . a Goldwater type of conservatism was the dominant political and emotional persuasion of the police. I encountered only three policemen who claimed to be politically liberal, at the same time asserting that they were decidedly exceptional."[24]

Since the police service abounds with such personnel, and since the current members decide who will be hired, it follows, then, that there's a tendency to exclude those applicants who somehow are different. Promotions are then made from the ranks of those who are able—and allowed—to enter the police service; they thereby enter positions of influence; and the whole system perpetuates itself.

Professor A. C. Germann, California State University, Long Beach, has stated that "the greatest police state exists within the police agency." Those who manage to enter the system and are then perceived as not "fitting in" are often made the subject of pressure tactics from peers and superiors so that they eventually resign in disgust, thereby helping to preserve the pool of traditionalists. It should further be noted that the well-educated officers are better able to leave the police service to seek more rewarding careers while the poorly educated have little choice but to remain, thereby being available when promotions are made. And the cycle is complete.

Internal political pressures are numerous and varied in nature. They are abundant and strong in the peer group, they are common and powerful downward in the hierarchy, and they are rare and weak upward in the organization. In short, the power structure tends to prevail.

Politics in Action in the Criminal Justice Field

We have seen how the police are a part of the governmental system and, therefore, can't be separated from politics, including the politics of power. It's been theorized that police, power, and politics involve influences which are both external and internal to the police organization. To illustrate these points, certain specific issues of current interest will be explored.

The Law and the Unpopular Social critics, civil libertarians, legal scholars, and even a few criminal justice professionals are among those who charge that the agencies of criminal justice have historically lent themselves as political tools—machines used against the unpopular, against the questioners of the status quo, and against those whose politics were ahead of the times. Such charges suggest that the slogan "to protect and serve" should read "to protect and serve the popular," and that the phrase "protectors of liberty" should accurately read "protectors of the status quo."

William Domhoff, a University of California psychologist, sees federal law enforcement as closely tied to "members of the power elite."[25] Professor A. C. Germann, discussing local law enforcement, has stated:

> *Some police have values and standards more appropriate to the days of public hangings, and a very limited social awareness. Some police have more readily identified with the duty of maintaining* order *than with the duty of maintaining* liberty*. . . and some police have been identified as "the last puritans" with the predilection toward moralizing.*[26]

Howard Zinn, a political scientist at Boston University, sees a dichotomy between theory and practice:

> *Justice is a grand word in the United States. It calls to mind enormous marble columns, the black-robed dignity of the Supreme Court, the promises of the Bill of Rights. We think of eloquent decisions interpreting the Constitution that fill weighty volumes in the library, called the* U.S. Reports. *These decisions seem to spell out a historic procession toward greater and greater freedom in America. That is the justice we read about. But there is another kind of justice, which we* live.[27]

That law enforcement personnel are not neutral in political terms is suggested by the American Civil Liberty Union's (ACLU) Ed Cray, who claims: ". . . the police have emerged as a bold, even cocky band of political activists."[28] This may be particularly disturbing if the late Chief William H. Parker's evaluation of police personnel is correct: "Most of the police of America are 'conservative, ultra-conservative and very right wing.' "[29]

Are these concerns about America's justice system totally without merit, or are they founded in fact? Is it hysterical to be concerned about the misuse of our criminal justice system for political purposes, or does history show this to be an area which democratic men and women ought to focus their attention on? Charles Goodell, former United States Senator from New York, has explored this question in his book, *Political Prisoners in America.* Goodell gives a historical overview of the issue, from which a handful of illustrations are selected and discussed here.

In 1798, the Sedition Act was passed. It outlawed "any false, scandalous or malicious statement about the president or Congress made with the intent to bring them into contempt or disrepute or to stir up opposition to any law or presidential act." Thus, opposition to the Sedition Act itself was a criminal offense. Enforcement of the act occurred strictly along partisan lines by the Federalists against the Republicans, and the judges used the trials to expound on religion, politics, and morality. Jefferson urged use of the Act against the press: "I have therefore long thought that a few prosecutions of the most prominent offenders would have a wholesome effect in restoring the integrity of the presses. Not a general prosecution, for that would look like a persecution, but a selected one."[30] While it would be tempting to assume that such attitudes could only have existed many generations ago, it's obvious how comfortable a recent president would have been with such a law which would have prevented the press from kicking him around.

In the 1850s, the Fugitive Slave Law was used to prosecute those who on moral grounds opposed the institution of slavery. Congress had previously passed a resolution which in modern terms would have been called a "gag-rule": ". . . all petitions, resolutions, papers relating in any way to the subject of slavery shall . . . be laid upon the table and no further action whatever shall be had thereon."[31]

The Selective Service Draft Act—including the Espionage Act of 1917 and its amendment, which came to be known as the Sedition Act of 1918—made it a twenty-year felony to make statements with the intent to interfere with the military, to obstruct the sale of U.S. bonds, or to make statements intended to bring the government into disrepute. A New Yorker who, on the Fourth of July, distributed copies of the Declaration of Independence with the written question attached, "Does your government live up to these principles?" was sentenced to a term in prison.[32]

The International Workers of the World, a group whose 100,000 members were dedicated to organizing labor before unionism was seen as an acceptable institution, was systematically persecuted. When the IWW, or the "Wobblies," as they were called, engaged in nonviolent efforts to exercise free speech, they were beaten by police and vigilantes and jailed for disorderly conduct. Conservative California Republicans, through political pressure, were able to bring the Justice Department into action against the IWW. Later, in 1913 in Wheatland, California, the sheriff's department opened fire on the workers' mass meeting, killing several members as well as some public officials. As a result, two Wobblie organizers were convicted of murder. The federal government later brought in troops who made mass arrest of union members, detained them without charges, and raided union offices and meetings. These efforts were followed up by the FBI which, in 1917, raided IWW offices and members' homes across the nation. Fearing that their members might retaliate with force, the IWW tried to mail a resolution to the membership urging them not to engage in sabotage; the mailing itself was banned because it contained the word "sabotage." From 1917 to 1919, over a thousand Wobblies were arrested, half were indicted, and hundreds were given sentences ranging from ten to twenty years.[33]

A particularly well-known IWW organizer was Joe Hill, a Swedish immigrant who later became somewhat of a folk-hero about whom ballads were written. He was executed in Utah in 1915 for murder, despite his claim of innocence and national and international efforts to reexamine the case. It's evident that his union activities were troublesome to the Mormon Church and the copper interests. We may never know the facts of the case for, strangely, his file disappeared from the court after his death.[34]

Around 1920, the Immigration Act of 1903 became a useful tool of government with which Attorney General Mitchell Palmer accused people of engaging in "evil thinking." The Immigration Service and the Justice Department cooperated in a series of nationwide sweeps, rounding up socialists, union organizers, and other unpopular segments of the population. These activities represented some of the early achievements of J. Edgar Hoover, who saw the denial of bail as essential because he feared that pretrial release of the arrestees would give their attorneys an opportunity to prepare a defense. When Assistant Secretary of Labor Louis Post advocated due process for the arrestees, Hoover charged him with being in sympathy with radical elements, and impeachment proceedings were instigated in Congress against Post. Immigration officials arrested not only aliens but all types of persons, including U.S. citizens found in the company of the suspects. At the Hartford, Connecticut jail, persons requesting to visit their jailed friends and relatives were themselves seized and jailed.[35]

It was also during this time that Sacco and Vanzetti were sentenced to death for murder by a judge who proclaimed in the courtroom that while there was reasonable doubt as to their guilt, he would nevertheless convict and sentence them because their ideas were "foreign to American tradition." This era has been summarized as a period when Attorney General Palmer "converted the law of the United States into a tool of frenzy fed by public hysteria. . . ."[36]

The 1940s saw the interment without trial in concentration camps—or, as we chose to call them, relocation camps—of 117,000 Americans of Japanese ancestry.

Post-war hysteria was transferred to any person or any idea that could somehow be labelled as Communist. For example, when the late Paul Robeson was to give a concert at Peekskill, New York in 1949, the audience was literally stoned and beaten by vigilante mobs while the police stood idly by.[37]

The case of Julius and Ethel Rosenberg, now reviewed in greater calmness than prevailed during the fifties, has raised many questions by groups and individuals including prominent attorney Louis Nizer.[38] An Ann Arbor minister preached an Easter sermon on the case titled, "A Study in Contemporary Crucifixion."[39]

The civil rights movement may well have been sparked by Rosa Parks when, on December 1, 1955, she refused to move to the back of the bus, only to be arrested, jailed, and convicted of a crime. Other civil rights activists found themselves charged with such felony offenses as "conspiracy to obstruct business." Sit-ins, demonstrations, and freedom rides followed, with the police too often failing to give protection against ambushes, assaults, and burnings. It has even been charged that "the slayings of civil rights workers James Chaney, Andrew Goodman, and Michael Schwerner were carried out largely through the cooperation and planning of Mississippi officials."[40]

The Vietnam era made legal offenders of thousands of moral citizens. Those in the military who on moral grounds were unable to participate in certain military actions soon found that the Nuremberg doctrine—the doctrine which makes it mandatory to follow one's conscience rather than blindly obeying orders—was a doctrine which we claimed was binding when applied to the Germans in the Second World War but from which we now insisted that Americans were exempt. Civilians who voiced their opposition to the war became the target of both military and civilian authorities whose activities included surveillance, beatings, persecutions, and prosecutions. Thousands of citizens who simply exercised their First Amendment rights were filmed and in a variety of other ways recorded in intelligence banks. One Quaker who already had conscientious objector status and nevertheless, as a symbolic act, returned his draft card to his Selective Service Office, received three years in prison. Seven organizers of a sit-in in Oakland, California were charged with felony conspiracy to commit misdemeanor trespassing.

Two Catholic priests, Fathers Daniel and Philip Berrigan, brought their protest into a moral and philosophical perspective when they poured napalm on draft records under what Father Dan called "the apparently utterly absurd assumption that it is better to burn paper than children." He later explained, "We have chosen to be powerless criminals in the face of criminal power."[41]

When approximately half a million peaceful demonstrators marched to the Capital in Washington in April of 1971, Nixon's response was that he would in no way be influenced by public sentiment. In frustration, 100-200 young people remained in Washington and attempted to interfere with the government's "business as usual" by staging sit-downs in the streets. The police response was to indiscriminately arrest 12,000 citizens, few of whom had violated any law, and incarcerate them in jails and ballparks for days. The Justice Department official reported to have cooperated with the Washington police force in the planning of these illegal mass arrests was William Rehnquist who, shortly thereafter, was elevated to the Supreme Court by Nixon. The attorney general, John Mitchell, travelled about the country and lauded the mass arrests as a "a model for police work of the future."

Later, the Watergate era came equipped with illegal wiretaps, surveillance, "protective reaction strikes" abroad and at home, break-ins, government concern with the question of "how it will play in Peoria" instead of with the question of legality, and what was basically an attempt by Nixon to steal the United States Constitution from the people.

One of the individuals singled out during that time period for prosecution was Dr. Daniel Ellsberg, who embarrassed the government by releasing the Pentagon Papers to the press. Senator Charles Goodell comments on the case:

> *What were the charges? That Ellsberg gave the documents to the New York Times or the Washington Post? No. He was accused of espionage, spying for having enlisted friends to help him xerox the papers when he was trying to get a copy to the Congress of the United States a year and a half before the newspapers began publishing them. The criminal charges were brought against Daniel Ellsberg for political reasons. Nobody in government really cared about him copying the papers. That happens all the time. But publication by the New York Times was exceedingly embarrassing. Why? Because the Pentagon Papers were irrefutable proof that government leaders, well-intentioned or not, had lied to us.*[42]

Sadly, American history provides us with many other cases in which the criminal justice machinery has been set in motion in the interest of the politically powerful rather than in the interest of justice. One is reminded of the Latin American proverb:

> *For our friends, everything.*
> *For strangers, nothing.*
> *For our enemies, the law.*

What causes or allows criminal justice and other officials to use the weight of their awesome offices against those citizens whose politics, culture, or conscience make them march to a different drummer? One can suggest that a certain mentality must be at play. It is a mentality which, unfortunately, is alive and well among many officials in the criminal justice system across the country. We recently had on the west coast a police chief of a large metropolitan city who opposes granting a parade permit to a homosexual group because they are criminals and we don't grant parade permits to robbers and burglars;[43] who sees student demonstrations as the "the planned revolution to take over the United States...the whole thing is in the Bible";[44] who sees social disorder as having two specific causes, "the breakdown in self-discipline on the part of the American people" and the "elimination of the concept of hell from contemporary theology";[45] whose response to reports of torture by Mexican officials of persons arrested for drug offenses is that those officials "are to be highly commended for their additional vigor" and that people "get spoiled by being born and raised in America where there is the presumption of innocence in an arrest"; and who sees the solution to hijacking as hanging defendants at the airport "after a rapid trial...with due process of law... I would recommend we have a portable courtroom on a big bus and a portable gallows."[47]

Egon Bittner issues this warning in reponse to attitudes like these:

> *Today policemen direct, control, and discipline persons from all walks of life, and crudeness on their part places them in a position of significant disadvantage. To be sure, crudeness can yet prevail, but only at a cost sober judgment will find intolerable."*[48]

And there may be a price to pay for the progressive official. A few years ago, Joseph Paul Kimble was hounded out of his job as chief of police in Beverly Hills, California for being too progressive, too humanistic, too far ahead of his time to suit local politicians and some surrounding police officials. A few years ago, Tom Murton was fired as a warden of the Arkansas prison system for trying to reform the system. Murton warns:

> *... the true reformer, as opposed to the official reformer, must subordinate his profession success to his primary mission—doing what needs to be done for the benefit of his fellow men.*
>
> *...Real change is brought about by those who have both the vision and the power to effect it—hence, the most effective reformer is the person within the power structure. But he must move quickly, for the body politic will waste little time rejecting this foreign organism. Integrity is not a very marketable commodity, and the career crusader is not self-sustaining, because the occupation itself is self-defeating. The true reformer must accept each challenge with the knowledge that ultimately he will be consumed in the process.*
>
> *The cynic quickly steps forward to pose the question: "Is it worth it?"*
>
> *And by his answer, each man not only determines his destiny, but he also declares his view of man.*[49]

True justice, "the rendering to each his due," requires professional, objective judgment based on the alleged offender's actions, not his or her philosophy. Any deviance from this principle will seriously deter progressive criminal justice.[50]

Political Interference

Many individuals, groups, governmental agencies, and criminal elements have a strong interest in the way a police department operates. Often, they will engage in attempts to exercise political interference with the police department. The motivations of these individuals and groups are varied and range from an interest in law enforcement to economic and philosophical concerns.

The professional police agency prefers to be relatively autonomous and immune to improper influences. Wallace Sayre and Herbert Kaufman, urban politics experts writing about New York City, support this position but warn that it shouldn't be synonymous with freedom from accountability:

> *But the most important strategic method is to secure wide acceptance of an inviolate status, a taboo against "political interference" or the intervention of "special interest." Once armed with this status, the organized bureaucracy can assert boldly, or can depend upon the press or some other participant to assert for it, a claim to freedom from supervision. Few bureaucracies achieve the full flower of this inviolable status, but most of them strive for it. The teachers, the police, the medical and health groups, the social workers, and others have frequently found it either a shield or a weapon.*[51]

Nevertheless, political intereference with law enforcement is a fact of life and takes many forms. Like corruption, it is more prevalent in some areas of the country than in others. The east and midwest are particular problem areas, while the west (one major California city being a notable exception) generally has prevented improper interference and corruption from gaining a foothold.

Unfortunately, there's a tendency to avoid facing this problematic and serious situation. James Ahern, former chief of police in New Haven, Connecticut, warns: "the fourteen-volume study of the President's Commission on the Administration of Justice, undoubtedly the most comprehensive survey of the law-enforcement process ever done in America, completely ignores the greatest threat and detriment to fair and effective law enforcement. This threat is illegitimate political interference, often intimately connected with corrupt and criminal interference."[52] Ahern elaborates on local political interference as follows:

> *This means that political bosses control chiefs of police, who usually serve at the discretion of the mayors under whom they work and who therefore are highly vulnerable. Since bosses also control the boards that administer Civil Service examinations and determine advancement under that system, they are able to subvert Civil Service. Through the chief they can control who is assigned to such vital areas as vice, gambling, and narcotics investigations, and whether the department's Detective Division attempts to combat organized crime. Since they control promotions, the chief owes his to them more*

> *often than not, and any deviation from their policies or desires is sure to handicap the career of any officer in the department.*
>
> *This arrangement assures that the political boss can do numerous favors for politically important people. He can have parking and traffic tickets fixed, he can assure that minor violations of numerous laws—from obstruction of public streets to liquor-law violations—are ignored, and he can deliver extra police protection for favored neighborhoods. He can do a great deal more as well.*
>
> *Political bosses control courts and prosecutors—or at least some of them—just as they control other segments of city governments. Whether elected or appointed, judges come by their positions politically. If they are appointed, the connection is direct. If they are elected, someone must agree to put them on the party ticket, and that person is the boss.*[53]

But political interference does not always come from local gangsters and politicians. Sometimes it can originate with governmental officials on various levels. James Ahern has made an excellent contribution to the understanding of such issues with his book, *Police in Trouble.* When the Black Panthers and their sympathizers planned a demonstration in New Haven in 1970, Chief Ahern was faced with the question of how best to organize the policing of that event. But both state and federal officials wanted to "get a piece of the action," partly due to emotional reasons, and partly because they saw the situation as one containing political mileage. While Ahern wanted to maintain a low profile to avoid violence, the mayor's attitude was "it's too bad we can't just get the bastards." And the head of the state police insisted on approaching the event with maximum force. President Nixon assigned over 3,500 infantry and paratroopers without ever consulting the city officials. J. Edgar Hoover entered the picture by distributing intelligence information to the President and other federal officials, even though the intelligence consisted only of "raw data"—i.e., unverified rumors. Hoover also publicly named the Panthers as "the greatest internal threat to the security of the country."[54]

Such were the conflicts that there were even arguments about who would be in command. Ahern finally won the right to be in charge of the police operation; however, the head of the state police violated this agreement by not keeping his troopers out of sight:

> *At ten o'clock, after many thousands of demonstrators had gathered on the Green, a state police bus pulled up at the front entrance to City Hall. The troopers filed out and marched into formation, opening and closing the breeches of their shotguns and slamming metal around. A stream of militaristic orders echoed across the wide expanse of grass. State Police Commander Mulcahy had always believed in shows of force, and whether planned or inadvertent, this was a show of force par excellence. It looked like a deliberate challenge, and it brought the demonstrators surging to the fence of the Green, yelling and spilling into the street.*[55]

Chief Ahern, due to his skillful planning and careful negotiations with state and federal officials, managed to keep interference from other agencies at a minimum and the result was that his low profile policy prevailed and the demonstration took place without any major incidents.

It must be recognized, then, that political interference can and does come from a variety of sources, private as well as public. It requires a dedicated, professional, competent, and courageous police administrator to deal properly with such interferences.

Corruption*

Police corruption is a phenomenon which goes far back in history. There have always been some police officers who were dishonest while others were honest. The question that must be answered, then, is where does police corruption currently exist and to what extent?

In many American cities, corruption among police officers is a way of life. Officers accept payoffs from bars, prostitutes, pimps, organized crime figures, and others with the understanding that the bribers can expect non-enforcement of the law. Some officers accept bribes from narcotic dealers and then rob the "dope pads" at gunpoint, knowing that the dealers can't report the act to the police department. Certain officers themselves engage in the sale of narcotics. In some cities, motorists can avoid a traffic citation if they have a $10 bill handy. The list is endless.

Some officers make a distinction between serious corruption and petty corruption by assigning themselves labels:

> *The overwhelming majority of those who do take payoffs are grass-eaters, who accept gratuities and solicit five- and ten- and twenty-dollar payments from contractors, tow-truck operators, gamblers, and the like, but do not aggressively pursue corruption payments. "Meat-eaters," probably only a small percentage of the force, spend a good deal of their working hours aggressively seeking out situations they can exploit for financial gain, including gambling, narcotics, and other serious offenses which can yield payments of thousands of dollars.*[56]

This writer suggests a perhaps puritanical view of police ethics, i.e. that for an officer to accept anything of value, whether a $1000 payment or a free meal, is unethical and can, even in minor, innocent cases, give at least the appearance of impropriety.

One former police colleague, now a police chief in northern California, was rejected as an applicant for a chief's position in an eastern state when the city council learned that his policy would be to prosecute officers engaging in even minor dishonesty. The same person decided to decline the offer of a chief's position in a mid-western state because he feared that the regional corruption could taint his professional image.

In another case, a police officer who was dismissed from his position on a Colorado police department was prosecuted and convicted of committing a theft while on duty. Nevertheless he had no difficulty in obtaining a police officer's position on a metropolitan police department in Southern Michigan.

---

*The reader is referred to Chapter 12, *Police Corruption*, in which this problem is treated in detail, including its nature, causes, extent, and prevention.

It can be said, then, that police corruption does exist in various degrees of seriousness and that the phenomenon tends to be associated with specific regions and cities.

It would not be betraying any confidence if one were to point to New York City as one of the serious examples of a city saturated with police corruption. The Knapp Commission was appointed to investigate allegations of police corruption in New York City. It concluded its investigation in 1971.[57] Its central conclusion was that,

> *Police corruption was found to be an extensive, Department-wide phenomenon, indulged in to some degree by a sizable majority of those on the force and protected by a code of silence on the part of those who remained honest.*[58]

But the Knapp Commission was not the first investigative body to look into New York police corruption. As early as 1844 and several times since, New York Police Department has been the subject of similar investigations.

> *In each case, the investigators turned up substantial evidence of corruption, which was greeted by public expressions of shock and outrage. While some reforms usually followed each of these periodic scandals, the basic pattern of corrupt behavior was never substantially affected and after the heat was off, it was largely back to business as usual.*[59]

One commission commented that, "corruption is so ingrained that the man of ordinary decent character entering the force and not possessed of extraordinary moral fiber may easily succumb."

The Knapp Commission found that corruption fell into three categories:

> *The "pad" refers to regular weekly, biweekly, or monthly payments, usually picked up by a police bagman and divided among fellow officers. Those who make such payments as well as policemen who receive them are referred to as being "on the pad."*
>
> *A "score" is a one-time payment that an officer might solicit from, for example, a motorist or a narcotics violator. The term is also used as a verb, as in "I scored him for $1,500."*
>
> *A third category of payments to the police is that of gratuities, which the Commission feels cannot in the strictest sense be considered a matter of police corruption, but which has been included here because it is a related—and ethically borderline—practice, which is prohibited by Department regulation, and which often leads to corruption.*[60]

The Commission found that the two major sources of payoffs were organized crime and legitimate business.

> *Organized crime is the single biggest source of police corruption, through its control of the City's gambling, narcotics, loansharking, and illegal sex-related enterprises like homosexual afterhours bars and pornography, all of which the Department considers mob-run. These endeavors are so highly lucrative that large payments to the police are considered a good investment if they protect the business from undue police interference.*

> *The next largest source is legitimate business seeking to ease its way through the maze of City ordinances and regulations. Major offenders are construction contractors and subcontractors, liquor licensees, and managers of businesses like trucking firms and parking lots, which are likely to park large numbers of vehicles illegally.*[61]

Two smaller sources are private citizens, such as traffic violators and small-time criminals caught in a minor offense.

Commissions have come and commissions have gone. Yet, there is no evidence to suggest that conditions in New York or elsewhere have improved.

James Ahern, not addressing himself to any particular city, points out that corruption is not limited to the police service but that other areas of the criminal justice system are also suspect:

> *Judges are typically faithful party members who have run for other offices and failed, or who have been willing to serve the machine's interests in private law practices or in business capacities. This means that, below the federal level, they are seldom first-rate legal talents; they have had to make their way by means of influence rather than by legal brilliance or even legal competence, and they are compromised before they begin. The judge has considerable power to do favors for people which in turn lubricate the boss's machine.*
>
> *Prosecutors are in much the same position as judges. However they come by their positions, they are seldom first-rate talents, and often their activities will be more or less controlled by the bosses who put them into their positions. They have virtually unlimited discretion as to which cases to prosecute and which to drop. Prosecutors often have political ambitions on which bosses can play and tend to use their public positions as steppingstones to higher office.*[62]

It can be concluded, then, that police corruption ranges from being rampant in some cities and regions to being virtually non-existent in others. The key to this situation appears to be the fact that historically, corruption gained a foothold in some areas and not in others. Where it did not get a beginning, it was never allowed in. But what of the cities where it is more common than not? The famous police administration expert, O.W. Wilson, was selected by the City of Chicago as a reform police superintendent. And even he was unable to eradicate corruption.

The problem is a difficult one for it involves not only police personnel of all ranks but also city officials, politicians, organized crime with all its influence, and otherwise law-abiding citizens seeking an easy way out. Only by making the matter a major departmental priority with vast undercover operations, the strictest disciplinary system, and ruthless mass prosecutions can there be hope for restoring the integrity of the police departments in question.

Affirmative Action

Since this chapter deals with police and politics and since a section has been devoted to Politics in Action, it would seem inappropriate not to include the decidedly controversial issue of affirmative action.

The original definition of affirmative action may simply have been "the absence of discrimination." President Lyndon Johnson's 1965 Executive Order No. 11246 required federal contractors to "take affirmative action to ensure that hiring practices were not discriminatory because of race, color, religion, or national origin."[63]

Affirmative action has, however, taken on force and effect far beyond its original meaning. It's now a system which, in the opinion of many, is used to discriminate outright against Caucasians, particularly males. It must be made clear that no responsible person denies that Blacks and women have historically been denied equal opportunity. Fortunately, their situation has improved dramatically in recent years—perhaps not as fast as some would like, but no society in human history has ever been able to boast of total justice. It must further be made clear that no person of good will today advocates discrimination against Blacks and women. What can and must be advocated is true equal opportunity.

Unfortunately, affirmative action as practiced today doesn't provide equal opportunity but instead has resulted in a new and different form of discrimination which must raise serious questions regarding issues of justice, morality, personnel standards, employee morale, and constitutionality. As sociologist Paul Riedesel observes:

> *There is no justice in the conspicuous preference shown in the screening and hiring of new faculty today; it is defended in reified [abstract] terms but does not conform to any moral principle which recognizes the dignity and worth of each person.*[64]
>
> *I hope only to prick the consciences of those concerned with human rights and to perhaps stir up courage to resist sheepish conformity to unfair dictates from above. To take this perspective does not mean abandoning efforts to achieve equity.*[65]

Another basic question must be asked: Who is a member of a minority group? A San Francisco police official comments:

> *First, we must decide exactly who is a minority group member and who is not. In this area, the EEOC's arbitration efforts produced some rather arbitrary results—an apparently unavoidable situation. It was decided, for example, that policemen claiming American Indian ancestry were not "minority group" members unless they could demonstrate at least one-fourth Indian blood and adoption of an essentially "American Indian life style." And myraid similar problems are immediately suggested: At what point does a person of Chinese ancestry become a "minority group" member? Must he have one-eighth Chinese blood? One-sixteenth Chinese blood with a Chinese accent? Does it make any difference if the prospective minority group members earn over $30,000 per year?*
>
> *Second, we must somehow reconcile some individuals' concurrent membership in more than one minority group with our hypothetical scheme for calculating representation. For example, how should we count a Black woman with a Spanish surname? And once we have decided how to count her, do we then grant her threefold preference in our quota system? Whatever we do in these regards, we cannot avoid being somewhat arbitrary.*[66]

Sociologist Daniel Bell has asked, "Why not expand our definition [of a minority group] in order to provide quotas for groups characterized by certain political and religious beliefs as well?[67] Once we embark upon a policy of preferential treatment for certain groups, we open up a multitude of basic questions regarding justice and fairness.

The morality of affirmative action may well be questioned. Is it proper to utilize a system which may have a divisive effect upon our society? Rabbi Irving Spiegel, New York Times contributor, writes: "The polarization of ethnic groups that we have witnessed is making American into a divided community—instead of unifying and strengthening it, we are underscoring our differences and sowing seeds of internal hatred.[68] Paul Riedesel, University of Tulsa Sociologist, observes that affirmative action punishes an innocent generation: "The losers are new white male Ph.D.s paying for the sins of their academic fathers. Patchen has already noted the ludicrous nature of efforts to make up for discrimination of Type A individuals against Type B individuals by imposing new discrimination of Type D individuals against Type C individuals. . . We have reified Women and Minorities, and ascribed to them independent rights, over and above those inhering to the individual.[69] The motivation for affirmative action doesn't save it. Writes one columnist: "The purpose is compassionate; the effect is intolerable."[70]

Concurrent with affirmative action in police agencies has been a reduction in the quality of incoming personnel. To illustrate this fact, let's cite three sample test questions from a test which Detroit Police Department states is "directed to the minority community."[71]

One multiple choice question gives as possible answers the numbers 53, 58, 29, 57, and 16. The question is, "Which of the five numbers is larger than 55?" The sample test explains that "this determines how well you think." A second question is situational: "You see a badly crippled teenager being beaten by a younger uncrippled boy. What do you do?

a. Do nothing, but remain present.

b. Call the police, and report the fight.

c. Ask the younger uncrippled boy to stop fighting and pick on someone his match.

d. Beat up the uncrippled boy yourself.

e. Walk away and say nothing.

The correct answer is (c). This test measures your "social insight." A third question lists four colors—green, yellow, red, and blue—and calls for the candidate to identify the first letter of each word and place it in a circle. There is a ten second time limit on that question.

A news account explains how Detroit Police "dipped deep into the promotional list to promote blacks with low scores over whites with higher scores.[72]

The following comments are selected from interviews with New York City police officers: "Standards have declined. . . we need federal funds and we have to take the good with the bad. . . in the academy they mugged people in full uniform. . . we have guys coming in on the job who are convicted criminals, convicted felons. . . (in the academy there was) spontaneous and mindless acts of destruction; stealing of guns, typewriters, uniforms. . . muggings, academy walls marred with graffiti; profanity; insubordination; methadone addiction; indifference to grooming standards; and a general expression of contempt for everything and everybody. . . the kids in the academy are nodding. . . anybody who knows a junky can see they guys are junkies. . . some guys arrested for armed robbery. . . the average IQ went down to 70."[73] The comments are endless and can't be brushed off as unfounded or as symptoms of bias.

In the case of *Commonwealth v. O'Neill* [348 F. Supp. 1084, 1972], the court ordered that, because seventy percent of the Blacks failed a background investigation, compared with thirty percent of the whites, the police discontinue all background investigations. In 1975, the U.S. Equal Employment Opportunity commission held that the payment of higher salaries to college graduates in police departments constituted discrimination against Blacks.[74] The Academy of Criminal Justice Sciences adopted a resolution opposing the decision, calling it "a devastating blow to the hope for upgrading of law enforcement."[75] Anthony Balzer of the San Francisco Police makes a pointed comment: "The tax-paying community, it seems to me, is entitled to the services of the most qualified police candidates and supervisors available." [76]

The moral problems are legion. Officers, both Black and white, share in the concern regarding the reduced quality of personnel entering the police service. Often they see their prestige—and, indeed, their careers—damaged, they lose their work enthusiasm, and they begin to talk more frequently of job change or of retirement. White officers find it demoralizing to realize that years of college education seem to be of little or no value in obtaining promotions. Their careers, their self-image, their family lives and their income and future plans are seriously affected. In the words of one New York officer: "Yes, the standards have declined to the extent that I think it is ridiculous. It makes me feel that I no longer want to be associated with the Police Department or that I don't want to have anyone know that I am a policeman."[77]

The constitutional questions are of major importance. Is the Constitution indeed colorblind? Can the due process and the equal protection clauses of the Fourteeneth Amendment be ignored if done so in a compassionate cause? Legal opinion is beginning to hold that they cannot.

In *Hiatt v. City of Berkeley*, the state court found the city guilty of unlawful discrimination through its affirmative action program which gave hiring and promotion preference to members of "underutilized" groups.[78] The Pennsylvania Third Circuit Court of Appeals, in ordering a police department to discontinue its system of racial quotas, stated: "Opening the doors long shut to minorities is imperative, but in so doing, we must be careful not to close them in the face of others, lest we abandon the basic principle of non-discrimination that sparked the effort to pry open those doors in the first place."[79] In a case brought against Georgetown University for granting sixty percent of its scholarship money to the eleven percent minority student body, the U.S. District Court found in favor of the white plaintiff whose claim was that his civil rights had been violated. Judge Oliver Basch commented: "There is no justification for saying that a 'minority' student with a demonstrated financial need of $2000 requires more scholarship aid than a 'nonminority' student."[80] And, in Detroit, U.S. District Judge James Churchill ruled against the city for "discriminating against 36 white firemen when the city bypassed them to promote black firemen with less seniority." The judge commented that he was in sympathy with the emotional and philosophical arguments presented by the city, but that the issue was a matter of law.[81] Even the American Civil Liberties Union, an organization known for its sympathy for the plight of minorities, voted to represent officers of the Detroit Police Department as plaintiffs in a case where the city passed over the names of seven white police sergeants to promote Black officers with lower test scores.[82]

One case which has received major national attention is *DeFunis v. Odegaard*.[83] DeFunis, a white law school applicant, was denied admission to law school while 36 minority applicants with lower test scores were admitted. The trial court granted an injunction, ordering the school to admit DeFunis. Therefore, when the case reached the U.S. Supreme Court a few years later, DeFunis was about to graduate, and the Supreme Court ruled that the case was moot because the suit was not a class action, and the plaintiff would complete school regardless of the outcome. Justices Brennen, Douglas, White, and Marshall dissented on the grounds that the case represented an important constitutional issue.

A more recent case of similar nature is that of *Bakke v. The Regents of the University of California*.[84] Allen Bakke was one of 3,737 applicants for admission to the medical school at University of California. One hundred spaces were available, with 84 being selected through the normal admissions process and 16 spaces being reserved for minority applicants.

When Bakke was not admitted, he claimed that his right to equal protection under the Fourteenth Amendment had been violated. The trial court refused to grant Bakke an injunction because it found that Bakke, although qualified, had not scored high enough to be admitted. At the same time, however, the trial court ruled that Bakke's constitutional rights *had* been violated. The case was appealed to the California Supreme Court, which struck down the challenged "special admission program." The decision of the court said, in part:

> *In this case we confront a sensitive and complex issue: whether a special admission program which benefits disadvantaged minority students who apply for admission to the medical school of the University of California at Davis offends the constitutional rights of better qualified applicants denied admission because they are not identified with a minority. We conclude that the program, as administered by the University, violates the constitutional rights of nonminority applicants because it affords preference on the basis of race to persons who, by the University's own standards, are not as qualified for the study of medicine as nonminority applicants denied admission.*

The court, recognizing the dangerous consequences of reverse discrimination, added this warning: "This divisive effect of such preferences needs no explication and raises serious doubts whether the advantages obtained by the few preferred are worth the inevitable cost to racial harmony."

The United States Supreme Court has now decided the *Bakke* case in favor of Bakke. It is hoped that before too long, the American public will see the many associated and new issues of affirmative action settled, at least from a legal standpoint.

What we may expect from the court may well lie in the following comment by Justice Stevens: "Racial discrimination is as bad when practiced against whites as against blacks. Discrimination against Americans of Polish, German, or Italian ancestry is just as indefensible as discrimination against Americans of African ancestry. The fact that a political group . . . has suffered its own special injustice . . . does not make one such group different from any other in the eyes of the law."[85] A virtual chorus of legal scholars join in this sentiment. Professor Alexander Bickel of Yale University Law School, in his amicus brief in the *DeFunis* case, filed on behalf of the Jewish Anti-Defamation League, argued:

> *A racial quota derogates the human dignity and individuality of all to whom it is applied. A racial quota is invidious in principle as well as in practice. Though it may be thought here to help "minority" students, it can easily be turned against those same or other minorities. The history of the racial quota is a history of subjugation, not beneficience.*
>
> *The evil of the racial quota lies not in its name but in its effect. A quota by any other name is still a divider of society, a creator of castes, and it is all the worse for its racial base, especially in the society desperately striving for an equality that will make race irrelevent, politically, economically, and socially.*[86]

Albert Shanker, writing in the *New York Times*, presents this quote: "For a democratic society to systematically discriminate against the majority seems quite without precedent. To do so in the name of non-discrimination seems mind-boggling. For humane and liberal minded members of the society to espouse racial discrimination at all seems most remarkable."[87]

In summary, "affirmative action" in the present meaning is the opposite of "equality." Affirmative action is seen by many as unjust in that it discriminates against the innocent; its contributes to a reduction of the quality of public service personnel, thereby creating major morale problems and robbing the taxpayers of the best service available; and it is a flagrant violation of the due process and equal protection clauses of the Fourteenth Amendment to the U.S. Constitution.

In a democratic society we must strive for equality. Regardless of race or sex, we can not permit some people to be more equal than others.

A Look Into The Future

When one begins to speculate on what the American police service of tomorrow will be like, two areas of particular concern come to mind. One is *police leadership*, the other *professionalization*. These two issues are of particular interest not only because they are important in and of themselves (which they are) but also because they form a basis for a variety of related matters. The quality of police leadership affects many things, ranging from enforcement priorities to civil liberties, and from scientific management to relations with the community. Likewise, the state of professionalization is related to many issues ranging from personnel standards to ethics, and from education to community cooperation.

Police Leadership There are now over 40,000 separate law enforcement agencies in the United States. All but a few hundred are local police and sheriff's departments.

> *The vast majority of these agencies consists of three men or less, working on a part-time basis, compensated by fees, selected or elected without regard for physical or mental qualifications, untrained, unsupervised, undisciplined, and poorly equipped.*[88]

While the foregoing describes police officers in general, an evaluation of police leadership would not be much more optimistic. As viewed by many criminal justice professionals and academicians, the majority of American police administrators are ignorant, socially unaware, poorly educated, unfamiliar with management techniques, unable to engage in any planning beyond day-to-day operations, and unwilling or unable to think, manage or lead effectively. These people have reached the chief's level by being around for a long time and by not rocking the boat. They have generally done nothing to prepare themselves for a position of leadership and are essentially the same persons they were when they held patrol officer rank. One should hasten to add that there are many exceptions to this generalization. We've had such police chiefs as Bernie Garmire in Miami, Joe Kimble in Beverly Hills, and Joe McNamara in Kansas City. But these professional leaders don't cancel out the fact that the general picture is indeed a dim one.

Lest the reader think that this description is an isolated, pessimistic evaluation of America's police chiefs, it should be pointed out that the view is shared by many observers of the American police scene. For example, Professor A. C. Germann, California State University, Long Beach, commenting on police leadership, states:

> *Many police administrators are narrow-minded, tunnel-visioned, parochial individuals who haven't had a new idea in fifty years and are frightened of innovation. Reform can only come over the dead bodies of some Neanderthal incumbents who are ineffective, semi-comatose and moribund.*[89]

James Ahern, an unusually frank and courageous former police chief, makes this comment on police leadership:

> *Officers who have worked their way up through police-department ranks to become assistant chiefs, chief inspectors, and captains find themselves in middle-management positions in multi-million-dollar enterprises without the*

training, and often without the inclination, to handle mangement and planning problems. In most police departments ranking officers have become clerks or petty bureaucrats by default. Often the administrative structure is cluttered with leftover paper figures from previous political situations. The result is that the bureaucracy runs itself, but little else.

This difficulty often extends to the chief of police himself. As the Herder report pointed out, "An important cause, however, is the management climate of the department. The Chief of Police apparently does not see himself as an administrator. Rather, he appears to see himself as the 'head cop.' He is far more sensitive to interpersonal aspects of his role than he is to the executive aspects." The report went on to say, "The basic executive functions of planning, organizing, directing and controlling are not being carried out adequately in the department at the present time.'"[90]

Ahern evaluates the rise to the chief's position as follows:

At this point he wants little more than to survive. If he can move up in the ranks as he grows older, he will be more than satisfied. Wherever he ends up, his primary function will be to do favors for people. As he does, he finds himself building political walls that cement him into his own position. He gets paid a little more, he works a lot less, and he is as happy shuffling paper as he can be within the structure of the police department. If he is lucky, and if he does not make too many enemies, he may become a chief inspector, an assistant chief, or even chief of police. If he does, he will have received little or no more training or education than the cop on the walking beat, and he will have gained no wider perspective on the police department and its role than a decade of street experience and another decade of "indoor" work have given him. Although there are some notable expections, especially in larger cities, most chief of police are no more than fifty-year-old patrolmen. Whether he is a fifty-year-old chief or a fifty-year-old patrolman, the cop who has been on the force for twenty-five or thirty years has long since ceased to question or doubt the ways of the closed fraternity. He has been taken care of or absorbed by the hierarchy. He is no longer climbing three flights of ghetto steps wondering whether someone is waiting behind the door to smash his skull in. Although he sympathizes heartily with the men who still do climb the stairs, his primary attitude is usually hate for those who may be standing behind the doors. He is unwilling and unable to speak out for meaningful police reform that will alleviate the conditions under which he worked when he first joined the force and under which the majority of his fellows still work. He cannot comprehend a larger social perspective which, were he able to adapt and articulate it, might in the end give him some of the support he so desperately needs.[91]

Boston's Police Commissioner, Robert J. diGrazia, shocked America's police chiefs with his candor when, in a speech before an Executive Forum to Upgrade the Police, he made the following comments:[92]

Mere survival—that's the goal of most of us and that's one major thing wrong with police leadership. For the most part, we police chiefs have no vision of ourselves beyond that of being survivors with gold braid...

As police chiefs, most of us have allowed ourselves to be the underlings of American municipal government, somewhat as pet rocks unable to move, grow, change or innovate.

> *Contrast us as police chiefs with city managers, budget directors, school superintendents. Most of them got where they are by moving upward from one locality to another, encountering at each stop new challenges, fresh perspectives, different insights into their callings. Almost all of us got where we are as police chiefs by being immobile, climbing the promotion ladder of one department, suffering from the insularity and folkways of a closed system of advancement.*
>
> *Most city managers, school superintendents, and budget directors got where they are after obtaining a thorough education. Most of us were good police officers who become chiefs because we were able to perform well on a three-hour, paper-and-pen test on Saturday morning.*
>
> *And having reached the position of police chief by ways mostly irrelevant to the exercise of police leadership, do we take risks and truly lead? Seldom. Rather, we seek to assure that our voyage on the departmental ship be a smooth one, at least until we reach our retirement port.*
>
> *Bruce Smith, one of America's most perceptive commentators on the police, described police chiefs as being like the ballast of a ship—they contribute little to the speed of the vessel but add greatly to its stability.*

With police chiefs being as weak as they often are, it's no wonder that politicians are usually able to manipulate them. Professor James Q. Wilson, Harvard University, maintains that there's a relationship between the political climate in the city and the policing style adopted by the police chief. Wilson observes that these styles fall into three categories:

- The legalistic style (arrest and prosecution oriented);
- The service style (performing a variety of services to the community with enforcement having a lower priority); and
- The order maintenance style (don't rock the boat, step in only when absolutely necessary.[93]

While some responsiveness to community wishes is no doubt desirable, a certain amount of professional judgment and independence must still be maintained by the truly professional police chief. A step in the right direction would be the appointment of a city manager or city administrator, a professional manager who, as a city executive, answers to the mayor and the city council. Such a professional link between the city politicians and the police chief would generally permit a cleaner, more proper and independent, yet still accountable leadership of the police agency.

With the picture as bleak as it appears to be, how can improvements be accomplished for American police leadership? Obviously, standards must be raised significantly. Experience in itself is important, but not to the exclusion of other consideration such as management skills and education. Thomas Adams, Santa Ana College, Santa Ana, California, has stated: "Some officers have ten years' experience. Other officers have one year's experience ten times over." Many police chiefs fall into the second category. Experience must be combined with management training and higher education. The National Crime Commission recommended in 1967 that police management personnel, "as an immediate goal," hold baccalaureate degrees. While that seems to be a reasonable requirement, there's little evidence that anyone has every paid much attention to the commission. In fact, most police chiefs seem to be unfamiliar with the commission's report.

While medical, legal, and other professional groups have concerned themselves greatly with standards for members of their profession, no one in the police field has taken a similar position. The International Association of Chiefs of Police has been long on rhetoric and short on actual development of meaningful standards. Commissioner di Grazia commented in his speech:[94]

> *...the IACP, which is a collection of police chiefs, remained almost totally silent on the issue of establishing qualifications for becoming or remaining a police executive. There were resolutions over the years which decried the brief tenure of chiefs and which spoke out against political interference. But, if I am not mistaken, the resolution passed in 1968—which is the most recent one I could find on the subject of leadership improvement—while calling for supervisory and command training, remains a gesture. There has been no serious talk that I have heard which would call for chiefs to be more than appointed to be eligible to belong to the professional association.*

Since the police field itself is reluctant to establish minimum standards for police administrators, the impetus apparently has to come from elsewhere. Without suggesting the creation of a national police force, perhaps federal and state standards need to be established by law. Statutes can certainly be created (we seem to be able to create them for every other problem in the nation), and, with the vast amounts of grant money awarded by the Law Enforcement Assistance Administration (mostly wasted on gadgets which have little impact upon the crime picture), we have opportunities to attach certain requirements to those grant awards. On the state level, it's particularly ironic that we have specific training standards for barbers and cosmetologists, but anyone can be appointed chief of police or elected sheriff.

In addition to establishing requirements for management training and higher education, mobility must be permitted. At present, most police officers are tied to their departments because of non-transferable pensions. This causes in-breeding and ensures that police officials will always lack the experience of having served in a variety of agencies. It's similar in nature to forcing a physician to practice in one hospital for the duration of his or her career. And, if that physician dared to transfer to another hospital, he or she would be forced to start over again as an intern with loss of all prior benefits. One can imagine what such a system would do to the medical profession; it does exactly that to the police field. Lateral entry for all ranks, with transfer of pension and other benefits, is a must if the police occupation is every to become the police profession.

On the assets side of the ledger, there are bright spots on the horizon. The recent appearance of Executive Development Programs across the country is bringing into sharp relief the increasingly difficult role that must be fulfilled by the police chief executive. Courses in this important areas are now appearing in criminal justice programs at the university and college level. In addition, the International Association of Chiefs of Police has drawn the blueprints for a continuing series of Executive Development Workshops. Typical of these executive training conferences was the Workshop held at West Point, New York, June 20-24, 1977, which covered the following areas:

The Police Executive in a Changing Society: While the basic mission of the police within society remains unchanged, dominant societal interests and standards are constantly affected by technologial and social developments. Ways and methods are examined for police leadership to remain sensitive and responsive to emerging needs and expectations.

Management Strategies and Leadership Styles: Management strategies are described and evaluated for police application. Examples include management by objectives, grid management, participatory management, and comparison of democratic versus autocratic leadership styles.

Problem-Solving and Decision-Making: The decision-making process is analyzed, with emphasis placed on the role of communications and participation for effective implementation, and discussion of organizational and psychological factors that influence the process.

Overview of Labor Relations Problems: The labor movement within law enforcement is a critical concern of the police executive. A framework is provided for recognizing and dealing with labor relations issues such as unionization and related aspects of personnel management.

Personnel Management Issues: Key subject material is singled out, including recruitment and selection of police personnel, training programs, education and the police, personnel evaluation, promotions, and personnel development.

Police Discipline: Methods of personnel control with reference to effective communication, employee morale, control of corruption and internal friction; detection and correction of problem areas.

Police Productivity: Productivity concepts that can be applied to all aspects of police work; guidelines for measuring work performance, program effectiveness, and employee efficiency.

The general objectives of Executive Development Programs include:

1. Development of an understanding of the role and function of the executive.
2. Development of a management philosophy.
3. Development of a managerial style.
4. Construction of an intellectual frame of reference from which to anticipate, analyze, and solve organizational problems.
5. Development of an ability to understand the behavioral problems in organizations and the effects of managerial styles and techniques on organizational effectiveness.
6. Development of an awareness of the numerous internal and external pressures which modify the role of the police executive.
7. Familiarization with research methods and data analysis.

8. Development of an awareness of the assets and liabilities of computers and other hardware.
9. Familiarization with contemporary and new trends in police management.

Pressure continues to mount for academic excellence as an important element in the qualifications of the police chief executive. As early as 1974, the Police Chief Executive Committee of the IACP recommended, among other things, that:

1. Every state or local jurisdiction should require that new police chief executives of agencies with a personnel strength of more than 75 officers have at least four years of college education (baccalaureate degree) from an accredited college or university.
2. Every state or local jurisdiction should require that new police executives of agencies with a personnel strength of less than 75 officers have at least two years of education at an accredited college or university. In addition, such jurisdictions should require that new police executives have at least three years of education at an accredited college or university by 1978, and at least four years of such education by 1982 should be required of the new police executive.*

The proliferation of criminal justice programs at the degree level is reassuring. An increasing percentage of police personnel have a university background, and this means a great deal in terms of a personnel bank from which to draw candidates for the Chief's position.

Change is slow and tortuous, but there is nothing permanent but change, and the trend is unmistakeable. While the present is generally gloomy, however, the future appears to be little better. There's no sign that the police community itself, the federal government, state government, or even the public is demanding minimum standards for the nation's police leaders. Certainly, presidential commission reports, one after another, and accompanying state reports, all make "recommendations" for upgrading American police, including the leadership. But these reports, largely unknown to the uninformed administrators, appear to have had little if any practical effect. Criminal justice students study them in collegs and universities, and the consultants to the commissions collect their fees, but other than that the reports seem to do little other than gather dust on shelves. Perhaps the worst problem of all is that, while the reports produce no effect, they do create the illusion of change. In fact, it can be said that these reports are being issued *in lieu* of accomplishing changes.

---

*The composition of the Committee was significant; it included nine Chiefs of Police, two Sheriffs, one active head and one former head of a State Police System, a Deputy Associate Director for the Federal Bureau of Investigation, a Superior Court Judge, two immediate Past Presidents of the International Association of Chiefs of Police, a management consultant, and the current President of the IACP.

Professionalization

The term "profession" or "professionalization" is used freely. Just what is a profession? What makes one field a profession and another not?

A profession must include at least the following five elements: (1) systematic theory; (2) authority; (3) community sanction; (4) ethical codes; and (5) a culture. Many other definitions of professions also include a high level of education.[95] The obvious question, then, is whether the current police field qualifies as a profession. One must admit that there's no systematic theory; in fact, not even much of a system exists. Authority does exist, but mainly because of the right to use force rather than any professional authority *per se*. The community hasn't sanctioned or approved the police as a full profession. A code of ethics for law enforcement does exist on paper and is handed out in recruit academies, but has not otherwise gained widespread influence. The police do form a specific culture, often to the detriment of relations with "the outside world." And higher education has not only not been achieved but is widely resisted. The conclusion must be, then, that the American police service is far from being a true profession, and any claim that it is a profession is an illusion.

The President's Commission on Law Enforcement and the Administration of Justice (popularly known as the National Crime Commission) made six recommendations for police training and education in its 1967 report, *Challenge of Crime in a Free Society.* These recommendations were:

1. Police departments should recruit more actively on college campuses.
2. The ultimate aim of all police departments should be that all personnel with general enforcement powers have baccalaureate degrees.
3. Police departments should take immediate steps to establish a minimum requirement of a baccalaureate degree for all supervisory and executive positions.
4. Police salaries must be raised... in order to attract college graduates to the police service.
5. All police officers must receive a minimum of 400 hours of recruit training.
6. Every officer should have at least one week of intensive inservice training a year.[96]

This writer conducted research in 1975 to investigate two questions: (1) To what extent have these recommendations been implemented? and (2) What are the attitudes of the nation's police chiefs toward such standards?[97]

A random, stratified sample of 400 police departments in cities having at least 10,000 population was selected and questionnaires were sent to the chiefs. Three hundred and forty-four responses were received—an unusually good response rate of 86 percent. Since the sample was scientifically selected, it can be assumed that the responses are representative of all American police departments in cities with over 10,000 population.

The findings were as follows: With respect to recruiting on college campuses, 19 percent indicated compliance (they had actually implemented the recommendation), with 67 percent being in favor (they believed it to be a desirable goal). On the issue of a bachelor's degree for all police officers, it was found that 0.3 percent had such a requirement and 0.9 percent were in favor of such a requirement. With respect to a baccalaureate degree for supervisors and executives, the responses indicated that 0.3 percent followed such a standard, with 7 percent feeling that it's an appropriate requirement. Offering salaries to compete with business and industry for college graduates was complied with by 42 percent of all agencies, with 77 percent being in favor. The recommendation that at least 400 hours of recruit training be required was followed by 45 percent, with 65 percent approving of such a standard. And, finally, the requirement of a minimum of one week's annual inservice training was claimed to be followed by 55 percent of the respondents, with 95 percent favoring such a standard.

Some comments must be made on these findings. If 67 percent favor college campus recruiting, why are only 19 percent claiming to be doing so? And, to make another point, knowing police departments to be what they are, it's difficult to believe that 55 percent actually offer or even require one week's annual inservice training. One is tempted to assume that some respondents threw in roll-call training as fulfilling this requirement.

Finally, it's interesting to observe that, while most police chiefs (77 percent) would like to offer salaries satisfactory to college graduates, they strongly oppose educational requirements. Only 0.3 percent require a bachelor's degree for patrol officers and even for supervisors and executives; only 0.9 percent even wish to demand it for patrol officers; and only 7 percent see it as an appropriate standard for supervisors and executives. It must be remembered that the commission's report, which came out in 1967, urged compliance for patrol officers as a long-term goal and for management as an immediate goal.

As a concluding observation on this study, it must be noted that police chiefs are generally in favor of training (self-defense, teargas use, firearms training, riot formations, etc.) while their opposition to higher education could hardly be any stronger. What accounts for this dichotomy? It must be assumed that since police chiefs are generally uneducated, insecure, and threatened, they have a fear of education and the educated. On the other hand, technical training poses no threat to them. The danger they see in educated personnel is that those individuals could enter the department and question organization, administration, outmoded practices, and outdated enforcement policies.

The absence of professional police officers is described by Ramsey Clark, former U.S. Attorney General:

> *To combat crime amid the prevailing social unrest that changes constantly in its form and content, we dispatch the police, who are undermanned, undertrained and usually from backgrounds and with attitudes that are not sympathetic to or understanding of the people or the issues they confront. To be disciplined, cool and even-handed under such circumstances is exceedingly difficult, but these traits are essential to effective performance—and to justice.*

Clark continues:

> *Tomorrow only a highly professional, broadly skilled, sensitive, temperate police force, deeply traditioned to be fair, to adhere strictly to the law itself and to enforce it firmly, can assure safety, liberty and human dignity. We must start to professionalize our police now and build fast. The control of every type of crime depends upon it.*[88]

The fact that we have so many thousands of separate police agencies—each one constituting its own little empire, and many not communicating with each other—is a major obstacle to professionalization. While almost no one is advocating a national police force or even the use of state police to the exclusion of local departments, a strong case can certainly be made for legislation which will make regional police departments mandatory. Legislation is exactly what it would take, for those in charge of the mini-empires—the chiefs of small and medium-sized police departments—have a vested interest in opposing regional policing. Clark sees this situation as a major problem:

> *The fragmentation of police jurisdictions alone makes excellence impossible and effectiveness limited. The nation has a crazy-quilt pattern of 40,000 police jurisdictions—remnants of history. Major urban areas need a single police service with strong local ties tailoring local action to local need. Yet many major urban counties have scores of police jurisdictions within their borders. St. Louis County has more than a hundred. To have a number of police departments in a single county or urban area rarely makes sense. How does the small police force handle a big parade or major disorder, a riot or a thousand protesting students? How many jurisdictions will a fleeing bank robber or drunken driver pass through in five minutes? How well coordinated can police radio networks be? If gamblers can choose among dozens of police departments before locating illegal operations in a community, how much are the risks of corruption increased? What is the career opportunity for a bright and ambitious young officer in a twenty-man force?*[100]

A further obstacle to professionalization is the trend among police officers to affiliate with labor unions. Some officers have joined the Fraternal Order of Police, some the International Brotherhood of Police Officers, others the American Federation of State, County, and Municipal Employees, yet others the International Brotherhood of Teamsters.[101] The legal basis for police unions is explained as follows:

> *Prior to 1960 the right of police employees to organize and engage in collective bargaining depended on the approval of local administrative and legislative officials. Beginning in 1959, with the passage of the Wisconsin collective bargaining law, a number of states adopted legislation authorizing collective bargaining for police employees. Courts have held that police and other public employees have a constitutional right to join labor organizations. Public employees, however, do not have a constitutional right to collective bargaining. The courts have held that collective bargaining for public employees cannot take place without legislative authorization.*[102]

It must be understood that there are many reasons why police officers have decided to join unions. In far too many cases, the city administration either disregaded or abused the police department and its officers so badly that the officers simply had to seek protection in unions as a matter of self-defense. The officers' rights were disregarded by some cities, and their legitimate requests for adequate wage and fringe benefits were ignored. In a few cities, police chiefs and city officials even launched vicious campaigns against those officers who dared stand up for basic employee rights. In one Michigan city, officers claim that the chief wiretapped their telephones, demanded undated letters of resignation from new officers, and otherwise conducted a campaign of harassment against the police. There can be no doubt that some chiefs and city officials acted so arbitrarily as to force police personnel into unions as a form of self-protection.

On the other hand, police unions have in some cities become so powerful that their demands have become totally unreasonable. Wages in some cities have now exceeded salaries paid to highly educated and skilled professionals. This is particularly ludicrous when one realizes that many police officers, particularly some of those hired in recent years under affirmative action programs, are functionally illiterate, have criminal records, and could not withstand the background investigations conducted in reputable agencies.

Police unions, then, are a fact of life. They are here for a reason and they are no doubt here to stay. Nevertheless, union excesses remain deplorable. Furthermore, the search for professionalism must be considered abandoned once police officers join the Teamsters. Once union activity has led to police strikes, the refusal to protect citizens' lives and property, the ultimate in police immorality has been reached.

What the future holds is, of course, linked to some of the issues discussed here: leadership, education, professionalism, etc. But the basis for the future course of the police service may lie in the political philosophy and climate of the years ahead.

American society may move toward a more *repressive* scenario or a more *humanistic* scenario. In the repressive scenario, Professor A.C. Germann sees crime as increasing, a trend toward more police personnel and equipment, greater use of data intelligence banks, more surveillance, reliance on police fortresses and military equipment, and alienation of non-conformist groups. In the humanistic scenario, however, emphasis falls on police-community cooperation, use of the social sciences to solve problems, professionalization of police to the extent that law enforcement is equal in status to law and medicine, the addition of laws to preserve the environment and to protect consumers against fraud, and the elimination of statutes related to "morals offenses."[103]

The direction we take depends on all of us. In the words of Dr. Germann:

> *Now is the time for humanistic academics and humanistic police chiefs to lead the way. Even though our students and citizens are anxious, they are ever receptive to the idea of humane and progressive change, particulary when*

espoused by intelligent and compassionate professors and by intelligent and compassionate criminal justice leaders. The nation in waiting. Speak out! Lead! The classroom is waiting. Speak out! Lead! The criminal justice system is waiting. Speak out! Lead! The local community is waiting. Speak out! Lead! The future of law enforcement can be a matter of great pride instead of horrible embarrassment! Speak out! Lead! NOW![104]

Summary

We have recognized that the relationship between police and the various forms of politics are numerous and complex. Not only do politics play an important part in the intra-agency processes of law enforcement, but there is also an exchange (incoming and outgoing) of influences, pressures, and power plays between police and their environment.

The use of power is, like any tool, neither good nor evil but can be evaluated based upon its use and the perception of its use. In any event, the exercise of power has always existed and always will.

Throughout American history, the criminal justice system has played a significant role in the maintenance of the political, economic, and cultural status quo. It's a part of our history which unfortunately can be viewed with total pride. We must also come to certain conclusions regarding some current issues in American law enforcement. Police corruption is a serious problem in certain parts of the nation, a phenomenon which is recognized but about which little is done. In the quest for equal employment opportunities for all regardless of race and sex, we may well have overstepped the permissible moral and legal limits, a situation which has given rise to a backlash in public sentiment and which may bring us court decisions with far-reaching effects. Police leadership is seriously lacking with only minor signs of improvement. This situation is particularly problematic because of the increasing number of well-educated police officers who seek professionalization but are largely rebuffed by the system.

An understanding of these issues and their ramifications is imperative for the serious observer of American criminal justice.

Topics For Discussion

1. **What is power? Is it always evil or good? What are some of the methods used to exercise power? How does power differ from authority?**

2. **What is meant by the statement that influences upon the police agency are internal as well as external (incoming and outgoing)?**

3. **Has the criminal justice system always been used fairly and impartially against American citizens? If not, what are some representative examples of abuse?**

4. **To what extent is police corruption still with us? What forms does it take, and why does it flourish in some cities while not in others?**

5. **To what extent is affirmative action an important political issue for police administrators? Why can it be said to be an issue affecting personnel, morale, and constitutional law?**
6. **Evaluate today's police leadership.**
7. **What is a profession: Is the American police service a profession? Why or why not? What role does higher education play?**

References

1. Charles D. Hale, *Fundamentals of Police Administration* (Boston: Holbrook Press, Inc., 1977), p. 6.
2. Bernard L. Garmire, ed., *Local Government Police Management* (Washington, D.C.: International City Management Association, 1977), p. 20.
3. Garmire, p. 20.
4. Delbert C. Miller and William H. Form, *Industrial Sociology* (New York: Harper & Brothers, 1951), p. 310.
5. C. T. Hardwick and B. F. Landuyt, *Adminstrative Strategy and Decision Making* (Cincinnati: South-Western Publishing Co., 1966), p. 92.
6. Frederick C. Mosher, *Democracy and the Public Service* (New York: Oxford University Press, 1968), p. 1.
7. Paul M. Whisenand and R. Fred Ferguson, *The Managing of Police Organizations* (Englewood Cliffs, N.J.: Prentice-Hall, Inc., 1973), p. 136.
8. Hardwick and Landuyt, pp. 113-4.
9. Hardwick and Landuyt, pp. 117-8.
10. Hardwick and Landuyt, pp. 127-9.
11. Hardwick and Landuyt, p. 130.
12. John M. Pfiffner and Frank P. Sherwood, *Administrative Organization* (Englewood Cliffs, N.J.: Prentice-Hall, Inc., 1968), p. 75.
13. Pfiffner and Sherwood, p. 25.
14. Whisenand and Ferguson, p. 206-7.
15. Hermand Goldstein, *Policing a Free Society* (Cambridge, Mass.: Ballinger Publishing Co., 1977), p. 141.
16. Noval Morris and Gordon Hawkins, *The Honest Politician's Guide to Crime Control* (Chicago: The University of Chicago Press, 1969), pp. 3, 27.
17. Morris and Hawkins, p. 2.
18. James F. Ahern, *Police in Trouble* (New York: Hawthorn Books, Inc., 1972), p. 97.
19. Ahern, p. 97.
20. Ahern, p. 96.
21. James Q. Wilson, *Thinking About Crime* (New York: Basic Books, Inc., 1975), p. 118.
22. Goldstein, p. 118.
23. Garmire, p. 21.
24. George E. Berkley, *The Democratic Policeman* (Boston: Beacon Press, 1969), p. 173.

25. G. William Domhoff, *Who Rules America* (Englewood Cliffs, N.J.: Prentice-Hall, Inc., 1967), p. 129.
26. A.C. Germann, "Community Policing: An Assessment," paper presented to the Southern California Police Training Officers' Association, Westminster, Cal., February 28, 1968.
27. Howard Zinn, *Justice in Everyday Life* (New York: William Morrow and Co., Inc., 1974), p. ix.
28. Ed Cray, *The Enemy in the Streets* (Garden City, N.Y.: Anchor Books, 1972), p. 1.
29. *Los Angeles Times*, November 7, 1964, pt I, p. 16.
30. Charles Goodell, *Political Prisoners in America* (New York: Random House, 1973), pp. 34-5, 42.
31. Goodell, pp. 46-9.
32. Goodell, pp. 55-7.
33. Goodell, pp. 65-74. See also Patrick Renshaw, *The Wobblies* (New York: Doubleday and Co., 1967).
34. See Barry Stavis and Frank Harmon, *The Songs of Joe Hill* (New York: Oak Publishers, 1960) and Barry Stavis, *The Man Who Never Died* (New York: Haven Press, 1954).
35. Goodell, pp. 75-86.
36. Jethro K. Lieberman, *How the Government Breaks the Law* (Baltimore: Penguin Books, 1973), p. 75.
37. For a complete account of the events, see Howard Fast, *Peekskill U.S.A.* (New York: Civil Rights Congress, 1951).
38. See Louis Nizer, *The Implosion Conspiracy* (Greenwich, Conn.: Fawcett Publications, 1973).
39. Erwin A. Gaede, "A Study in Contemporary Crucifixion: The Rosenberg-Sobell Case" (Ann Arbor, Mich.: First Unitarian Church, 1966).
40. Lieberman, p. 75.
41. For an insight into this philosophy, see Daniel Berrigan, S.J., *No Bars to Manhood*; (New York: Bantam Books, 1970) and Daniel Berrigan, *Absurd Convictions, Modest Hopes* (New York: Vintage Books, 1973).
42. Goodell, pp. 147-8.
43. "Homosexuals Receive ACLU Aid in Parade Permit Fight," *Los Angeles Times*, June 13, 1970, Pt. II, p. 1.
44. "Los Angeles: The Chief," *Newsweek*, April 26, 1971, pp. 31-2.
45. William J. Drummond, "There is More to Chief Davis Than Meets the Ear," *West* (Los Angeles Times Supplement), August 15, 1971, p. 10.
46. *Los Angeles Times*, January 16, 1976, Pt. II, p. 2.
47. "Hang Hijackers at the Airport, Davis Suggests," *Los Angeles Times*, July 8, 1972, Pt. I, p. 1.
48. Egon Bittner, *The Functions of the Police iModern Society*, (Chevy Chase, Md.: National Institute of Mental Health, 1970), p. 120.
49. Tom Murton and Joe Hyams, *Accomplices to Crime* (New York: Grove Press, Inc., 1969), preface.

50. The foregoing material was adapted from a presentation made by Erik Beckman before the Academy of Criminal Justice Sciences, annual meeting, Dallas, Texas, March 25, 1976.
51. Wallace S. Sayre and Herbert Kaufman, *Governing New York City: Politics in the Metropolis* (New York: W.W. Norton and Co., 1965), p. 406.
52. Ahern, p. 92.
53. Ahern, pp. 101-2.
54. Ahern, pp. 48-57.
55. Ahern, p. 61.
56. "Patterns of Corruption," in Arthur Niederhoffer and Abraham S. Blumberg, eds., *The Ambivalent Force* (Hinsdale, Ill.: The Dryden Press, 1976), p. 150.
57. For the commission report, see *The Knapp Commission Report on Police Corruption* (New York: George Braziller, 1973).
58. "Patterns of Police Corruption," in Niederhoffer and Blumberg, p. 149.
59. Ibid., p. 149.
60. Ibid., pp. 150-1.
61. Ibid, p. 151.
62. Ahern, p. 102.
63. U.S. Commission on Civil Rights, "Affirmative Action: Some Notes," *Civil Rights Digest*, 7, Spring 1975, p. 52.
64. Paul L. Riedesel, "Justice and Affirmative Action," *ASA Footnotes*, Vol. 3, No. 4, December 1975, p. 2.
65. Riedesel, p. 2.
66. Anthony Balzer, "A View of the Quota System in the San Francisco Police Department," *Journal of Police Science and Administration*, Vol. 4, No. 2, June 1976, p. 128.
67. Balzer, p. 128.
68. Irving Spiegel, "Two Rabbis Assail Quota System," *New York Times*, March 25, 1973, p. 66.
69. Riedesel, p. 2.
70. James L. Kilpatrick, "The DeFunis Syndrome," *Nation's Business*, 62, June 1974, pp. 13-14.
71. Personal communcation from the Recruiting Division, Detroit Police Department, January 29, 1976.
72. "38 Police Promoted in Rush," *Detroit Free Press*, January 14, 1977, p. 7-A.
73. Nicholas Alex, *New York Cops Talk Back* (New York: John Wiley and Sons, 1976), pp. 41-46.
74. 348 F. Supp. 1084, 4 FEP cases 970 (E.D. Pa. 1972).
75. Resolution, Academy of Criminal Justice Sciences, March 21, 1975.
76. Balzer, p. 129.
77. Alex, p. 30.
78. "Discrimination in Affirmative Action," *Monthly Labor Review*, June 1975, p. 58.
79. National Civil Service League, *Judicial Mandates for Affirmative Action*, (Washington, D.C.: National Civil Service League, 1973), p. 15.

80. "School Guilty of Reverse Bias," State Journal, July 29, 1976, p. A-6.
81. "White Firemen Win City Bias Suit," *Detroit Free Press*, February 11, 1976, p. A-1.
82. "Detroit ACLU Sides With Police," *Civil Liberties News Letter*, Vol. 16, No. 3, Fall 1975, p. 1.
83. 507 P2d 1169.
84. 132 Cal. Rptr. 680.
85. *Detroit Free Press*, November 30, 1975, p. 14-C.
86. Brief for the Anti-Defamation League as Amicus Curiae, DeFunis vs. Odegaard, U.S. , 94 S.Ct. 1704 (1974).
87. Albert Shanker, "How Order No. 4 Promotes Employment Quotas," *New York Times,* March 18, 1973, p. 7.
88. A. C. Germann, Frank D. Day and Robert R. J. Gallati, *Introduction to Law Enforcement and Criminal Justice* (Springfield, Ill.: Charles C. Thomas, 1976), p. 118.
89. A. C. Germann, "Community Policing."
90. Ahern, p. 78.
91. Ahern, p. 29.
92. Robert J. diGrazia, speech before the Executive Forum on Upgrading the Police, Washington, D.C., April 14, 1976.
93. For a complete account, see James Q. Wilson, *Varieties of Police Behavior* (Cambridge, Mass.: Harvard University Press, 1968).
94. diGrazia, speech.
95. Ernest Greenwood, "The Elements in Professionalization," in Howard M. Vollmer and Donald L. Mills, eds., *Professionalization* (Englewood Cliffs, N.J.: Prentice-Hall, Inc. 1966), p. 9.
96. The President's Commission on Law Enforcement and the Administration of Justice, *The Challenge of Crime in A Free Society* (Washington, D.C.: U. S. Government Printing Office, 1967), pp. 91-123.
97. Erik Beckman, "A Study of Police Implementation and Attitudes Related to the National Crime Commission's Recommendations for Police Education and Training," doctoral dissertation, Wayne State University, December 1975.
98. Ramsey Clark, *Crime in America* (New York: Simon and Schuster, 1970), p. 138.
99. Clark, p. 150.
100. Clark, p. 132.
101. Garmire, p. 312-313.
102. Garmire, p. 314.
103. A. C. Germann, "Law Enforcement: A Look Into the Future," in Niederhoffer and Blumberg, pp. 351-354.
104. Ibid., p. 355.

Annotated Bibliography

Ahern, James F. *Police in Trouble.* New York: Hawthorn Books, Inc., 1972. A candid account of a police chief's experiences in an Eastern city, including comments on corruption, incompetence, and political interference.

Clark, Ramsey. *Crime in America*. New York: Simon and Schuster, 1970. An evaluation from a liberal standpoint of crime and criminal justice in the U.S., social and economic comments on crime, and our need to reform the system.

Goldstein, Herman. *Policing a Free Society*. Cambridge, Mass.: Ballinger Publishing Co., 1977. An evaluation of modern policing. Includes such issues as the police role, crime, discretion, political processes, and corruption.

Morris, Norval and Hawkins, Gordon. *The Honest Politicians's Guide to Crime Control*. Chicago: University of Chicago Press, 1969. A discussion of the overreach of the criminal law and how various acts should be legalized to lighten the load of the criminal justice system.

Neiderhoffer, Arthur and Blumberg, Abraham S. *The Ambivalent Force*. Hinsdale, Ill.: Dryden Press, 1976. A reader containing articles written by many respected authors on a variety of issues including the police role, police values and culture, discretion, the legal system, and the future of law enforcement.

Wilson, James Q. *Thinking About Crime*. New York: Basic Books, 1975. Thought provoking comments on crime and criminological theories, shattering many myths.

Wilson, James Q. *Varieties of Police Behavior*. Cambridge, Mass.: Harvard University Press, 1968. A study of policing in certain communities and the conclusion that the policing style and philosophy is related to the political powers in the community.

12

POLICE CORRUPTION
The Ethics of the Situation

Chapter Objectives

The study of this chapter should enable you:

☑ To offer and illustrate a practical definition of police corruption.

☑ To describe and illustrate the types of corrupt activity

a. The extortion/accommodation/crime typology

b. Isolated versus system-supported corruption.

☑ To describe the historical background as to the forces which have shaped corruption and the meaning that term has taken over the past hundred years in the United States.

☑ To indicate the extent of police corruption.

☑ To describe the processes which lead police into corrupt activity.

☑ To describe anti-corruption activity and the requisites for appropriate administrative action.

a. Political forces, the research establishment and the newspapers against corruption

b. The necessary police agency policies and practices (1) Policy positions. (2) The requirement and reward structure. (3) Agency counter-measures to corruption. (4) The importance of ethics.

Introduction

For the first hundred years of their existence, local police in America had few recognized guidelines for their operations. They acted in conformity with the public morality of their times when they took orders from the political groups which had established them. Political orders often called for what we now see as clear abuses of police power (for example, election frauds or the protection of houses of prostitution and barrooms). The early local police in many communities were involved in widespread corruption, mainly at the order of machine politicians and as part of an overall pattern of political corruption. However, political graft never made the headlines that were always there for any charges of police misconduct. All policing was the constant target of opposition politicians and of the muckrakers (the writers of the Reform Movement), who were most concerned about the political controllers of the police. Although individual police acts were publicized, police agencies received little notice except when charges were being made against them. The American public was most likely to hear of police organizations when it read politically inspired accounts of corruption.

Police corruption was as real during the years up to the 1960s as the attempts to study or meet it were unreal. Since that time, the problems of corruption have changed; we have begun to understand and discuss corruption in more realistic terms. We recognize that corruption is widely found in institutions other than the police, and we are beginning to understand that the study of police corruption may provide us with valuable information about the control of all criminal abuses of governmental power. It is against this background that the following chapter has been written.

What is Police Corruption?

The words "police corruption" have been used with different meanings by many different people. Therefore, writings on the subject often deal with different but obviously related ideas. In this chapter, we'll use one definition which seems to fit most of the accepted instances. When we speak of police corruption, we're referring to *police officers participating in criminal activities for money or some cash equivalent and in some way involving the police role, powers, or knowledge.*[1]

This definition specifies that only criminal acts will be considered as corruption. Thus, it doesn't include the frequently mentioned case of the police officer having a free cup of coffee. We'll speak about this later, and it should be clear that there's no intention here to support even minor unethical behavior. However, we want to separate out the particular kind of unethical behavior which is usually thought of as corruption.

While extortion and bribery are the crimes which are most usually designated as corrupt activity, there have also been instances in which police officers have taken part in burglaries or robberies or have actually worked to set up or participate in gambling operations or other illegal activities. We also consider these actions to be corrupt.

The reason for specifying that corruption is criminal activity *for profit* is also important. Complaints of illegal police action sometimes cite the improper use of force, or technicalities about searches or arrests. These are serious charges, but in and of themselves aren't necessarily related to corruption. The police officer who gets into an argument and then illegally uses fists or nightstick against another person, or who makes an unjustified search of a suspect, is wrong—sometimes criminally wrong. But this officer is neither a thief nor an extortionist, as long as there is no question of the officer's doing the illegal actions to get money or something else of financial value.

The following cases would be examples of police corruption according to this definition:

- Patrol Officer A takes two hundred dollars from a person he has arrested and agrees to deter his testimony in court so that the case will be dismissed.
- Officer B agrees to allow illegal parking on her post in return for free meals.
- Patrol Officers C, D, and E, who all work a particular post, agree to accept ten dollars each every week in return for not reporting that a dice game is held every evening in a particular location.
- Patrol Officer F arrests a known narcotics dealer and finds that he has a large amount of heroin in his possession. Officer F takes five thousand dollars from the dealer to release him and make no record of the arrest.
- Patrol Officers G, H, and I are called to a liquor store which has been burglarized. At a time when her two partners aren't in sight, Officer H takes a bottle of whiskey and hides it in her car for her own personal use.
- Patrol Officers J and K identify several businesses where large sums of money are left overnight. On an evening tour, when they know that they will be unobserved, they burglarize one of these stores.
- Patrol Officer L wants to buy a snowmobile. She goes to one dealer who has a large number of trucks. L has frequently warned the dealer to keep his trucks from double parking or blocking the sidewalk, and has given several summonses to the drivers for these violations. It would be worth a lot to the dealer if his drivers were allowed to commit these violations, at least at times when parking space is at a premium. The dealer tells L that he has a snowmobile which is marked down and sells it to her at a very low price. Both L and the dealer know, in fact, that the snowmobile is of the latest type and could easily be sold for its list price.

We come to difficulties in approaching the problem of police corruption when we try to consider the cases of unethical behavior that resemble others which we label corrupt but lack some important element of our definition. The following activities wouldn't be considered as corrupt according to the definition we've established, but each case represents a situation which should be examined carefully by the officials involved.

- Investigator A has been conducting a lengthy burglary investigation at a residence. Lunchtime arrives, and the family invites him to join them for a sandwich and coffee. He accepts. If this is—as it appears—an honest invitation and there's no question of A's report being affected by any obligation he might feel, then there's no corruption involved.

- Patrol Officer B is allowed by the rules of the police department for which she works to take a job as a security officer in a supermarket. She is allowed by the police department to wear her uniform on this off-duty assignment. The manager of the store gets into an argument with a customer, and the officer takes the manager's side in a way which most police officers would evaluate as biased.

This situation represents that would be called a *conflict of interests*; that is, the officer operating under high ethical standards should not allow himself or herself to take unfair action under any circumstances. However, this particular case would not involve corrupt activity according to the definition we've established.

- The police of Community A decide that they're going to bring their wage demands to the attention of the public in a very forceful manner. They begin a "ticket blitz" in which they give out hundreds of summonses to members of the community for violations which would ordinarily have gone unnoticed.

This kind of behavior has often been used by individuals or small groups to enforce private demands, and constitutes corrupt behavior if it is done by an individual or a group for personal gain. However, society at this time accepts that such activities by an employee group may be illegal but that they don't represent corrupt behavior in the terms that we're considering here.

- Patrolman Q stops a motorist for going through a stop sign. In the conversation that follows, Q discovers that the motorist is a "nice person" who also belongs to the same church he himself attends. He warns the motorist not to commit the violation again and releases her without giving her a ticket.

Again, one can question the ethics of the matter, but there's no question of corruption.

The Types of Corruption Activities

The examples given above are illustrative of both corrupt activities and some borderline situations. At this point, we would like to draw some distinctions among the kinds of corruption. We will use two kinds of distinctions. First, we will differentiate among the kinds of actions which are called corruption; second, we will discuss the different ways in which corrupt activities are viewed by those within police agencies.

Kinds of Corrupt Activities We can distinguish three types of corruption:

1. *Official extortion.* The police officer forces another person to pay to avoid some official action which should be taken, or to receive a service which the officer should perform as a regular part of his or her duties. An

illustration of this type of corruption would be the case of the person who's arrested and then released when he or she pays the officer a sum that the officer demands. Not only criminals are subject to official extortion, however. For example, consider the case of a restaurant which wants to sell wine and beer with its meals. A police-approved license procedure is involved, and any delay can cost the licensee a lot of money. In a case like this, a corrupt officer might let it be known that he or she won't operate quickly and helpfully unless he or she is paid.

2. *Accommodation.* Many corrupt activities involve a relatively congenial relationship between the briber and the bribe taker. A bookmaker may want to take bets without being disturbed and may be willing to pay thousands of dollars a month for the privilege. Or, the person in charge of a loading dock at a department store in a busy commercial area may have been told by his or her employers to try to get the police to overlook a considerable amount of traffic blockage by trucks coming into this loading dock. The employers know that the difference between having the police overlook a considerable amount of congestion and having the police require the trucks to follow the law may be worth a lot of money in a relatively short time. Therefore, the representatives of the department store may want to pay off the police for overlooking the traffic violations. The police may justify accepting the bribery with the position that the store is important to the economic welfare of the community.
3. *Other police crime.* In addition to extortion or collusion arrangements, the police are, by the nature of their duties and the powers they have, in a position to use police power or information gained through policing to commit crimes. The most common of such activities are thefts. Police have come into situations where money or valuable merchandise is openly available to them, and where there may be no way to account for things which are taken. Two very common examples of this might involve actually burglarizing premises or participating in narcotics-related crimes. We'll discuss the narcotics crime situation in a later section.

In the case of burglarized premises, particularly where a store is involved, police officers may be called into a store which has been burglarized at some hour when there are no other people around to observe them. There have been times when police officers have taken liquor, or clothing, or merchandise. Very often, they have excused their thievery by saying that the insurance company was going to pay for anything that was missing and that there was no real harm in what they were doing. In other cases, police officers have formed burglary rings. Some police have acted as lookouts, while other have broken into and burglarized stores selected ahead of time.

It's important to recognize that a police officer may commit crimes as a private individual and that these crimes would not necessarily constitute corruption—*if* they were not involved in some way with the police officer's knowledge or powers as a police officer. Thus, a police officer might become involved in a financial manipulation scheme which had no connection at all to anything he or she had learned or done as a police officer. This would be a crime, but it would not represent police corruption.

Isolated and System-Supported Corruption A second and extremely important distinction among corrupt activities distinguishes those which are isolated from those which are supported by a network of expectations and accomodations within the police organization itself.

Isolated Corrupt Activity. This occurs when an officer or small group of officers has carried out some criminal activity which was not suggested by other police people or in any way supported by them. For example, a police officer who's badly in need of money may be offered money by a person whom he or she has stopped for a traffic offense. The officer could have every reason to believe that no one else would ever find out about the incident.

The officer carrying out such an isolated course of criminal activity is very much alone. Assuming that the department in which he or she works is an "honest" department, he or she knows that discovery will result in both legal penalties and the contempt and disapproval of his or her coworkers. Many people can put aside the danger of being arrested and convicted of a crime, but comparatively few people are willing to risk being cut off by the people with whom they associate constantly and whose opinions they value.

Thus, the isolated police criminal is in a very restricted situation. The chances are that he or she can never go very far with criminality. From the viewpoint of evaluating an entire department, it's obvious that a situation where there's only occasional isolated corruption is very different from and much less serious than a situation in which such criminality is widespread and supported.

System-Supported Corruption. The individual who is an isolated criminal within a police organization is in a difficult and usually short-lived position. It's almost impossible for isolated corruption to exist over a long period of time without the department finding out that something wrong is going on. If that awareness is present, and if the department doesn't move promptly and firmly to correct the condition, we have evidence of what we would call a much more serious condition—system support of corruption.

System support can take many forms, but basically it's that form of corruption which exists within a police organization when an officer who commits a criminal action for money or who even thinks about that possibility can: (1) reasonably expect that other police officers will support him or her; or (2) feel that corrupt actions are required in order to just get along in the department or to achieve any rewards within the organizational structure.

The most serious case is when the department procedures or policies either require or reward corrupt activity. In the past, it was anticipated in some police departments (and, in some agencies, the expectation is still there) that an officer would develop criminal informants who would only give information if they were paid in one form or another for providing that information. It was usually suggested that the main "pay-off" to the criminal informants would be some recommendation to the prosecutor for special consideration on the grounds that the informant had supplied valuable information. It becomes obvious, however, that the chances of legally getting information on a continuing basis from a criminal informant in exchange for court leniency are almost nonexistent. First, the good, continuing informants don't get arrested very often. Second, a police department can't hold the threat of some past criminal action over the head of the informant for a long period. That constitutes blackmail no matter how it's described. In reality, continuing informants—the people who are almost invariably consulted in vice, gambling and narcotics cases (the cases where corruption is most often found)—will usually only work with the police if they are paid in either money or narcotics.

Payment with narcotics is always a crime. However, it's possible to make a money payment in a perfectly legal manner. The department can be given money for informants and pass this out with care and full record in special cases. The FBI worked with a very large informant budget for many years. Unfortunately, few municipal agencies can get more than token funding for such activities.

This actually means that the officer is paying the informant money (or, with addicts or drug sellers, narcotics instead of money), and these payments are not supplied by the department. Such money ordinarily comes from pay-offs to the police; narcotics are obtained in raids or arrests where the police illegally withhold drugs which are seized.

The payment with narcotics is sometimes excused as necessary in dealing with drugs. Unfortunately police officers who start making illegal narcotic deals for good purposes often decide that they are going to personally benefit from the transactions. Any department which allows unsupervised diversion of narcotics to "pay informers" must recognize that the possibility of substantial corruption is present.

Such a situation is one way in which corruption can be forced or supported by departmental practices, but there are other ways. For example, in some police departments throughout the country, it has been departmental policy to reward individuals who have "flaked" (that is, planted evidence on) persons who were thought to be guilty anyway.

If a police agency follows practices and policies which support corruption, it's obvious that, although a few may resign, many people within the organization will soon come to believe that a great deal of corrupt behaviour is acceptable. Even the people in the organization who are not personally involved will know that they themselves are subject to the same demands and the same reward systems as those officers who act in a corrupt manner in response to the department's pressures. In an organization like this, illegal activity on the part of police officers isn't thought of as something which no decent person would do; more realistically, the officer who rejects any criminal participation may be though of as a "Holy Joe" or even as a dangerous nonconformist. This type of condition is usually described as a *subculture of corruption.* In such a subculture, kinds of behavior which are unacceptable in the larger society can be both approved and aided.

When corruption is uncovered, it's usually reasonably evident whether the perpetrator was acting with the support of a system (or at least believed that that support was there) or as an isolated criminal. However, the belief that the individual was an isolated criminal is, of course, what a corrupt agency wants everyone to accept so that that agency can avoid further investigation of its activities. Thus, it's usually in the interest of the agency to claim that an individual who was charged as corrupt is either innocent or, at worst, represents a "rotten apple." It's mainly for this reason that the exposed case of corruption is often handled as though the only problem is to determine the guilt or innocence of the individual who is charged. That determination is always important, but even more important is the question of whether the police system supported that activity.

The Background of Corruption

Much of what's been written on corruption has been based on views which have reflected the different police worlds which have existed within the United States at various times. For a long period in our history, policing—like many other types of work in those days—operated on the premise that the ways of doing police work which had been developed over a long time were right and didn't merit further examination on an individual basis. Some of these practices might have been perfectly justified but, under close examination, some would have been found to be inconsistent with other accepted practices, and others would have been obviously inappropriate.

For people who live by tradition or by the rules, there are important benefits that go along with this approach. Individual situations don't have to be examined to determine what's right or wrong when everyone knows that the established way is the right way. Being wrong doesn't involve doing something which is objectively examined and found to be wrong; instead, it involves simply *not* doing what tradition requires. It should be clear that we all live to some extent according to prescribed patterns which we don't question. However, in the departments of up to 30 years ago, the police lived according to standards of an isolated police world and, in many cases, that was almost the only world they lived in. They didn't have the extensive contacts outside "the job" which are widely found in police groups today. Some of them could believe that a "reasonable amount" of corrupt activity was justified as long as the police officer involved wasn't "greedy" or didn't take "dirty money." An officer might take money from gamblers or for doing a favor without feeling that he or she was involved in corrupt activity.

It should be very quickly noted that even in departments which were widely corrupt, there were many scrupulously honest police officers who might have considered impractical or just "religious" by their less conscientious coworkers, but they were accepted, too. The important thing to remember here was that for many of the people in organizations like these, acts which we think of as being corrupt were regarded as perfectly acceptable. Of course, this wasn't—and isn't—only a police problem. One can examine many different occupations and find a similar tolerance of, and even a belief in the necessity of, bribery or extortion.

This whole situation was strongly influenced by the first years of policing. Most of the local police agencies were created in the last half of the nineteenth century and—this is very important—they were created under the power of the municipalities at a time when municipal administration was at its lowest ebb in terms of political corruption. The last quarter of the nineteenth century was, in particular, a time when machine politics dominated most cities throughout the country. The police agencies in such cities were generally recognized as the creatures of the political machines.

It would be a mistake to think of the political machines as being entirely evil. To the immigrant coming from a rural world and having few skills marketable in the city, patronage jobs (including those on the police department) were important. The local ward captain could get help when some kind of a license or permit was needed. When the family needed coal or food or legal help because the father had been arrested after a drinking bout, the local politicians helped with no questions asked as long as there was the assurance that the family's votes would be delivered when the "boss" wanted them. All told, the politicians varied widely, but they were not effective unless they were acceptable to their constituents, and being acceptable usually meant helping when help was needed. In a time without social welfare systems or formal ways for bringing the immigrant from outside into society, the political machine offered advice, assistance, jobs—basically a way of coming into this New World.

It was a period of which Robert Fogelson could write that the police represented a kind of cushion between a body of laws representing the public morality of the dominant political group—the rural, native-born, moralistic, Protestant world—and the customs and beliefs of the new groups of immigrants who didn't share that ethic.[2] Basically, the earlier tradition held that a high standard of morality in everyday life could be demanded and enforced only if the police were properly directed and supported. Thus, there was a great emphasis on trying to enforce morality and on the legislation of "victimless crimes." The new immigrant masses simply didn't accept the laws foisted on them by the rural and upper-class societies. The merchants of the Jewish ghetto weren't about to obey the observance of the Sunday closing laws. The people of the city, along with a great many of the visitors who at home supported the laws regulating morality, wanted the brothels and the free-running saloons kept open. Fogelson maintains that the early and extensively publicized corruption scandals (particularly those uncovered by the Lexow investigation of 1894 and the Curran committee in 1911) were attempts by the ministers and good government advocates who dominated the reform movements to attack the political powers of the cities which were so closely tied to the lower-class, immigrant societies. The battleground was the province of the municipal police.

In those days, the concept of police corruption was unclearly defined. It was just part of the political whole. The reformers seldom won the elections, and they were even less likely to win reelection. The machines usually stayed in power, and the investigations which came up every twenty or so years in the big cities usually resulted in the appearance of reform. No realistic possibility of change ever existed, and the corrupt activities were as much a part of that world as were the political machines which thrived during the same period.

Thus, until World War I, what we consider as corruption was largely a standardized way of getting along in the society of that time. World War I broke up the patterns that had existed for almost a quarter of a century before it. The wake of the war introduced Prohibition under the auspices of the Volstead Act (also known as the Eighteenth Amendment). Prohibition had an extraordinarily corrosive impact on American policing. It transformed the patterns of illegal police activity from what had basically been a form of social and political accommodation to a relationship with a new and very different source of corruption, the forerunners of organized crime. In the years of Prohibition (1919-1933), police departments across the United States were badly scarred by the absolute amorality of the Prohibition world. The impact on corruption was similar to, but probably much more virulent than, the impact of narcotics on the corruption pattern of the 1960s. Suddenly, enormous sums of money were available from liquor runners and, just as vicious, Prohibition whiskey was easy to get, which resulted in great numbers of alcoholics in police ranks.

By 1933, when Prohibition was repealed, the moral climate of law enforcement throughout the United States had suffered greatly. For almost fourteen years, large numbers of the American public from every walk of life had consistently and openly violated the law. The basis for an organized crime empire had been established. In addition, the Prohibition experiment had demolished the Reform Movement. The reformers could no longer even define corruption or the activities which could be carried out to stop it. In this way, the alliance of the Protestant moralists, the good government advocates, and the native-born Americans of the early western and northern European stocks (the group which had largely dominated the movement against corruption since the 1890s) lost its effectiveness as an important political power. The political forces were still important in many communities, but in some, the police themselves had become important politicans. In other cases, as in New York during the LaGuardia regime, the police inherited the power to control the corruption when the Tammany Hall machine was driven out of office. Thus, in many cities, the police officers were actually in positions of political power rather than simply being creatures of the politicians.

The year 1933, which saw the end of Prohibition, was a bad time for America for a good many reasons. We were in the heart of the Depression. Policing was not a particularly prominent part of the national life, and with the Reform Movement no longer fighting the political machines, there were few people who could speak authoritatively on corruption-relevant problems. That vacuum was filled by a group of noted police leaders who did not stress corruption or any other unpleasant aspect of policing. Rather, they emphasized the need for an honest and positive approach which they labeled "professionalism." In retrospect, it seems that these eminent police officers had important things to say, but they did not have much of an impact.

The people who began to take the leadership in speaking out about policing were the "professionals," men like August Volmer and O. W. Wilson. Their careers were founded on successful fights against corruption and the professional label became the focus for important reform activity. Their administrations no longer tolerated corruption, brutality or bias in the day-to-day policing. Corrupt police officers resigned, were fired or went to jail. Berkeley, in particular, became a "training ground for police chiefs."

World War II followed, and after it came the period during the 1950s when the United States seemed to coast along on the forces and ideas which had been established. In all those years from the mid-1930s to the mid-1960s, the basic politican-police-organized crime relationship lived quietly and well in its many local variations. Although corruption scandals broke out periodically, it was generally assumed that police corruption was more or less vaguely tied to political intervention and that a certain amount of corrupt activity was inevitable. Following some proven or even merely publicized charge of police corruption, the usual prescription was to chase out one group of corrupt officers, and then install another group who would not be exposed as corrupt for another ten or fifteen years. Generally, it can be said that during these years the traditional patterns of policing went along largely unchanged in most of the cities in the country, but that in some—particularly in the west—a new professionalism was beginning to give police operations a new shape.

The real breakdown of the traditional ways occurred during the years from the end of the 1950s through the 1960s. In that decade, life in America changed greatly. Even more drastic than the general change was the change in the institution of policing. The police at the end of the 1950s were a largely anonymous, custom-bound group in parts of which corruption patterns were deeply ingrained. Within a few years, the Black, student, and anti-war protests were to present policing with a series of challenges such as the field never before had to face. Persons as varied as Dr. Martin Luther King, "Bull" Conners, and Tom Hayden brought to the police problems which involved them in national headlines. The Supreme Court issued decision after decision which sharply changed standard police views about the rights of accused individuals. *Mapp v. Ohio, Kerr v. California, Katz v. U.S., Terry v. Ohio, Escobodeo v. Illinois, Miranda v. Arizona*, and a host of other cases represented the first serious federal challenges to local police practice. The universities came into the picture, and with them the police science and criminal justice faculties and students. Police unions came along and proposed new relationships between the line officers and the power structures within which they operated. Suddenly, the old traditions began to pass away, and along with them went the easy acceptance of such corruption-supporting ideas as the "Blue Wall," the "rotten apple" theory of police corruption and, in general, the whole idea that corruption was something that had always been there and always would be, and that very little could be done about it.

We were well into the change-filled era when in April 1970 a major police scandal broke out in New York City. The scandal led to the creation of the so-called Knapp Commission. The report of that commission marked a major break in the tradition of corruption investigations over the years. It was searching, thorough, and—most unusual—it was obviously intended to change long-existing graft patterns. In addition to providing a great deal of detail and many recommendations, the report indicated that up until that date the patterns of corrupt activity had changed little in the preceding twenty years. The Knapp Commission found the ties between gambling, narcotics, prostitution, parking, construction, the pay-offs from bars and grills, and the pattern of intradepartmental payments, along with a variety of less obvious patterns of corruption (Knapp, pp. 71-169). When the Emergency Crime Committee of the Chicago City Council issued the Kohn Report in 1952, it had found the same kinds of criminal activities on the part of the Chicago Police (Kohn, 1953, pp. 5-69). Twenty years and a thousand miles made no difference in the types of corrupt activities reported. However, the Knapp Commission did note one important new trend—that of the rise in narcotics corruption-related problems.

At the time of this writing, seven years later, it's obvious that New York City policing has gone through many changes, the beginnings of which were noted in the Knapp Commission Report. Many of the same forces behind change have acted on police forces all over the country. The police world which the report documented has already changed. The gambling "pads" and the widespread monthly payoffs, which marked the most significant and systematic link to corruption in the days from the 1930s up until the Knapp era, have seemingly disappeared. The small-time bookmaker or policy runner is in competition with government-sponsored off-track betting. Sports gambling is more important than gambling on the horses, at least when one is considering the preferences of gamblers small enough in the size of their operations to deal with corner bookmakers.

In the past ten years, there has been an important change in the long-existing climate of organizational support for police corruption. In the aftermath of the Knapp Commission and of a number of studies which have analyzed the corruption problem, the myths that corruption was a necessary part of policing and that the police officer had to be protected by his fellow officers against any charges of corruption have weakened to the point of disappearance. This has left the corrupt police officer with far less opportunity for support from his or her colleagues than he or she might have anticipated in earlier days. The corruption investigations were much deeper than the old surface whitewashings which had always been the official reaction to corruption investigations. The major scandals of recent years—in Denver, New York City, and Philadelphia—were not treated as they would have been in the "old days." They made large waves in their communities and have resulted in substantial changes in policies and practices. Now, when the subject of corruption comes up, the police ask about what corrective measures can be taken. Anti-corruption is now not only the legal approach, but also the necessary approach for administrators in today's police world.

The Extent of Police Corruption

When we try to estimate the extent of police corruption, we are forced to deal with only general impressions and isolated bits of information. It's usually said that corruption is most often found in the old cities of the northeast, the south, and the midwest; however, there are departments everywhere with at least some measure of corruption. But large and small departments alike are involved.

In 1976, Dr. Harry W. More, Jr., of San Jose State College, conducted a Delphi projection study in which he engaged in a continuing series of questionnaire and answer relationships with the members of a panel of one hundred persons who were either experts in the study of police corruption or practitioners who had had to deal with the question of police corruption in an operating situation. The Delphi research approach is designed to bring together the opinions of people who have a wide range of expertise (the group which is questioned is called the panel) about corruption matters. The members of the panel are asked several rounds of questions, beginning with very general questions about corruption, and progressing to much more specific questions. After each round, the results of the answers are analyzed and fed back to the members of the panel, along with the next questions, which call for more specific answers. Thus, each person in the panel is given the chance to get the opinions of all the other specialists on the questions that have been asked (More, 1976, passim). The result is that, as the panel members progress through the successive stages, their thinking is sharpened and they arrive at opinions which are usually more precise than those they had when the Delphi project began.

More's report indicated that about one-third of his panel members believed that corruption had increased during the past ten years, while about one-half believed that corruption had stayed at a relatively constant level. Most of the panelists (78.4 percent) anticipated that corruption would level off and begin to decrease during the next twenty-five years.[3] It seems likely that the system supports for corruption, insofar as they've often been based on political corruption, have probably weakened. There's also evidence of a decreasing willingness on the part of the police to take a viewpoint about corruption which is greatly different from that held by the general public.

Why Do Police Officers Become Involved in Corruption? Most attempts to explain the reason for police involvement in corrupt activities stress the fact that corruption is usually learned within the police organization and is supported by practices and pressures within the organization. This is, of course, another way of saying that police officers usually become involved because of the system support given to corruption.

Isolated Corruption It's important to remember that corrupt activity is usually carried out either because it pays off or because weak people are pressured into following the example of others. Generally speaking, the kinds of personal, unique motivation which may be involved if a patrol officer uses force against someone who has angered or hurt him or her are not present in corruption cases. Corruption is learned behavior, and, even when very great sums are involved, is a kind of behavior which will not be followed by many police officers unless their behavior is supported by the climate of the agency in which they are working. In money matters, the isolated pressures for criminal involvement are less important, but there are cases where money pressures result from the personal needs of individual police officers. Police officers get into financial problems just as other people do. When this happens, a very few seem to feel pressured into criminal activity. They're not usually very effective criminals, and the kinds of criminal actions which they commit are often unreal and usually unsuccessful. A few examples can give some idea of the nature of these isolated police criminal activities.

In one California community, where the police had a very high reputation for honesty, a young policeman got himself heavily into debt. He didn't know what to do, and eventually seemed to break under the pressure.[4] He walked into a bank in civilian clothes, held up the teller, took the money, and then walked outside and waited, seemingly unable to take any action to get away. He was, of course, arrested and convicted.

In an eastern city, the police were presented with a burglary of an elaborate vault system which would ordinarily be considered burglar-proof. Obviously, the burglars knew the exact layout of the alarm system. A short time later, a similar and equally unlikely vault burglary took place. The case had, of course, very few mysteries. Obviously, only somebody who had access to the security diagrams for both of the locations could have managed the burglaries. This person turned out to be a police officer who had somehow gotten the security information and then shared it with a professional burglar. He made sixteen thousand dollars from the joint venture, but his arrest and conviction made it a particularly expensive undertaking.[5]

Narcotics is an area where the high value of the contraband and the great sums of cash involved present unusual opportunities for isolated police criminality which can take bizarre forms. In one New York City case, the parents of a young woman who had become a narcotics addict turned her over to the police. The officer assigned to the case betrayed his responsibilities in a singular instance of corruption. Instead of helping the young woman, he began supplying her with narcotics. A short time later he introduced the woman to "Solly," a narcotics wholesaler. They told her that they had 100 bags of heroin which she was to sell. When she protested, she was told to cooperate or they would "take care of her kids." The proceeds from the sale were split three ways among the woman, the officer, and Solly, who —it later turned out—was another narcotics officer. When an official complaint was made, the plot thickened even more. The policemen kidnapped the woman and held her in an apartment for several days in a futile attempt to stop the investigation. The two later went to prison.[6]

To sum it up, there are occasional instances of strictly isolated crimes but, in general, corruption in the police department occurs because system supports exist for that kind of behavior. The ways in which a system may support the corrupt behavior of members of a police agency vary greatly. At worst, the whole organization can be like a criminal gang in which the only serious question is whether the individual operates according to the rules of the gang. In such cases it becomes difficult for anyone to press a charge of corrupt activity against any police officer; serious attempts may be made to block any investigation, and police or political power may be used to harass those who complain. Sometimes the system pressure rises, such as when the agency requires the officer to perform illegal acts or to actually get bribe money so that expected and expensive activities such as buying information can be carried out even though the department can't pay for them. Sometimes the support comes when the department rewards activities which could only have occurred corruptly. Most often, however, the causes are poor leadership, poor control, and the criminal subculture which may have developed among the officers with whom a corrupt officer works. Peers are often poor examples; they press the officer to join in illegal actions, and they support him or her in corrupt activities by refusing to press criminal charges and by blocking complaints. In particular, the people with whom one works give approval or disapproval. That is very important. Most people need the support of their coworkers if they're going to do things which society doesn't accept.

In an adult world, we're all responsible for the criminal actions we take. However, if the system is as important as we've said it is, then a great part of the blame for a corruption-supporting system must be placed on the executives in an organization in which corruption develops. Blame also must be placed on political forces which support corruption within the organization. Generally, the guilty ones aren't arrested. They run less risk of being branded as corrupt than do those officers who are identified and then lose their positions and the respect of the community. It may be that some of these executives or politicans who create conditions which support corruption don't realize that they're having this effect. Many don't recognize the seriousness of not taking firm positions and rigorously opposing corruption.

It should be obvious at this point that corruption is a subject that's almost as broad as is the question of economically motivated crime in the general society. However, there is a substantial difference. The financial manipulator in the stockmarket, or the person who perpetrates a "con game," or a thief within the general community has the advantage of being able to find his or her life-support system in a world which may be almost entirely divorced from that of his or her victims. Every police officer must find a large part of his or her reference world—the people whose opinions are personally important—within the agency itself.

The Struggle Against Corruption We have considered a number of background questions and concerns of the corruption problem. At this time we'd like to examine the forces which attempt to control corruption. We'll note that while there are important forces external to the agency, the real work of meeting the corruption problem is the responsibility of the police agency. Consider first the external forces.

The most obvious source for corruption control would be expected to be the political controllers of the police. The police are an agency of the local government and, as such, their work is supervised by the executive and the legislative branches of that local government. In addition, some state agencies and even federal agencies have investigative authority in corruption matters.

Unfortunately, however, most local police agencies were established during the years when local government was controlled by political machines. Thus, local government control has often encouraged corruption rather than acted as a control against it.

That situation seems to be changing, however. Reform executives, particularly those who are brought into office after a political scandal, require effective police chiefs, and effectiveness is not associated with corruption. Thus, the major political pressures today are different from those which shaped policing up until now.

Although many of the more vigorous mayors and managers are demanding greater accountability from their police, the major accountability changes have resulted from the introduction of new types of management control by staff units within local and state government. It isn't uncommon now for a police agency to have to deal with municipal or state groups which are concerned with budget and performance standards, with other agencies which are responsible for conducting the negotiations with the police union, with state and federal agencies which serve as conduits for federal monies through the mechanisms of grants or studies, and with other existing agencies having new or expanded functions. All of these supervisory relationships have at least occasional impact on the corruption problem, but their lack of coordination fragments their total impact.

Another group which will have considerable impact on the study and development of new ideas for meeting corruption is composed of the academics and researchers who study the problem from the universities and research institutes. Much corruption exists because we don't know enough about policing and, in particular, about some of the regulatory areas (e.g., gambling vice, enforcement of various ordinances, etc.) to be able to propose controls for them. Within the past few years, the federal government has funded major studies on corruption by the Rand Institute and by the John Jay College of Criminal Justice. From their work and from the doctoral dissertations or the isolated research activities conducted under the auspices of the Police Foundation and by a few isolated researchers, there has been emerging a more ordered picture of the corruption field and the actions taken against corruption.

In addition to the political powers and theoreticians, another prominent group of people in the community often take an important role with regard to corruption problems. The reporters and publishers of the newspapers in most communities are interested in the way in which the police react to all of their problems, including corruption. From the days of the 1890 Lexow Commission to the 1970 Knapp Commission investigation in New York City, to the Watergate scandal, conscientious newspaper reporters have created a major force "concentrating on the practices that stop government from functioning in the public interest."[7]

Police relationships with the newspapers haven't always been the best. Sometimes reporters or publishers have been unfair, and it's a common police complaint that the newspapers publish the unfavorable news about policing while saying very little about the good work that the police do. To some extent this is the nature of the newspaper business. Newspapers aren't sold because of stories on properly performed routine. On the other hand, stories about scandals, such as corruption, do build up newspaper sales. The police have to see the news media as one form of the public conscience. They must live with and learn from whatever is printed, but the newspaper accounts will be shaped by the reputation which the police build with the public and the news media through years of integrity in the business of carrying out policing. That reputation is the police agency's greatest protection against irresponsible reporting.

Agency Policies and Practices to Meet Corruption

Although there are many important things which remain to be done by the political authorities and by the theory builders, and although it's important that the newspapers publicize corrupt practices, the major task of combating corruption must be accomplished within the individual police agencies. It must be done in the "now." No administrator can wait for theories to be developed or for other forces outside the department to do the job for him or her. If those outside forces have to expose corruption, it probably means that the police administrator is ineffective.

Particularly since the New York City scandal of 1970 and the resulting Knapp Commission Report, we're more concerned with the relationship of administrative practices and procedures to corruption than we were formerly. The Knapp Commission Report (pp. 196-264) and the author's 1972 study of the New York City anti-corruption campaign are among recent studies which have stressed administrative relationship to the problems of corruption. We know that much of the corrupt practice occurs in areas where there's unclear understanding as to how policing should be carried out, or where the tradition has been that it's just not wise to look too closely at how such things as gambling control, the supervision of bars and cabarets, or the enforcement of the laws against prostitutes and homosexuals, are actually carried out. In these enforcement areas, the conventional police enforcement practices have often been of questionable legality (and the point should be made that this is still a problem). It has often been assumed that the police job with regard to these regulatory areas could not be carried out legally. Thus, for large areas of police administration there have been inadequate guidelines for proper performance.

The administrators have the prime responsibility for preventing corruption or meeting any that can't be prevented. However, in a world largely shaped by political realities, even honest and effective administrators find it difficult to fight corruption. The problem begins with the need (which exists for any activity which we would like to accomplish by the use of goals and measured activity) to define the nature and extent of the problem before developing a program to meet it. Some of the difficulties arise because it isn't easy to determine the extent of the corruption problem or its nature. Beyond that, however, many sincere and honest officials believe that revelations about corruption, particularly when they are still unproven, damage the police image and morale. This is the problem which is faced by a police administration that is competent enough to recognize that there is a strong likelihood of the existence of corruption before overwhelming evidence is presented that that corruption is there.

When the administration is unclear as to the nature or extent of the corruption problem, and/or the administrators prefer not to discuss the corruption within the agency, there is the tendency for the administrators to accept the "rotten apple" theory. It's easier to accept the belief that if corruption exists, then the corrupt police officer who's obvious enough to get caught is an evil person, than it is to recognize that he or she was most likely shaped by the forces that he or she lived with on the job.

The job that administrators face when they must deal with the threat of corruption is difficult, but there are guidelines for them. Basically, we would expect them to take four kinds of action:

1. Clearly state their policy positions with regard to corruption and its control, publicize those positions, and then enforce them.
2. Carefully study the ways in which the police in their agency learn and are supported in or prevented from carrying out corrupt activity. The job here is to make sure that nothing in the department policies or practices requires or rewards corrupt practice.
3. Establish vigorous countermeasures to uncover and take action against any evidence of corruption.
4. Develop and carry out an ethical course of police administration, including the publicizing and enforcement of a rigorous code of ethics.

1. The Necessary Policy Statements

a. *A strong and clear statement against corruption must be made and enforced.* Too often, police administrators neglect to make very clear to the public and to the police: (1) the kind of behavior that's regarded as corrupt; and (2) the attitude of the administration toward corruption. This doesn't mean that threats and half-accusations should be made. A good police executive has got to be tough enough and open enough so that the official position is clear. In a good police department, everyone should know that corruption is a kind of treason and will be treated accordingly. Corrupt police officers will be arrested and vigorously prosecuted.

b. *Deep and clear lines of communication should be established from the police to all of the legitimate groups within the communities.* Much corruption is enabled because there's no communication between the police and groups which are most affected by police criminality. It isn't unusual to have people who live in the poverty areas of the city believe that no one will listen to any complaints that they make. By making it clear to all members of the community that the department won't tolerate police crime, the police department can gain the public support which comes when all citizens know that their police department supports them against dishonest police officers. This can enable the honest police executive to resist political or other pressures toward corrupt action. Such channels to the community allow the departmental executives to know what's going on in the community, and also to bring back to the community their own sense of the necessity to reduce corruption. Just as important, the building up of lines of communication to the community decreases the isolation and defensiveness of the police. It's more possible for the police administration to lead and work effectively with non-defensive police officers.

c. *The relationship of the police to political authority must be clarified.* The police are administratively responsible to the local executive and to the local legislature. Obviously, political interference, particularly that which is in support of corrupt practice, cannot be tolerated. However, it's important to recognize that there's a big difference between illegitimate interference and legitimate administrative control. The police should be responsible to those who represent the public, particularly for explaining the measures that the police are taking against corruption.

There should be a clear understanding with the political powers that any time the department is expected to deviate from its established policies and procedures, that kind of deviation should only be made through political contact with the police chief. There may be good reason for asking for some deviation from established practice, but the chief must be the person who makes the exception. It's particularly important that no person or group has the power to give immunity to specific individuals involved in narcotics or illegal gambling. This doesn't mean that the mayor, manager, local council, or police chief can't *legally* and *openly* deemphasize a particular general area of enforcement or discontinue a particular enforcement practice. For example, when the New York City Police Department ordered its officers to stop acting as complainants in homosexual solicitation arrests, that decision seems to have been entirely proper. By this action the administration recognized the need for a correction of practices which had often resulted in corruption. Similarly, many police organizations throughout the country are ordering their officers not to make arrests for the possession of one or two marijuana cigarettes. This is legitimate selective enforcement; it isn't the same as authorizing a particular marijuana dealer to operate.

d. *There should be no attempt to have the police enforce obviously unconstitutional or illegal laws or ordinances.* In many localities, local laws similar to those which have been declared unconstitutional elsewhere have not been repealed. In some instances, such laws have been enforced even though everyone has been aware that they no longer had legal validity.

e. *Responsibility for anti-corruption activity should be very decentralized.* In many instances, corruption has been fostered in police departments because only a small group of people in a special unit has had any responsibility for enforcing the laws against corruption. Corruption is everybody's business. The police officer who knowingly allows another member of his or her department to commit a crime is a partner in that crime. Every officer and every supervisor should have the responsibility for taking vigorous action whenever an incident of corruption is uncovered.

f. *Integrity and efficiency must be considered as being equally essential.* It hasn't been unusual to hear police protests about reformers "handcuffing the police," or to hear statements that the city will be taken over by the criminals unless the police are allowed to follow old and outlawed patterns of conduct. The point is that everyone should know that the kind of integrity which is required for effective job performance is part and parcel of the same kind of integrity that is involved with honest job performance.

g. *There should be policies which facilitate department cooperation with other agencies against corruption.* In many cases, police agencies have considered that their internal affairs are strictly their business. It must be recognized that in conducting corruption investigations, particularly those which are widespread, other local, state or federal agencies may have important interests in the investigation.

It is also true that in many instances there are examples of corruption in the judiciary and, in some cases, in detention or even probation or parole settings. Whenever such activities are discovered, the police agency should have the responsibility for bringing them to the attention of the proper authorities.

h. *There should be a policy of openness about corruption.* Corruption is facilitated when excessive secrecy exists. This can lead to covering up instances of corruption within an agency with the belief that what the public doesn't know won't hurt it. Secrecy also leads to a great many misconceptions which impede the development of policing. Some of the beliefs which secrecy promotes are as follows: "You don't bring outsiders into police problems or let them know about problems. Police problems are unique. Only a police officer can understand police problems. You never talk about corruption except in vague generalities or even admit that it exists." These and a number of other harmful cliches—all aided by the emphasis on secrecy—lead to ineffective problem-solving by the police.

i. *The broad corruption picture is important.* In a nationwide study on police corruption which was conducted by the author in 1967 for the President's Commission on Law Enforcement and Administration of Justice,[8] it was concluded that crime in general and corruption in particular were almost universally approached by the police on a case-by-case basis. The police considered case A as isolated from case B, as isolated from case C, and so forth. There was never an attempt to try cases together and thus to get at the system support of an incident. It's only in examining the total picture of a problem such as corruption that broad problems can be isolated and studied.

2. The Examination of the Requirement and Reward Structure

The point has been made that the most extensive problems of corruption are found in the agencies where the agency policies or requirements actually result in corrupt practice. Much of our preceding discussion can be seen in this light. Fundamentally, it's essential to examine the kinds of agency requirements in areas where there has been a history of corruption. The following are examples of the questions which need to be answered:

- Is the use of criminal informants carefully supervised?
- Is there a procedure for supervising the court presentation and the quality of the cases made by persons dealing with vice, gambling, and narcotics? (Such monitoring is usually on a spot-check basis.)
- Is any licensing procedure which the police are engaged in checked to determine whether it is carried out effectively, without unusual delays, and without favoritism toward, or bias against, any licensee or applicant?

3. The Counter-Measures

Every agency, no matter how large or how small, should have some individual or unit responsible for carrying out for the department the specific control activities designed to combat corruption. In very small agencies this may be an additional function given to the chief or some trusted subordinate. William McCarthy, a former Deputy Police Commissioner in New York City during the Knapp Commission days and one of the most vigorous and effective of the anti-corruption administrators, suggested that in any department of a hundred or more, a special unit concerned with internal affairs is required.[9]

In a very large police organization, the Internal Affairs Unit may handle the more important investigations or those involving several commands while it acts as a central supervising unit for those cases which can be effectively handled by field units. There is value in having field units responsible for investigations which don't require unusual skills or equipment. The units become involved in the work and there is no chance that corruption is thought of as being the business of some remote central office. The Internal Affairs Division is in one way an intelligence division and in another a unit directed toward a special kind of investigation.

Intelligence should not be confused with the compilation of large files of information used only in isolated cases. The whole effort should be to make use of all records both as case records—that is, as relating to a particular person or situation—and also as records which can be used to establish an information base for management. Case records for corruption situations are usually very complete in departments where proper attention is given to these matters. The more serious problem is that it's very difficult to extract from these records the kinds of information which management needs to make its decisions. Thus, records usually only give case-by-case results rather than the "big picture." The overall perspective which management does require will vary from city to city, but there are some record summaries and extractions which are important.

Among the investigation innovations which Commissioner McCarthy introduced into New York City were the use of "turn-arounds" and "field associates." The "turn-arounds" were officers who had been apprehended in corrupt activity and who were given the opportunity to save their jobs or at least to gain a police recommendation for reduced sentence if they cooperated with the Internal Affairs Division. This meant that people who were part of the corruption system were required to inform on the system or face the loss of job and pension rights, or even jail. The results of this practice were spectacular. There was the obvious benefit of the apprehension of a considerable number of corrupt officers who could not have been captured without the aid of one of their criminal conspirators. In addition, a major benefit was the destruction of the belief that other members of the department could be trusted by a police officer who wanted to be corrupt.

The "field associates" was another and equally dramatic program. It recruited young officers who were coming into the Department to serve as undercover operators for the Internal Affairs Division even though they were assigned to special units (including the Internal Affairs Division) or to various field units. The instructions given to these undercover operators were very specific. They were not to report any non-corrupt activities, even such serious matters as drinking on duty or sleeping or lateness. However, they were to report anything at all that looked as though it involved the illegal exchange of money for some police favor—in short, the kind of corruption of which we are speaking in this chapter. Great care was taken to preserve the secrecy of the field associates, whose identities weren't even known to Commissioner McCarthy. The result was that the rumor spread through the Department that there were a great number of these undercover agents and their work did result in some important arrests.

The idea behind both "turn-arounds" and "field associates" was, of course, to destroy the effectiveness of the corruption-supporting "system." There have been objections to both of these programs on the grounds that they destroyed the trust that police officers need to have in each other. However, it must be recognized that in the situation which existed when these devices were introduced, trust was very commonly used to facilitate crime by corrupt police officers. A great deal of fear was introduced into the awareness of the corrupt, resulted for those aware of departmental corruption, but there was never any question that those who were not criminally involved were ever injured by the undercover operation. These were bitter medicines for a very difficult sickness in the policing of that time. They helped in discrediting the old idea that there was some kind of an obligation for honest police officers to support those who were corrupt.

There have been other attempts to develop programs which tested the honesty of police officers in a number of ways. These have usually been labelled "integrity testing." In New York City and other cities, experiments have been set up in which people were hired to act as drunks or poor people who in some way might be victimized. In one city there had been a complaint that police officers stole money from elderly poor people on the day when relief checks were distributed. Actors impersonated the people who were most likely to be victimized and offered a trap for anyone who might be inclined to steal from them. In other tests, money or some other valuable item was left where a police officer might find it, or it was turned in to a police officer by some individual who claimed to be leaving town immediately. The idea was that if an officer was inclined to steal, these opportunities offered him or her very good chances to do so. In some cases, the results of integrity testing operations were used as more of a "compliance index"; that is, the test items involved were of small value and no effort was made to identify particular individuals. The objective was only to check on the general level of honesty among the group tested.

4. The Importance of Ethics

In our society, the study of ethics and the use of ethical codes in administration has not been well developed. However, some guidance in ethics is essential if officers are to meet the wide variety of conditions which may be presented to them on any one day and still act properly and in a way that allows them to have the respect of themselves and of others. Basically, the code of ethics should allow a person guidance in answering questions to which honest people could give different answers. The code which is presently being developed for the American Academy for Professional Law Enforcement (AAPLE) is probably the most developed official police code which has come to the attention of this writer. It is worthy of considerable study.

Ethics has particular importance to the officer who is serious about avoiding even the appearance of corruption. Following the code tends to leave the officer in a position where the questionable activities which often lead to corruption are simply avoided. A code of ethics would, for example, speak about avoiding "conflicts of interest." These are situations in which the officer finds him or herself with what we call a "divided loyalty"; that is, he or she has obligations to individuals who would expect him or her to operate in other than the best ethical manner. The code might cover such problems as the use of public information, avoiding obligations to grant favors, avoiding wrong appearances, and the importance of setting a good personal example.

For many years it was assumed that it was only important to develop codes which regulated the conduct of individuals. We are now more and more aware that organizations, even governments, should be acting according to ethical principles. It's easiest for a police officer to act ethically when the organization for which he or she works is operating ethically. Research by this author would indicate that the surest indication of ethical behavior on the part of the organization is a constant dedication to serve the interests of all legitimate groups in the community which is its responsibility. The cause of ethics in policing will be substantially benefited as we come to greater agreement on the specific job of the police. Understanding the needs of the community in the terms of a particular definition of police function will give us a better awareness of the job which must be accomplished in a particular community. It can then be assumed that the organization is acting ethically when it devotes all of its energies to meeting that job legally and effectively.

It's important in determining organizational rectitude that the organization develop with its own personnel the reputation for actively trying to follow the most correct course of action as it carries out its mandate. The organization must be seen by its employees as sincerely and toughly engaged in a continuing effort to be effective and to be right.

In particular, it's important that the police attempt to determine and satisfy the legitimate needs of those who live in the poorer sections of the community. These are usually the areas in which there is the most frequent contact with the police but in which the police are most disliked and mistrusted. These are also the areas in which the gambling, vice, and drug activities which are most commonly associated with corruption are the most frequently found.

The agency's reputation for fairness in dealing with its employees is also important. This should not be considered as equivalent to the administration being soft or unwilling to use discipline or the necessary authority of command. The objective is mutual respect within the organization tied to the goal of doing the right thing, both as an organization and as individuals. This is extremely important to every member of the department. Respect and honor within the agency should lead, for each individual in the department, to a position of respect and honor to the community.

We have mentioned the importance of administrative control and direction, of a standardized code of ethics, and of developing the necessary standards so that the work of the agency can be carried on with efficiency and rectitude. It should be recognized that all of these forces constitute a constant training activity to which each member of the force is exposed and which is most effective when it's consistent and comprehensive in its relationship to all of the areas which pose temptation or strain.

Beyond the generalized training impact, it's also possible to develop what have been called *integrity training programs*, and a number of agencies have worked effectively in this area. Sometimes these offerings are called *ethical awareness programs*. They all involve attempts to present to the police officers, usually in a relatively informal setting, structured training which clarifies some of the ethical dilemmas involved in policing and to suggest answers to them. It's important in all such activities that the officers actively participate in the training exercise. There is no value if the officers are just talked to or preached at. The officers must contribute their own experiences and apply the study material presented to their personal experiences. Then they must come to accept the value of the observations. Real ethical development only comes through the officer-student's effort in trying to develop an awareness as to how he or she and other officers whom he or she can recognize as being in similar situations can meet the ethical problems which they have in common. Such workshops have often been extremely useful.

We have mentioned the most obvious reward that an ethically operating agency can expect—that is, respect and support within its community. But police officers are individuals, and a proper ethical climate is invaluable for the welfare of each individual officer. It's important that the police officer feel a measure of pride in the work his or her agency does accomplish and, even more, in what it *tries* to accomplish. Each officer must know that the people who most need help are being given that help; each officer must feel satisfied with himself or herself and know that he or she is doing a necessary job in the community and doing it well.

Summary

We have attempted in these pages to define police corruption and to describe the different kinds of activity covered by that term. We have noted that most serious and widespread corruption is system-supported rather than being caused by "rotten apple" individuals.

The recognition that "The System Is The Problem" adds a new dimension to the need for anti-corruption response. An adequate effort against corruption must include efforts to shape the police agency in its conduct and in the way it treats and shapes the officers who have been historically considered as the sole target of anti-corruption measures. The focus probably must shift from the line officer and the injunctions to him or her against vice and for virtue to a new emphasis on administrative action to ensure that neither policies nor procedures support corruption.

It must also be recognized that corruption control is everybody's business. Every citizen, police officer or civilian, must recognize that the seed of corruption is like an ever-present and deadly germ. It is as near as greed; it has destroyed the lives of hundreds as many police officers as have been killed by criminals. No individual can afford to be anything but totally opposed to corruption, and eternally vigilant against it.

Topics For Discussion

1. If we want police officers to relate to and represent the people of the community, should police be expected to have a different standard of ethics than the good people in the community?

2. The point has been made in the chapter that when the questioned activity is not both (1) criminal and (2) for money or some cash equivalent, it isn't corrupt according to the definition. Obviously, this doesn't imply approval of police criminal activity which isn't committed for money or of police acceptance of money without violating the law. It just means that they are different problems.

A. What are some examples of:

1. Illegal police activity *not* committed for some cash (or equivalent) return?

2. Situations in which police are given money and no crime is involved?

B. What problems could we anticipate from such activities?

3. Police unions have sometimes enforced traffic laws vigorously just to publicize their union demands. What are the problems in relating such practice to any definition of corruption?

4. In recent years there have been many accounts of activity by local, state, or federal officials not in police work which would be corrupt according to the definitions discussed in this chapter.

A. Give some examples.

B. Are there differences between the situations with which these officials must deal and the police problems which make these non-police activities more or less excusable than they would be if committed by a police person?

5. Assume that you've just been employed by a police department. On one of your first working days you observe a fellow officer involved in some action which seems suspicious to you.

A. How would you evaluate the situation?

B. What would you do?

6. Is there any necessary or usual relationship between police brutality and police corruption?

References

1. William P. Brown, *The Police and Corruption*, President's Commission on Law Enforcement and Administration of Justice, 1967.

2. Robert Fogelson, *Big City Police* (in publication, 1977).

3. Harry W. More, Jr., "Delphi Analysis of Police Corruption," 30 pp. multilithed, 1976.

4. Brown, *The Police and Corruption*, p. 46.
5. Brown, *The New York City Police Department Anti-Corruption Campaign* (School of Criminal Justice, State University of New York at Albany, 1972).
6. Brown, *The New York City Police Department Anti-Corruption Campaign.*
7. David Burnham, "The Role of the Media in Controlling Corruption," Criminal Justice Center Monograph 3 (New York: John Jay Press, 1976), p. 1.
8. Brown, *The Police And Corruption*, pp. 140-41.
9. McCarthy, p. 44.

Annotated Bibliography

American Academy for Professional Law Enforcement, 444 West 56th Street, New York, New York 10019: "Ethical Standards in Law Enforcement," 10 pp. mimeo, 1977. This is a brief but comprehensive statement of ethical standards which bear upon the line officer and the administrator. It has been developed by practitioners and it has an unusually rigorous statement of principles and practices which should be followed.

Brown, William P., *The Police and Corruption* (196 pp.). Report of a nationwide study commissioned by the President's Committee on Crime and the Administration of Justice. Published as an appendix to the Commission Reports (1967). This was the first major study of the corruption problem in the United States. It was based on in-depth interviews with over 50 top police administrators in this country and Canada.

———, *The New York City Police Department Anti-Corruption Campaign—October 1970-August 1972* (185 pp.). Report of a preliminary study of the New York City Department. Published at the School of Criminal Justice, 1972. This report places in context the important anti-corruption activity which was taken by Commissioner Patrick Murphy in New York City during the first part of his tenure in that police agency. The work contains a thematic analysis of the policies and procedures undertaken in what was probably the most widespread and long-lasting anti-corruption drive ever mounted in this country.

Burnham, David, Criminal Justice Center Monograph 3, "The Role of the Media in Controlling Corruption," New York: John Jay Press, 1976. This is a brief but interesting statement of the powers of and the limitations on the press in its investigations of corruption. As an investigative reporter for the *New York Times*, Mr. Burnham was instrumental in breaking the original story which stirred the Knapp Commission investigation and the Murphy regime in the New York City Police Department.

Commission to Investigate Allegation of Police Corruption and the City's Anti-Corruption Procedures (New York, N.Y.), *The Knapp Commission Report on Police Corruption*, New York: George Braziller, 1972. The Knapp Commission report contains one of the most carefully documented accounts of the nature of police corruption in a major city.

Fogelson, Robert, *Big City Police* (In publication, 1977). Professor Fogelson is a renowned historian who has studied the history of the police/political relationships in the period from 1890 to recent days. His views of corruption and its historic and organizational settings are among the most sophisticated available.

McCarthy, William, Criminal Justice Center Monograph 5, "A Police Administrator Looks at Police Corruption." New York: John Jay Press, 1976. This is a brief but excellent statement by an administrator who was a skilled, uncompromising and highly effective foe of corruption.

More, Harry W., Jr., "Delphi Analysis of Police Corruption," 30 pp. multilithed, 1976. The Delphi technique for assembling professional opinions as to the implications of police corruption has been used by Dr. More in an innovative and useful study.

Sherman, Lawrence W., *Police Corruption: A Sociological Perspective*, New York: Anchor Books, 1974. The fifteen readings which Professor Sherman presents discuss historical, organizational and social science views of corruption.

Index

D

E

F

G

H

I

J

K

L

M

N

O

P

R

S

T

U

V

W

Y

Z

†